Online Education for Lifelong Learning

Yukiko Inoue
University of Guam, Guam

INFOSCI

Information Science Publishing

Hershey • London • Melbourne • Singapore

Acquisition Editor: Kristin Klinger
Senior Managing Editor: Jennifer Neidig
Managing Editor: Sara Reed
Assistant Managing Editor: Sharon Berger
Development Editor: Kristin Roth
Copy Editor: April Schmidt
Typesetter: Michael Brehm
Cover Design: Lisa Tosheff
Printed at: Yurchak Printing Inc.

Published in the United States of America by
Information Science Publishing (an imprint of Idea Group Inc.)
701 E. Chocolate Avenue
Hershey PA 17033
Tel: 717-533-8845
Fax: 717-533-8661
E-mail: cust@idea-group.com
Web site: http://www.idea-group.com

and in the United Kingdom by
Information Science Publishing (an imprint of Idea Group Inc.)
3 Henrietta Street
Covent Garden
London WC2E 8LU
Tel: 44 20 7240 0856
Fax: 44 20 7379 3313
Web site: http://www.eurospan.co.uk

Library of Congress Cataloging-in-Publication Data

Online education for lifelong learning / Yukiko Inoue, Editor.
p. cm.
Summary: "This book provides theoretical understanding of the essential link between open and lifelong learning and online distance education. It also offers a critical discussion of distance, open and lifelong learning, with a focus on new and emerging challenges of online distance education in global learning communities"--Provided by publisher.
Includes bibliographical references and index.
ISBN 978-1-59904-319-7 (hardcover) -- ISBN 1-59904-321-0 (ebook)
1. Continuing education--Computer-assisted instruction. 2. Distance education. 3. Open learning. I. Inoue, Yukiko.
LC5225.D38O55 2007
374.00285--dc22

2006033758

British Cataloguing in Publication Data
A Cataloguing in Publication record for this book is available from the British Library.

To old friends, good friends, and the best friends

Online Education for Lifelong Learning

Table of Contents

Foreword

There can be little doubt that "online education" has provided significant opportunities and enhanced access to courses, knowledge, and information for people engaged in lifelong learning. Over the past decade, online education has provided an important and potentially innovative means of enhancing teaching and learning experiences within the context of lifelong learning. Online education has now evolved from a marginal form of education to a commonly accepted and increasingly popular means of providing lifelong learning opportunities to a wide range of learners. Online education provides a valuable means for lifelong learners to participate in learning regardless of geographic location (place-independent) theoretically "24 hours a day" (time-independent), thus providing access to lifelong learning which may not otherwise be possible. In addition, online education can provide anonymity of characteristics such as gender, race, age, social status, and special needs, which can reduce the feeling of discrimination and provide equality of social interaction among learners.

Online education has gone through significant changes in terms of both available technology and the ways in which online technologies can improve the quality of learning and opportunities for learners. Connolly and Stansfield (in press) identify three distinct generations of online education. The *first* generation, which was based mainly on the passive use of the Internet (circa 1994-1999), focused primarily on the conversion of course material to an online format, basic mentoring via e-mail and low-fidelity streamed audio and/or video. The *second* generation (circa 2000-2003) was characterized by the use of more advanced technologies with high-bandwidth access, rich streaming media and virtual learning environments (VLEs) providing access to course material, communication facilities, and student services. VLEs became capable of supporting a constructivist form of learning encouraging more reflection and rigorous thinking, which helped learners make connections among ideas and to construct internal, coherent knowledge structures. The *third* generation (since 2003) is characterized by more collaborative learning environments based more on constructivist epistemology, promoting reflective practice through tools such as e-portfolios, blogs, wikis, games-based online learning, and highly interactive online simulations. We are also now starting to see the development of mobile learning with the wider adoption of devices like PDAs, mobile phones, and smartphones. Above all, online education is providing much greater freedom and flexibility for lifelong learning in that the very latest knowledge and information can be delivered and tailored to the needs and context of the learner, at a time when they need it (just-in-time learning) to a place of their convenience (work, home, or on the move).

The knowledge-driven society is increasing demand for continuing professional development in which employees need to update their skills and knowledge and evolve to meet the changing demands of industry and commerce. The demand for higher education is expanding exponentially throughout the world, which is an indication of the trend towards globalization, which, due to the changing nature of employment, a job for life is no longer the norm. As a result of globalization and a push for mass higher education from both government and society, and in responding to the needs of learners and employers for greater flexibility, continuing education and lifelong learning, institutions across the world are under increasing pressure to integrate new technologies associated with online education into existing teaching, learning, administrative, and student support services.

In addition to significant technological changes, online education has managed to successfully develop past much of the hype and unrealistic expectations that plagued it in the mid- to late-1990s and contributed to the failure of a number of high profile online education initiatives across the world. We are now entering a crucial stage in the evolution of online education in which it is starting to become part of mainstream teaching and learning, with learners now having access to hundreds of thousands of online courses throughout the world.

If online education for lifelong learning is to be sustainable, this presents a number of key economic, social, pedagogic, and technological challenges that learning providers must address. Specific issues such as ensuring that online education provides for cost effective lifelong learning are vital to ensuring its long-term sustainability. The issue of how online education is costed and funded is vital for many educational institutions across the world with limited resources. There are challenges in addressing the needs of learners from diverse backgrounds whose cultural experiences might be different from the dominant educational culture which underpins their online course. This is particularly relevant within the context of the international delivery of online courses and franchising or joint partnership agreements between educational institutions in different countries and continents.

While technology might be leading change at a rapid pace, it could be argued that too little attention is being paid to exploring the new forms of pedagogy made possible by online education. It is vital that effective staff development is provided within educational institutions so that online learning tutors and developers change the way they think about teaching and learning and how to employ emerging technologies to enhance learning. Online education is only as good as the people who provide and deliver the learning experiences and support. Having the most up-to-date and innovative technologies in itself will not guarantee success and learner satisfaction.

Yukiko Inoue's book provides invaluable insight into the key issues surrounding the use of online education for lifelong learning. Experienced and esteemed authors from around the globe have contributed chapters that cover the full spectrum of technological, pedagogic, social, and economic issues relating to online education for lifelong learning. Key issues are explored from both a theoretical and practical perspective. This publication provides essential reading to all stakeholders involved in online learning whether they are tutors, researchers, academics, administrators, senior managers, or policy-makers. Online education for lifelong learning is about sustainability and working towards achieving long terms strategic goals rather than providing short term quick fixes.

I myself have been closely involved in online education for lifelong learning for over a decade in a variety of different roles as a content developer, tutor, academic support, program leader, researcher, and author. I have seen firsthand how online education has provided access to lifelong learning opportunities that otherwise would not be possible for managers in full-time employment. In addition, I have seen part-time students within an online learning environment flourish and consistently perform better than the face-to-face students (Connolly, MacArthur, Stansfield, & McLellen, in press).

Many of us have learned valuable lessons from the hype and failures of the recent past and online education for lifelong learning is gaining greater acceptance within many educational institutions. However, there is still much work to be done before online education reaches maturity and realizes its full potential for lifelong learners from preschool age, throughout school and university education, during employment, and into retirement. In addition, if many of the obstacles and issues are to be addressed, then it is essential that stakeholders are informed and make decisions based on the latest thinking and developments in online education and lifelong learning. This book provides a key resource and essential reading in helping people stay informed and enhance their online education provision. Yukiko Inoue and the contributing authors are to be congratulated on this publication, which is timely and highly relevant.

Mark Stansfield
School of Computing
University of Paisley
Scotland, UK

***Mark Stansfield**, PhD, is senior lecturer in the School of Computing at the University of Paisley in Scotland. Stansfield received his doctorate in information systems and has had papers published on online learning, games-based e-learning, information systems, and e-business in a number of international journals that include the* Journal of Further and Higher Education, *the* Journal of Electronic Commerce Research, *and the* Journal of IT Education. *He also serves on the editorial boards of several international journals. Stansfield has been involved in online education at postgraduate level for over a decade, particularly with the online MSc Management of eBusiness program at the University of Paisley.*

References

Connolly, T. M., MacArthur, E., Stansfield, M. H., & McLellan, E. (in press). A quasi-experimental study of three online learning courses in computing. *Computers and Education.*

Connolly, T. M., & Stansfield, M. H. (in press). From eLearning to games-based eLearning: Using interactive technologies in teaching information systems. *International Journal of Information Technology Management.*

Preface

The age of distance learning and new forms of e-learning is here. The rate at which a variety of institutions are entering the distance learning arena is increasing rapidly. In spite of the increased popularity and presence of online learning opportunities, however, many researchers and practitioners are decrying the lack of a research-validated framework to guide their design. Other researchers and practitioners point out that what works in effective traditional learning environments may or may not work in online environments ... . Educators, researchers, and policymakers continue to argue for updated learning and schooling models and the increased use of new and emerging electronic learning (e-learning) technologies that can better prepare students for an increasingly global, changing, and complex world. (Mccombs & Vakili, 2005, p. 1582)

"E-learning," sometimes referred to as online learning, Web-based learning, distance learning, and technology-based learning, is a concept that has garnered significant global attention; the importance of e-learning is therefore universal (Waight, Willging, & Wentling, 2004).

This publication, *Online Education for Lifelong Learning*, seeks to capture critical dynamics and challenges in the context of online education for lifelong learning. Higher education is particularly exploring the new possibilities offered by open and distance learning. Indeed open and distance learning is not limited to adult continuing education but is considered a frontier created by online-learning communities to enhance *access* to and *success* in higher education.

All learners, in the electronic information age of today, as reviewed by McGrath (2004), need the following four sets of skills so that they can successfully negotiate the 21st century:

1. **Digital-age literacy** (basic, scientific, economic, and technological literature; visual and information literacies; and multicultural literacy and global awareness);
2. **Inventive thinking** (adaptability, managing complexity, and self-direction; curiosity, creativity, and risk taking; and high-order thinking and sound reasoning);
3. **Effective communication** (teaming, collaboration, and interpersonal skills; personal, social, and civic responsibility; and interactive communication); and
4. **High productivity** (prioritizing, planning, and managing for results; effective use of real-world tools; and ability to produce relevant and high-quality products).

Online Distance Learning Environments

The institutional or organizational structure of higher education is changing to emphasize academic accountability, competency outcomes, outsourcing, content standardizing, and adaptation to learner-consumer demands (Howell, Williams, & Lindsay, 2004): "funding challenges are increasing with fewer resources to meet expanding *lifelong-learning* demands. Distance education is becoming more abundant, especially online, and location independent, increasing the need for effective course-management systems and teaching strategies that utilize technology" (p. 16). As noted earlier, the higher education community is finding itself on the edge of a new era of online learning. Online learning has been promoted as being more cost effective and convenient than traditional educational environments as well as providing opportunities for more learners to continue their education (Richardson & Swan, 2003).

Allowing students to participate regardless of geographic location, independent of time and place, online education has progressed to the point where students no longer need to be able to meet face-to-face in order to complete a degree program or a course. Richardson and Swan further identify six specific advantages offered by online learning environments:

1. Convenience and flexibility are offered by "anytime, anyplace, anywhere."
2. Accessibility means that students have access to courses and course materials "24 hours a day" (time independent), regardless of location (place-independent), making them far more convenient than the traditional educational experience.

3. Asynchronous learning allows students to reflect upon the materials and their responses before responding, unlike traditional classrooms.
4. Students can work at their own pace, which is especially important for non-native speakers.
5. The ability of personal identities to remain concealed means that all students, regardless of race, sex, disability, or appearance are on equal ground.
6. With the option of multiple representations of a concept embedded in an online course, students can store and retrieve information more effectively.

Richardson and Swan, at the same time, make it clear that (1) Web-based or online learning environments are *not* as effective as traditional learning environments because of the lack of face-to-face interactions or rapport, and that (2) students taking online courses feel disconnected from other classmates because of the lack of facial and vocal expressions and other features common to traditional classroom environments including direct communication and feedback.

Challenges of Online Instruction

It is true that adequate feedback assists both the instructor and students in improving the quality of e-learning, primary because online education instructors are required to be a facilitator, guide, mentor, and coach rather than an authoritative source of knowledge (Lawhon & Ennis-Cole, 2005). The use of distance learning technologies for delivering courses in higher education has thus challenged faculty to reconsider their firmly rooted concepts of "instruction." In other words, as many faculty members are just now emerging from an excessive dependence on the lecture method, new challenges to completely reassess how instruction will be conceptualized are arriving at the main gates of college and university campuses (Travis & Price, 2005).

Another challenge for faculty members is to promote individual teaching strategies and to find ways for technology to enhance the student's ability to read, write, reflect, and synthesize course materials; that is to say, instructors who are successful in mentoring student-teacher communications utilize a variety of techniques or materials to create a more positive online learning environment (Lawhon & Ennis-Cole, 2005). The most daunting challenge for distance education faculty may be the extensive increase in time that faculty must commit to course preparation, grading and feedback, and interaction and rapport (Travis & Price, 2005). Additionally, it should be noted that libraries (which become identified as sites for lifelong literacy and are committed to education, especially to lifelong learning) have expanded their functions. Such functions include the following: (1) helping individuals learn to write and to use communication technologies and helping them learn to read "visually"; and (2) providing alternative learning sites for specific populations (Yancey, 2005).

Higher education today must combine its traditional roles of extending the boundaries of knowledge and passing on that knowledge to students with a commitment to make higher learning available to all through massively extended university outreach and the provision of opportunities for mass higher education through using media, educational technologies, libraries, and distance education (Dodds, 2003). Further, higher education must be understood as a "globalizing process" because, derived from Cobb's (1999) notion that an educated populace is a vital resource for national growth and development in a global economy, an important task of institutions of higher learning is to assist students in participating in the global economy.

It should be further emphasized that American higher education has changed with regard to educational goals and the means used to attain them. In addition to a diversified student population in terms of ethnicity, social status, and expectation, the proportion of nontraditional older students is increasing significantly. In this environment, higher education has a mission to provide adult learners with reeducation or retraining such that they are able to remain competitive in the workforce of the increasingly technologically sophisticated society. The mission of higher education is changing in its relationship with mature-age students.

Lifelong Learning and Online Education

Although *lifelong learning* continues to be a somewhat diffuse term, it is obvious that people learn their whole lifelong, experiencing *new* things, and acquiring *new* knowledge and *new* skills through conversations, from watching television and reading books, and through surfing on the Internet (Alheit & Dausien, 2002): "like breathing, this kind of learning occurs without their being aware of it" (p. 3). Lifelong learning, in essence, is the concept that refers to activities people perform throughout their lives to improve their knowledge, skills, and competencies in a particular field, given some personal, societal, or employment related motives (Field, cited in Koper, Giesbers, Rosmalen, et al., 2005). As Dodds (2003) maintains, universities can help individuals to become lifelong learners, recognizing that educational/learning opportunities are available throughout the individuals' lives. Dodds also emphasizes the startling growth of new technologies and of the popularity, and of open and distance learning delivery approaches. Online distance learning does provide answers to both the problem of availability (accessibility and cost) and the demand for flexibility (time, place, and pace) of higher learning; consequently, technology-mediated learning and distance learning are both becoming major vehicles for fulfilling the needs of lifelong learning in the knowledge age of today (Beller, 1998).

The confluence of the need for continuous learning and unprecedented technological innovations in communications has pushed distance education approaches to the forefront of contemporary educational practices (Garrison, 2000). As mentioned earlier, online distance education is a growing force in lifelong learning; in particular, "due to the rapid development of Web-based technologies, increasing bandwidth, decreasing costs, and widening access, online versions of distance education programs are becoming increasingly popular teaching strategies for colleges and universities to adopt" (Townsend & Wheeler, 2004, p. 127). Linn (1998), nevertheless, asks the following intriguing question: Can modern technologies allow instructors to design distance-learning environments with all the features of traditional courses? Currently, "changes are taking place very rapidly with little time to develop or analyze trends and relationships in the use of new and emerging information technology for enhancing learning" (Havice, Havice, Isbell, Grimes, & Wilson, 2004, p. 111).

Purpose of the Book

Online Education for Lifelong Learning provides a critical discussion of changing roles of college and university faculty members in terms of online learning delivery approaches and technological innovations, focusing on the appropriate use of technologies to make education and learning more *productive* and *personal*. Distance learning, online lifelong learning, and educational technology are *all* inseparable today. Three principal objectives of the book are:

1. As an adage goes, experience is the best teacher. Chapter authors are international and are eager to discuss and share their professional experiences and observations to make a positive impact on online lifelong learning. Their diverse experiences, practices, discoveries, and perspectives can be applied to any other settings or institutions of higher learning in the world.
2. This book discusses roles of today's universities particularly in terms of open and distance learning delivery approaches and technological innovations. These approaches and innovations empower universities to become genuinely "lifelong learning" institutions.
3. Focusing on practical applications of technologies (such as the Internet, and asynchronous communication tools), this book describes a new model for designing distance education for lifelong learning that would assist the readers in the design, development, implementation, and evaluation of their own online teaching-learning environments.

Organization of the Book

This book, consisting of 14 chapters, is divided into five sections: Introduction; Development and Implementation of Online Lifelong Learning; Learning Theories and Online Applications for Lifelong Learning; Tech-Knowledge and Communication Technologies for Lifelong Learning; and Case Studies in Online Education for Lifelong Learning. Specifically:

- **Chapter I** provides an overview of the current literature to inform the shared understanding of the concept of online education for lifelong learning based on the theorized notion that the term *lifelong learning* is increasingly important for college graduates to be able to take their place in the changing world and to be adaptable within the organization that employs them. This overview is represented in the following six themes: (1) lifelong learning; (2) self-directed learning; (3) technology and globalization; (4) open and distance learning; (5) online learning assessment; and (6) higher and adult education.
- **Chapter II** examines two key factors that influence the efficacy of online learning: student and teacher interaction and rapport. These two factors are heavily influenced by the stance that the learner takes. Online learning is opening up more possibilities for lifelong learning. This chapter provides a critical discussion of online education, the theories that ground this delivery system, and the challenges that one university faculty had in creating a community of learners in a technology-mediated learning environment.
- **Chapter III** explores ways in which information and communication technologies (ICT) might transform the learning experience through online delivery. After presenting a conceptualization of ICT use by educators in terms of *inaction, investigation*, *application*, *integration* and *transformation*, two diverse learning settings are examined to develop insights into the implications of online learning for lifelong learning: (1) the delivery of educational services to preschool children through to students (aged 15 years old) in Australia, and (2) the dimensions required for designing online learning for adult learners in higher education.
- **Chapter IV** presents a method for foreign language (FL) teachers to implement currently available technologies as instructional tools in a FL language classroom using the memory efficient approach (MEA) to enhance instruction, and help students to become lifelong FL learners. Introducing currently emerging technologies that can be utilized for instruction in a FL, the chapter will demonstrate a method to implement technologies in an advanced Japanese course as well as in an elementary Japanese course, using MEA.
- **Chapter V** investigates perceptions of teaching and learning in online instruction guided by the Vygotskian perspective of constructivist theory. The use of

constructivist approaches in online learning reflects agreement with educators who stress that good teaching is both a collaborative and a highly individual process. The chapter focuses on current research studies of online constructivist-based course developments and applications and then proceeds to the authors' practical inquiry project, which examined both instructor perspectives on creating and facilitating online learning communities and students' perceptions of their online constructivist experiences.

- **Chapter VI** introduces a new model for designing instruction using the state-of-the-art venue, that is, an archetype for effective instructional design for lifelong learning. The escalating infusion of online education to promote lifelong learning has triggered a re-examination of teaching and learning not witnessed since perhaps the advent of the printed textbook. Today, distance education, in all its manifestations from programmed instruction to Web-based courses, requires instructors to employ new strategies in course design and delivery in order to engage students and promote learner-centered activities.
- **Chapter VII** illustrates theoretical issues and practical challenges to support lifelong learning, namely the development and use of self-regulation within online learning environments. This chapter proposes that a Vygotskian view of self-regulation may be more applicable to investigating self-regulation within the social and cultural context of online teaching and learning. Case studies, personal essays, and contemporary research focusing on self-regulation in face-to-face and online environments are utilized to examine, discuss, and illustrate key challenges and strategies to support lifelong learning within online environments.
- **Chapter VIII** is an attempt to build a framework based on the constructivist online synchronous communications approach to improve the learners' communication styles and abilities related with real-world problems. Individuals can become active participants in their knowledge constructions rather than passive receptacles. The authors also develop a framework according to the strategies of media richness theory, which declares that there must be a fit between information technologies and communication structures to reduce task-related ambiguity.
- **Chapter IX** describes how early childhood teachers can support the development of young children's love for learning through educational technology, and how one early childhood education program promoted college students' learning through online video conferencing technology. Useful suggestions for educational software for children as well as Web sites for both children and teachers are included.
- **Chapter X** talks about how to build online knowledge networks between universities and communities for lifelong learning. Online learners indicate that diverse resources, multicultural experiences, and egalitarian opportunities open their minds and broaden their perspectives via new communication

technologies. The chapter, therefore, discusses the main characteristics of the university-community partnerships for lifelong learning to build online communities with new communication technologies.

- **Chapter XI** focuses on practical applications of emerging technologies in the delivery of professional development programs. The introduction of computers and new technology applications has changed the learning landscape, especially in higher education. From traditional university classroom learning to community-based adult continuing education programs, it is common to see the delivery of instruction that is now supported by online or distance learning technologies. Online learning has become a common strategy to deliver instruction, enhance access to educational resources, and achieve success in higher education.
- **Chapter XII** uses the importation of an American institution of information—"the library"—into the Pacific region of Micronesia as an example of a contextual-less, cross-cultural information transference that suggests the autonomous impact of distance education technology and protocols on indigenous and other interpretative communities. Such an impact negates the innate values of these communities as they pertain to concepts of *knowledge* and *information* derived from tenacious cultural and social values.
- **Chapter XIII** assesses the perceptions of adult learners in online distance learning programs regarding the instructional quality of Web-based courses via WebCT. The visual appeal of Web site and appropriateness of the course materials received the highest rating. The results were closely correlated to students' responses regarding the important aspects of instructional quality of online courses. The results also indicated other perceived aspects that affect students' views of the instructional quality of an online course, including interaction, design, convenience, feedback, and usability.
- **Chapter XIV** examines the effects of lifelong learning and online education in the role of an educator and a trainer, with a focus on the new capabilities and challenges that organizations, learners, and educators face in contemporary times. This chapter further describes a framework of competencies necessary for educators or trainers who practice their profession within new learning environments that already exist or that are going to appear in organizations, as needs for learning and knowledge managements are continuously increasing. For this particular purpose, a case study is presented regarding the way an online training system can be designed and implemented to support learning within a banking organization.

In summary, the goal of this book is to appeal to researchers, faculty members, and practitioners with a professional interest in distance, open, and lifelong learning environments or strategies using new and emerging technologies. Anyone working with online learners or anyone engaged in distance learning activities will also find this book useful.

Yukiko Inoue
Mangilao, Guam
September 2006

References

Alheit, P., & Dausien, B. (2002). The double face of lifelong learning: Two analytical perspectives on a silent revolution. *Studies in the Education of Adults, 34*(1), 3-22.

Beller, M. (1998). The crossroads between lifelong learning and information technology. *Journal of Computer-Meditated Communication, 4*(2). Retrieved August 12, 2006, from http://www.ascusc.org/jcmc/vol4/issue2/beller.html

Cobb, V. L. (1999). *An international comparison of teacher education* (ERIC Database #ED436486).

Dodds, T. (2003). *Universities, adult basic education, open and lifelong learning and new technology.* Retrieved August 12, 2006, from http://www.eldis.org/static/DOC13384.htm

Garrison, R. (2000). Theoretical challenges for distance education in the 21st century. *International Review of Research in Open and Distance Learning, 1*(1). Retrieved August 12, 2006, from http://www.icaap.org/iuicode?149.1.1.2

Havice, P. A., Havice, W. L., Isbell, C., Grimes, L., & Wilson, K. (2004). Bridging communities: Lifelong learning opportunities through distributed staff development. *The Quarterly Review of Distance Education, 5*(2), 111-116.

Howell, S. L., Williams, P. B., & Lindsay, N. K. (2004). *Thirty-two trends affecting distance education: An informed foundation for strategic planning.* Retrieved August 12, 2006, from http://www.westga.edu/~distance/ojdla/fall63/howell63.html

Koper, R., Giesbers, B., Rosmalen, P.-V., et al. (2005). A design model for lifelong learning networks. *Interactive Learning Environments, 13*(1-2), 71-92.

Lawhon, T., & Ennis-Cole, D. (2005). Advice from the trenches: Experienced educators discuss distance learning. *Journal of Faculty Development, 20*(2), 105-110.

Linn, M. C. (1998). Instances of distance learning: Cognition and distance learning. *Journal of the American Society for Information Science, 47*(11), 826-842.

McCombs, B. L., & Vakili, D. (2005). A learner-centered framework for e-learning. *Teachers College Record, 107*(8), 1582-1600.

McGrath, D. (2004). Equity revisited. *Learning & Leading with Technology, 32*(9), 36-39.

Richardson, J. C., & Swan, K. (2003). Examining social presence in online courses in relation to students' perceived learning and satisfaction. *Journal of Asynchronous Learning Networks, 7*(1), 68-88.

Townsend, M., & Wheeler, S. (2004). Is there anybody out there? Teaching assistants' experiences of online learning. *The Quarterly Review of Distance Education, 5*(2), 127-138.

Travis, J. E., & Price, K. (2005). Instructional culture and distance learning. *Journal of Faculty Development, 20*(2), 99-103.

Waight, C. L., Willging, P., & Wentling, T. (2004). Recurrent themes in e-learning: A narrative analysis of major e-learning report. *The Quarterly Review of Distance Education, 5*(3), 195-203.

Yancey, K. B. (2005, March-April). The people's university. *Change*, 13-19.

Acknowledgments

The production of a book is exciting but complex. The editor would like to thank all the staff at Idea Group Inc., especially Mehdi Khosrow-Pour, Jan Travers, Amanda Kirlin, Andrew Bundy, Jennifer Neidig, Jamie Snavely, and particularly Kristin Roth (who worked with me from start to finish), for their constant assistance and expertise throughout the whole production process from developing a book prospectus to completing the book editing procedure. I have thoroughly enjoyed working with such a reliable and high-energy publishing team at Idea Group Inc.

The production of a book involves many individuals. Special thanks go to all involved in the review process of book chapters, without whose comprehensive, critical, and constructive comments and suggestions the book production could not have been satisfactorily completed. Special thanks also go to Mark Stansfield at the University of Paisley in Scotland for his Foreword to the book. He was also one of the chapter reviewers. Stansfield has extensive experiences in online education for lifelong learning and I certainly value his contribution.

I would like to express my sincere appreciation to all the chapter authors who wrote, revised, clarified, and responded to my many inquiries during the editing process particularly. Many of the chapter contributors were also the chapter reviewers. This publication and its value are truly built around such excellent contributors from all over the world. Most of the contributors would not identify themselves as technologists; rather, they are using information and communication technologies to deliver or to reinforce the content in which they are experts focusing on online lifelong learning. Chapter authors have shared their own practices, applications, observations, discoveries, and challenges encountered in improving teaching and learning, while making a positive difference through online education for lifelong learning.

In closing, I would like to thank my colleagues at the University of Guam for their encouragement and useful suggestions during the development of this publication. I would further like to express my thanks to all the staff of the Interlibrary Loans Department at the University of Guam for their assistance to get references and materials that I needed. Finally, my special thanks go to Kazuko Onodera, a retired educator and my academic and lifelong mentor, who never lost faith in my scholarly endeavors and personal actualizations.

Section I

Introduction

Chapter I

Online Education for Lifelong Learning: A Silent Revolution

Yukiko Inoue, University of Guam, Guam

Abstract

The term lifelong learning *(which has played an important role in policy discussions as well as in studies of the sociology and economics of education) is increasingly important in the 21st century for college graduates to be able to take their place in the changing world scene and to be adaptable and creative within the organization that employs them. Lifelong learning has increasingly been cited but there is no shared understanding of its usage at the global level.The objective of the present chapter is to provide an extensive overview of the current literature to inform the shared understanding of lifelong learning in general and the concept of online lifelong learning specifically. The overview is represented in six themes: lifelong learning, self-directed learning, technology and globalization, open and distance learning, online learning assessment, and higher and adult education.*

Introduction

In the UK government's white paper, titled *21st Century Skills, Realizing Our Potential*, information and communication technology (ICT) was acknowledged as a "skill for life" along with good reading and math skills (NIACE, n.d.). ICT is a powerful and indispensable tool to enable education to face the challenges for lifelong learning. The term *lifelong learning* has played an important role in policy discussions as well as in studies of the sociology and economics of education; yet, the relationship of this term to the rapidly changing world of ICT has been considered much less frequently (Friesen & Anderson, 2004). Lifelong learning has increasingly been cited but there is no shared understanding of its usage at the global level (Medel-Añonuevo, Ohsako, & Mauch, 2001). As one example, the economic interpretation of lifelong learning "in the last ten years has become problematic for many practitioners who have come forward with such terms as Lifelong (L)Earning and Learning to Earn as their succinct criticism of the way the term is being promoted" (Medel-Añonuevo et al., 2001, p. 1).

It is more and more important in the 21st century for college graduates to be able to take their place in the changing world scene and to be adaptable and creative within the organization that employs them; and higher education has been through enormous change in the last 20 years (Peat, Taylor, & Franklin, 2005). In addition to a diversified student population in terms of ethnicity, social status, and expectation, the proportion of nontraditional older adult re-entry students is increasing significantly. In this environment, higher education has a mission to provide older adult learners with re-education or retraining such that they are able to remain competitive in the workforce of today's technologically sophisticated society.

The objective of the chapter, therefore, is to provide an overview of the current literature to enlighten the concept of online education for lifelong learning in the information age. This overview is represented in the following six themes:

1. Lifelong learning
2. Self-directed learning
3. Technology and globalization
4. Open and distance learning
5. Online learning assessment
6. Higher and adult education

Online Education for Lifelong Learning

Lifelong Learning

An article, titled *The Double Face of Lifelong Learning,* by Alheit and Dausien (2002) focuses on the tensions between two perspectives on lifelong learning (one is a reorganization of the education system, and the other is the aspects of a phenomenology of lifelong learning). Specifically:

Since the 1960s, the first perspective has formed the basis for an international policy of "lifelong learning," The background to this approach is the diagnosis that a faster pace of social changes, structural changes, and transformations involving a greater role for civil society require competencies and flexibility on the part of society's actors that can no longer be acquired at the speed and in institutionalized forms of "traditional" education and training. The second perspective focuses—in the sense of a subject-centered science of education—on the learning processes of individual social actors. Here, the lifelong learning perspective has heightened attention for non-formal, informal, non-institutionalized and self-organized learning. (p. 5)

The key educational question, as pointed out by Alheit and Dausien (2002), is no longer how certain material can be taught as successfully as possible, but which learning environments can best stimulate self-determined learning (and lifelong learning encompasses a variety of meanings, ideas, and connotations). Lifelong learning is *not* limited to "reproductive" forms of learning but also includes "productive" activities (i.e., learning-on-demand resulting from job specifications and current tasks covers the reproductive aspects of learning, whereas generative learning focuses on the productive aspects of active citizenship, participation in innovation, knowledge creation, and ongoing change); lifelong learning is also *not* limited to professional development or vocational training but affects any aspect of life (Allert, Richter, & Nejdl, 2004).

The concept of lifelong learning refers to the activities people perform throughout their lives to improve their knowledge, skills, and competence professionally, socially, and personally; in this regard, the following four implications can be explored when developing ICT networks for lifelong learners (Koper & Tattersall, 2004):

1. Lifelong learners are self-directed and are responsible for their own learning process.
2. Learners are typically engaged in a variety of formal and informal learning activities during their lifetimes.

3. In lifelong learning, the door is opened to exploiting the heterogeneity of learners by setting up learning communities in which novices collaborate with more experienced people.
4. It is necessary to maintain a record of an individual's growth in competency in a persistent and standard way to ensure that learners can search for new learning facilities that fit and extend their current knowledge and skills.

Lifelong learning, in essence, embraces the whole of the life course; motivation for, access to, and outcomes of learning vary greatly according to the different circumstances in which people find themselves at any given stage (Schuller, 2004). Lifelong learning "needs to promote effective educational opportunities in the many learning settings through which people pass, including home, school, work, and the larger political community" (Fischer, 1999, p. 7).

Today innovative technologies and business processes require the acquisition of new knowledge and skills to maintain high quality of *productivity* and *efficiency*. Adults would like to learn for improving their qualifications and bringing their skills up to date for a new line of work. Adults would also like to learn because of the rapidity and constancy of change in the society and because of lifelong learning dealing with changes in lifestyle or value systems.

Older adult students enrolled in community colleges, for instance, bring far more experience and practical information than younger adult students and such older adult students are particularly interested in knowing how *new* knowledge relates to what they already know (Whiteman, 2002). Therefore, as Whiteman describes:

> ... *effective approaches to helping adults learn include contributions from the students and their involvement in what is being taught and how it is being taught. In keeping with the mission of community colleges to encourage lifelong learning, it is important to encourage and support adult students' involvement in their own learning.* (p. 7)

Based on the notion that many community college students have grown up with technology and they expect technology to be a significant part of their learning experience, Frey and Donehue (2003) conducted the faculty technology survey. Their survey results have revealed that (1) most faculty members are between "very comfortable" and "moderately comfortable" in using computers (specifically, word processing, Internet search engines, spreadsheets, databases, and presentation software), and that (2) faculty members would need some help to feel comfortable in using graphics software and desktop publishing. Moreover, their survey indicated that faculty with the ability to teach both "online" and "face-to-face" courses are a valuable asset for their college, primarily because both community college learners and their potential employers not only expect but also demand the use of technology in the curriculum and instruction.

Self-Directed Learning

Lifelong learning (i.e., a continuous engagement in acquiring and applying knowledge and skills in the context of self-directed problems) should be grounded in descriptive and prescriptive goals; in other words, learning should be embedded in the pursuit of intrinsically rewarding activities; and, skills and processes that support learning as a lifetime habit must be developed (Fischer, 1999). It is commonly recognized that as stress increases and accumulates with life-changing events, the adult's motivation to engage in learning experiences increases. *Self-directed learning*, *critical reflection*, *experimental learning*, and *learning to learn* can be identified as four major, unique, and exclusive adult learning processes; subsequently, lifelong learning has become increasingly important, facilitated by the development of real-time multimedia applications available via the Internet and computer-mediated learning (Huang, 2002).

The current shift towards computer-mediated teaching and learning places college and university instructors under an enormous amount of pressure to gain expertise not only in emerging new media but also in the innovative pedagogical approaches: "the acquisition of empathic and pedagogically appropriate skills for the online environment must now come high on the list of teaching competencies" (Creanor, 2002, p. 57). A paradigm shift is taking hold in American higher education that includes the shift from institutions of *instruction* to institutions of *learning*, creating powerful learning environments, improving the quality of the exiting students, and viewing faculty as primarily "designers" of learning methods and environments (Goetz, 2004).

In Japan, for instance, proactive attention to the use of media in lifelong learning was addressed in the 2000 Lifelong Learning Council Report, titled *Measures to Promote Lifelong Learning Using New ICT* (Sakamoto, 2002). In reality, however, the use of media and ICT in Japan is "restricted to video or databases of books and materials, or to the use of e-mail in the distribution of teaching materials. ... A noticeable trend in media use has been the shift from communications satellites and terrestrial media to the Internet" (Sakamoto, 2002, p. 15).

There are many synonyms used for computer-mediated learning (e.g., distributed learning, e-learning, distance education, and online learning) but it can be defined by the following five standards: (1) the instructor and students are separated by distance; (2) the instruction is delivered via computer technologies; (3) the communication is interactive (the teacher and the student send and receive feedback);

(4) the learning is done asynchronously (the delivery therefore does not take place simultaneously); and (5) the instructor delivers the content via a computer and the students respond at a later time (Whiteman, 2002).

The emergence of worldwide communications networks and powerful computer technologies has redefined the concept of distance learning. Bourne, Harris, and Mayadas (2005), for instance, identify five pillars of quality online learning: (1) learning effectiveness (in such areas as social interaction and the creation of learning communities); (2) student satisfaction; (3) faculty satisfaction; (4) access (problems in access were due largely to lack of connectivity but have been largely solved); and (5) cost effectiveness (costs for creating and running online courses have plummeted over the decade). Online learning has obvious disadvantages (e.g., the impersonal nature of learning and technical problems including breakdown in multimedia software and insufficient processor speed) but definitely advantages (e.g., flexibility in length and time of study; automated assessment and feedback; and discussion between remote users, which facilitate *self-directed learning*) (Medford, 2004).

Oncken and Wass's (1974) concept of the metaphorical monkey (which represents the way that responsibility for learning is distributed between teacher and student) and Grow's (1991) self-directed learning model are both effectively merged and then conceptualized in the four-stage staircasing model by Flores and Flores (2003) as illustrated:

- **Stage 1:** The dependent learner (teacher as authority: student needs close supervision); the learner sees direction, motivation, and education as the responsibility of the teacher.
- **Stage 2:** The interested learner (teacher as motivator: student works well with consistent supervision); the learner considers that direction, motivation, and education as the responsibility of the teacher.
- **Stage 3:** The involved learner (teacher as facilitator: student works well with regular teacher input); the learner accepts direction, motivation, and education as the responsibility of the teacher.
- **Stage 4:** The independent learner (teacher as consultant: student directs own learning); the learner knows direction, motivation, and education as the responsibility of the teacher.

An important principle of lifelong learning is therefore "the ability for *self-direction*; the reality, however, is that students are at various stages of dependence means that online teachers need to recognize the variety of learners present in their online classrooms and implement strategies to guide them toward such independent learning" (Flores & Flores, 2003, p. 239). Regarding the responsibility of the teacher, Moore (2003) observes:

Whether the technology has been effective or not has been dependent on the knowledge and skills of teachers who employ them, and to an even greater extent on the readiness of educational organizations to provide the conditions under which their teachers can develop and apply those skills. This brings into sharper focus the question whether the teaching and learning processes in distance education are significantly different. (p. 38)

Technology and Globalization

Globalization, which has become a major theme in social discourse in recent years, is a complex phenomenon but is an economic phenomenon, as noted by Jarvis (1999):

Globalization is related to the power of the economic institution and its effects on the whole world, as information technologies and rapid transport systems have turned it into a global village, although the term "village" is a little misleading since the world cultures are far less homogeneous than those of a single village. (p. 249)

As lifelong learning and knowledge become ever more important to economic well-being, women and men find themselves juggling not only work and family but also demands of further schooling and education throughout their lives (Kramarae, 2001). Distance education offers new opportunities for many women to achieve educational goals. Kramarae further provides a discussion as to (1) why women pursue the *third shift*, (2) how they manage to balance *work*, *family*, and *education*; and (3) what would make distance learning easier for them. In other words, most women work one shift at the office or factory, a second shift at home, and now "education" is considered a third shift, in addition to paid work and work in the home, for many female students.

Based on the fact that the increasing orientation towards *education* and *lifelong learning* as important factors in the global competition between nations and companies, Illeris (2003) addresses intriguing questions: What is learning? How can it be promoted? Why does teaching not always result in learning? Illeris defines "learning" in the following terms:

Learning can no longer be conceived of as merely the acquisition of a syllabus or curriculum. If one examines job advertisements or interviews personnel managers, it becomes obvious that general skills and personal qualities are considered at least as important as professional qualifications. In contemporary everyday life, such skills and qualities are also essential both to manage the complex functions of modern life and to maintain the common and democratic functions of society. Thus, what should be learned in education as well as in working and societal life is a complex totality of traditional and up-to-date knowledge, orientation and overview, combined with professional and everyday life skills and a broad range of personal qualities such as flexibility, openness, independence, responsibility, and creativity. (p. 397)

In the Austrian context, for instance, *globalization* and *internationalization* are considered as providing multiple opportunities for higher and adult education (Allport, 2000):

- *A nation can provide its citizens with the necessary broad-based skills to engage with an international economy through tertiary education on the lifelong learning model;*
- *Educational institutions can earn valuable private income through the investment made in education by both national and international students;*
- *By forging stronger links with the world of work, higher education institutions can be job creators, promoting new employment in information-based industries in a global economy;*
- *Global knowledge networks can enhance research productivity and expand research training opportunities; and*
- *Through international cooperation and exchange, universities can promote tolerance and understanding of different cultures, advance knowledge through research, and enhance participatory citizenship.* (p. 38)

Randall Fielding (2002), the editor of *Design Share* and an architect specializing in educational facility planning and design, describes basic yet innovative ideas about learning in his article, *Personalized Learning Space in a Global Context,* as follows: (1) every student learns all the time (learning occurs inside and outside of class; every setting provides a learning opportunity); (2) direct experience decisively shapes individual understanding (the brain's activity is in direct proportion to its engagement with stimulating environments; concrete experiences solidify understanding of abstract concepts); (3) individuals learn by establishing and reworking patterns, relationships, and connections; and (4) change in the environment is stimulating.

In the knowledge-driven era of today, higher education *is* a precondition to full and satisfying participation in the global economy and society and, in essence, the rate of participation in higher education globally continues to rise (EDUCAUSE, 2005):

Today's colleges and universities continue to prosper and adapt by letting many flowers bloom. Differing institutional structures have emerged to address the chang-

ing educational and economic needs of changing populations. New information technologies are developed and adapted to serve differing learning styles. Higher education institutions have moved far away from the ivory tower and now extend into the very fabric of the diverse societies in which they operate. (p. 5)

Open and Distance Learning

Beginning in the 1970s and 1980s, stimulated by the example of the UK Open University, governments around the world began to see open and distance education as a vehicle for achieving national development goals, resulting in an improvement "in the qualifications of the workforce to operate in a new economic climate and improving access and equity for individuals who previously had been excluded from education beyond school" (Calvert, 2005, p. 228).

The term *open and distance learning* (for the detailed open and distance learning terms, see Appendix A) appeared in 1991 (for example, in the 1970s, the term "open" meant that people did not need a high school diploma in order to enroll at a distance university) but does *not* always describe the same reality (Blandin, 2000). Learning systems based on networks are not considered open and distance learning in the Anglo-Saxon countries but are considered under different categories such as Web-based training (WBT) and technology supported learning (TSL) when the emphasis is put on the technology in use, or more generally as online learning systems (Blandin, 2000). Although definitions of *e-learning* vary, e-learning is generally defined as the use of network technologies to design, deliver, administer, and extend learning.

Additionally, the terms *online education* and *distance learning* refer to a system and process of connecting students, teachers, and learning resources when they are not in the same location as mentioned previously. Distance education has been tied to ICT for many years in the United States, initially after the establishment of an efficient postal system (Kramarae, 2001):

In the past several decades, the format of distance education has changed from primarily paper-based instruction to integrated multimedia (such as the delivery of courses via TV programs) to the use of networked computers (the Internet) and the Web. Internet-based distance education is becoming the major delivery method in the United States. (p. 4)

The commonly accepted concept of distance education is that it is a practice in which the learner and the instructor are separated in space and/or time, but it does not include the more recent conceptualization of the field that defines distance in

Table 1. Structure of the WebCT bulletin board composed of three categories (Source: Du, Harvard, & Li, 2005, p. 213)

Framework General Process	Bulleting Board Categories	Category Design
Information	Technical	Flexible peer discussion
Methods	Theoretical	Structured topic discussion
Cognition	Comprehensive	Collaborative task discussion

social terms—namely, the *transaction* and *interaction* between the learner and the teacher and among the learners (Saba, 2005).

Many distance learning courses experience high attrition rates resulting from factors such as students feeling *isolated*, *unmotivated*, *overwhelmed*, and *unchallenged*; therefore, as one of the strategies, online discussion in distance education might be imperative for student learning in general and for deep learning in particular (Du, Havard, & Li, 2005). Table 1 illustrates a framework for deep learning for dynamic online distance education.

The structure of the above WebCT bulletin board is composed of three categories (technical, theoretical, and comprehensive) and students engage in discussion as part of assignment completion: "Based on the framework and the dynamic discussion strategy proposed, student participation is encouraged in all aspects of the requirements for course completion. … Dynamic discussion is an integral part of an online course" (Du et al., 2005, p. 216). Concerning online discussion strategies, Beuchot and Bullen (2005) note, "researchers have begun only recently to look into the social dimension of online communication and their impact on the quality of interaction. Course designers and online instructors need to understand how students interact and how groups develop in computer-mediated environments" (p. 67).

One technology with potential for use in distance learning in Australia is broadband videoconferencing (Smyth, 2005): "There is great potential for broadband videoconferencing to add richness and flexibility to learning environments for distance students and to provide greater opportunities for teachers and students to engage interactively in their disciplines" (p. 816). This is because videoconferencing (1) improves teachers' and students' access to other teachers and students, thereby reducing the isolation of remote learners by facilitating the development of support networks, and (2) enhances the experiences of full-time students by providing them with opportunities to interact with peers or experts working professionally in the field.

In the practice of distance education, government agendas are supplanted by institutional agendas (the clientele shifts from undergraduate second-chance learners to fee-paying postgraduates); the methods are under challenge by the online revolution (Calvert, 2005):

Distance education, once a discrete field, is now operating in a context of convergence. Its methods have been incorporated into mainstream educational processes without the distance. The vehicle for this is online technology. In fact, distance education is becoming synonymous with non-contiguous online learning and the latter is dominating the research agenda. New researchers in the area do not ground their work in the accumulated body of distance education theory and research. (p. 227)

As regards distance education in practice, pointing out two issues of distance education (one is concerning the practice or methods of distance education, and the other is concerning research and scholarship), Calvert (2005) notes that the con-

Table 2. Traditional mode vs. online mode

Dimension	Traditional Mode	Online Mode
Assessment tasks	▪ The details of the assessment tasks are provided at the first class. ▪ Discussion about assessment tasks continues at subsequent classes. ▪ Assessment products are submitted directly to the teacher. ▪ The teacher returns feedback and marks directly to the students.	▪ The details of the assessment tasks are provided online. ▪ The teacher facilitates discussion about assessment tasks online. ▪ Assessment products are submitted online and the teacher downloads. ▪ The teacher returns feedback and marks online.
Resources	▪ Workshop-style presentations and discussions are a key source of information. ▪ Printed handouts are also provided.	▪ Electronic resources provided through the subject Web site are the key information source. ▪ Many journals are available through the library's online collection.
Activities	▪ Students attend workshop-style classes. ▪ Class focus on discussion activities, student presentations, and group activities.	▪ Individual and group online activities are designed as subtasks to help learners complete assessment tasks. ▪ Online discussion activities are used for sharing ideas and feedback.
Schedule	▪ The schedule is organized around the regular class meetings with weekly activities.	▪ The schedule is organized around the slots of time needed to complete the assessment tasks.
Interactions	▪ Face-to-face meetings are the main opportunities for interaction. ▪ One-on-one communication occurs during face-to-face sessions and through consultation times by phone.	▪ Continuous interaction occurs through online communication technologies. ▪ Students have opportunities to use communication tools to support collaboration and discussion.

temporary scene is different from the old scene chiefly in three ways: (1) there are more distance education players (i.e., many traditional campus-based universities now offer distance courses in fields of high demand or niche areas where they have particular strengths); (2) institutions are targeting different types of students (e.g., in the 1980s, most distance education students were in undergraduate courses); and (3) with online technologies to facilitate communication, administration, the distribution of learning resources and marketing, and institutions are looking to transnational markets for students.

The changes within higher education have brought about changes to the role of the instructor and the nature of instruction involved in *online* education as well as in *distanc*e education. The online classroom is different from the traditional classroom setting in several significant ways, including content delivery, self-initiated learning, and lack of face-to-face human interaction (Milheim, 2004). The comparison by Bennett and Lockyer (2004, pp. 235-236) is quite useful to understand holistically the characteristics of both ways of instructional methods (see Table 2).

Teachers perform, in online environments, as facilitators of student learning, but the techniques they employ to achieve that facilitation role are quite different. Bennett and Lockyer further note that online instructors need to:

- Design and facilitate collaborative and cooperative activities for learners who are working in different places, at different times, and with varying facilities
- Develop a schedule and study guide around milestones rather than classes
- Manage an electronic assignment submission and feedback process
- Create and integrate a greater range of electronic resources
- Develop skills and strategies for using computer-mediated tools as the primary means of communication

While online interactions support flexibility and convenience, synchronicity provides for more efficient and natural interaction, as maintained by Boettcher (2005):

When we gather in the physical classroom, we bundle many types of experiences; we combine lecture demonstrations, discussions, question-and-answer sessions, and large and small group activities. And, although many of the traditional synchronous tools were designed with the "lecture" or "presenter" paradigm in mind, the newer synchronous tools are more specialized and have been designed for collaborative interactions. ... The kinds of instructional experiences that this type of synchronous tool can support include a live videofeed that enables learners to hear and see a faculty member leading a discussion, performing short concept demonstrations, conducting review sessions, or hosting live interactions with guest experts. (pp. 21-22)

The growth of the Internet and online learning will be a continuous challenge to institutions of higher education. A survey by Song, Singleton, Hill, and Koh (2004) focused on two questions: What are the components of online learning environments that learners recognize as helpful in the learning process? And, what are the components of online learning environments that learners identify as challenging? As a result, the participants identified the following components as helpful: design of the course, comfort with online technologies, and time management. Difficulties understanding instructional goals and technical problems were both identified as challenges in online learning environments. Consequently, the following factors are important: (1) effective instructional design for online courses (that is, the design should focus not only on the technological aspects of the course but also on the goals, objectives, and expectations for the learners); (2) time management strategies (when learners are accustomed to learning in more static, real-time contexts, this can create significant time management issues); and (3) assisting students with establishing community or feelings of connection in online contexts.

Online Learning Assessment

Bradshaw, Powell, and Terrell (2005) describe the development and assessment of online communities at Ultralab (which is part of Anglia Polytechnic University and has been running online projects from pilot phase through the large-scale implementation using online learning communities for over 10 years) for students engaged in masters-level programs, doctoral research, and continuing professional learning as follows:

It considers the ways in which the engagement of learners, and their consequent participation, is seen to be dependent on several factors—the learners' perception of purpose, their sense of identity and trust, framing of learning activities, interactions from learning facilitators and tutors, and the information architecture of the learning space. The term community of enquiry *is used to indicate the key purpose of the community—that of practitioner-based enquiry, or research.* (p. 205)

The online course assessment by Steinweg, Davis, and Thomson (2005), on the other hand, indicates that there are no statistically significant differences in the changes in knowledge, in the changes in dispositions, and in the skill performance of learners enrolled in the online and traditional sections in a special education course. As an implication of the assessment, according to Steinweg et al. (2005), "the consistency in the content presented and the structure of the online and traditional sections of the course would be a factor of the similar outcomes" (p. 70); and, "the need for certified special education teachers and the demand for online classes to provide the necessary coursework in an easily accessible manner will likely continue to grow" (p. 71).

Garrison and Cleveland-Innes (2005) assessed the depth of online learning, with a focus on the nature of online interaction in distance-education course design. Their findings suggest: (1) the challenge is how to design and facilitate online learning experiences in order to create the cognitive presence consisting of deep learning and understanding; and (2) it is important to provide engaging questions, focus discussions, challenge and test ideas, model appropriate contributions and to ensure that the discourse is progressive. From a design and organizational perspective, their findings further suggest defining clear expectations and selecting manageable content, structuring appropriate activities (both collaborative and individual), and conducting assessment congruent with intended goals—the fostering of a deep approach to learning.

It is also important to recognize that the online student is *not* a "homogenous entity but a fragmentation of different backgrounds, learning needs, aptitudes, abilities, and degrees of self-direction. Emphasizing such diversity by actively creating an environment that can adjust to meet these demands is the challenge to online college educators" (Flores & Flores, 2003, p. 246).

The online environment affords unprecedented opportunities to shift the role of university faculty from "plan and deliver" to "listen and support," and the advantage of this shift is that students may learn more because the faculty focus on the development of the students' understanding and learning (Doubler, Grisham, & Paget, 2003). In many online classes, however, over 50% of students will drop or fail, and this results in an ideological half-truth (physical presence is essential to learning and, after all, education is best in the face-to-face environment); nevertheless, an essential factor is *not* the physical presence or absence of teachers and students but the students' capacity to direct their own learning (Flores & Flores, 2003).

Calvert (2005) emphasizes that distance education itself and its international research scene are both *not* characterized by mutual identity and that the research on distance education is scattered. Calvert suggests the following issues or questions facing distance education that form useful guidance for research:

- Transnational distance education is attractive to institutions because of its revenue-generating potential. What inhibits its growth?
- How should institutions cater to the differing expectations of on- and off-campus students in an online environment?
- How can institutions facilitate the innovation that teachers bring to distance education when the institutions standardize practices with learning management systems such as WebCT and Blackboard?

- What are the long-term implications for academic workload and the nature of teaching?

The reflective and collaborative properties of asynchronous, text-based distance online learning are well adapted to deep approaches to learning (cognitive presence); therefore, there is a strong need to study the qualitative nature of online interaction in terms of teaching and learning approaches, and further study is very much needed to understand the nature of online interaction that will support high levels of learning (Garrison & Cleveland-Innes, 2005).

Asynchronous distance learning is the most ambitious form of e-education, yet distance teaching that necessarily involves greater faculty workloads than classroom teaching represents the imposing barrier to participation in "e-education" in general and "distance learning" specifically (Dibiase & Rademacher, 2005). Moreover, according to Dibiase and Rademacher, successful online course implementation should focus on the following:

- Setup and coordination including tasks associated with readying new implementations of the course within the course management system and ongoing tasks related to administration and coordination;
- Content development and maintenance including all changes to course content such as corrections, revisions, and additions to text and graphics;
- Communication including daily communications with students via threaded discussion, e-mail, and occasional telephone calls or in-person conversations; and
- Assessment and feedback including development and revision of rubrics, evaluation of projects published in e-portfolios, and grade reports and comments sent to individual students.

Higher and Adult Education

Faculty members who teach in traditional modes tend to think that a quality instructional experience requires students to attend face-to-face lectures within the university, despite the fact that there is no research to support the idea that the classroom is the optimal place in which to learn; actually outcome comparisons between students who have studied in a traditional manner and those at a distance have found "no significant difference" (Ebersole, 2003).

ICT and technology-based learning have quickly become educational "hot topics" over the last decade; educationalists around the world have been quick to herald ICT as a transformatory arena for secondary and postsecondary education and training

(Gorard, Selwyn, & Madden, 2003). Twenty years of information technology (IT) innovation (from the introduction of personal computers to the spread of the Internet and e-mail) have transformed higher education and have altered the communications, administrative, research, and teaching landscapes of universities (Roach, 2004). The goals of higher education are enhanced student learning and increased satisfaction for both instructor and learners, and nothing is more important to teaching students to take responsibility for lifelong learning (Harrison, 2004). The highest priority for today's higher education teachers, administrators, and policy makers, therefore, should be making their students effective "lifelong learners," providing students with the ability to acquire new skills and knowledge; and eventually students have to develop their ability to control the learning process. Historically, in the world of education (Gustavason, 2002):

> *... a radical redefinition of the central concepts of dialogue (lifelong learning and knowledge) took place in the mid 1980s, especially in terms of policy and practice; high technology production places more investment in knowledge than do mechanical or industrial production—the amount of knowledge invested in high technocratic products is greater than that invested in traditionally industrial products and such innovations occurred in the mid 1980s. During the 1990s, progressivism has increasingly been given an IT signature. The teacher becomes a tutor or a coach. Knowledge is no longer seen as a "package" but rather as something one will find in catalogues, on the Internet or in databases.* (p. 19)

At present, almost all institutions of higher education offer some form of distance teaching and learning in the United States; there were an estimated 3,077,000 enrollments in all higher education courses and an estimated 127,400 different higher education distance courses were offered during the academic year 2000-2001 (Saba, 2005): "If current trends continue, it will be just a matter of time before distance education becomes the dominant form of teaching and learning" (p. 257). It may *not* happen in the near future. Nonetheless, it is the reality that besides the daunting task of learning how to use the specific technology, university faculty members are routinely confronted with the never-ending changes in software and hardware, a lack of support personnel, overloaded classes, varying technology skills of students, and increased commitment of time necessary for preparation and student interaction (Travis & Price, 2005).

Future Trends

Pointing out that the urgency to define a clear vision for American higher education system has never been greater than it is today, Nair (2003) identifies four key change agents or trends that American higher education needs to be mindful about: (1) *technology-driven growth of information and communication* (which continues to be fueled by quantum leaps in technological advancement); (2) *globalization* (underlying the two trends—technological advances and an acceleration of globalization—is competition); (3) *competition* (in a global marketplace, education itself is becoming a commodity); and (4) *accountability* (the lack of adequate performance measures tied to funding hurts the higher education institutions financially).

Higher education in contemporary times must be understood to be a globalizing process because the ongoing faculty development of those currently in the teaching force is the key to educational enhancement which, in turn, helps students to live and work in an increasingly global world, and because that education is becoming a global commodity, having a definite practical application, such as information technology as utilized on the Internet (Inoue, 2004).

Based on an integrative literature review (the illustration of the 21st century will not be those who cannot read and write but those who cannot *learn*, *unlearn*, and *relearn*, for example), Howell, Williams, and Lindsay (2004) recognize 32 trends for future directions of online distance education which include the following:

Student/Enrollment Trends

- Higher education learner profiles, including online distance and adult learners, are changing.
- Percentage of adult, female, and minority learners is increasing; retention rates concern administrators and faculty members.

Faculty Trends

- Traditional faculty roles are shifting or "unbundling."
- Need for faculty development, support, and training is growing.
- Instructors of distance courses can feel isolated.

Academic Trends

- Knowledge and information are growing exponentially.
- There is a shift in organizational structure toward decentralization.

- Education is becoming more seamless between high school, college, and further studies.
- Higher education outsourcing and partnerships are increasing.

Technology Trends

- Technological devices are becoming more versatile and ubiquitous.
- There is growth in Internet usage.
- Technological fluency is becoming a graduation requirement.

Economic Trends

- Funding challenges are the top IT concern for many institutions.
- Lifelong learning is becoming a competitive necessity.
- Internet is becoming dominant among other distance-education media.
- Distinction between distance and local education is disappearing.

The most fundamental and perhaps the most decisive change in the 21st century will take place in education; indeed, the school for the 21st century must be vital in all aspects—vital in the meaning of virtual, individualized, tutored, and active learning, and has to be based on a learner's concept and not on a teacher's concept (Free, 2000).

Recent issues in prominent distance-learning journals have established the need for administrators to be informed and prepared with strategic plans equal to foreseeable challenges because many trends in higher education will influence the future of distance learning in many ways. For example, as noted by Howell et al. (2004): (1) traditional faculty roles, motivation, and training needs are shifting while workload, compensation, and instructional issues continue to deter them from distance learning participation; (2) the Internet and other information technology devices are becoming ubiquitous while technological fluency is becoming a common expectation; and (3) distance education is becoming more abundant, especially online, and location independent, increasing the need for effective course-management systems and teaching strategies that utilize technology.

Summary and Conclusion

Research shows the growing demand for online distance education worldwide as the main driving force for borderless education, emphasizing a demand from a new group of learners, working adults (earning and learning), for lifelong, relevant, "just-in-time," and flexible learning opportunities (Wende, 2002). Accommodating the fact that many of today's mainstream students combine jobs with full- or part-time study and family life, this explains that distance education will become the dominant mode of higher education (Calvert, 2005).

The student population in many institutions of higher education has doubled in size and this has led to an increase in the diversity of the student groups (Peat et al., 2005). Institutions of American higher learning, from now on, will be more responsive to a student body that is no longer traditional in its composition. This group includes working students, older adult re-entry students, part-time students, students for whom English is a second language, and professionals seeking to update their knowledge and who may not see themselves as students.

Higher education faces an era of mass graduation at a time of rapid ICT development; consequently, future opportunities and choices may deal with five issues: (1) access (with ICT, higher education can widen access to include students at a distance and to accommodate groups unable to attend at specific times); (2) engagement (promoting engaging learning and enquiry using ICT); (3) community (through online communities, ICT can be used to promote community); (4) pedagogy (ICT provides an opportunity for rethinking the curriculum and developing the pedagogy for adults); and (5) cost (some propose that ICT might be used solely to reduce unit costs and to capture a growing international market but some would say that changes in the use of ICT in higher education are slow) (Millwood & Terrell, 2005).

Contributions of ICT and distance education to the development of individual learners, and eventually of lifelong learners, are enormous but, as White (2005) states:

> *For distance education to play a key role in the future provision of educational opportunities, sustained attention needs to be given to those who are most involved in distance education—the learners. Most informed understanding of the circumstances of learners, their needs, and the ways they respond to distance learning opportunities is an important basis for developing and providing quality-learning experiences and for contributing to the development of individual learners. Research has a crucial role to play in the viability of this position.* (p. 177)

Teacher-student interactions have always been regarded as a crucial variable determining learning in distance learning environments (Offir, Barth, Lev, & Shteinbok, 2005): "online collection of data regarding students' performance, combined with an analysis of the teacher's interactions during each individual lesson, enable researchers to identity patterns of teacher interactions that support effective student learning" (p. 165). Therefore, administrators and faculty are expected to adjust to new paradigms of online instruction: "a misperception of the role of technology in instruction, regarding it as a teaching method rather than a delivery tool, continues to thwart effective technology use" (p. 99), and faculty truly need to engage their creative abilities for distance learning situations (Travis & Price, 2005).

For students and instructors, through Internet facilities, communication goes beyond the spatiotemporal particulars of their lives, and helps them shape multiple identities and pursue a variety of opportunities and challenges (Papastephanou, 2005). Eventually, perhaps, the Web site of the course will become an "open door" to the classroom, and the Web site will create a "sense of community" among class members (currently, professors try to create a "sense of community" in the classroom) (Koepke, 2000). Certainly, it is a useful and intriguing notion.

Acknowledgment

The author is grateful to Mark C. Goniwiecha at the University of Guam for his critical suggestions on the earlier draft of this chapter.

References

Alheit, P., & Dausien, B. (2002). The double face of lifelong learning: Two analytical perspectives on a silent revolution. *Studies in the Education of Adults, 34*(1), 3-22.

Allert, H., Richter, C., & Nejdl, W. (2004). Lifelong learning and second-order learning objects. *British Journal of Educational Technology, 35*(6), 701-715.

Allport, C. (2000). Thinking globally, acting locally: Lifelong learning and the implications for university staff. *Journal of Higher Education Policy and Management, 22*(1), 37-46.

Bennett, S., & Lockyer, L. (2004). Becoming an online teacher: Adapting to a changed environment for teaching and learning in higher education. *Educational Media International, 41*(3), 231-244.

Beuchot, A., & Bullen, M. (2005). Interaction and interpersonality in online distance forums. *Distance Education, 26*(1), 67-87.

Blandin, B. (2000). *Open and distance learning: An overall survey at the beginning of 2000.* Retrieved July 23, 2006, from http://www.eden-online.org/contents/publications/New_ Learning/ODL_Within_The_World_of_VET.pdf

Boettcher, J. V. (2005). Designing for the virtual interactive classroom. *Campus Technology, 18*(9), 20-30.

Bourne, J., Harris, D., & Mayadas, F. (2005). Online engineering education: Learning anywhere, anytime. *Journal of Engineering Education, 94*(1), 131-146.

Bradshaw, P., Powell, S., & Terrell, I. (2005). Developing engagement in Ultralab's online communities of enquiry. *Innovations in Education and Teaching International, 42*(3), 205-215.

Calvert, J. (2005). Distance education at the crossroads. *Distance Education, 26*(2), 227-238.

Commonwealth of Learning. (2000). *The concept of open and distance learning.* Retrieved July 23, 2006, from http://www.col.org/resources/startupguides/intro_learning.htm

Creanor, L. (2002). A tale of two courses: A comparative study of tutoring online. *Open Learning, 17*(1), 57-68.

Dibiase, D., & Rademacher, H. J. (2005). Scaling up: Faculty workload, class size, and student satisfaction in a distance learning course on geographic information science. *Journal of Geography in Higher Education, 29*(1), 139-158.

Doubler, S. J., Grisham, L., & Paget, K. F. (2003, January). *Emerging faculty role.* Paper presented at the American Association of Colleges for Teacher Education Annual Meeting, New Orleans. (ERIC Database #ED473257)

Du, J., Havard, B., & Li, H. (2005). Dynamic online discussion: Task-oriented interaction for deep learning. *Educational Media International, 42*(3), 207-218.

Ebersole, J. (2003). It's not whether to innovate, but how. *Adults Learning, 15*(1). Retrieved July 23, 2006, from http://web15.epnet.com/citation.asp?tb=1&_ug=sid-DF4FD738%2D8A9F%2D4E0D%2D8

EDUCAUSE. (2005). *The pocket guide to U.S. higher education.* Boulder, CO; Washington, DC: Author.

Fielding, R. (2002). *Personalized learning space in a global context.* Retrieved July 23, 2006, from http://www.designshare.com/Research/AIA/Cambridge/Personal_Global_3.htm

Fischer, G. (1999). *Lifelong learning—more than training.* Retrieved July 23, 2006, from http://www.l3d.cs.colorado.edu/~gerhard/papers/lll99.pdf

Flores, J., & Flores, B. (2003, March). The gradual student. *Teaching English in the Two-Year College (ETYC)*, 239-247.

Free, C. (2000). *The future of vocational education*. Retrieved July 23, 2006, from http://www.eden-online.org/contents/publications/New_Learning/ODL_Within_The_World_of_VET.pdf

Frey, B., & Donehue, R. (2003). Making the transition from traditional to cyberspace classroom. *PAACE Journal of Lifelong Learning, 12*, 69-84.

Friesen, N., & Anderson, T. (2004). Interaction for lifelong learning. *British Journal of Educational Technology, 35*(6), 679-687.

Garrison, R. D., & Cleveland-Innes, M. (2005). Facilitating cognitive presence in online learning: Interaction is not enough. *The American Journal of Distance Education, 19*(3), 133-148.

Goetz, J. R. (2004). *Confessions of an early Internet educator* (DETC occasional paper). Washington, DC: The Distance Education and Training Council.

Gorard, S., Selwyn, N., & Madden, L. (2003). Logged on to learning? Assessing the impact of technology on participation in lifelong learning. *International Journal of Lifelong Education, 22*(3), 281-296.

Grow, G. (1991). Teaching learners to be self-directed. *Adult Education Quarterly, 41*(3), 125-149.

Gustavason, B. (2002). What do we mean by lifelong learning and knowledge? *International Journal of Lifelong Education, 21*(1), 103-23.

Harrison, R. F. (2004). The school library: The educational extension (administrator's perspective). *Teacher Librarian, 31*(3), 63.

Howell, S. L., Williams, P. B., & Lindsay, N. K. (2004). *Thirty-two trends affecting distance education: An informed foundation for strategic planning*. Retrieved July 23, 2006, from http://www.westga.edu/~distance/ojdla/fall63/howell63.html

Huang, H.-M. (2002). Toward constructivism for adult learners in online learning environments. *British Journal of Educational Technology, 33*(1), 27-37.

Illeris, K. (2003). Towards a contemporary and comprehensive theory of learning. *International Journal of Lifelong Education, 22*(4), 396-406.

Inoue, Y. (2004). Higher education: A globalizing process (revised version). In L.-H. N. Chiang, J. Lidstone, & R. A. Stephenson (Eds.), *The challenges of globalization: Cultures in transition in the Pacific-Asia region* (pp. 59-72). Lanham, MD: University Press of America.

Jarvis, P. (1999). Global trends in lifelong learning and the response of the universities. *Comparative Education, 35*(2), 249-257.

Koepke, M. L. (2000). Portfolio development: Multimedia presentations for designers. In D. G. Brown (Ed.), *Teaching with technology* (pp. 178-182). Bolton, MA: Anker.

Koper, R., & Tattersall, C. (2004). New directions for lifelong learning using network technologies. *British Journal of Educational Technologies, 35*(6), 689-700.

Kramarae, C. (2001). *Excerpts from the third shift: Women learning online.* Retrieved July 23, 2006, from http://darkwing.uoregon.edu/~cheris/third%20shift.pdf

Medel-Añonuevo, C., Ohsako, T., & Mauch, W. (2001). *Revisiting lifelong learning for the 21st century.* UNESCO Institute for Education.

Medford, A. (2004). Online learning. *Quality in Primary Care, 12,* 87-9.

Milheim, K. L. (2004). Strategies for designing on-line courseware. *International Journal of Instructional Media, 31*(3), 267-272.

Millwood, R., & Terrell, I. (2005). Overview: New technology, learning and assessment in higher education. *Innovations in Education and Teaching International, 42*(3), 195-204.

Moore, G. M. (2003). *From Chautauqua to the virtual university: A century of distance education in the United States* (Information Series No. 393). Columbia, OH: Center on Education and Training for Employment, Ohio State University. (ERIC Database #ED482357).

Nair, P. (2003). *Imperatives for change in higher education: Planning the future of the American campus.* Retrieved July 23, 2006, from http://www.designshare.com/Research/Nair/HigherEd/imperatives_higher_ed.htm

National Institute of Adult Continuing Education (NIACE). (n.d.). *ICT skill for life.* Retrieved July 23, 2006, from http://www.niace.org.uk/Research/ICT/ICT-skillforlife.htm/

Offir, B., Barth, I., Lev, J., & Shteinbok, A. (2005). Can interaction content analysis research contribute to distance learning? *Educational Media International, 42*(2), 161-171.

Oncken, W., & Wass, D. L. (1974, November-December). Management time: Who got the monkey? *Harvard Business Review*, 75-80.

Papastephanou, M. (2005). Difference-sensitive communities, networked learning, and higher education: Potentialities and risks. *Studies in Higher Education, 30*(1), 81-94.

Peat, M., Taylor, C.E., & Franklin, S. (2005). Re-engineering of undergraduate science curricula to emphasize development of lifelong skills. *Innovations in Education and Teaching International, 42*(2), 135-146.

Roach, R. (2004). Technology: Riding the waves of change. *Black Issues in Higher Education, 21*(9), 92-95.

Saba, F. (2005). Critical issues in distance education. *Distance Education, 26*(2), 255-272.

Sakamoto, T. (2002). E-learning and educational innovation in higher education in Japan. *Education Media International, 39*(1), 9-16.

Schuller, T. (2004). Visual imagery, lifecourse structure and lifelong learning. *Studies in the Education of Adults, 36*(1). Retrieved July 23, 2006, from http://web35.epnet.com/citation.asp?tb=1&_ug+sid+DFDC1135%2D4E4B%2

Smyth, R. (2005). Broadband videoconferencing as a tool for learner-centered distance learning in higher education. *British Journal of Educational Technology, 36*(5), 805-820.

Song, L., Singleton, E. S., Hill, J. R., & Koh, M. H. (2004). Improving online learning: Student perceptions of useful and challenging characteristics. *Internet & Higher Education, 7*(1), 59-70.

Steinweg, S. B., Davis, M. L., & Thomson, W. S. (2005). A comparison of traditional and online instruction in an introduction to special education course. *Teacher Education and Special Education, 28*(1), 62-73.

Travis, J. E., & Price, K. (2005). Instructional culture and distance education. *Journal of Faculty Development, 20*(2), 99-103.

Wende, M. (2002). *The role of U.S. higher education in the global e-learning market*. Retrieved July 23, 2006, from http://www.utwente.nl/modelsofchange

White, C. (2005). Contribution of distance education to the development of individual learners. *Distance Education, 26*(2), 165-181.

Whiteman, J.-A. M. (2002). *The adult learner in the computer mediated environment.* (ERIC Database #ED467889).

Appendix: Open and Distance Learning Terms and Definitions

Source: Commonwealth of Learning. (2000). *The concept of open and distance learning*. Retrieved July 23, 2006, from http://www.col.org/resources/startupguides/intro_learning.htm

- **Basic Education:** The provision of teaching and learning opportunities that enable learners to obtain primary-level skills in reading, writing, and numeracy.
- **Cable Feed:** Broadcast material sent via a fixed cable or a community antenna.
- **Computer-Assisted Learning:** A learning method that uses a computer system to present individualized instructional materials.

- **Computer-Based Learning:** A generic term for the various kinds of stand-alone (that is, non-networked) learning applications that involve computer software.
- **Computer-Mediated Learning:** In the context of teaching and learning, the use of electronic mail, computer conferencing and the World Wide Web to deliver learning material and provide learners and teachers with opportunities for interaction. Also called networked learning.
- **Continuing Education:** Education that is usually not for credit, but which can be delivered on campus or at a distance.
- **Correspondence Education:** Education that relies on print-based, self-study materials with communication through postal services.
- **Deep Learning:** An intention on the part of the learner to develop his or her understanding and to challenge ideas; contrast surface learning.
- **Digital:** Information stored in the form of 0s and 1s; digital information may include video, audio, graphics and text.
- **Distance Teaching:** A term that emphasizes the teacher's role in the distance education system
- **Distributed Learning:** A term that emphasizes learning rather than the technology used or the separation between teacher and learner; distributed learning makes learning possible beyond the classroom and, when combined with classroom modes, becomes flexible learning.
- **Electronic Mail (e-mail):** the exchange of information from one computer to another using software that is designed to store and forward messages received or sent.
- **External Studies:** Instruction that takes place somewhere other than a central campus, such as a classroom remote from campus, and that includes a variety of delivery options, including home-study and telecommunications.
- **Flexible Learning:** A term that emphasizes the creation of environments for learning that have the following characteristics: convergence of open and distance learning methods, media and classroom strategies; learner-centered philosophy; recognition of diversity in learning styles and in learners' needs; recognition of the importance of equity in curriculum and pedagogy; use of a variety of learning resources and media; fostering of lifelong learning habits and skills in learners and staff.
- **Hypertext Mark-Up Language:** The protocol used to create documents for publication and distribution on the World Wide Web; html consists of tags, added to text documents, which format and create links to other www resources.
- **Independent Study:** A mode of learning in which learners work through their study materials independently of other learners.

- **Information Highway:** A term developed as a way of describing the joining together of once-separate telephone and television technologies and computing systems into a single global network of networks.
- **Interactive Television:** Television broadcasts that are combined with some form of telecommunications link to enable viewers to respond to what they are watching.
- **Internet:** The worldwide collection of computer networks that use a common communications protocol and addressing scheme to share resources with one another; owned by no one, it is maintained collectively by the individual national, regional, commercial and institutional networks that make up the Internet; it is a learning, information and business tool.
- **Learner-Centered Education:** An educational philosophy in which the integrity and freedom of the individual is primary; therefore, the teaching and learning process provides flexible sequences of study, negotiated objectives and content, negotiated learning methods, negotiated methods of assessment and a choice of support mechanisms.
- **Lifelong Learning:** A philosophical concept in which learning is viewed as a long-term process beginning at birth and lasting throughout life; a conceptual framework within which the learning needs of people of all ages and educational and occupational levels may be met, regardless of their circumstances.
- **Listserv:** An e-mail system that automatically sends messages to all subscribers on specific mailing lists, especially interest groups.
- **Media Designer:** Sometimes called the visual designer; the person on the course team who bears responsibility for the illustrations, page layout, formatting and integration of print with other media.
- **Multimedia:** Learning technologies that involve the whole range of audio, visual, text, and graphics media available, integrated into a package that has been effectively designed from an instructional point of view.
- **Networked Learning:** A type of learning in which learners and instructors use computers to exchange messages, engage in dialogue and access resources; the interaction can occur in real-time (synchronously) when learners and instructors are communicating at the same time from different places or in delayed-time (asynchronously) when they are not linked at the same time.
- **Networking:** The process of creating, expanding and maintaining relationships with other agencies.
- **Open and Distance Learning:** A way of providing learning opportunities that is characterized by the separation of teacher and learner in time or place, or both time and place; learning that is certified in some way by an institution or agency; the use of a variety of media, including print and electronic; two-way communications that allow learners and tutors to interact; the possibility of

occasional face-to-face meetings; and a specialized division of labor in the production and delivery of courses.

- **Open Learning:** An educational philosophy that also emphasizes giving learners choices about media, place of study, pace of study, support mechanisms, and entry and exit points.
- **Self-Instruction:** A process in which materials take learners step-by-step through an instructional process; self-assessment exercises are a central feature and instruction can be paper-based or computer-based.
- **Single-Mode Institution:** An institution that has been set up solely to offer programs of study at a distance.
- **Technical or Vocational Training:** Training that is designed to prepare technicians, middle management, and other skilled personnel for one or a group of occupations, trades, or jobs.
- **Technology-Based Education:** In the context of teaching and learning, a system in which a media other than print has a major role.
- **Video Conference:** A technological arrangement in which television monitors, cameras, and microphones are linked so that people in three or more sites can all see, hear, and speak to one another.
- **Video Disc:** A disc on which video and audio signals are recorded for television use; a video disc requires a video player compatible with the video disc.
- **World Wide Web (WWW or Web):** A communication protocol of the Internet that deals with text, audio, video, animation, graphics, and color—anything that a computer program can produce.

Section II

Development and Implementation of Online Lifelong Learning

Chapter II

Can You Hear Us Now? Stances Towards Interaction and Rapport

Susan J. Wegmann, University of Central Florida, USA

Joyce K. McCauley, Sam Houston State University, USA

Abstract

This chapter examines two key factors that influence the efficacy of online learning: student and teacher interaction and rapport. These two factors are heavily influenced by the stance that the learner takes. Online learning is opening up more possibilities for lifelong learning. This chapter will provide a critical discussion of online education, the theories that ground this delivery system, and the challenges that one university faculty had in creating a community of learners in a technology-mediated learning environment. "Let's put our Reading Masters courses online," the Dean suggested. "We need to move our graduate course offerings into the twenty-first century. Can't be left behind." She left the six of us in the conference room to talk over her proposal. But what was there to discuss? The answer was "No." It just wasn't possible. We'd lose that personal connection with our students that our university is known for. We'd lose those rousing discussions and meaningful interactions. Why, the students wouldn't even see each other, let alone see us. How could we encourage lifelong learning when we weren't even sold on the idea? The whole idea was impractical, unworkable, and inconceivable. Putting our courses online? Out of the question!

That was four years ago. Since then there have been a few changes in our attitudes toward online teaching and learning. We now have face-to-face courses and an online Master of Education in Reading program, both identical in content and rigor—and both reflecting our pedagogical beliefs in the importance of the affective factors in creating a community of learners. This chapter shares our observations and new understandings as we examined the reactions and interactions of our students in our online courses.

Introduction

Lifelong distance learning is no longer a novel experience but rather an expected offering of most institutions of higher learning and is gaining strength and popularity in graduate programs across the nation (Lao & Gonzales, 2005). Between 1995 and 1997, the number of classes offered online in two- and four-year institutions has nearly doubled, according to the U.S. Department of Education (2002). In the 1999-2000 school year, 124,240 people earned a master's degree in education (U.S. Department of Education, 2000). Of these students, approximately 12% participated in some form of online learning. The National Center for Educational Statistics (2003) reported that in 2000-2001, 89% to 90% of public two- and four-year degree-granting institutions offered some form of distance education. Additionally almost half of the four-year institutions offered online degrees.

This chapter is a description of one faculty's journey to develop an online program, as well as an exploration of the nature of online interaction and rapport. Believing that instructor and student stance highly influences the online experience, we will offer some suggestions after describing an analysis of our students and instructors.

The benefits of online learning have been widely explored in the literature (Benbunan-Fich & Hiltz, 1999; Maher & Jacob, 2006). The one benefit heard most often is the elimination of the need to travel to go to classes (Barkley & Bianco, 2001). Students find themselves "in class" with others from all over the state and nation that results in an exchange of a wide variety of ideas, experiences, and opinions. As one graduate student of ours remarked, "Being with such admirable educators from different states has made me realize that we truly do have a powerful force across this country." Distance learning also allows students to choose when, where, and how long they will engage in course materials thus allowing for more control over learning preferences (DeRouin, Fritzsche, & Salas, 2005; Laferrière, Lamon, & Chan, 2006; Lin, Cranton, & Bridglall, 2005). This can be seen in a quote from a final course evaluation:

The convenience of coming home after work and getting comfortable to study is certainly a plus. I have the luxury of waking up early or staying up late to time the ebb and flow of my creative "juices." Even the slight additional fees are cost-effective when you compare the gas mileage, wear and tear on my car, and the hour and a half commute time.

And finally, online learning fits into the lifestyles of today's learners who are increasingly mobile. "They are the ones who will pursue and ultimately demand mobile learning resources and opportunities" (Wagner & Wilson, 2005, p. 1) to continue learning throughout their lives.

How a university transitions to online coursework varies, but any change is often met with some worries and concerns (Beller & Or, 1998). For example, in the scenario (from the quotation), our faculty had developed a sound Master of Education in Reading program that was nationally accredited and resulted in successful pass rates for their graduates on the Reading Specialist Exam for their state. The faculty continued to assess and improve the coursework and was pleased with the positive and encouraging responses to the program by the candidates. In the fall of 2000, the directive came from the administration to consider offering the program in an online format. After much research and discussion, the faculty decided to experiment with the online format, one course at a time.

The first course was developed during the Spring 2001 semester and was delivered online in the summer of 2001. Each semester, courses were added. Also, each semester the faculty shared ideas, research, challenges, and student responses. By Spring 2003, the 36-hour Master of Education in Reading program was fully delivered online.

For the past three years, the program has been offered online and face-to-face concurrently. Students can take every course online, except for one three week period on campus in which candidates complete an assessment and remediation internship and attend seminars. All classes are taught by tenured and tenure-track reading faculty. Typical students in this program are employed as teachers or support personnel who would usually attend classes at night. The program is supported by Blackboard, a computer program that allows instructors to house lectures, PowerPoint presentations, asynchronous discussion board questions, and other materials necessary for delivering course content. Students are given weekly assignments (usually a reading task and a writing/response task that is e-mailed to their professor) and asked to respond to their peers on a chat-room-type of discussion board. Asynchronous (comments, questions, and answers that are posted and later accessed by others) is preferred over synchronous communication (conversations occurring in real time). Often, professors ask students to work on small group projects tailored to the students' interests along with reading additional materials and mandatory class readings. Students are also asked to complete semester-long projects that include literature reviews, PowerPoint presentations, and/or use other formats to display their learning.

Semester by semester as the faculty converted their face-to-face courses to the online format, they were careful to keep the integrity of their course content by using the same objectives, readings, assignments, and experiences. Some rubrics were modified in order to reflect the online nature of the assignments; however they were kept as close as possible to the face-to-face versions. The faculty was unsure, however, that the affective factors were sustainable as well and some worried about the level of interaction and rapport. In elementary classrooms, teacher-to-student and student-to-student interaction and rapport are both critical in order to motivate students to learn (Simpson & Galbo, 1986). Reasoning that interaction and rapport influences and motivates adult students as well, other teacher-educators across the nation are also concerned about whether the interaction and rapport found online is as powerful as in face-to-face settings (Killian & Willhite, 2003; Martinez & Sweger, 1996; Wegmann & McCauley, 2006).

Our faculty asked many questions during the development of the first few courses: Would their students like Internet-based instruction? What would happen to the personal contact, the laughter, the asides, the quick stories to emphasize a point, the extended illustrations to clarify a difficult concept, the "how-are-things-going," and the informal before-class banter? All these are important to establishing an online learning community. All of these add to the richness of conversations. What would happen to these factors in courses where computer-mediated communication was necessary? As the courses were developed, the following questions were considered and monitored:

1. How can Web-based interaction facilitate communication, and are there opportunities for genuine discussions, grand conversations, or a participant stance online?
2. How can instructors establish rapport in an online course with students they never physically see?

The purpose of this chapter is to discuss these questions as we analyzed the interactions and rapport found in our online classes over the course of three years. Our classes averaged 12 students. Three courses in the online Master of Education in Reading program were analyzed: the first two (a foundation of reading course and a multicultural course in reading education) occurred in the first year of the program and the third (a course on instructional materials in reading) occurred during the second year. The rest of this chapter will address online interactions and discussions as well as the rapport that instructors and students need to establish.

Methodology

Data collection consisted of the constant comparison method. We surveyed three master's level online classes, asking students about the nature of discussions in their classes (Note: Samples of the survey questions are included in Appendix A). We followed the participant observation model in order to analyze discussion board contents. To focus on the interrelatedness of interactions, we chose one discussion board entry and mapped out the interactions found therein. We verified our analyses by interviewing the participants at a face-to-face end of the program meeting. As a theoretical background, we embrace Vygotsky's (1978) notion of social interactionism and Rosenblatt's (1994) transaction theory to understand both classroom interactions and reading processes. We also understand that a *participant stance* (Britton, 1993; Wegmann, 2001) is necessary in order to ensure *social presence* (Moore, 1991; Short, Williams, & Christie, 1976; Stein, Wanstreet, Calvin, Overtoom, & Wheaton, 2005). The purpose of this chapter is to describe the nature of online interactions and discussions. Conducting a quantitative analysis of online interactions (i.e., who interacted with whom, why, and quantifying how the instructor's stance influenced the interactions, in both undergraduate and graduate level classes) was beyond the scope of this chapter, yet we hope to do so in the near future.

How Can Online Interaction Facilitate Computer-Mediated Communication?

Interaction is an important component of any learning event (Dewey, 1938; Vygotsky, 1978) and has been identified as one of the major constructs in online learning (Li & Akins, 2005; Shovein, Huston, Fox & Damazo, 2005; Vrasidas, 2002). Simpson and Galbo (1986) defined interaction as "behavior in which individuals and groups act upon one another ... a continually emerging process, as communication in its most inclusive sense" (p. 38). The discourse sequences are mediated by the computer, adding to the complexity of computer mediated communication (Mondada, 2006). Distance educators have defined four types of interaction: (1) learner-teacher, (2) learner-content, (3) learner-learner, and (4) learner-interface (Hillman, Willis, & Gunawardena, 1994). This last aspect of interaction is unique to distance education and has come about only recently. Moreover, interactions do not just happen—they need to be an intentional part of the instructional design (Althaus, 1997; King & Doerfert, 1996; Saba & Shearer, 1994; Smith, 2005; Zhang, Perris, & Yeung, 2005). Thus, can online interaction actually facilitate communication, or does the computer-as-mediator between person and content inhibit true communication?

Some degree of interaction occurs in every teaching/learning experience. Most face-to-face classrooms reflect an initiate respond evaluate (IRE) pattern (Mehan, 1979).

Table 1. Discussion board entry and possible moves of participants

Participant, day, date, time	**Actual words of participants: Teacher-generated question on Discussion Board: How does Calkins work 'fit' with what you know about teaching writing in classrooms?**	**Possible moves identifying stance of participant**
Kristy Tuesday, Feb. 11, 9:45 pm	I think that Calkins can teach us to respond with belief. Believing that your student is a writer and that they have many reasons to write. She also showed that when responding to what may not seem like much of a writing, respond with a positive attitude. Also, to question the student and make them think further. Calkins' attitude made me think of Mathewson's theory and how making the student feel important and in a warm environment. I think that if we believe in our students' writing from the very beginning, we are giving them a head start.	Introducing a new topic Sharing opinion Connecting to other readings Sharing opinion, beliefs
Michael responds to Kristy Wednesday, Feb. 12, 8:24am	Students need to have meaning in their writing. I have to give mine topics that they are interested in or they cannot write half a page. I give them a topic they care about and they write two pages. I have very little time to do writing assignments in my class. I teach in the high school and all we focus on is the TAKS test. My students are getting tired of hearing about this test. Students also need positive reinforcement. If they know that you believe in them and that you are going to support them then they will perform for you.	Connecting to his own classroom experiences Introducing a new topic Sharing opinions, beliefs Connecting to his own thinking
Mary Ann responds to Kristy Wednesday, Feb. 12, 8:20pm	You know I agree that not all she says about how a teacher should teach can be applied in the real classroom. These professors have been out too long. When did she write the book? 1980. The test taking is crazy and in real life upper grade teachers need to help kids pass the test. I know in kinder I am like one of the teachers in the early part of the year, however in the later part of the year I am like the other teacher. Kids need to learn about Clay's principles and they must be taught how to use them. And the sooner they are exposed them in Guided reading and Guided writing the better it is for them. I use approximation but I need to tell you sooner or later they need to start making progress. I was happy to see the connection to Matthewson. I really see the Cambourne in Caulkin's work. Since I see so much of Cambourne's theory; Approximation, Expectations, Responsibility, etc. I have been wondering about these theorists: Clay, Cambourne and Calkins. Who came first? I see them modify and re-state the same thing. Only it seems that Cambourne describes the learning (reading and writing processes) more clearly. I wonder if he came last? What do you think?	Rapport building Sharing opinion, "us vs. them" Agreeing with Michael, Connecting to her own classroom Connecting to other readings Rapport building, Sharing opinion, Rapport building with Kristy Wondering Connecting to other readings Posing question to class

Table 1. continued

Caroline responds to Kristy Thursday, Feb. 13, 11:17am	Kristy, I think you have touched on one of the major points from the Calkins article—the point that oral language is developed in non-sequenced, whole-task basis, so writing should be thought of in the same way. I probably feel as I do because so much of my training and classroom practice was skills-based. I am really working to shift some of my paradigms to a more whole-task, non-sequenced point of view. If I were in the classroom regularly, I believe that working with children on purposeful writing tasks across the curriculum would help settle my qualms.	Rapport building Sharing opinions Connecting to her own thinking Revealing her own struggles
Frannie responds to Kristy Thursday, Feb 13, 5:56pm	Calkins draws two different views of teaching writing. I could see the Venn diagram in my head. What is important is what's in the middle here? Do both these views have merit? Of course they do. The end goal is to have successful writers. They need a little of both sides. They need structure and building blocks and they need freedom to experiment and "feel" their writing. This is where educators get hung up, there is no one way. A good teacher will take from both sides to find the appropriate mix of the two. If the teacher is wise and crosses her fingers, her choices 'should' take care of the assessment monster.	Suggesting a way to organize information Sharing opinion Connecting to other readings Responding to Michael's comments
Traci responds to Kristy Thursday, Feb. 13, 8:10pm	Your comment about questioning the student to make them think further reminds me of Carol Avery's book *And With A Light Touch...* It is filled with examples of her guiding students toward what they need to be doing in their writing. It's not about avoiding instruction, but using questioning and other techniques to draw it out of students so that they discover much of it for themselves.	Connecting to other readings
Kristy replies back to Traci Thursday, Feb. 20, 10:45pm	Sounds like an interesting book. I will have to check it out. I think students need every opportunity to think for themselves. Sometimes we hand them too many things with straightforward answers and do not give them a chance to think.	Building rapport with Traci Sharing opinions Connecting with her own thinking

Within the IRE pattern, teachers mainly initiate questions and evaluate students' answers to specific questions. Students typically respond to teacher-initiated questions. Experts in classroom discourse found that the IRE pattern, while pervasive, is not necessarily the optimum pattern for student learning (Cazden, 1988; Mehan, 1979). Instead, researchers argue that better interactions are found in genuine discussions (Dillon, 1994) or grand conversations (Eeds & Wells, 1989) in which students and teachers assume a participant stance (Wegmann, 2001), or use language in personally meaningful ways (such as exploring a possibility or investigating a personal inquiry). Considering Web-based interactions, in which the learning is mediated by a computer, the question becomes: Are there opportunities for genuine discussions, grand conversations, or a participant stance online?

According to Bakhtin (1986), all utterances are in answer to, continuation of, or in anticipation of, other utterances. This *dialogic chain* is one lifelong tool for learning and growing; interacting with others often sets the course for new learning. Historically, researchers have analyzed oral interaction patterns to determine the nature of utterances. In an online course, the discussion board is used extensively as the vehicle for interactions (Burnette & Buerkle, 2004; Waltonen-Moore, Stuart, Newton, Oswald, & Varonis, 2006). The chains of utterances on a discussion board may take place over the course of a few days or an entire semester. Instead of face-to-face discussions to analyze for interaction patterns, asynchronous discussion boards determine the nature of the utterances in one online course.

For example, the following discussion (see Table 1) took place over six days. Kristy, a student in her second semester of master's work, was responding to a book chapter written by Lucy Calkins in a course focused on writing processes and theories.

Realizing that the first interpretation is the act of writing it down (Mischler, 1991), we identified possible moves that participants could have been connecting to, as they were writing their responses. It immediately became clear that these participants were not routinely answering questions and responding to their peers. They were sharing opinions, introducing new topics, connecting to other texts. Students showed evidence that they were connecting the content of their reading assignments to:

- Their own thinking (Michael's response; Caroline's response; Kristy's last response),
- Their own classrooms (Mary Ann's response; Michael's response), and
- Other readings (Mary Ann's response, Traci's response, Frannie's response).

As students wrote, they were able to reflect on their readings and previous responses. Kristy's response at the end (as well as a personal e-mail communication about this particular episode) shows that she read the other responses and considered their perspectives. Also notable is the fact that the teacher's voice is absent from this excerpt. These students are not merely enacting an IRE discussion (Mehan, 1979). They were instead authentically voicing their opinions about theories, synthesizing their own ideas, and drawing attention to the aspects of the reading they found salient. Instead of the IRE pattern, this discussion board entry represents what some have termed a *participant stance* (Wegmann, 2001). The participant stance occurs when students use language to wrestle with intricate matters for various purposes. James Britton first coined the terms *participant* and *spectator* (1993) when writing about using language while musing over silent reading; however, these terms can be used effectively here as well, since online classes involve silently reading a text and responding in writing. Students enacting a participant stance, face-to-face or online, can be compared to participants at a sporting event because they use language as a tool for actively making sense of the world. No longer are they on the sideline as spectators talking *about* language, these participants are wondering, questioning, conjecturing, and generally using language to get things done.

Seen another way, this discussion board interaction can also be transcribed in Figure 1.

This transcription brings out the fact that the episode took place over 10 days, with most occurring within two days. It shows the complicated nature of interactions and shows that one discussion board entry can create numerous other replies. Kristy's response was met with five responses, three of whom created other responses. Bakhtin (1986) purported that all utterances are in answer to, and stimulate other responses. Mary Ann provided one such example of the dialogic chain (Bakhtin, 1986) when she responded to Kristy's answer. In her answer she also referred to Michael's response and challenged the class as a whole. (In reality, it could be reasoned that all participants challenged the class as a whole, because this discussion board was able to be read by all participants.) When Mary Ann responded to the end of semester questionnaire, she intoned that her fondest memory about the class was the interaction afforded by the discussion boards. The dialogic chain was clear: the instructor's question, Kristy's answer, Mary Ann's response (which included a challenge to the whole class), and so on.

Online asynchronous discussions may offer students time to reflect on peers' comments, sometimes resulting in profound ideas (another possible explanation for the widespread posting times in the previous example.) This time for reflection may be missing from face-to-face interactions and may give preference to certain personality types. Lin et al. (2005) conducted a study of asynchronous online environments as they relate to psychological types. Participants reported that the time they were given to reread and clarify their thoughts was valuable. Their main findings were driven by personality types and the ability of learners to feel a "copresence" in the online class. In the discussion board excerpt above, students felt a copresence because they were able to assume a participant stance while responding to the question posed, as well as engage other students in responses of their own.

The efficacies of asynchronous discussions that give time for reflection were supported by the end-of-semester comments from our students:

Figure 1. Graphic representation of one discussion board entry

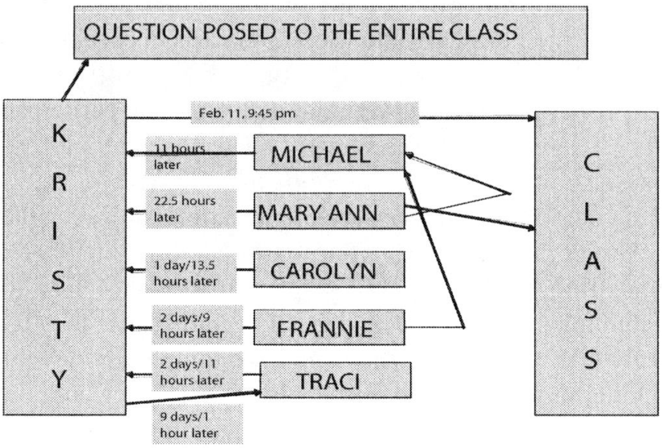

- "I feel like I am better able to express myself online. I am able to think and reflect on what I am going to say before I say it, which is something that I struggle with in person."
- "The online discussion forums gave me the chance to mull over my thoughts in response to other students' postings, giving my reflections much more depth than they would have had in a face to face setting."
- "Unlike spoken words which are often quickly forgotten once released, the written format on the discussion board allows me to thoughtfully craft my answers to your focus questions. I know I would not have been able to answer such questions in a regular class with the same depth. In addition, my response would be "lost in the wind." Instead, there is documentation of my reflection and those of my colleagues. I am able to print those out and reread them for further study or pleasure."

Online students, like all students, vary in motivation and linguistic-experiential reservoirs (Rosenblatt, 1994). Added to this, the language-in-use in online courses is written instead of oral, which complicates things further. For example, if students reply to a discussion board entry, there is little possibility for immediate feedback or self-correction. In contrast, if a student made a comment in a face-to-face class and his instructor frowned, he would be able to pick up on nonverbal cues and self-correct, modify, or support his answer. Tone of voice is also absent from online interactions. Cues like tone of voice and nonverbal communication can strengthen interactions. In an online platform, there are no opportunities for students to use these cues to modify their responses. Since these critical cue systems are missing, online interactions may be difficult to monitor and repair.

Because these cue systems relate to rapport that must be healthy in order for students to assume a participant stance online, we encouraged students to produce power points with added audio narration, chat with each other via phone, and use emoticons as they write. Emoticons are pictures made with computer keys that relate the emotional intent of the written statement. Here are several that our students have used:

Smile	**:)**
Frown	**: (**
Wink	**;)**
Laugh	**: D**
Mad	**>: (**
Indifferent	**: |**

Strategies like using emoticons and personal communications serve to strengthen interaction as well as rapport. Instructors reported that:

- "Student are enormously supportive of each other—truly they have formed a collaborative network in the 'ether!' They are able to explore ideas in small groups and generally end up in a better place than when they started."
- "I have noticed that since I began the semester by giving my students examples of 'full' responses to questions on the discussion board, they are really catching on. Now I expect so much of them (because of the rubrics and examples) and they often surprise me by how much interacting they do."
- "I can't say that teaching online is my favorite way to teach, but I have learned that discussion and interaction are 'different' not necessarily 'better.' I do think my use of rubrics has helped. I rely on my students to carry the discussions—and they do! It's all about the way we set up the class."

How Can Instructors Establish Rapport Online?

Developing rapport with students is one of the most important jobs of a teacher, in both online and face-to-face classrooms (Delucchi, 2000). Even though teachers might be well-versed in particular content areas, learning may not be supported if they do not have good rapport with their students. Adult educators need to establish adult-to-adult rapport with their students in order to create a positive learning environment (Imel, 1985). But, how can instructors establish rapport in an online course with students they never physically see? Can reading, writing, and responding take the place of rapport-building with informal conversations and quips? Because our students reported a high degree of satisfaction with the interaction and rapport we provided in our classes, we decided to offer some suggestions to others who may be about to embark on a similar journey. The rest of this chapter describes our successes and gives suggestions for improving interaction and rapport.

We realized quickly that instructors need to provide "multiple means of communication to support the need to engage in work and social interaction, both publicly and privately" (Haythornthwaite, Kazmer, Robbins, & Shoemaker, 2000, para. 3). Rapport in an online course may be supported by personal e-mails between students or students and instructors. According to the *Distance Education Instruction by Postsecondary Faculty and Staff: Fall 1998* (U.S. Department of Education, 1998), faculty members who taught in distance education courses appeared to interact with students more than their counterparts who taught in regular classes. This interaction came in the form of office hours and e-mails. Those professors who taught in distance education courses had office hours totaling 7.5 hours, compared to professors who taught in regular classes who spent on average 6.4 hours a week in office hours. Also faculty members who taught online spent on average 4 hours a week communicating to students by e-mail, compared to 2.6 hours a week for faculty members who did not teach online courses.

However, e-mail is not the only strategy that will encourage online interaction and rapport. Here are 10 strategies we have found to help in improving our online interaction and rapport:

1. Start each course with a "getting to know you" activity, requiring students to become acquainted.
2. Measure the technological savvy of participants before expecting them to perform. Stretch their awareness and skill, but not to the breaking point.
3. Hold regular office hours, both face-to-face and online. Consider setting up online hours in the evening, to meet the needs of your students' schedules.
4. Contact each student, each week, at least one time (e.g., e-mail, discussion board reply, and assignment response).
5. Consider using "track changes" or "add comment" feature of Microsoft Word documents to respond to assignments thoughtfully and meaningfully.
6. Respond to e-mails within 24 hours and assignments within five working days, if possible.
7. Build group assignments into the online course. Add rubrics that gauge participation levels and hold students accountable for writing to peers.

8. About halfway through the course, ask students to evaluate their satisfaction with their own interaction in the course.
9. Require students to contact each other at various times throughout the semester.
10. Use weekly rubrics to provide feedback to students that include things like depth of discussion board entries, responses to other students, contribution to the class discussions, course content, and so on.

Another technique we have found that increases rapport and interest is the format of course assignments. Adding in side comments and changing the type and color of font used can cause students to laugh or smile. Graphics also can enhance understanding (DeRouin et al., 2005) and add interest and humor. A few samples from our courses follow (see Figure 2).

Figure 2. Increasing rapport and interest with graphics

Give a couple of ideas to your colleagues as to how a teacher might activate or create schema in a classroom. You can even tell about some hot lesson you have already done where schema theory was just oozing out all over the place…even though you didn't know what it was at the time. ☺

AS YOU READ THROUGH THIS ASSIGNMENT, DON'T PANIC. IT'S ONE THAT IS WORKED ON OVER THE REST OF THE SEMESTER. JUST TAKE IT IN PIECES…ONE WEEK AT A TIME…AND YOU'LL DO FINE.

Some PRE-course thoughts…

This assignment will take you about an hour or two…so don't begin unless you have quiet time to sit and think.

Oh…. And you don't need to be naked like this fellow. ☺

Final Thoughts

The findings of our three-year analysis of online interaction and rapport cannot be appropriately generalized to any other context. However, over the course of the last three years, we have realized that the teacher's stance on interaction and rapport are complex issues of communication that are at the heart of the success of online classes. As Tannen (1995) maintains, "communication isn't as simple as saying what you mean" (p. 138). In an online course, computer mediated communication is not as simple as *writing* what you mean. One barrier to writing what you mean is *transactional distance*, or a psychological gap that may occur when teacher and students are separated geographically.

Transactional distance needs to be reduced by encouraging dialogue between both teacher-to-students as well as students-to-students. This dialogue may take the form of e-mails, discussion board entries, or personal phone calls. Dialogue may also take the form of a genuine discussion, which will look different from a face-to-face discussion. Our previous suggestions of the ways instructors can maintain a participant stance support the reduction of transactional distance. Online learning can support a different type of genuine discussion as well as support building rapport with students. The genuine discussion (Dhillon, 1994) formed online might appear different, but can be compared to face-to-face genuine discussion in content and practice. As one participant in our study reported:

For me, I was born into this technology driven world. This is the NEW age of technological communication. Talking without fingers is natural for me—good or bad isn't the question ... it is reality. So that being said, I feel that discussing online is a normal mode of communicating and is has proven to be a very valued way of communicating. I have learned so much from my colleagues in online discussions. I have been blown away with the amount of learning I do through online discussions. Sure some students might need to learn how to do it but because it is done on a daily basis it is easily done and done effectively.

This student obviously felt comfortable interacting online and taking the time to explain her thoughts in order to "construct interaction by acting in the world based on those meanings" (Vrasidas, 2002, p. 289). Thus, instructors designing online courses need to ensure that students have ample opportunity to respond to each other on discussion boards and in group activities (Ruan & Beach, 2005). If they are occupied in engaging, interactive assignments, students will potentially have positive interactions, thus building rapport and increasing the possibility of a participant stance.

Not all students will "buy into" the online platform, especially novice computer users. Teachers can facilitate this process by being sensitive to novice students (Meyen & Lian, 1997) and possibly holding face-to-face sessions to increase trust between students (Sainsbury & Baskerville, 2006). This sensitivity can build rapport as the students realize that their instructors are willing to scaffold their learning by providing them with additional help. This will also help to reduce the transactional distance between the teacher and learner as the learner assumes a participant stance in order to hone computer skills. If it is a matter of psychological preference against computer use, teachers need to be sensitive as well. As Lin et al. (2005) posit:

To prevent unintended external technology control over personal destiny and to enhance one's autonomy, we not only need to be aware of the benefits and drawbacks of the new technology for different users but also need to discover our personal blind spots and expand our capabilities. (p. 1810)

Online instructors should create courses that promote initial bonding as well as monitor and support continued interaction and participation. In highly effective programs, a great deal of scaffolding is provided for the candidates for interaction and rapport. When students transfer in the middle of a program without the prior scaffolding, problems may occur. As one instructor said, "Transient students who do not have the initial courses in the program struggle at the beginning 'to be present' to each other, in a way that the more experienced have come to expect."

What type of learners might prosper in an online platform? Gardner's (1993) multiple intelligences may direct further studies in online interaction and rapport. Certainly those who rely on inter and intrapersonal intelligences may find the online format does not allow for the "human dimension" and may suffer from the effects of transactional distance. Or rather, does the online platform create a different type of interpersonal communication—computer-mediated, instead of face-to-face?

Future Trends

Distance learning in education has opened the door for unlimited lifelong learning (McCombs & Vakili, 2005) that challenges and enriches, that transcends time and space, and that connects people and resources. As opportunities for online learning increase so must our understanding of online teaching (DeRouin et al., 2005; Wegmann, Price, Robbins, Miller, Higgins, & Breen, 2005). Rapport and interaction online are critical aspects of learning and must be supported and well understood if learning is to occur. We must not rely on technological savvy to make up for inadequate teaching, for "no technology can overcome poor teaching; poor teaching is actually exacerbated in distance education applications" (Barker, 1995, para. 8). Rather, we must seek to reduce transactional distance, scaffold our students' efforts, and promote a participant stance as we navigate learning online together.

As a faculty group, we decided to further investigate our online classes by surveying our students to determine their level of satisfaction with online interactions (see Appendix B). We hope that using an instrument like the one in Appendix B will gauge whether our students perceive a good sense of interaction and rapport in our online classes. This is only the first step in what we hope will be an ongoing effort to increase social presence and the participant stance in our classes.

Now we can say we have crossed our county, state, and national boundaries as we have brought students together in our cyber classrooms. It was a journey that began four years ago with trepidation and one that continues to be a challenge. But we are determined to create a community of lifelong learners by reducing transactional distance and increasing interaction and rapport. "Can you hear us now?" The answer is YES.

References

Althaus, S. L. (1997). Computer-mediated communication in the university classroom: An experiment with on-line discussion. *Communication Education, 7*, 158-174.

Bakhtin, M. (1986). The problem of speech genres. In M. Bakhtin (Ed.), *Speech genres and other late essays* (pp. 60-102). Austin: University of Texas Press.

Barker, B. O. (1995). *Strategies to ensure interaction in telecommunicated distance learning*. ACSDE Research Monograph. The Pennsylvania State University. Retrieved August 4, 2006, from http://www.csusm.edu/ilast/vcyear3/transactional/Barker.htm

Barkley, S., & Bianco, T. (2001). Learning experts examine shortfalls in onsite and online training. *Performance Improvement Journal, 40*(5). Retrieved August 4, 2006, from http://www.ispi.org/publications/pitocs/pimayjune2001e.htm

Beller, M., & Or, E. (1998). The crossroads between lifelong learning and information technology: A challenge facing leading universities. *Journal of Computer Mediated Communication, 4*(2). Retrieved August 4, 2006, from http://jcmc.indiana.edu/vol4/issue2/beller.html

Benbunan-Fich, R., & Hiltz, S. R. (1999). Educational applications of CMCS: Solving case studies through asynchronous learning networks. *Journal of Computer*

Mediated Communication, 4(3). Retrieved August 4, 2006, from http://www.ascusc.org/jcmc/vol4/issue3/benbunan-fich.html

Britton, J. (1993). *Language and learning.* Portsmouth, NH: Boynton/Cook.

Burnette, G., & Buerkle, H. (2004). Information exchange in virtual communities: A comparative study. *Journal of Computer Mediated Communication, 9*(2). Retrieved August 4, 2006, from http://www.ascusc.org/jcmc/vol9/issue2/burnett.html

Cazden, C. (1988). *Classroom discourse.* Portsmouth, NH: Heinemann.

Delucchi, M. (2000). Don't worry, be happy: Instructor likeability, student perceptions of learning, and teacher ratings in upper-level sociology courses. *Teaching Sociology, 28*, 220-231.

DeRouin, R. E., Fritzsche, B. A., & Salas, E. (2005). E-learning in organizations. *Journal of Management, 31*(6), 920-940.

Dewey, J. (1938). *Experience in education.* New York: Macmillan.

Dhillon, M. (1994). *Using discussion in classrooms*. Philadelphia: Open University Press.

Eeds, M., & Wells, D. (1989). Grand conversations: An exploration of meaning construction in literature study groups. *Research in the Teaching of English, 23*, 4-29.

Gardner, H. (1993). *Frames of mind: The theory of multiple intelligences.* New York: Basic Books.

Haythornthwaite, C., Kazmer, M. M., Robbins, J., & Shoemaker, S. (2000). Community development among distance learners: Temporal and technological dimensions. *Journal of Computer-Mediated Communication, 4*(2). Retrieved August 4, 2006, from http://www.ascusc.org/jcmc/vol6/issue1/haythornthwaite.html

Hillman, D. C., Willis, D. J., & Gunawardena, C. N. (1994). Learner-interface interaction in distance education: An extension of contemporary models and strategies for practitioners. *The American Journal of Distance Education, 8*(2), 30-42.

Imel, S. (1985). *Guidelines for working with adult learners. ERIC Digest, 77* (ERIC#ED299456).

Killian, J., & Willhite, G. (2003). Electronic discourse in preservice teacher preparation. *Journal of Technology and Teacher Education, 11*(3), 377-395.

King, J. C., & Doerfert, D. L. (1996). *Interaction in the distance education setting.* Retrieved August 4, 2006, from http://www.ssu.missouri.edu/ssu/AgEd/NAERM/s-e-4.htm

Laferrière, T., Lamon, M., & Chan, C. (2006). Emerging e-trends and models in teacher education and professional development. *Teaching Education, 17*(1), 75-90.

Lao, T., & Gonzales, C. (2005). Understanding online learning through a qualitative description of professors and students' experiences. *Journal of Technology and Teacher Education, 13*(3), 459-474.

Li, Q., & Akins, M. (2005). Sixteen myths about online teaching and learning in higher education: Don't believe everything you hear. *TechTrends, 49*(4), 51-60.

Lin, L, Cranton, P., & Bridglall, B. (2005). Psychological type and asynchronous written dialogue in adult learning. *Teachers College Record, 10*(8), 1788-1813.

Maher, M., & Jacob, E. (2006). Peer computer conferencing to support teachers' reflection during action research. *Journal of Technology and Teacher Education, 14*(1), 127-150.

Martinez, R., Jr., & Sweger, B. (1996). Plugged in: Long distance technology offers benefits and drawbacks to teacher education programs. *Vocational Education Journal, 71*(3), 30-31.

McCombs, B., & Vakili, D. (2005) A learner centered framework for e-learning. *Teachers College Record, 107*(8), 1582-1600.

Mehan, H. (1979). *Learning lessons.* Cambridge, MA: Harvard University Press.

Meyen, E., & Lian, C. (1997). Teaching online courses. *Distance Education, 12*, 166-175.

Mischler, E. G. (1991). Representing discourse: The rhetoric of transcription. *Journal of Narrative and Life History, 4*, 255-280.

Mondada, L. (2006). Participants' online analysis and multimodal practices: Projecting the end of the turn and the closing of the sequence. *Discourse Studies, 8*(1), 117-129.

Moore, M. G. (1991). Distance education theory. *The American Journal of Distance Education, 5*(3), 1-6.

National Center for Education Statistics (NCES). (2003). *Distance education at the degree granting post-secondary institutions: 2000-2001*. Washington, DC: Department of Education. Retrieved August 4, 2006, from http://nces.ed.gov/surveys/peqis/publications/2003017

Rosenblatt, L. (1994). *The reader, the text, the poem*. Carbondale: Southern Illinois University Press.

Ruan, J., & Beach, S. (2005). Using online peer dialogue journaling to promote reflection in elementary preservice teachers. *Action in Teacher Education, 27*(3), 64-75.

Saba, F., & Shearer, R. L. (1994). Verifying key theoretical concepts in a dynamic model of distance education. *The American Journal of Distance Education, 8*(1), 36-57.

Sainsbury, R., & Baskerville, R. (2006). *Distrusting online: Social deviance in virtual teamwork*. Paper presented at Hawaii International Conference on System Sciences, Honolulu.

Short, J., Williams, E., & Christie, C. (1976). *The social psychology of telecommunications*. London: John Wiley & Sons.

Shovein, J., Huston, C., Fox, S., & Damazo, B. (2005). Challenging traditional teaching and learning paradigms: Online learning and emancipatory teaching. *Nursing education perspectives, 26*(6), 340-343.

Simpson, R. J., & Galbo, J. J. (1986). Interaction and learning: Theorizing on the art of teaching. *Interchange, 17*(4), 37-51.

Smith, R. (2005). Working with difference in online collaborative groups. *Adule Education Quarterly, 55*(3), 182-199.

Stein, D. S., Wanstreet, C. E., Calvin, J., Overtoom, C., & Wheaton, J. E. (2005). Bridging the transactional distance gap in online learning environments. *The American Journal of Distance Education, 19*(2), 105.

Tannen, D. (1995). The power of talk: Who gets heard and why. *Harvard Business Review, 73*(5), 138-149.

U.S. Department of Education. (1998). Distance Education Instruction by Postsecondary Faculty and Staff. *National Center for Education Statistics* (NCES 2005-155). Washington, DC: U.S. Government Printing Office.

U.S. Department of Education. (2000). 1999-2000 National Postsecondary Student Aid Study. *National Center for Education Statistics* (NCES 2005-165). Washington, DC: U.S. Government Printing Office.

U.S. Department of Education. (2002). The Condition of Education, *National Center for Education Statistics* (NCES 2002-025). Washington, DC: U.S. Government Printing Office.

Vrasidas, C. (2002). A working typology of intentions driving face-to-face and online interactions in a graduate teacher education course. *Journal of Technology and Teacher Education, 10*(2), 273-297.

Vygotsky, L. S. (1978). *Mind in society*. Cambridge, MA: Harvard University Press.

Wagner, E. D., & Wilson, P. (2005). Disconnected. *Training and Development, 59*(12), 40-43. Retrieved August 4, 2006, from http://www.astd.org/astd/Publications/TDMagazine/2005.pdf/Contents_0512.htm

Waltonen-Moore, S., Stuart, D., Newton, E., Oswald, R., & Varonis, E. (2006). From virtual strangers to a cohesive learning community: The evolution of online group development in a professional development course. *Journal of Technology and Teacher Education, 14*(14), 287-311.

Wegmann, S. J. (2001). *Negotiating the real and the ideal: Four elementary teachers and the influences on their literacy teaching.* Unpublished doctoral dissertation, University of Florida, Gainesville.

Wegmann, S., & McCauley, J. (2006). *Stances to facilitate online interaction and rapport.* Paper presented at Society for Information Technology and Teacher Education, Orlando, FL.

Wegmann, S., Price, D., Robbins, M., Miller, M., Higgins, B., & Breen, L. (2005, November). *Developing and sustaining an online program.* Paper presented at College Reading Association, Savannah, GA.

Zhang, W., Perris, K., & Yeung, L. (2005). Online tutorial support in open and distance learning: students' perceptions. *British Journal of Educational Technology, 36*(5), 789-804.

Appendix A:
Sample of Survey Questions

1. *Do you think discussing during the online classes is a skill that students have to learn or do you think it's a pretty natural/normal mode of communicating?*

   I think it is a natural/normal mode of communicating…especially for the younger generation. I feel more comfortable sharing my views online as opposed to in person. It definitely improved my technology skills!

2. *If you think online discussions are something people have to LEARN to do, how do students in our graduate program learn the skill? What was it that was done in your online class(es) that helped the process?*

   I didn't answer that it is something that people learn to do, but I will tell you that in your class, having specific times and days for reflections, and responses (as well as a required number of responses) was helpful to establish routine and focus. The more I responded, the more comfortable I felt about the process. I truly appreciated that everyone received responses. I was also motivated to read all reflections because of the requirements. Some instructors do not ask students to make sure everyone gets a response, and sometimes you never know if you are on track, or your reflection is off the wall. It was also helpful that you responded to our reflections. Not all instructors do that either. Feedback is essential to the communication process.

3. *Did your feelings toward online discussions change from the beginning of your grad studies (RDG 530?) until now? If so, how?*

Yes, I was very apprehensive at first. Now, it is a natural extension of communication and learning for me. I was afraid to ask questions when I first began because I didn't want to look stupid. Now, I just ask away … and don't worry about what other people think. I'll probably never see them anyway!

Thanks for asking!

Appendix B: Pilot Survey for Online Interaction and Rapport

Computer Proficiency		
1	I have proficient computer skills.	1 2 3 4 5
2	I am proficient communicating by e-mail.	1 2 3 4 5
3	I am comfortable interacting on discussion boards.	1 2 3 4 5
4	I usually access the coursework from home.	1 2 3 4 5
5	I usually access the coursework from school, NOT where I work.	1 2 3 4 5
6	I usually access the coursework from school where I work.	1 2 3 4 5
7	I usually access the coursework a public library.	1 2 3 4 5
Online Dialogue		
1	The instructor creates opportunities to encourage dialogue among students online.	1 2 3 4 5
2	The instructor is prompt in responding to my questions or insights.	1 2 3 4 5
3	I expect a response online within one day.	1 2 3 4 5
4	The instructor quickly answers questions in e-mail.	1 2 3 4 5
5	The instructor encourages me to ask questions using e-mail.	1 2 3 4 5
6	I am satisfied with the learning strategies used by the instructor in e-mail.	1 2 3 4 5
7	I am happy with the online interactions of my peers in this class.	1 2 3 4 5
8	My peers interact at about the same level of thoughtfulness.	1 2 3 4 5
9	There was a good amount of dialogue in this class.	1 2 3 4 5

continued on following page

Online Rapport		
1	My instructor knows me well enough to answer my questions.	1 2 3 4 5
2	I could easily join in a face-to-face discussion with this instructor.	1 2 3 4 5
3	I feel like I know the instructor of this course.	1 2 3 4 5
4	I feel like I know my peers in this course.	1 2 3 4 5
5	The instructor replies to questions in discussion boards.	1 2 3 4 5
6	The instructor leads discussions in discussion boards.	1 2 3 4 5
7	I would like more opportunities to use discussion boards in this class.	1 2 3 4 5
8	I participate in group work in discussion boards.	1 2 3 4 5
9	I am satisfied with the discussion board activities in this class.	1 2 3 4 5
10	There was a good sense of rapport in this class among the students.	1 2 3 4 5
Stance Online		
1	My instructor asked us to complete engaging activities.	1 2 3 4 5
2	I find that I used higher-order thinking skills to complete activities.	1 2 3 4 5
3	The activities for this course made me think.	1 2 3 4 5
4	I often used outside sources to complete activities.	1 2 3 4 5
5	I felt my assignments were stimulating.	1 2 3 4 5

Chapter III

Online Learning and Lifelong Learning: Implications for Transforming Teaching and Learning

Glenn Finger, Gold Coast Campus Griffith University, Australia

Abstract

This chapter explores ways in which new and emerging information and communication technologies (ICT) might transform the learning experience through online delivery. After presenting a conceptualisation of ICT use by educators in terms of inaction, investigation, application, integration, and transformation, two diverse learning settings are examined to develop insights into the implications of online learning for lifelong learning—namely, the delivery of educational services to preschool children (aged 4 years old) through to Year 10 students (aged 15 years old) in rural and remote communities in Australia, and the dimensions required for designing online learning for adult learners in higher education. Through the presentation of a case study of a School of Distance Education in Australia, which reflects technological improvements using telephone teaching, and the affordances of improved connectivity, the case study demonstrates that this has enabled the use of more constructivist approaches to teaching and learning to transform the delivery of education to rural and remote students. Subsequently, this chapter provides a synthesis of the literature relating to the critical factors influencing learner satisfaction in online learning.

Introduction

The concepts of *lifelong learning* and *online learning* have become central to educational policies and curriculum development in Australia. This chapter explores ways in which new and emerging information and communication technologies (ICT) might transform the learning experience through online delivery. After presenting a conceptualisation of ICT use by educators in terms of *inaction, investigation, application, integration,* and *transformation,* two diverse learning settings are examined to develop insights into the implications of online learning for lifelong learning—namely, the delivery of educational services to preschool children (aged 4 years old) through to Year 10 students (aged 15 years old) in rural and remote communities in Australia, and the dimensions required for designing online learning for adult learners in higher education.

Through the presentation of a case study of a School of Distance Education (SDE) in Australia, which reflects technological improvements using telephone teaching, and the affordances of improved connectivity, the case study demonstrates that this has enabled the use of more constructivist approaches to teaching and learning to transform the delivery of education to rural and remote students. Subsequently, the chapter provides a synthesis of the literature relating to the critical factors influencing learner satisfaction in online learning. That synthesis identifies considerations for online learning related to the learner dimension, instructor dimension, course dimension, technology dimension, design dimension, and environmental dimension.

Lifelong and Online Learning

Accompanying and contributing to the centrality of *lifelong learning* and *online learning* has been the emergence of new and emerging technologies known as ICT and the implications of the knowledge economy. For example, in 2000, the Ministerial Council for Education, Employment, Training and Youth Affairs (MCEETYA) which enables a collaborative approach between Australian State and Territory, and New Zealand governments, endorsed the report *Learning in an Online World: The School Action Plan for the Information Economy* (MCEETYA, 2000). In the same year, the Department of Education, Training, and Youth Affairs (DETYA) in Australia released *Learning for the Knowledge Society: An Education and Training Action Plan for the Information Economy* (DETYA, 2000). Both documents provided an educational vision which "was based on the understanding that ICT have the potential to transform all aspects of school education and contribute to the achievement of all learning goals" (MCEETYA ICT in Schools Taskforce, 2005, p. 3).

MCEETYA established the MCEETYA ICT in Schools Taskforce (MCEETYA, 2002) which has the responsibility for "ensuring that the nature and role of ICT in contemporary learning is investigated and understood" (MCEETYA, 2003, p. 3). Specifically, the MCEETYA ICT in Schools Taskforce is required to regularly report to MCEETYA about the goals set down in *Learning in an Online World: The School Action Plan for the Information Economy* (MCEETYA, 2000) in terms of five key action areas—*people, infrastructure, content and services, supporting policies,* and *enabling regulation*. Similarly, in New Zealand, the *Digital Horizons: Learning through ICT* (Ministry of Education, 2003), built its framework for action around six key action areas—*learners, teachers, leaders, Māori, families, communities, businesses and other stakeholders, curriculum and learning resources,* and *infrastructure*. These policy positions provide a strong sense of visions for education systems, schools, teachers, students, and communities for teaching and learning in an online world.

An interesting development has been the research strategy developed by the MCEETYA ICT in Schools Taskforce (MCEETYA, 2003; see http://icttaskforce@mceetya.edu.au) which involved consultation with all state and territory jurisdictions in Australia, the Australian Association for Research in Education, the Australian Council for Educational Research, the Australian Research Council, the Deans of Education, and the Department of Education, Science and Training. The resulting research strategy builds on the priority research areas for ICT research identified in *Learning in an Online World 2003-06* (cited in MCEETYA, 2003)—namely, the changing nature of schooling, student learning, equity issues, teacher development, and monitoring progress. In particular, the research strategy (MCEETYA, 2003, p. 5) states that ICT research related to ICT use and impact in each of those areas should consider the following overlapping dimensions:

- ***Conditions for learning:*** *providing the conditions necessary for effective student, staff, and community engagement;*
- ***Learning possibilities:*** *exploring how to transform, enrich, and extend learning;*
- ***Educational effectiveness:*** *ensuring effective curriculum, pedagogy, student learning, assessment, and school transformation; and*
- ***Equity:*** *providing appropriate student, staff, and community access, participation, and satisfaction as well as improving achievement.* (MCEETYA, 2003, p. 5)

Moreover, in recent times as we move into the 21st century, curriculum documents for use in Australian schools reflect responses to the demands for students to be futures-oriented, and to be effective thinkers in an increasingly complex, technological world. An underlying driver for curriculum design and implementation is the assumption that students must be equipped with skills for *lifelong learning*, have a capacity for critical thinking, and develop deep intellectual engagement. For example, to illustrate this, the Queensland Studies Authority (QSA), an intersystemic curriculum development and approval authority in Queensland, a state within Australia, indicates that all curriculum documents are designed to assist students to become lifelong learners. The identified valued attributes of the lifelong learner are:

- *Knowledgeable person with deep understanding*
- *Complex thinker*
- *Creative person*
- *Active investigator*
- *Effective communicator*
- *Participant in an independent world*
- *Reflective self-directed learner* (QSA, 2003, p. 3)

Those attributes require students to acquire and process information using thinking skills which are necessary tools in a society characterised by rapid change, with many alternatives of action and numerous individual and collective choices and decisions challenging the students' existence (Young, 2005). Many educators believe that specific content knowledge will not be as important to tomorrow's workers and citizens as the ability to learn and make sense of new information (Gough, 2002). The important implication is that this promotes transformations to teaching and learning.

Transforming Teaching and Learning

Many education systems and educational researchers throughout the world have traditionally framed initiatives and investigations on the assumption that the model for schooling involves students and teachers being physically located in a school. That model implicitly suggests that the teachers and the students travel to a physical setting (schools and classrooms) from their homes to engage in face-to-face teaching and learning situations. The emergence of new technologies characterised by computers and the Internet offer new possibilities to transform existing models.

In conceptualising the stages of progress by teachers, Trinidad, Newhouse, and Clarkson (2005) describes these stages as moving through *inaction*, *investigation*, *application*, *integration*, and *transformation*. As displayed in Table 1, Trinidad et al. include a "critical use border" between application and integration, as this is seen to be "critical" for enabling ICT to support the learning environment.

Table 1. Stages of teacher development (Source: Trinidad et al., 2005, p. 8)

	Description of Key Difference(s)
Inaction	At this stage, there is a general lack of action and/or interest.
Investigation	At this stage, the teacher has developed an interest in using ICT with students and is beginning to act on this interest.
Application	At this stage, the teacher is regularly using ICT with students and knows how to do so competently and confidently.
	Critical Use Border
Integration	At this stage, the use of ICT becomes critical to the support of the learning environment and the opportunity for students to achieve learning outcomes through the learning experiences provided.
Transformation	At this stage, the teacher is able to take on leadership roles (formal and informal) in the use of ICT and be knowledgably reflective on its integration by themselves and others.

The stages conceptualised in Table 1 assist analysis of policies and initiatives relating to online learning. The *Learning Technologies Plan for ACT Government Schools and Preschools 2004-2006* is subtitled *Transforming the Way We Teach and Learn* (ACT Government, 2004) and presents "a practical vision of how learning technologies can help to transform preschool and school-age learning in the ACT over the next three years" (p. 1). Similarly, the Department of Education Tasmania (DET) emphasises "Transforming schools in the changing world of the twenty-first century involves developing the capacity to engage all students more deeply in their learning, broadening the learning environment and making authentic connections between the curriculum and the community" (DET, 2005, p. 1). Therefore, moves to online learning align and reflect the use of ICT to transform teaching and learning.

In her doctoral thesis, Doig (2005, p. 38) noted that Goodlad (1984) differentiates between improving the schools we have through innovation that is incremental, and *beyond* the schools we have through radical innovation. Doig suggests that incremental innovation deals more with continuous improvement within the school or *first order change*, while radical innovation deals with changing education from a systems perspective or *second order change* (Ellyard, 2001; Senge, 1990). The model presented by Doig in Figure 1 usefully portrays the movement of change from "having an effect only on an individual, to having a major effect on a whole system; and from changes being small to those that are deeply disruptive" (p. 38).

Doig builds upon this conceptualisation of innovation by incorporating the stages in the implementation of ICT in schools synthesised by Russell and Finger (2004) in which they identify three stages in the literature (see also DEST, 2002; Dwyer, Ringstaff & Sandholtz, 1991; Jonassen, 2000; Kraver, 1997)—*skill acquisition*, *en-*

Figure 1. Conceptualising theories of innovation in education (Source: Doig, 2005, p. 38)

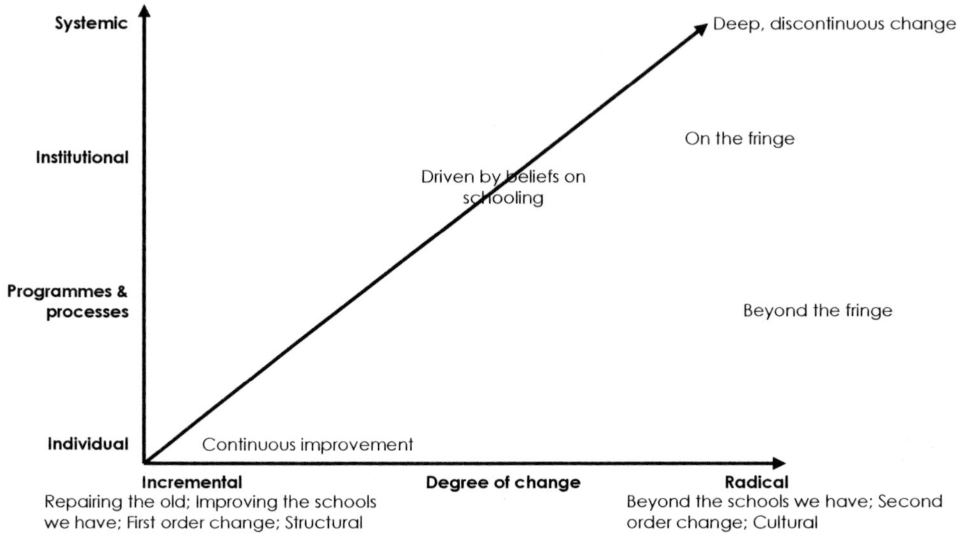

hancing teaching and learning, and *transformative practices*. According to Russell and Finger (2004), *skill acquisition* refers to the use of ICT as a tool for use across the curriculum or in separate subjects where the emphasis is on the development of ICT-related skills, knowledge, processes, and attitudes. *Enhancing teaching and learning* refers to ICT use as a tool for enhancing students' learning outcomes within the existing curriculum and using existing learning processes, and *transformative practices* relates to when ICT becomes an integral component of broader curricular reforms, which will change not only *how* students learn but *what* they learn and is an integral component of the reforms, which will alter the organisation and structure of schooling itself. That model can be built upon further by drawing upon the stages of teacher development proposed by Trinidad et al. (2005, p. 8) shown earlier in Table 1.

By referring to Figure 2, it can be theorised that, while online learning can be situated at any point in the model—from individual to systemic, from inaction to transformation—the model enables the analysis of online learning initiatives to determine the impact and purpose of those initiatives, that is, to identify whether or not the purpose of the online learning initiative is to assist with skill acquisition, enhance teaching and learning, or to transform teaching and learning.

Figure 2. Conceptualising innovation in education and ICT use (Source: Doig, 2005, p. 41)

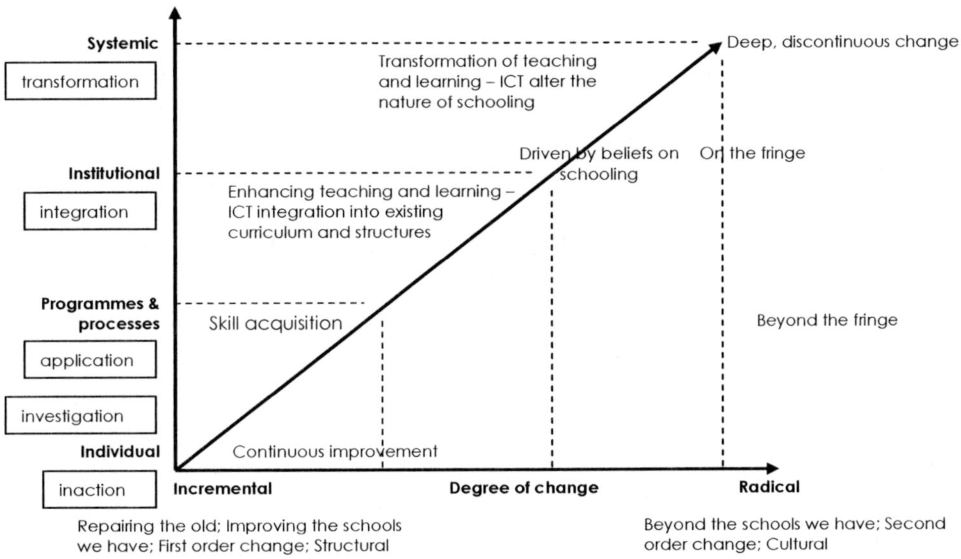

Case Study: Charleville School of Distance Education

While many schools in Australia and throughout the world have enhanced the technological provisions and learning experiences for their students, there exist cohorts of many young people in rural and remote regions of Australia for whom their main means of communication has been high frequency (HF) radio. In marked contrast to the level of communication infrastructure available to young Australians who can readily connect to the rest of the world through broadband Internet connectivity, the reality for the families in rural and remote areas of Australia is that large distances prohibit physical attendance at a school location on a daily basis. Infrastructure costs prohibit the provision of communication systems that people take for granted in more populated regions of Australia. This case study of the Charleville SDE, located in South West Queensland in Australia, attempts to capture the realities of life for students in that remote region and, at the same time, present research evaluating the introduction of telephone teaching and the possibilities of online learning aimed at transforming teaching and learning of those students.

The Charleville SDE is approximately 750 km west of Brisbane, the capital city of the state of Queensland in Australia, and is the largest town in the southwest of the outback region of Queensland. The Charleville SDE (formerly the Charleville School of the Air) was established in 1966, and today provides distance education services to over 300 rural and remote students from Preschool to Year 10 living throughout Southern Queensland. Curriculum content delivered through SDE covers the curriculum prescribed for all Queensland Government schools. This requires schools to address eight key learning areas (KLAs) adopted by the Australian Education Council and the Queensland School Curriculum Council (QSCC). Those KLAs include English, health and physical education, languages other than English, mathematics, science, studies of society and environment, technology, and the arts. Thus, students enrolled at the Charleville SDE engage in learning activities encompassed by that framework on the assumption that those KLAs which were affirmed in the Adelaide Declaration (MCEETYA, 1999) fully address the learning which is expected to be offered in schools Australia-wide.

While the rural and remote students are expected to engage in the same curriculum framework as other Australian students, the delivery of programs is different due to students' inability to physically attend a school site in the traditional sense. Delivery of curriculum programs is provided through print materials, on-air lessons, and field services that provide face-to-face contact with students. Building on a foundation of the remote families linked to the Royal Flying Doctor service, on-air lessons have traditionally been provided using HF radio. Beginning in 1997, the SDE began to trial the use of telephones as an alternative to the HF radio and now delivers all core lessons via telephone. At home, students are issued with a modified telephone that includes a head set and microphone facility that enables the student to participate in the lesson. The student might communicate with the teacher and other students by pressing a button that enables clear communication by eliminating background noise in the student's home environment.

The phone also has a loudspeaker facility, which allows a home tutor to listen to the lesson. A key role is played by the home tutors—often students' mothers—who are seen as important facilitators and coordinators of learning. In homes, children and their families establish a space for a "schoolroom" where planned learning activities occur with the supervision and support of the home tutors. The important technological shift from HF radio to telephone teaching also enabled the introduction of Internet connection and data transfer between the students and their teachers. This represented a significant move forward to an online learning environment which opens up possibilities for synchronous and asynchronous teaching and learning, and possibilities for new means for accessing information and communication.

Challenging the Reader: The Schoolroom in Rural and Remote Communities in Australia

The author wishes to make it clear from the outset that it is impossible to proceed in this case study by following the trend of "sanitised" accounts often found in educational journals and books. To help set the context, the following image gained on a visit by the author to one of the closer properties to Charleville has been sketched.

Distances in these remote areas of Australia are difficult to comprehend for people from populated cities. The closest neighbour in these areas may be more than 200 km away. The rugged dirt roads make it necessary to use a four-wheel drive vehicle for traveling to the properties. Wet weather usually prevents travel on the dirt roads so it is necessary to follow the convention of making a radio call ahead of arrival in order to check weather conditions and that the family will be home. Upon arrival, the author was met at the gate by welcoming smiles of a father and some sons emerging under their cattleman's hats. The father explained that the property was several kilometres from the letterbox at the gate. The journey to the letterbox was only undertaken once each week, weather permitting, as the mail only arrived each Thursday. On arrival at the family home, the isolation and the primitive structures in which the family lived made it difficult to believe this was Australia in the 21st century. Amidst the rapidly changing technological environments found elsewhere in Australia, the author's host family had no town water or power. They relied totally on their own means of generating electricity and provision of water. The family related how they could shower using only one litre of water each, their toilet had only two walls, and their home was some distance from "the schoolroom."

The "schoolroom" where the children's lessons take place was a make-shift building away from the main home building. The schoolroom floor was a mix of concrete and dirt. Tree trunks supported the roof and the ventilation was adjusted by branches of different lengths. "Bushy," one of the older sons had just come in from the paddock to take up his position at a desk and placed on his headphones in readiness for his Year 10 mathematics lesson. The teacher, after checking which students were present, said that he had decided to start the lesson with the lyrics of the Johnny Farnham song "We're Not Gonna Sit in Silence" as a reminder of how distance education helped to ensure that the teacher and student voices were not silenced.

The Research Focus

The focus of the research described here draws upon a study conducted by Hobbs, Finger, and Torrisi-Steele (2000) which evaluated the benefits of telephones over HF radio for on-air lessons at the Charleville SDE and to a subsequent follow-up study by Rotolo (2001) which investigated the extent to which the introduction of telephone teaching had resulted in a more constructivist teaching and learning environment for students. Student, home tutor, and teacher perspectives of the telephone teaching experience and subsequent moves to online learning are presented in the following discussion.

Findings and Perspectives

Home tutors, like teaching staff reacted positively to the use of telephone teaching rather than HF radio. Participation in telephone lessons was less frustrating for home tutors in that they were able to clearly hear all communication between student and teacher. Furthermore, since students were also able to hear more clearly, there was less time wasted clarifying teacher instructions during lesson time. Strong support for the use of telephone rather than HF radio was grounded in the observation that telephone teaching had substantially improved student's motivation, enthusiasm, and learning through improved clearer communication and the facilitation of more conversational forms of teacher-student and student-student interaction (Hobbs et al., 2000). The minimal training requirements to use the home telephone system were also cited as a major advantage of the telephone system.

Consistent with findings for home tutors, an analysis of survey responses from students indicated that they felt that telephone lessons were superior to lessons conducted using HF radio (Hobbs et al., 2000). Student support for the use of telephone lessons rather than HF radio was strong, feeling that all on-air lessons should be conducted via telephone. The positive differences of telephone teaching over HF radio were cited by students in terms of how much was learnt, speed of setting up, more efficient time use during lesson, increased opportunity for participation and lesson's being more enjoyable (Hobbs et al., 2000). Like the students and home tutors, teaching staff at the Charleville SDE wholeheartedly supported the use of telephone technology over HF radio for lesson delivery. Clarity of communication and the natural conversation environment supported by the telephone providing opportunities for more efficient lesson time usage and for the use of a wider variety of teaching strategies.

The results obtained appear to support the underlying principles of Garrison's (1993) theory of transactional constructivism, and lend support to Hardy and Olcott's (1995) views of the goals of telephone teaching, that is, "to produce high-quality interaction, facilitate student autonomy and interdependence in the learning process, and foster a commitment by faculty to a rich learning experience" (p. 53). This study reported that the teachers at the Charleville SDE had moved to utilising teaching strategies and facilitating interactions that reflect the major tenets of a constructivist teaching and learning philosophy.

Overall, the results obtained showed that the teachers were utilising teaching strategies and learning activities that reflected the major tenets of a constructivist teaching and learning philosophy. The most utilised strategies were those relating to the teachers' ability to cater to the individual needs of students, and to make use of students' background knowledge. These results support Garrison's belief that in a constructivist environment, teachers need to recognise the dynamic nature of learning and the need for flexibility during the implementation or learning phase.

According to these results, it would appear that the sustained two-way communication provided by the telephone has enabled this challenge to be met by the teachers at the Charleville SDE.

The study found that the teachers were utilising students' prior knowledge that supports Brown, Collins, and Duguid's (1989) belief: "probably the most important issue in designing constructivist environments is authenticity, the extent to which the environment faithfully reflects the ordinary practices of the culture" (p. 21). The results also lend support to what Anderson and Garrison (1995) found in their study to be a successful teleconference whereby the success of the teleconferences were, in part, "dependent on the teachers' ability to provide learning activities appropriate to students' needs" (p. 41).

Importantly, the strong result obtained in regard to the teachers' beliefs that they were providing students with opportunities for reflection, both on their own ideas, and on the ideas of others significantly supports a major tenet of Garrison's theory of transactional constructivism, whereby meaningful and worthwhile knowledge is constructed and validated through both individual reflection and social discourse. Although there is the contentious issue of whether or not the telephone is a medium which can support reflection (Laurillard, 1993), the finding in this study that, according to the teachers, student self-reflection was occurring, provides further evidence that the telephone teaching and learning environment at the Charleville SDE is a constructivist one.

Overall, the results obtained showed that the teachers believed that telephone teaching and learning environment supported the development of a community of learners through both teacher-student and student-student interaction. Improved interaction has been highlighted by Dymock and Hobson (1998) as an important component of effective learning. This notion is supported by Garrison and Shale (1990), who state that the increased two-way communication and interaction brought about as a result of telecommunication technologies, such as the telephone, is likely to have the most significant impact upon the effectiveness of learning at a distance. Further, Garrison (1993) argues, "without sustained interaction, the learner has few opportunities to develop deep understanding and is not encouraged to do more than assimilate information" (p. 205). Overall, the findings suggested that the telephone teaching and learning environment at the Charleville SDE, as measured by teachers' perceptions of the elements of teaching strategies and interaction, was found to be substantially constructivist in nature.

From HF Radio to Telephone Teaching to Online Learning

Garrison states that technologies and distance education are inextricably linked, and that all forms of distance education are mediated by technology (Garrison, 1985). As observed by Garrison (1985), "the development of the generations of distance education represents, in systems terminology, a hierarchical structure with an increasing differentiation of technological capacity for integrating unique delivery systems" (p. 236). *First generation* education delivery made use of the printed word and the postal system resulting in slow and sparse two-way communication between learner and teacher (Nipper, 1989). Telecommunications such as HF radio, telephone, and teleconferencing opened the way for the *second generation* of delivery systems. The term "telecommunications" refers to the "use of wire, radio, optical or other electromagnetic channels to transmit or receive signals for voice, video, and data communications" (Olgren & Parker, 1983, p. 330). Computer technologies made possible the third generation of delivery systems for distance education. The *third generation* of education delivery systems is characterised by a greater emphasis on the use of communication technologies to facilitate dialogue between participants in the educational process (Kirkwood, 1998). Technologies such as communication networks and satellite technologies support new forms of real time interaction with two-way videoconferencing, or one-way video and two-way audio communication (Passerini & Granger, 2000). *Fourth generation* distance education is driven by the emergence of Internet technologies. "Internet technology empowers the joint exploration of the delivery mechanisms of previous generations, adding stronger collaborative learning elements" (Passerini & Granger, 2000, p. 3). Passerini and Granger (2000) suggest a hybrid design model that merges step-by-step and objectivist methodologies with flexible design and constructivist strategies, resulting in a richer learning environment.

The development of high performance communication technologies can promote the creation of exciting and innovative pedagogies in distance education. While the move to telephone technology, when used as the primary means of contact between teacher and student, is a second generation technology, it has provided a foundation for the development of infrastructure to support new technologies such as the Internet.

Access to Online Learning

Since telephone teaching was introduced in 2001 replacing HF radio lessons, enhancements to on-air telephone teaching have been investigated with the IDL pilot from July to November of 2005. IDL involves the use of interactive multimedia used synchronously in real time delivered via the Internet. Teachers can develop lesson content, demonstrate concepts, develop individualised tasks, and share student work (Charleville SDE, 2005; see http://www.charlevisde.qld.edu.au/site/curriculum.htm).

Moreover, teachers and students now have access to online learning resources developed by Education Queensland such as those provided by *The Learning Place* (Education Queensland, 2005a; see http://education.qld.gov.au/learningplace/). Resources include chat rooms, comic chat, forums, blogs, project rooms, QMOOnity, voice conferencing, and data conferencing. Within *The Learning Place* there is *The Curriculum Exchange* which provides teaching and learning resources, including online learning objects which teachers can select for their students to use. *The Learning Place* offers a range of online courses for Education Queensland staff and students through the Blackboard™ learning management system. Schools, teachers, and students can now actively access and participate in ready-to-go courses. Also within *The Learning Place*, Education Queensland has developed the Virtual Schooling Service (VSS) (Education Queensland, 2005b; see http://education.qld.gov.au/learningplace/vss/) which uses innovative delivery strategies and a range of learning technologies to support students at a distance. The VSS has become an internationally and nationally recognised exemplar of excellence in distance education.

In terms of the conceptualisation in Figure 2, the move to online learning reflects a substantial transformation of teaching and learning for distance education students in rural and remote communities in Australia. Until the turn of the century, delivery of education services was largely *first generation* (Nipper, 1989), the introduction of telephone teaching during 2000-2001 reflected *second generation* technologies, while access to the Internet has seen a rapid expansion of learning opportunities and forms of delivery and interaction reflecting moves to *third* and *fourth generation* technologies.

As we move toward online learning environments, guidance is needed to enhance the probability of developing effective teaching and learning in those new environments. The following sections of this chapter explore dimensions of learner satisfaction in online learning environments in higher education to provide insights into the implications for effective online learning.

Dimensions of Learner Satisfaction: Implications for Online Learning

As established earlier in this chapter, ICT and, in particular, the Internet has resulted in online learning. Added to this has been the advantage of teachers and learners to more easily engage in the interactions between learners and materials, learners and teachers, and learners with other learners in the learning process. The limitations of time and space through the asynchronous network model (Katz, 2000, 2002; Trentin, 1997) have been overcome. Online learning has become synonymous with e-learning, and both are used synonymously and interchangeably here. Online learning has "already proved a major influence in creating more flexible campus-based structures as well as distance-education provision for learners" (Roffe, 2004, p. 52) as illustrated in the generational changes outlined in the case study of the Charleville SDE.

Roffe indicates that everyone who attempts to provide distance education has the challenge of overcoming the separation between teacher and learner which is referred to as "transactional distance" (Roffe, 2004, p. 53). According to Roffe, transactional distance depends upon three variables—dialogue, structure, and autonomy. Those variables are dependent upon the people involved, the content of the teaching, and the aims and methods of teaching (Roffe, 2004, p. 53). Accompanying the push for online learning provision, more recently, higher education institutions have also needed to address the challenge of demands for efficient and effective funding usage from all stakeholders, public, and political groups. Rahm and Reid (1997) note that higher education institutions have been actively seeking opportunities to expand and apply their educational resources more publicly and efficiently. Online learning has been seen by many higher education institutions to address this challenge (Tsichritzis, 1999). As Roffe (2004) indicates, there is now interest evidenced by the many investigations into e-learning by many interest groups, including governments, professional organisations, commercial and educational communities. However, as Park, Russell, Finger, and Jo (2004) have indicated, "there is a growing concern and fear that money spent on the new technological infrastructure might be diverted away from the employment of lecturers" (p. 100). Park et al. warn that there is also growing evidence that infrastructure and associated costs such as hardware, network, technical support, and Internet cots tend to increase rather than diminish. They cite the example of one higher education institution which had Internet costs in 1995 of $50,000, but with expanded use of online learning by academics and students had increased to $1.5 million in the space of five years (Park et al., 2004, p. 100).

Chou and Liu (2005) have commented that new learning models have become enabled through ICT, particularly through the use of multimedia and hypermedia. In combination with databases, Web programming languages, and digital educational materials such as learning objects, online learning supports the design of teaching materials with various features such as hyperlinks, multimedia, interactivity, and communication. Therefore, while online learning has often been accompanied by optimistic expectations, it is important to examine research on the effectiveness of online learning and theorise the dimensions which might be conceptualised to guide and inform the design and implementation of online learning. The following discussion attempts to provide a synthesis of some of that research.

Sun, Tsai, Finger, Chen, and Yeh (in press), undertook an extensive review of the relevant literature related to learner satisfaction and identified the dimensions evident from that literature review. Those dimensions included learner dimension, instructor dimension, course dimension, technology dimension, design dimension, and environmental dimension. I would suggest that these dimensions interact and influence each other. For example, the learner, course, technology, and environmental dimensions might influence expectations for the instructor and the design dimension.

In taking the learner dimension as an example, the need to focus and understand the learner dimension aligns with Roffe's warning that e-learning does not equate with

Figure 3. Dimensions of learner satisfaction: Synthesis of the literature related to dimensions of online learning (Source: Sun, Tsai, Finger, Chen & Yeh, in press)

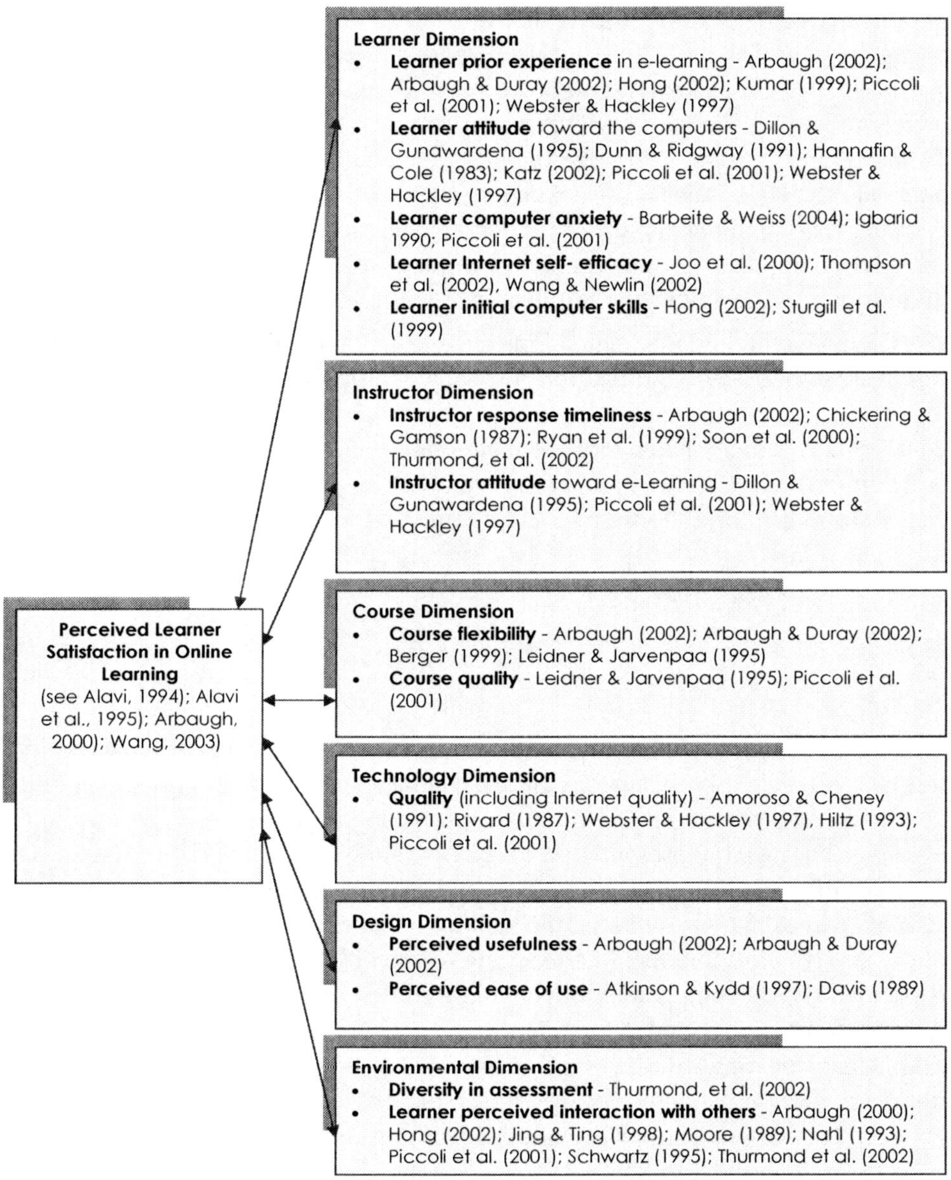

electronic learning, but requires an understanding of the human purpose of learning. Roffe suggests that in designing e-learning or online learning, the designer has to "find the optimum match between educational content and the potential learner" (Roffe, 2004, p. 3). Roffe argues that this has to do with other "e" words such as engagement of the learner, ease of use, empowerment, and execution (Roffe, 2002, pp. 40-55). Sun et al. also highlight research which indicates that prior experiences of learners influence learner satisfaction in e-learning (Arbaugh, 2002; Arbaugh & Duray 2002; Hong, 2002; Kumar, 1999; Piccoli, Ahmad & Ives, 2001). They postulate that as learners have more experience in online learning environments, those learners might become more proficient and therefore increasing their learning satisfaction. Figure 3 provides a model which synthesises research related to those dimensions and identifies the implications emerging from that literature review.

These dimensions and the related issues identified in the literature and presented in Figure 3 provide useful implications for consideration when designing online learning. Together with the case study of the Charleville SDE, which demonstrated the generational changes in delivery of educational services to rural and remote students, these dimensions present a compelling argument for going beyond the technological considerations in order to transform teaching and learning using ICT.

Conclusion

This chapter has provided conceptualisations related to the use of ICT, especially the Internet, for education systems, schools, teachers, and students to move from *inaction*, to *investigation*, *application*, *integration*, and *transformation* of teaching and learning. Through the presentation of the case study of the Charleville SDE, which provides educational programs to rural and remote students within a geographical area of Queensland in Australia, the technological changes and challenges in moving from HF radio to telephone teaching to the affordances of online learning. In particular, those changes were conceptualised in terms of four generations of educational delivery reflected in four identifiable technological advances, concluding in the most recent *fourth generation* characterised by online learning which is enabling transformational changes in the way those students learn. The transactional distance between teacher and learner is being bridged through new technologies.

Subsequent to the case study, a synthesis of the review of relevant literature about dimensions which inform learner satisfaction in online learning was presented. Implications were identified in the model which graphically summarised that synthesis. As we move into the 21st century, we have technologies which were unavailable several decades ago. This is an exciting time for educators and for learners as we transform teaching and learning in an increasingly online world. The world in the next decades will certainly be a far different world from that of today. The challenge is to encourage and equip learners to be *lifelong learners* in that *online world*.

References

Alavi, M. (1994). Computer-mediated collabrative learning: An empirical evaluation. *MIS Quarterly, 18*(2), 159-174.

Alavi, M., Wheeler, B. C., & Valachich, J. S. (1995). Using IT to re-engineer business education: An exploratory investigation to collaborative teleclearning. *MIS Quarterly, 19*(3), 293-312.

Amoroso, D. L., & Cheney, P. H. (1991). Testing a causal model of end-user application effectiveness. *Journal of Management Information Systems, 8*, 63-89.

Anderson, T. D., & Garrison, D. R. (1995). Transactional issues in distance education: The impact of design in audio teleconferencing. *The American Journal of Distance Education, 9*(2), 27-45.

Arbaugh, J. B. (2002). Managing the on-line classroom: A study of technological and behavioral characteristics of Web-based MBA courses. *Journal of High Technology Management Research, 13*, 203-223.

Arbaugh, J. B., & Duray, R. (2002). Technological and structural characteristics, student learning and satisfaction with web-based courses: An exploratory study of two on-line MBA programs. *Management Learning, 33*, 331-347.

Atkinson, M., & Kydd, C. (1997). Individual characteristics associated with World Wide Web use: An empirical study of playfulness and motivation. *DATA BASE for Advances in Information Systems, 28*, 53-62.

Australian Capital Territory (ACT) Government. (2004). *Learning technologies plan for ACT government schools and preschools 2004-2006: Transforming the way we teach and learn*. Tuggeranong ACT: Australian Capital Territory. Retrieved August 5, 2006, from http://www.deyfs.act.gov.au

Barbeite, F. G., & Weiss, E. M. (2004). Computer self-efficacy and anxiety scales for an Internet sample: Testing measurement equivalence of existing measures and development of new scales. *Computers in Human Behavior, 20*, 1-15.

Berger, N. S. (1999). Pioneering experiences in distance learning: Lessons learned. *Journal of Management Education, 23*, 684-690.

Brown, J. S., Collins, A., & Duguid, P. (1989). Situated cognition and the culture of learning. *Educational Researcher, 18*(1), 32-42.

Charleville School of Distance Education (SDE). (2005). *Curriculum*. Retrieved August 5, 2006, from http://www.charlevisde.qld.edu.au/site/curriculum.htm

Chickering, A. W., & Gamson, Z. F. (1987). Seven principles for good practice in undergraduate education. *AAHE Bulletin, 39*, 3-6.

Chou, S. W., & Liu, C. H. (2005). Learning effectiveness in a Web-based virtual learning environment: A learner control perspective. *Journal of Computer Assisted Learning, 21*, 65-76.

Davis, F. D. (1989). Perceived usefulness, perceived ease of use and user acceptance of information technology. *MIS Quarterly, 13*, 319-340.

Department of Education, Science and Training (DEST). (2002). *Raising the standards: A proposal for the development of an ICT competency framework for teachers*. Canberra: Department of Education Science and Training.

Department of Education Tasmania (DET). (2005). *Education, training, and information: Learners and learning.* Retrieved August 5, 2006, from http://www2.education.tas.gov.au/Nav/Topic.asp?Topic=Learners+and+learning

Department of Education Training and Youth Affairs (DETYA). (2000). The way forward—higher education action plan for the information economy incorporated. In *Learning for the knowledge society—an education and training action plan for the information economy.* Retrieved August 5, 2006, from http://www.edna.edu.au/highered/actionplan/

Dillon, C. L., & Gunawardena, C. N. (1995). A framework for the evaluation of telecommunications- based distance education. In D. Stewart (Ed.), *17th World Congress of the International Council for Distance Education* (pp. 348-351). Milton Keynes, UK: Open University.

Doig, C. (2005). *Innovation in education in designated character schools: A case study of the directors of discovery 1 and unlimited Paenga Tawhiti.* Unpublished doctoral dissertation, Griffith University, Gold Coast, Queensland, Australia.

Dunn, S., & Ridgway, J. (1991). Computer use during primary school teaching practice: A survey. *Journal of Computer Assisted Learning, 7*, 7-17.

Dwyer, D., Ringstaff, C., & Sandholtz, J. (1991). Changes in teachers' beliefs and practices in technology-rich classrooms. *Educational Leadership, 48*, 45-52.

Dymock, D., & Hobson, P. (1998). Collaborative learning through audio conferencing and voicemail: A case study. *Distance Education, 19*(1), 157-171.

Education Queensland. (2005a). *The learning place.* Retrieved August 5, 2006, from http://education.qld.gov.au/learningplace/

Education Queensland. (2005b). *Virtual schooling service*. Retrieved August 5, 2006, from http://education.qld.gov.au/learningplace/vss/

Ellyard, P. (2001). *Ideas for the new millennium* (2nd ed.). Melbourne: Melbourne University Press.

Garrison, D. R. (1985). Three generations of technological innovations in distance education. *Distance Education, 6*(2), 235-241.

Garrison, D. R. (1993). Quality and access in distance education: Theoretical considerations. In D. Keegan (Ed.), *Theoretical principles of distance education* (pp. 9-21). New York: Routledge.

Garrison, D. R., & Shale, D. (1990). *Education at a distance: From issues to practice.* Malabar, FL: Krieger.

Goodlad, J. I. (1984). *A place called school.* New York: McGraw-Hill.

Gough, N. (2002). The long arms of globalisation. In W. E. Doll & N. Gough (Eds.), *Curriculum visions* (pp. 167-178). New York: Peter Lang.

Hannafin, J. J., & Cole, D. D. (1983). An analysis of why students select introductory high school computer coursework. *Educational Technology, 23*, 26-29.

Hardy, D., & Olcott, D. (1995). Audio teleconferencing and the adult learner: Strategies for effective practice. *The American Journal of Distance Education, 9*(1), 44-60.

Hiltz, S. R. (1993). *The virtual classroom: Learning without limits via computer networks*. Norwood, NJ: Ablex Publishing Corporation.

Hobbs, T., Finger, G., & Torrisi-Steele, G. (2000). *Evaluation of the Charleville School of distance education whole school telephone teaching pilot.* EdData.

Hong, K.-S. (2002). Relationships between students and instructional variables with satisfaction and learning from a Web-based course. *Internet and Higher Education, 5*, 267-281.

Igbaria, M. (1990). End-user computing effectiveness: A structural equation model. *OMEGA, 18*, 637-652.

Jing, M., & Ting, E. (1998). *Course design, instruction, and students' online behaviours: A study of instructional variables and student perceptions of online learning*. Paper presented at the Annual Meeting of the American Educational Research Association (pp. 13-19), San Diego, CA.

Jonassen, D. (2000). *Computers as mindtools for schools engaging critical thinking* (2nd ed.). Columbus, OH: Merrill Prentice Hall.

Joo, Y. J., Bong, M., & Choi, H. J. (2000). Self-efficacy for self-regulated learning, academic self-efficacy, and Internet self-efficacy in Web-based instruction. *Educational Technology Research and Development, 48*, 5-17.

Katz, Y. J. (2000). The comparative suitability of three ICT distance learning methodologies for college level instruction. *Educational Media International, 37*, 25-30.

Katz, Y. J. (2002). Attitudes affecting college students' preferences for distance learning. *Journal of Computer Assisted Learning, 18*, 2-9.

Kirkwood, A. (1998). New media mania: Can information and communication technologies enhance the quality of open and distance learning? *Distance Education, 19*(2), 228-241.

Kraver, T. (1997). *Emerging learning technology report.* Retrieved August 5, 2006, from http://www.altp.org/SSP/EmergingLearningTechnologyReport.htm

Kumar, A. (1999). Learner characteristics and success in Indian distance education. *Open Learning, 14*, 52-58.

Laurillard, D. (1993). *Rethinking university teaching: A framework for the effective use of educational technology.* London: Routledge.

Leidner, D. L., & Jarvenpaa, S. L. (1995). The use of information technology to enhance management school education: A theoretical view. *MIS Quarterly, 19*, 265-291.

Ministerial Council on Employment, Education, Training and Youth Affairs (MCEETYA). (1999). *The Adelaide declaration on national goals for schooling in the twenty-first century*. Adelaide, South Australia. Author.

Ministerial Council for Education, Employment, Training and Youth Affairs (MCEETYA). (2000). *Learning in an online world: The school action plan for the information economy.* Retrieved August 5, 2006, from http://www.edna.edu.au/onlineworld.pdf

Ministerial Council for Education, Employment, Training and Youth Affairs (MCEETYA). (2002). *Information and communication technologies taskforce.* Retrieved August 5, 2006, from http://www.curriculum.edu.au/mceetya/taskforce/task223.htm

Ministerial Council for Education, Employment, Training and Youth Affairs (MCEETYA). (2003). *Research strategy. Learning in an online world.* Carlton South, Victoria: Curriculum Corporation. Retrieved August 5, 2006, from http://icttaskforce.edna.edu.au/documents/research/research_strategy.pdf

Ministerial Council for Education, Employment, Training and Youth Affairs (MCEETYA) ICT in Schools Taskforce. (2005). *Learning in an online world: The school education action plan for the information economy progress report 2004*. Retrieved August 5, 2006, from http://www.icttaskforce.edna.edu.au/documents/learning_online_progress_04.pdf

Ministry of Education. (2003). *Digital horizons: Learning through ICT*. Wellington: Learning Media.

Moore, M. G. (1989). Three types of interaction. *The American Journal of Distance Education, 3*, 1-6.

Nahl, D. (1993). Communication dynamics of a live interactive television system for distance education. *Journal of Education for Library and Information Science, 34*, 200-217.

Nipper, S. (1989). Third generation distance learning and computer conferencing. In R. Mason & A. Kaye (Eds.), *Mindweave: Communication, computers, and distance education* (pp. 63-74). UK: Pergamon Press.

Olgren, C. H., & Parker, L. A. (1983). *Teleconferencing technology and applications.* Artech House Inc.

Park, S., Russell, N., Finger, G., & Jo, J. (2004). The virtual university: Prospects and problems. *Information Technology, Education and Society*, *5*(1), 97-112.

Passerini, K., & Granger, M. J. (2000). A developmental model for distance learning using the Internet. *Computers & Education, 34*, 1-15. Retrieved August 5, 2006, from http://www.elsevier.com/locate/compedu

Piccoli, G., Ahmad, R., & Ives, B. (2001). Web-based virtual learning environments: A research framework and a preliminary assessment of effectiveness in basic IT skill training. *MIS Quarterly, 25*, 401-426.

Queensland Studies Authority (QSA). (2003). *Technology years 1 to 10 syllabus.* Brisbane, Queensland: The State of Queensland.

Rahm, D., & Reed, B. J. (1997). Going remote: The use of distance learning, the World Wide Web, and the Internet in graduate programs of public affairs and administration. *Public Productivity and Management Review, 20*, 459-471.

Rivard, S. (1987), Successful implementation of end-user computing. *Interfaces, 17*, 25-33.

Roffe, I. (2002). E-learning: Engagement, enhancement and execution. *Quality Assurance in Education, 10*(1), 40-50.

Roffe, I. (2004). *Innovation and e-learning: E-business for an educational enterprise.* Cardiff: University of Wales Press.

Rotolo, C. (2001). *Telephone teaching: Towards a constructivist approach.* Unpublished undergraduate education honours thesis, Griffith University, Queensland, Australia.

Russell, G., & Finger, G. (2004, July 5-8). *Teacher education in an online world: Future directions.* Paper presented at the Australian Council for Computers in Education 2004 Conference, Research, Reform, Realise the Potential, Adelaide, Australia.

Ryan, M., Carlton, K. H., & Ali, N. S. (1999). Evaluation of traditional classroom teaching methods versus course delivery via the World Wide Web. *Journal of Nursing Education, 38*, 272-277.

Schwartz, R. A. (1995). The virtual university. *American Society for Engineering Education Prism, 5*, 22-26.

Senge, P. (1990). *The fifth discipline: The art and practice of the learning organization.* New York: Doubleday.

Soon, K. H., Sook, K. I., Jung, C. W., & Im, K. M. (2000). The effects of Internet-based distance learning in nursing. *Computers in Nursing, 18*, 19-25.

Sturgill, A., Martin, W., & Gay, G. (1999). Surviving technology: A study of student use of computer-mediated communication to support technology education. *International Journal of Educational Telecommunications, 5*, 239-259.

Sun, P., Tsai, R. J., Finger, G., Chen, Y., & Yeh, D. (in press). What drives a successful e-learning? An empirical investigation of the critical factors influencing learner satisfaction. *Compters and Education*.

Thompson, L. F., Meriac, J. P., & Cope, J. G. (2002). Motivating online performance: The influences of goal setting and internet self-efficacy. *Social Science Computer Review, 20*, 149-160.

Thurmond, V. A., Wambach, K., & Connors, H. R. (2002). Evaluation of student satisfaction: Determining the impact of a Web-based environment by controlling for student characteristics. *The American Journal of Distance Education, 16*, 169-189.

Trentin, G. (1997). Telematics and on-line teacher training: The POLARIS project. *Journal of Computer Assisted Learning, 13*, 261-270.

Trinidad, S., Newhouse, P., & Clarkson, B. (2005, November 27-December 1). *A framework for leading school change in using ICT: Measuring change.* Paper presented at the Australian Association for Research in Education Conference – AARE '05 Education Research Creative Dissent: Constructive Solutions, UWS Parramatta, NSW, Australia.

Tsichritzis, D. (1999). Reengineering the university. *Communications of ACM, 42*, 93-100.

Wang, A. Y. (2003). Assessment of learner satisfaction with asynchronous electronic learning systems. *Information and Management,* (41), 75-86.

Wang, A. Y., & Newlin, M. H. (2002). Predictors of Web-student performance: The role of self-efficacy and reasons for taking an on-line class. *Computers in Human Behavior, 18*, 151-163.

Wang, H. (2003). Mathematical theory of molecular motors and a new approach for uncovering motor mechanism. *IEE Proceedings Nanobiotechnology,* 150, 127-133.

Webster, J., & Hackley, P. (1997). Teaching effectiveness in technology-mediated distance learning. *Academy of Management Journal, 40*, 1282-1309.

Young, B. (2005). *A model for ICT in the UAE.* Unpublished doctoral dissertation, Griffith University, Queensland, Australia.

Chapter IV

Technology, Lifelong Learning, and Effective Foreign Language Instruction Under the Memory Efficient Approach

P. Tokoyo Kang, University of Guam, Guam

Abstract

This chapter presents a method for foreign language (FL) teachers to implement currently available technologies as instructional tools in a FL language classroom using the memory efficient approach (MEA) to enhance instruction, and help students to become lifelong FL learners. Providing historical backgrounds of the FL acquisition or learning theory as well as technological implementation for FL instruction, the chapter suggests MEA with eclectic methodology for FL instruction. Under the MEA, the methods for "skill-using" and "skill-getting" (Rivers, 1985) are employed; thus, appropriate methods as well as appropriate instructional tools—technological and nontechnological—are selected according to the learning objective or goal. In addition, introducing emerging technologies that may be utilized for instruction in the FL area, the chapter will demonstrate a method to implement technologies in advanced Japanese courses as well as in elementary Japanese courses using MEA.

Introduction

The movie *Matrix* fascinates me as a foreign language (FL) teacher. The movie demonstrates that a FL teacher can virtually use changing situations by opening virtual reality (VR) doors to provide FL practice environments for students. They will be able to practice the language, complete self-assessment tests, take a final exam, and use it as lifelong FL learning tool as a virtual field trip in the target language's country. Current technologies are not capable of creating *Matrix* level VR stages at this time, but we are in the digital age and VR is right around the corner. We continually improve the power of our first language; however, a FL requires a stronger constant effort to maintain proficiency. The FL attrition rate is many times greater than a first language attrition rate. One mission of a FL teacher is "developing the skills and attitudes of lifelong learners among all ... [their] students" (Dodds, 2001, p. 3). Universities also have a mission that FL teachers support, simply because "university learning can and should be open to people of all ages (post-school)" (Dodds, 2001, p. 1). Current technological developments have brought FL teachers new tools to accomplish these missions. Although their reasons are varied, many teachers do not take advantage of these new technologies in their classrooms.

Every teacher has a learning theory, explicit or implicit, to support a teaching methodology. Technological tools are employed according to the teacher's methodology. Thus, how to use technological tools effectively depends on the learning theory. Many FL acquisition theories have been proposed and each theory has its own methodology. The theories do not seem to be related because FL acquisition theories have focused on only a few aspects of FL learning, but not on the overall process. After evaluating the overall FL learning process, these methodologies may be unified under a single enhanced approach based on a learning theory.

This chapter will explain a cost, time, and labor effective method to use technologies in the FL classroom instruction under the memory efficient approach (MEA) (Kang, 1993). This approach will help and encourage students to continue learning the FL after graduation through self-motivated lifelong learning. MEA, which is the outcome of human parser FL learning theory, encourages a FL instructor to be eclectic in terms of methodology.

There are four additional sections and a summary. First, I will address the need to implement technologies in FL instruction with a brief historical overview of FL learning, acquisition theories, and recent theories of computer-assisted language learning (CALL). Second, I will propose implementation of Kang's MEA (1993) and discuss how effectively technology can be implemented under the MEA. Third, I will identify some of the emerging technologies relevant to FL teaching and lifelong learning. Finally, I will exhibit technologies I use to teach Elementary Japanese II (JA102) and an advanced 4th year Japanese (JA490). Use of these technologies enhances my classroom instruction and the student's lifelong learning. The summary will recap the main points and stimulate addition thoughts.

Overview

As mentioned previously, there are many FL teachers who do not motivate their students to use computers for learning the target language. One may raise a question: Are they technophobes? Cuban (2001) finds that teachers (not specifically FL teachers, but in all subjects at school) are *not* technophobes because they use computers in their daily lives. Lam (2000) also answers "No" to the question. Then, why are FL teachers not using computer technology? Lam reports several reasons including that some FL teachers do not see how computer technology could be useful for language teaching. This kind of skepticism toward technological implementation is understandable based on an audiolingual laboratory experiment that failed in 1970s. This attempt is well known to many FL teachers and will be discussed in the following section.

FL teachers may ask whether using technology is worth the time, labor, and expenses consumed for implementation in classroom teaching, as Garrett (1991) does. Some FL teachers who want to integrate computer technology into the classroom are often discouraged because the hardware and software crucial for classroom instruction is not available to them. Omoto, Fukai, and Schneider (2002) identify what Japanese language teachers need to implement technologies in class: (1) technical support for troubleshooting; (2) much broader bandwidth to receive large audio and video files; those audio and video files are necessary for the Japanese language instruction, but just not available; (3) development of more courseware for class use so students can participate in collaborative learning; and (4) resources to take advantage of authentic reading material on the Internet (e.g., reading newspapers on the Internet utilizing an online dictionary) and training for those resources. My requirements are from (1) to (3) and should be met soon, although they are not just Japanese language needs. CALL is expected to develop additional courseware with more consideration of FL curricula. This chapter focuses on taking advantage of authentic reading material on the Internet and discussing simple, cost-effective, time-effective, and labor-effective ways to make the most use of authentic reading materials on the Internet that require little training.

Technology and FL Learning Theories/Hypotheses

As we have seen in the previous section, those FL teachers who do not use computer technology for their instruction raise the question: How could computer technology be useful for FL teaching? Warshauer and Meskill (2000) and Salaberry (2001) raise the following similar questions (concerning technology-driven vs. principle-oriented pedagogies): Does advanced technological development bring us effective

FL teaching? And, is increased technological sophistication correlated to increased effectiveness to achieve pedagogical objectives? Warshauer and Meskill (2000) started with the concern about recent enthusiasm in using computer technology in the FL classroom. Their concern is because this enthusiasm grows from the assumption that our students can learn their target language more effectively merely because they are using advanced technology. Historically speaking, technological implementation has not brought as much positive influence as expected. A well-known case is audiolingual method (ALM) based on the learning theory of Skinner's behaviorism and structural descriptive linguistics in 1970s. Most of the universities in the 1970s had expensive audiolingual (new technology at that time) language labs to provide students with audiolingual structural lessons. Learning outcome of these lessons was discouraging. According to Warshauer and Meskill, the failure is not "audiolingual" technology (FL teaching tool) but the "audiolingual" method. Salaberry's answer is that "a principle-oriented [pedagogical] approach uses the new technologies only to the extent that they serve a pedagogical purpose. Yet, their answers are not satisfactory, simply because what failed is *not* the method or pedagogical approach but the FL *learning theory/hypothesis* behind the method or pedagogical approach. In other words, the FL learning theory based on Skinner's behaviorism has responsibility for the failure of "audiolingual" method. The learning theory might have been successful in terms of only one learning objective, learning grammatical prosody of the target language, but failed in terms of the other learning objectives. This is an extreme way to explain language learning or acquisition process.

Foreign or second language acquisition theories have been changed from one extreme to another or have focused only on a few aspects of the FL acquisition process. In the 1950s and 1960s, the grammar-translation method was the dominant FL teaching method with the hypothesis that a FL is learned by memorizing vocabulary, and by consciously learning grammar to translate written FL texts. How did students learn the sounds of a FL? In the late 1960s and 1970s, ALM based on Skinner's learning theory emerged, which took into the consideration the difference between the learner's first language and the target language. Skinner's learning theory assumed that language is learned by imitation, repetition, and reinforcement as habit formation and that language is acquired by listening to native speakers' spoken, but not written, language. Therefore, the ALM does not teach how to read and write in the introductory and intermediate FL courses. In other words, according to the ALM, phonology of the target language should be consciously learned, especially for enhancing speaking and listening skills.

Chomsky (1965, 1975, 1982) proposed the innateness of linguistic competence (a child is born with a language faculty device called *universal grammar*). Chomsky strongly denies Skinner's hypothesis that language acquisition is a type of habit formation. Based on this, Chomsky's acquisition theory, the natural approach (Krashen, 1985), is suggested. Under the natural approach, a FL is learned naturally as a first language learning. The natural approach strongly rejects rote learning, imitation, and repetition, but promotes immersion method, and ignores the difference between the learner's first language and the target language due to innate universal grammar. When the learner is a young child, the immersion method may not intimidate the learner so much, but when it comes to an adult learner, the method may create a very intimidating learning environment. Thus, Krashen must have claimed no error-correction because it may increase the learner's anxiety. The Chomskian learning theory has two distinctions: competence and performance. The theory's interest is couched in linguistic competence, but not linguistic performance. Language use or the use of linguistic skills such as speaking, listening, reading, and writing belongs to "performance" but not to "competence."

In the 1980s, the communicative approach without grammatical error correction was proposed. This approach focuses on FL use for communication, or functional use of a FL, that is, linguistic "performance." Although the proponents of the communicative approach were not satisfied with the natural approach, the communicative approach also discourages FL teachers from correcting the learners' linguistic errors as the natural approach. The approach put "more emphasis on language in context, language in use for a purpose, language to *do something* with [for example, greeting, invitation, apologies], not just language form for its own sake" (Lightbown, 2000, p. 435). Communicative language teaching (CLT) is the first FL teaching approach to allow students to use their target language as a tool as native speakers do. The CLT approach has been criticized because grammatical accuracy is not required.

In the early 1980s, another FL teaching method called content-based (task-oriented) method emerged from the immersion method. The content (or task) based FL teaching also let the students use their FL as a "tool," like a native speaker. This content-based/task-oriented approach also tacitly assumes that a FL is acquired as a first language. It also assumes that students have obtained communicative skills in the FL to complete a given task. It is well known that the diversity in adult language learners is far bigger than that in the child language learners (e.g., Felder & Henriques, 1995; Skehan, 1989). However, both CLT and the content-based/task-oriented teaching methods have inherited the ignorance of the well-observed diversity gap, as their ancestor—the immersion method—did. As a result, they paid attention to the aspect of "skill-using" (Rivers, 1981), but not "skill-getting" (Rivers, 1981).

How to view and use the technologies for FL instruction also has changed from one extreme to another as FL learning/acquisition theory has. Under behaviorism, the computer was viewed as a mechanical tutor that never grew tired or judgmental and allowed students to work at an individual pace (Warschauer & Healey, 1998). The recent researchers of CALL also look at "skill-using" part of language learning. Warschauer and Healey further propose the integrative approach in the following way:

Task-oriented, project-oriented, and content-oriented approaches all sought to integrate learners in authentic environments, and also to integrate the various skills of language learning and use. This led to a new perspective on technology and language learning ... a perspective which seeks both to integrate various skills (e.g., listening, speaking, reading, and writing) and also integrate technology more fully into the language learning process. (p. 2)

The integrative approach by Warschauer and Healey integrates only those instructional methods for skill-using. For beginners, it is not clear how an authentic environment brings positive effects on its target language learning. For advanced students, due to Japanese characters called *kanji* (Chinese characters) to participate in a chat (in text) room for native speakers of Japanese is not an easy task because they are reading the sentences wrote by the native speakers (cf. LeLoup & Ponterio, 2003) fast enough, or their mental *kanji* dictionaries do not have enough *kanji* to enjoy text chatting with the native speakers. Another researcher on CALL, Wang (2005) touts the constructivist learning approach. Constructivist theory of learning, which hypothesizes that social interaction will enhance individual learning, is developed from Piagetian psychology of learning. Its focus seems to solve problems collaboratively using a FL. Thus, Wang's constructivist approach also focuses on "skill-using."

What the FL learning/acquisition theories, as well as CALL, do not take into consideration are the following two ideas. First, unrealistically, they simply ignored the difference in the FL students' proficiency levels. The beginners need a higher proportion of time for skill-getting, while, in the advanced FL class, the proportion of time spent for skill-using is in general higher. Second, again unrealistically, they ignored the language specific aspects of learning. In the classroom of a FL like Japanese, even in an advanced class, the characters (*kanji*) learning as vocabulary learning (skill-getting) still takes high proportion of student's learning to read authentic reading material on the Internet.

To close this section, the question (How could computer technology be useful for FL teaching?) needs to be answered. As discussed, technologies including computer technology are nothing but tools. The usefulness or effectiveness of the tools will be realized when we find a method to use them effectively. To find out how to use these tools effectively, we should have good knowledge about the tools to take advantage of their capabilities. We, FL teachers, are always looking for new teaching materials, new activities, new methodologies, or new tools. Any instructional tools or materials, however, cannot be effective for student learning, unless activities using those tools and material are incorporated in the curriculum. In the digital age, we can extend the tool-searching area into technological field and learn what current technological tools can do. Especially, when it comes to lifelong self-motivating FL learning, technological tools available on the Internet are indispensable

Memory Efficient Approach (MEA)

The FL learning theory endorsed in this chapter is (Kang, 1993), which argues for MEA. If the attentive listener tries to comprehend linguistic inputs, the parser in the listener's brain will be activated. Uncertainty, unfamiliarity, or ambiguity cause extra burden on a FL learner's short-term memory. This extra burden is caused by unknown words or phrases and the capacity of short-term memory is limited (Miller, 1956). The short-term memory is tasked beyond its capacity and the parser is not able to process all the unknown words and phrases. If the capacity of short-term memory cannot process all the information, a learner's parser has difficulty learning ways to process new structures. When learners become unattentive, the capacity of their short-term memory will not be fully used. Comprehension of structure is not attained when the learners' parser fails to process input sentences.

HP learning theory agrees with Chomsky's universal aspects of syntax of languages. The HP theory also agrees with Skinner's behaviorism in terms of the following: (1) paying attention to language specific aspects; (2) the hypothesis that phonological learning is the first of all; and (3) language learning is habit formation. The HP theory assumes a child is born with a set of language processors, including a parser. According to the HP theory, what to learn is the following: (1) parsing algorithms for a FL when the FL is different from student's mother tongue in terms of heading parameter—bottom-up parsing algorithm for a head final language (e.g., Japanese) or top-down parsing algorithm for a head-initial language (e.g., English); (2) phonological or prosodic phrases as "comprehension units" (Kang, 2003); and (3) morphology and vocabulary. Parsing algorithms that tell how to analyze syntactic structures of input sentences cannot be learned consciously, so the parsing algorithms are not something that a teacher can teach. On the other hand, phonological phrases, or phonological phrase boundaries can be learned consciously, as well as morphology and vocabulary.

MEA recommends brief grammar teaching for each level of FL classes and learning vocabulary (skill-getting) to let our students properly engage and learn in "skill-using" activities.

MEA is an "eclectic" teaching methodology. Whether it is a digital age or any other age, one of the main concerns for the FL teacher is the following inquiry: Will their instructions work effectively for the students' target language learning? Effective instruction should be eclectic to improve memory efficiency by integrating all methodologies mentioned previously and any new methodologies that will improve memory efficiency (to my knowledge, Rivers is the first FL teacher to suggest "eclectic" methodology for FL teaching). FL students are expected to learn vocabulary and grammatical form prior to participating in "skill-using" activities such as communicative, task-oriented, immersion, collaborative, integrative, and socioconstructive activities. Under the MEA, "skill-getting" activities are as important as "skill-using" activities. With good knowledge of relevant vocabulary and grammatical form, student parser will be able to parse sentences memory efficiently that used to be incomprehensible. Although the integration of four skills—speaking, listening, reading, and writing—is not new, the MEA's rational for the four-skill integration is new because of the learning effectiveness of activities using more than one of the four skills (Felder & Henriques, 1995). Furthermore, as noted by Stice (cited in Felder & Henriques, 1995):

A point no educational psychologist would dispute is that students learn more when information is presented in a variety of modes than when only a single mode is used. The point is supported by a research study carried out several decades ago, which concluded that students retain 10 percent of what they read, 26 percent of what they hear, 30 percent of what they see, 50 percent of what they see and hear, 70 percent of what they say, and 90 percent of what they say as they do something. (p. 28)

Now, we are already in the digital age as well as our current and future students' lives. When it comes to teaching those digital-age students (they are "digital native" but their teacher's generation is called "digital immigrants"), as described by Prensky (2001), are we ready to give them effective instructions for their FL learning?

Today's students—kindergarten through college—represent the first generations to grow up with this new technology. They have spent their entire lives surrounded by and using computers, videogames, digital music players, video cams, cell phones, and all the other toys and tools of the digital age. ... Computer games, email, the Internet, cell phones and instant messaging are integral parts of their lives. (p. 1)

It appears to be a challenge for FL teachers to have those students in the classroom. The teacher's generation also played games with *different tools* from computer, TV, or a cell phone. For FL teachers, adopting (language) games are nothing new (e.g., Wright, Betteridge, & Bucky, 1983); only "tools" have been changed. For example, crossword games or scrabble games are played on a paper or on the board, but now, on the Internet, and on cell phones as well. Digitized language games are welcome as self-study material for the FL classes, especially under MEA, as long as they are suitable for learning objectives of the classes (see Warner, 2004, for interesting categorization of language games).

Games/quizzes are categorized as goal-oriented activities, whose goal is to get a higher score. To achieve the goal the students will try the games/quizzes again and again until they attain the high score they want to get. In other words, the repetition of language games/quizzes will naturally take place without feeling bored, and creates more memory efficiency, which MEA welcomes. Especially, MEA embraces such game/quiz-style CALL for relevant vocabulary or grammatical learning used as a learner's self-assessment tools.

FL teachers will be ready to implement the technologies, if CALL fits learning objectives (Salaberry, 2000), if the outcomes of the students' learning due to the employment of the technologies for some course objectives will be better than those using any other instructional tools, and if the implementation is cost-effective, time-effective, and labor-effective.

It is a well-known fact that diversity in adult language learners is far greater than in child language learners (e.g., Felder & Henriques, 1995; Skehan, 1989). This is another reason for the suggestion of MEA, which strongly encourages FL teachers to be eclectic in terms of FL teaching methodology, to motivate them; motivation is the most important because student's strong motivation makes the student attentive to linguistic stimulus.

Emerging Technology for FL Classroom Instruction and Lifelong Learning VR

One cutting-edge technology is VR. Video games and computer games are very popular among the digital generation, as mentioned earlier. Those games are created with VR technology and are commercially made, but not with educational purpose, because the technology is expensive and needs to be paid off with big profits. Commercially made VR games are mostly action-oriented, but not verbal communication-oriented. To my knowledge, there is one exception, the game called SIMs. SIMs is available in different languages including a Japanese version (see Purushotma, 2005 for a detailed explanation of how SIMs can be useful for FL learners). FL teachers may like to have one in their language lab to let their students play it.

To create FL learning software implemented with VR must be difficult without governmental financial assistance. Yes, there is one, amazingly sophisticated innovative software with a VR game program called "Rapid Tactical Language Training System." This is developed for Arabic language learning by the University of Southern California for the U.S. Army. This has a speech recognition system to correct learner's pronunciation by a virtual tutor, and nonverbal communication in Arabic culture is also incorporated. This kind of technology seems far from reachable for FL teachers at low budget institutions like mine. However, the technologies introduced next are free or affordable.

Podcasting with iPod or iTune and Newspaper Readers

Podcasting is the way to automatically download audio files onto an iPod, computer (through iTune), or mobile phone (through iTune). iTune (free downloading for Mac and Windows is available on the Web) and iPod are originally used to download music. Their usage has expanded by virtue of new devices and software to convert text files to audio files. If such sites as newspapers or blogs, according to Chinnery (2006), have machine readable texts on their Web sites, one can download audio files of those articles through iTune whose version is higher than 4.9. What can podcasting do with FL learning and teaching? Podcasts are (often homemade) audio/radio shows on culture, news, or life that are made available for download on the Internet (Godwin-Jones, 2005). The Web sites of BBC or *BusinessWeek* allows us to download their podcasting for free. For Japanese Web sites, Nikkei (business) newspaper starts to podcasting to computers, iPods, and mobile phones in 2005. Those podcastings on the Internet can be used for teaching material to improve listening comprehension in advanced levels of FL classes such as German, French, and English for native speakers of Japanese.

Speaking of a newspaper reader/speaker, in Japan, Fujitu company developed an evolutionary newspaper reader and speaker, called WebUC. Although the device is right now only accessible to readers of the Asahi Newspaper, this has a great potential to be made available for any Japanese Web pages. This is ideal for those students in advanced Japanese courses. WebUC will write the reading of *kanji* in *hiragana* above the *kanji*, which enables even junior high school students to read the newspaper. It also has a zoom feature, whereby the characters on the paper can be magnified. It can also read the newspaper articles out loud. However, the English version of Windows XP cannot make it work; we probably need Japanese Windows. The WebUC was originally developed for people with disabilities or senior citizens in Japan. However, this technological innovation has a great possibility to be improved more and to expand its application to all Web pages written in Japanese, even to homemade Web pages on the Internet, which also greatly helps students learn Japanese as a FL, especially with their lifelong learning.

Cell Phones and Japanese Language Games

The quality and functions of cell phones have rapidly improved. They are more popular in Asian countries than in the United States. For example, in Japan, they are one of the indispensable things for daily life even for junior high school students. With cell phones, in Japan users can send and receive e-mail messages, as well as take and send pictures by e-mail immediately. With cell phones using iTune, the podcasting of the Nikkei newspaper will also be available.

People can play games with cell phones inexpensively. The game called *mojirisu* is a kind of "Scrabble." Each time a block of a character (*hiragana*) shows up on the top of the screen. The player needs to find a slot to put a new block and make some word with the block insertion. If it makes a word with other existing blocks, the pop-up window tells the player what the word is, not only in *hiragana* but also in *kanji*. Then, those blocks composing the word will disappear. The faster a player loses the blocks, the better the player is. Unfortunately, this game is received only by Japanese cell phones with the specific mode. This is the offspring of the first Japanese scrabble, *mojipittan* (exact match of characters!) for Playstation. If it were sold on a CD, this might be one of the language games a FL teacher like myself would want to have in the language lab for Japanese general vocabulary learning. Cell phone functions will definitely be expanding and probably will assist FL learning and teaching. There will come a time when we tell our students to bring their cell phones to class (Prensky, 2004) and connect them to the virtual (FL) language lab. One of the great things about this virtual lab is that it will not cost anything to an educational institution.

Internet: Online TV and Radio

Truly current, up-to-the-minute video by native speakers using the language for real communication can make the language and culture come alive for students (LeLoup & Ponterio, 2004, p. 3). Although there are not so many online TVs (video), I have found the following: Shortwave Broadcasts LIVE On The Internet, French TV Channel TF1 (see LeLoup & Ponterio, 2004), Japanese Internet Radio/TV, Yomiuri Stream, and Nikkei Broadband News. When the cost of wide-bandwidth becomes more affordable for FL teachers, online TV broadcasting will be one of the most attractive teaching materials, especially for those students at the intermediate high, or advanced levels. There are multilanguage radio broadcastings such as Japanese NHK's news broadcasting called Radio Japan Online. We can listen to the radio in Japanese, English, Arabic, Bengali, Burmese, Chinese, French, German, Hindi, Indonesian, Italian, Korean, Malay, Persian, Portuguese, Russian, Swahili, Swedish, Thai, Urdu, and Vietnamese.

Pop-Up Online Dictionary with Automated Vocabulary Quizzes

Recent technological development has also brought us wonderful online dictionaries. What I am going to touch on is the revolution in online dictionaries, the advent of "pop-up/jump" dictionaries with tests/quizzes. To my knowledge, currently there are three pop-up dictionaries: Ultralingua, WordChamp, and POPjisyo. Ultralingua has only European language dictionaries, but not Asian language dictionaries. On the other hand, WordChamp outperforms Ultralingua in terms of the number of languages supported. The impressive listing includes Bengali, Bulgarian, Burmese, Cambodian, Catalan, Chinese (Cantonese), Chinese (Mandarin), Croatian, Czech, Danish, Dutch, English, Farsi, Finnish, French, German, Greek, Hebrew, Hindi, Hungarian, Indonesian, Irish, Italian, Japanese, Korean, Kurdish, Latin, Lithuanian, Malay, Marathi, Norwegian, Pashto, Polish, Portuguese, Punjabi, Romanian, Russian, Sanskrit, Serbian, Sindhi, Singhalese, Slovak, Spanish, Swahili, Swedish, Tagalog, Tamil, Telugu, Thai, Tibetan, Turkish, Ukrainian, Urdu, Vietnamese, and Yiddish (LeLoup & Ponterio, 2005).

The article in Figure 1 is from Asahi Newspaper. The WordChamp's Japanese English dictionary highlights *kanji* words or phrases. However, there are several *kanji* vocabulary that are not highlighted; this means the dictionary does not have the unhighlighted word. If we move the cursor to some highlighted *kanji* word, its reading is given in *hiragana*, and the meaning in English. This pop-up dictionary has more surprises. As seen in the pop-up box, we can add the word to the test. By clicking the speaker icon beside the *kanji* word, one can hear the sound for pronunciation of the *kanji* compound word, although how to read it is written in *hiragana* under the *kanji* compound word in the left box, as seen in Figure 1.

Our last pop-up dictionary is Popjisyo ("pop-dictionary" in English). It shows not only the vocabulary translation from Japanese to English, but from Japanese to Chinese, and from Japanese to Japanese in a pop-up window, as seen in Figure 2. This dictionary has several *kanji* matching games opened by clicking a menu bar

Figure 1. WordChamp (Source: Asahi Newspaper, May 24, 2006)

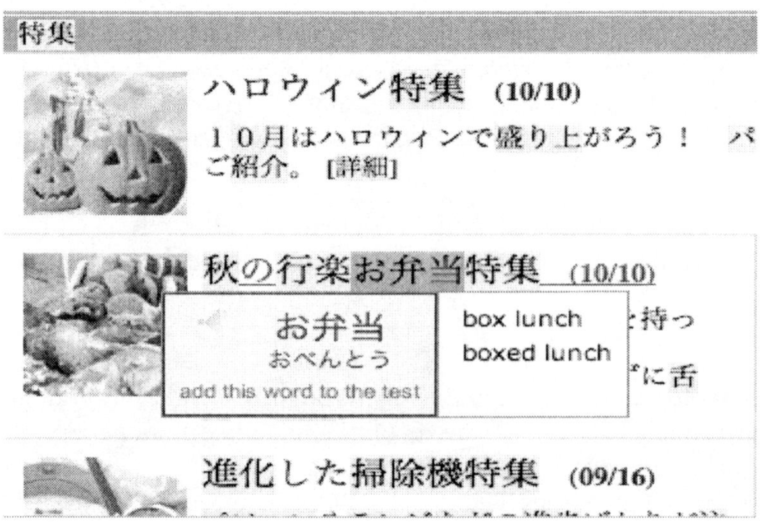

on the top of the inside of this Web page. Besides, this Popjisyo automatically creates a word list of the very Web page one is reading. The Popjisyo can be accessed through a cell phone also, without any charge. The Popjisyo has the following language dictionaries: English to Japanese; English to Spanish; Japanese to English; Japanese to German; Japanese to Chinese; Chinese (Mandarin) to English; Chinese (Cantonese) to English; Korean to English; and English to Korean. Just type in a URL you want to read and it will open the Web page under Popjisyo. The weakness of this dictionary is that the dictionary does not know the phrase boundary when comes to *hiragana* writing parts.

These pop-up dictionaries, although they are not yet perfect, open up the possibility for our students to read more and more authentic material available on the Internet, especially to read newspapers, even for the students learning Japanese language, too. This is a tool to encourage advanced students to continue their FL learning after graduation to improve literacy skill.

Moodle (Modular Object-Oriented Dynamic Learning Environment)

Moodle has brought another revolution to FL instruction because FL teachers want to have the course management and assessment tools. A low budget university like

Figure 2. Popjisyo (Source: Game Watch: June 14, 2005)

the author's cannot afford to have expensive Blackboard or WebCT. Brandle (2005) shows how learning management system works in the Spanish case, although it is unknown for a FL like Japanese—and assessment tools without any cost by the advent of Moodle (moodle.com). Moodle is a template-based system that FL teachers can fill in the contents. The learning theory behind Moodle is "socioconstructive" theory of learning, which hypothesizes that social interaction will enhance individual learning, developed from Piagetian psychology of learning. There is a caveat. It is in general not labor-effective or time-effective to use a course management system (Morgan, 2003). In Morgan (p. 4), on the other hand, many faculties found that the CMS helped them include more interactive materials, allowing them to address diverse learning styles.

The Integration of Technologies into Elementary Japanese II (JA102) Class: Effective Implementations in Terms of Cost, Time, and Labor

When the students finish the course (Elementary Japanese II), they will meet the foreign language requirement of general education here at the University of Guam. My motivation for implementing technological educational techniques in my elementary Japanese language classes is to encourage those students who stop taking higher levels of Japanese courses to motivate lifelong Japanese language learning after graduation. People living in a place like Guam—where the majority of tourists come from Japan—never know when the knowledge of Japanese language will open opportunities in the job market.

For Skill-Getting Internet: Supplemental Teaching/Learning Material for the Textbook

I have adopted the textbook *Genki*, "how are you?/I am fine." When I started using this textbook in the Elementary Japanese courses, there was only one CALL Web site for this textbook use, the "self study" site of Genki-Online. Then, the site of Genki Exercise was created and I used it for vocabulary learning objectives. Later the Web site *Usagichan* "rabbit" was added for *kanji* learning with stroke order movies. Now, all of the old and new CALLs useful to the textbook users are on the Japan Times' *Genki* Web site, although all of the CALL programs are useful and effective for skill-getting; learning for (1) *kana* characters (Japanese alphabets), (2) vocabulary, (3) grammar; conjugation quizzes of adjectives and verbs, and (4) *kanji* characters. Among them, the following two CALLs for learning *kanji* characters are revolutionary innovative: *Usagichan* and *Kanji* Alive.

Kanji (Chinese Characters) Learning: Stroke Orders and Compound Words for the Objective of Learning About 90 *Kanji*

Usagichan and *Kanji* Alive are excellent Web sites as "beginner's *kanji* dictionaries" for those students in an elementary or an intermediate Japanese course. These CALL programs are new and different in terms of stroke order movie for each *kanji*. First, in the *Usagichan*'s case, the screen for stroke order movie for a *kanji* pops up on the page of *kanji* list. The students can see both screens at the same time. The quick time movie can show the stroke order of a *kanji* again and again, if a student clicks the start button repeatedly. Second, this shows the list of example compound words with the very *kanji*, if we click "Go!" In the case of *Kanji* Alive, by one's clicking the button under "Kanji display," seen in the Figure 3, the Kanji Alive shows the stroke order of hand written *kanji* in animation. Additionally, if students click on the speaker beside an example word, they can hear the pronunciation of the word. Clicking an example word shows its meaning in English. Another feature of Kanji Alive that *Usagichan* does not carry is the information about the radical of a *kanji* on the same screen.

Figure 3. Kanji Alive (Source: Kanji Alive Overview: July 20, 2005)

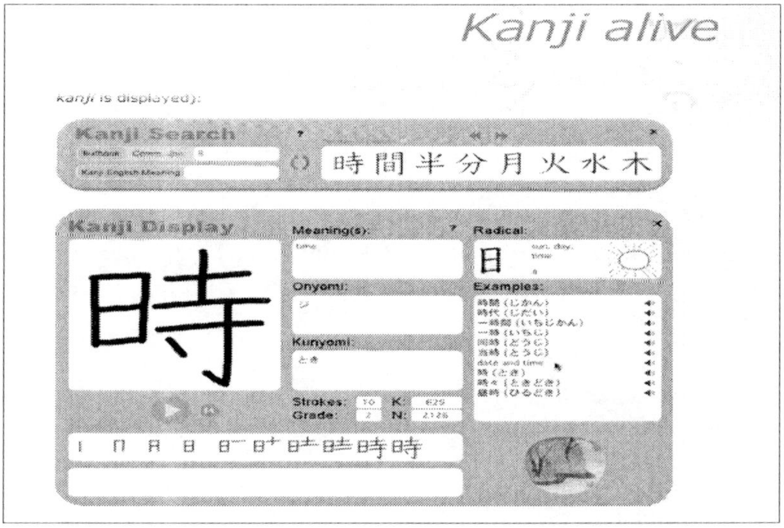

This method of providing *kanji* writing will make *kanji* learning much easier for students, because the students can learn how to write *kanji* memory efficiently. Another great thing is that these two Web sites are free of charge and open to anyone to access.

For Skill-Using

Most of the skill-using activities are performed in the classroom without any specific current high techs.

Japanese Word Processor and Internet (Task-Oriented)

Japanese word processor in MS Word and Internet are used for the following objectives: to make a simple flyer for a party or for sale, and to make a greeting card in Japanese. To make an electronic greeting card (especially in the Fall semester, New Year's, or Christmas cards), Internet is used to show greeting card samples in Yahoo Japan and in Yahoo U.S. Making a greeting card in Japanese is an activity to learn the culture by understanding the similarities and differences between the two cultures through greeting cards such as Japanese New Year's and Western Christmas cards.

For Skill-Getting and Skill-Using Courseware on the Internet: CyberMap III: The Objective to Demonstrate to Ask/Give Direction in Japanese (Vocabulary and Grammar Learning and Task-Oriented)

It is not easy to find an appropriate courseware that fits into individual FL course's lesson plan. CyberMap III is the only one I can use. I have adopt this for my JA102 classes because this CALL program created by Keiko Schneider makes it easy to learn not only vocabulary and grammar (skill-getting), but also how to give/get directions in Japanese (skill-using); memory efficient (see Kang, 2002 for how students evaluate the implementation of this as supplementary teaching material). The CyberMap III has plenty of playfulness, and takes advantage of the functions of Flash; the programmer has also created animations of a boy walking along the streets according to directions.

A Video Film: "Yan and the Japanese People" for Beginners: Immersion and Goal (Cultural Understanding) Oriented

The lifestyles in the film are a little dated, but the video film is still highly effective not only for listening comprehension material for this second-semester course, but also for learning Japanese culture (skill-getting; goal-oriented). Besides, what is important is that the students enjoy the film because they can understand most of the conversations (50%-80%) of each episode in the film by virtue of the pictures. The high rate of successful comprehension leads to a strong motivation for Japanese language learning, and encourages students to study more.

WWW on the Internet About Japanese Culture (Goal-Oriented)

For elementary Japanese courses, the Internet is one of the best tools to use for cultural (goal) instruction. To understand well the dialogues in a lesson of the textbook, give an assignment of writing answers in Japanese to simple questions in Japanese regarding *Kabuki*—Japanese classical musical theater plays—searching an English Web site about *Kabuki* on the Internet.

CDs for the Textbook (Learning Prosodic-Grammar: cf. ALM)

Most of the contents of the CDs are good for skill-getting and used for self-study, except for the listening comprehension exercise of each lesson in the CDs, which are given as an assignment.

We can make audio files very easily by Audacity (freeware) to upload in Moodle to create listening comprehension questions/quizzes, or upload to the instructor's Web page to allow anyone to access to the listening comprehension quizzes.

Course Management Tool: Moodle

The implementation of Moodle is now under preparation, as the course management tool and as the student learning assessment tool, for this course. Moodle is attractive, especially because it has templates of quizzes that are easy to add contents with or without time limit, or with or without feedback, which we can use for the learning assessment.

Japanese Through Current News Media: Advanced 4th Year Japanese

This course is conducted in Japanese—immersion method—using only technological teaching materials. The technologies utilized in this class are Internet (mainly), TV (NHK) news that I recorded at home, video with TV commercial films (rented from Japan Foundation at Los Angeles), and podcasting of Nikkei newspaper through iTune. The motivation for employing only technological instructional tools came from one of the objectives of this course—to learn Japanese through news media—and the students' difference in their proficiency. Japanese newspapers are freely available on the Internet. Popjisyo has emerged and it is also free. NHK news is available through cable TV if I record it at home. The TV commercial video can be rented from Japan Foundation for free. *Hiragana Megane* "hiragana glasses (hiragana converter)" is available on the Internet and it does not cost anything.

In this semester, I have only two students in this class, whose proficiency levels are different. One finished both 4th year Japanese courses (JA401 and JA402) and needed one higher Japanese class. I call this student Student A. Additionally, last summer, she came back from Japan after about six-month stay there. The other (Student B) has just finished 3rd Year Japanese II and has never visited Japan, although she has a part-time job using the Japanese language with Japanese tourists here on Guam. The difference in their proficiency is reflected on their difference in the goals in terms of the Japanese language proficiency tests. The goal of Student A after this class is to pass the first level (the highest level) of the Japanese proficiency tests. On the other hand, the goal of Student B is to pass the second level of the test. Technological instructional tools are assisting them well to study at their own paces. Especially, the computer technology utilized for the FL (Japanese language in this case) instruction has advanced well for teaching the students with different proficiency levels and at individual paces, using multiple technological tools in a variety of ways. Another objective of this course is to get the students well prepared for the lifelong Japanese language self-study process needed to continuously improve their Japanese literacy. For lifelong Japanese literacy learning, these technological tools on the Internet will be especially useful for leading them to their ultimate goal to obtain such literacy skills as high as a Japanese native speaker's.

For Skill-Getting: Internet Pop-up Dictionary: Popjisyo to Robust Mental Kanji Dictionary (Character and Vocabulary Learning, and Translation Method)

I have selected Popjisyo over WordChamp, because Popjisyo is freely applicable to more Web pages, especially for its dictionary from-Japanese-to-English, without any charge. By virtue of the availability of the dictionary on the Internet, the students do not have to consult with a traditional *kanji* dictionary. To consult with a traditional dictionary, the students would have to already know *kanji*'s radical, stroke number, or reading. What the students need to do, however, is just move the cursor over an unknown *kanji* word to get the meaning as well as the reading or the stroke number. In other words, the pop-up dictionary will encourage the students to read more and will lead the students to efficient and effective learning of the target language with a tool they can use the rest of their lives.

Internet: Hiragana Megane: To Learn Kanji Reading (Vocabulary and Character Learning)

This CALL technology can put each *kanji*'s reading in the parentheses beside the *kanji* instantly in a second! Student B needs this tool frequently, while Student A does not need it so often.

Internet: Gahoh (Character Learning)

This is another wonderful Web site where we can find *kanji*'s stroke order according to the *kanji*'s reading. However, it had been difficult for me to introduce this Web page to my students to encourage them to use this tool, because there had been no way to find a *kanji*'s stroke order without knowing its reading. Thanks to the Popjisyo (in the case of Student A) or *Hiragana Megane* (in the case of Student B), now I can introduce the Web tool to my students because now it is easy for them to find the *kanji* to get its stroke order movie at the *gahoh* after finding the reading with *Popjisyo* or *Hiragana megane.*

For Skill-Using (Immersion) Internet Newspapers (Reading and Listening Instructional Material)

As reading material, an online Japanese newspaper, Yomiuri Newspaper is mainly used because the students are expected to listen to Yomiuri STREAM. Podcasting of Nikkei newspaper will be tried in 2005. The rational is that after class, the students can easily access it with a computer because the podcasting is free of charge. Another rational is to introduce students to additional sources of learning materials that will keep them studying Japanese after their graduation.

TV: NHK News (Mainly Listening Comprehension Material)

Yomiuri Stream's sound and picture quality is lower than those of TV (NHK) news. If the quality is not good, it is difficult to learn and comprehend the news correctly.

This is why I use this old technology for listening comprehension activities. When I show it for the first time in the class, Student B exulted because she found that she was able to read *kanji* words on the screen and comprehend them.

For Skill-Getting and Skill-Using (Immersion)

Japan Foundation has 51 award-winning TV commercial films available for a Japanese teacher. The motivation to use the films is to let the students learn Japanese contemporary culture (skill-getting; goal-oriented), using the skills of Japanese language. The other purpose of this is to make the students relaxed and enjoy the commercial and learn Japan's pop-culture. However, questions like the following the students have to answer: (1) Whose hearts/minds does this commercial try to catch? Young children? Teenagers? Young adults? The middle aged? Or the silver aged? And (2) Why do you think so? Best of all, the students love the commercials.

Conclusion

Although current technological developments have not reached the high level of the *Matrix* movie, the developments have brought highly sophisticated educational tools to FL teachers, even for Japanese language courses. Proposing MEA, I have demonstrated how technological tools can be used to make FL instruction more effective and enjoyable. In terms of methodology, being eclectic, a FL teacher needs to examine whether currently available tools—regardless whether technological or not—can help students achieve a learning objective of a FL course memory efficiently. Then, teachers examine whether the technological tools serve the task better or not. If the technological tools serve the objective better, I recommend FL teachers to take advantage of the technological instructional tools. Some students spend a great deal of time and money traveling to Japan just to expand their FL skills. Now, with all these technological tools, even students that cannot afford to travel to Japan can immerse themselves in the FL environment to continue a lifelong educational experience or just to brush-up once in a while. This chapter predicts that it will soon become a simpler and simpler procedure for FL instructors to implement new technologies in their classrooms. Some of the new technologies introduced in this chapter may be outdated when this chapter is published, but the reader can be sure that there will be better tools available very soon. The reader should use them to the fullest advantage of the students.

References

Brandle, K. (2005). Are you ready for Moodle? *Language Learning and Technology, 9,* 16-23. Retrieved August 5, 2006, from http://llt.msu.edu

Chinnery, G. (2006). Emerging technology: Going to MALL. *Language Learning and Technology, 10*. Retrieved August 5, 2006, from http://llt.msu.edu

Chomsky, N. (1965). *Aspect of the theory of syntax*. Cambridge, MA: MIT press.

Chomsky, N. (1975). *Reflections of language*. New York: Pantheon Book.

Chomsky, N. (1981). *Lecture on government and binding*. Dordrecht: Foris Publications.

Cuban, L. (2001). *Oversold and underused: Computers in the classroom.* Cambridge, MA: Harvard University Press.

Dodds, T. (2001). *Universities, adult basic education, open and lifelong learning and new technology: Resources for change in developing countries?* Retrieved August 5, 2006, from http://literacy.org/products/ili/pdf/UTLPdodds.pdf

Felder, R. M., & Henriques, E. R. (1995). Learning and teaching styles in foreign and second language education. *Foreign Language Annals, 28*(1), 21-31.

Garrett, N. (1991). Technology in the service of language learning: Trends and issues. *Modern Language Journal, 15*, 74-101.

Godwin-Jones, B. (2004). Emerging technologies: Language in action: From Webquests to virtual realities. *Language Learning and Technology, 8*(3), 9-14.

Godwin-Jones, B. (2005). Emerging technologies: Messaging, skype and podcasting: Disruptive technologies for language learning. *Language Learning and Technology, 9*(3), 9-12.

Kang, P. T. (1993*). Parser strategies of adult English speakers learning Japanese as a second language.* Unpublished doctoral dissertation, University of Texas at Austin.

Kang, P. T. (2002). CyberMap exercise III: As a computer assisted teaching (CALT) material, Part 2: Implementation. In *Proceedings of CASTELJ 2002.*

Kang, P. T. (2003). *Surface X-bar theory, prosodic structure and first language acquisition*. Paper presented at the conference (UG Principles and Input: How do we get Plato's heaven into Skinner's box?) at the Linguistic Society of America's Linguistic Summer Institute, Michigan State University.

Krashen, S. D. (1985). *The input hypothesis.* London: Longman.

Lam, Y. (2000). Technophilia vs. technophobia: A preliminary look at why second language teachers do or do not use technology in their classrooms. *Canadian Modern Language Review, 56*, 389-420.

LeLoup, J. W., & Ponterio, R. (2003). *Second language acquisition and technology: A review of the research.* Retrieved August 5, 2006, from http://www.cal.org/resources/digest/0311leloup.html

LeLoup, J. W., & Ponterio, R. (2004). On the net: Internet television news in the classroom TF1: Improved features makes sites more useful. *Language Learning and Technology, 8*(2), 3-6.

LeLoup, J. W., & Ponterio, R. (2005). On the net: Vocabulary support for independent online reading. *Language Learning and Technology, 9*(2), 3-7.

Lightbown, M. P. (2000). Anniversary article classroom SLA research and second language teaching. *Applied Linguistics, 21*(4), 431-462.

Miller, G. (1956). The magical number seven, plus or minus two: Some limits on our capacity for processing information. *The Psychological Review, 63*, 81-97.

Morgan, G. (2003). Faculty use of course management systems. *ECAR* (EDUCAUSE Center for Applied Research), 1-6.

Omoto, Y., Fukai, M., & Schneider, K. (2002). *Survey on the use of computer and the Internet in Japanese classes in northern California.* Paper presented at the SEATJ 2002 Conference. Retrieved August 5, 2006, from http://www.sabotenweb.com/conference/SEATJ2002/

Prensky, M. (2001). Digital natives, digital immigrants. *On the Horizon, 9*(5). Retrieved August 5, 2006, from http://www.marcprensky.com/writing/default.asp

Prensky, M. (2004). *What can you learn from a cell phone?* Retrieved August 5, 2006, from http://www.marcprensky.com/writing/default.asp

Purushotma, R. (2005). Commentary: You're not studying, you're just… *Language Learning and Technology, 9*(1), 80-96.

Rivers, W. (1981). *Teaching foreign language skills* (2nd ed.). Chicago: University of Chicago Press.

Salaberry, R. (2000). Pedagogical design of computer mediated communication task: Learning objectives and technological capabilities. *Modern Language Journal, 84*, 28-37.

Salaberry, R. (2001). The use of technology for second language learning and teaching: A retrospective. *Modern Language Journal, 85*, 39-56.

Skehan, P. (1989). *Individual differences in second language learning.* London: Edward Arnold.

Stice, J. E. (1987). Using Kolb's learning cycle to improve student learning. *Engineering Education, 77*, 291-296.

Terry, R. (n.d.). *Technology and language instruction.* Retrieved August 5, 2006, from http://www.richmond.edu/~terry/tech.htm

Wang, L. (2005). The advantages of using technology in second language education. *T. H. E. (Technology Horizons in Education) Journal Online.* Retrieved August 5, 2006, from http://www.thejournal.com/

Warner, C. N. (2004). It's just a game, right? Type of play in foreign language CMC. *Language Learning and Technology, 8*(5), 69-87.

Warshauer, M., & Meskill, C. (2000). Technology and second language teaching. In J. Rosenthall (Ed.), *Handbook of undergraduate second language education.* Mahwah, NJ: Lawrence Erlbaum. Retrieved August 5, 2006, from http://www.albany.edu/etap/Faculty/CarlaMeskill/Publication/mark.pdf

Warschauer, M., & Healey, D. (1998). Computers and language learning: An overview. *Language Teaching, 31*, 57-71.

Wright, A., Betteridge, D., & Bucky, M. (1983). *Games for language learning.* Cambridge, MA: Cambridge University Press.

Appendix: URLs of WWW

- Rapid Tactical Language Training System http://www.isi.edu/isd/carte/proj_tactlang/

Podcasting

- German https://depts.washington.edu/llc/olr/german/GER_011/index.php
- French http://www.podcast.net/tag/french/newest
- English for native speakers of Japanese http://mainichi-podcasting.cocolog-nifty.com/weekly/

Online Newspaper and Newspaper Reader

- WebUC (freeware; http://www.asahi.com/information/service/webud.html)
- Asahi Newspaper (http://www.asahi.com)
- Yomiuri Newspaper www.yomiuri.co.jp

Online TV

- Shortwave Broadcasts LIVE On The Internet http://www.multilingualbooks.com/online-radio-japanese.html
- French TV Channel TF1, http://www.tf1.fr/ (see LeLoup & Ponterio, 2004)
- Japanese Internet radio/TV, http://www.dxworld.com/sw_live.html
- Yomiuri Stream http://www.yomiuri.co.jp/stream/
- Nikkei Broadband News http://www.nikkei.co.jp/bb/index.html

Online Radio

- Japanese NHK's news broadcasting called Radio Japan Online http://www.nhk.or.jp/rj/index_e.html

Online Pop-Up Dictionaries

- Ultralingua http://ultralingua.net/
- WordChamp http://www.wordchamp.com
- POP jisyo.com http://www.popjisyo.com/WebHint/Portal_e.aspx
- Game watch http://watch.impress.co.jp/game/

Textbook Genki Series

- Genki-Online http://www.genki-online.com
- Genki Exercise http://www.lyon.edu/webdata/users/mpeek/japanwebpages/GenkiExercises.htm
- Usagichan http://www.csus.edu/indiv/s/sheaa/projects/genki/index.html
- Usagichan's stroke order site http://www.csus.edu/indiv/s/sheaa/projects/genki/index.html
- Kanji Alive http://kanjialive.lib.uchicago.edu
- Japan Times' Genki Web site http://genki.japantimes.co.jp/self/self.html

Courseware

- CyberMap III http://www.sabotenweb.com/classes/mapex3/

Kanji Learning

- Hiragana Megane http://hiragana.jp/
- Gahoh http://gahoh.marinebat.com/modules.php

Section III

Learning Theories and Online Applications for Lifelong Learning

Chapter V

Constructivism Online: Vygotskian Applications for 21st Century Learning in Higher Education

Candace Kaye, New Mexico State University, USA

Erica Volkers, Central New Mexico Community College, USA

Abstract

In higher education, the use of constructivist approaches in online learning reflects agreement with educators who stress that good teaching is both a collaborative and a highly individual process. Online constructivist application also suggests congruence with adult learning theory and educational programming designed for experiential and inquiry-based learning. The objective of this chapter is to investigate perceptions of teaching and learning in online instruction guided by the Vygotskian perspective of constructivist theory. The chapter first focuses on current research studies of online constructivist-based course development and application and then proceeds to the authors' practical inquiry project, which examined (1) instructor perspectives on creating and facilitating online learning communities and (2) students' perceptions of their online constructivist experiences. The authors conclude with a discussion of their findings, contributions to the field and suggestions and challenges for the principled use of a constructivist approach to online teaching.

Introduction

In higher education, instructors/researchers who explore the uses of constructivist approaches in online learning for the acquisition of knowledge are in agreement with educational philosophers such as Noddings (1992) and Palmer (1998) who stress that good teaching is a complex and highly personal process. For example, according to Palmer (1998), "to educate is to guide students on an inner journey toward more truthful ways of seeing and being in the world" (p. 6). The same instructors/researchers also find themselves in accord with educational reformers (e.g., Merriam & Caffarela, 1991; Richardson, 1999) who suggest that constructivist-based programs are more congruent with adult learning theory and that educational renewal is possible only if educational programs are designed to be experiential, inquiry based (Norlander-Case, Reagan, & Case, 1999) and achieved through dialogue (Vella, 2002).

Practitioners of constructivist approaches in online program design and implementation understand that while higher education faculty can design a successful curriculum, students must be directly involved in guiding and understanding their own journeys toward learning. By creating such experiences, higher education faculty are able to develop principled forms of instruction guided by a process first suggested by Vygotsky in his design of learning within a zone of proximal development (ZPD) (Collins, Brown, & Newman, 1989).

The following Vygotskian concepts are particularly germane to building online coursework: (1) collaborative experiences among students or between students and teachers are necessary for students to advance through their individual ZPD (Vygotsky, 1978); (2) social interaction as a cognitive amplifier (Bruner, 1966) transforms socially shared activities into internalized cognitive processes; and (3) the most efficient instruction is when students engage in activities within a supportive learning environment and receive appropriate guidance (Vygotsky, 1978). Additionally, these concepts resonate with the following interdependent themes of Vygotskian theory as applied to technology-based learning: "reliance on a developmental method, the association between higher mental processes and their origin in social processes and the idea that mental processes can be understood if we understand the tools and signs that mediate them" (Dixon-Krauss, 1997, p. 176).

The objective of this chapter is to investigate perceptions of technology-based learning opportunities (i.e., online instruction in higher education) in terms of instructional design and application guided by principles of Vygotskian constructivist theory that consistently focus on building student-centered and collaborative learning communities. The chapter consists of two sections. The authors first review research studies of perceptions of constructivist online design and application, concluding with a synthesis of issues, best practices, and challenges as reflected by the literature review. For the second section, the authors discuss their own twofold inquiry project which investigated (1) their own perspectives on creating online learning communities and (2) their student perceptions of online constructivist learning. The chapter concludes with a discussion of the findings of their inquiry, its contribution to the field, and a commentary on the challenges for the principled use of a constructivist approach online in the 21st century. Suggestions for future research opportunities within the domain of online teaching and learning are offered.

Background

The following background discussion has a twofold purpose of (1) focusing the contents of the chapter discussion and (2) introducing the authors' investigative inquiry. Additionally, an analysis of current research is discussed, including a descriptive synthesis of emerging themes of online constructivist models of instruction focusing on the learner's active participation in constructing meaning. This focus is consistent with the Vygotskian perspective: "passivity of the student is the greatest sin from a scientific point of view, since it relies on the false principle that the teacher is everything and the pupil nothing" (Bozhovich & Slavina, 1972, p. 165).

As online learning has become increasingly integrated into the delivery of learning experiences in higher education, multiple perspectives on the use of constructivist theory and Vygotskian approaches have begun to emerge for both design and implementation and reflect a variety of definitions and descriptions.

Definitions of Online Constructivism in the Literature

Crumpacker (2001) describes constructivist online approaches as being active, as each student is responsible for discovering, constructing, practicing, and validating acquired knowledge via active exploration and interactive social collaboration. For educational success, he further suggests that such collaborative pedagogy using constructivist principles shifts the focus from assistive teacher-student interaction found in face-to-face learning experiences to the pivotal role of building supportive peer relationships in technology-based teaching.

Experiential learning as a defined constructivist framework is used as an approach in online course design by Nunes, McPherson and Rico (2001), whose design elements are described as a "blend of activities that promoted reflective practice within an active learner environment conducive to collaborative learning" (p. 4). Additionally, Williams (2000) asserts that online instruction that defines the use of a constructivist theoretical perspective must specifically use methods and strategies that assist learners in actively exploring complex topics. Thus, Williams asserts that the constructivist content must be well-defined so that knowledge connects to the context under study and to the experiences that the learners bring to that context. Ermer and Newby (1993) and Wilson (1993) offer further definition to the use and elements of constructivist theory in online design:

1. Emphasis on identifying the context in which skills will be learned and applied as applications of learning in meaningful contexts.
2. Emphasis on learner control and capability of the learner to manipulate information. Premise is for the learner to actively use what is being learned.
3. Need for information to be presented in a variety of ways. For reinforcement of important content, design process allows for revisiting content at different times in rearranged contexts for different purposes and from different perspectives.
4. Support for the use of problem-solving skills that allow the learner to expand their thinking beyond the information given.
5. Assessment focuses on transfer of knowledge and skills.

Ortiz (2004) describes design elements for constructivism online as "rooting educational activities in a realistic situation that embodies the knowledge and skills that students need to learn" (p. 672). She further describes this pursuit of knowledge as becoming dynamic, based on encouragement of collaboration and communication among learners as an integral part of the process. Additionally, she suggests that in a well-formulated design for online coursework, learners are encouraged to bring prior experiences and current understanding, while negotiating and refining their understanding through continuous reflection within both content and process. Ortiz concludes that the resulting learning becomes an informed student-activated response to the construction of meaning.

Descriptions of Vygotskian Approaches to Online Teaching and Learning

A basic tenet of constructivist theory is that learning is a process of conceptual change whereby individuals construct new understandings of reality (Whittle, Morgan, & Maltby, 2000). However, the Vygotskian perspective offers the concept that collaboration among learners fosters the social construction knowledge and that evidence of knowledge-building activity is embodied in both the tone and content of group discussions (Graddy, 2003). Stepich and Ertmer (2003) discuss use of computer-mediated communication tools to develop a sense of community and such knowledge building thorough active interaction, collaborative learning opportunities, sharing of resources, and peer expressions of support.

Wang and colleagues (2001) discuss the asynchronous nature of online communication as giving the opportunity for reflection and revision, a component of Vygotskian application. This opportunity is in direct contrast to student required immediate reaction to learning activities, often found in behaviorist pedagogical methodology.

Responsibilities of the Instructor and Student

Collis (1998) defines specific responsibilities of students in Vygotskian-based collaborative communities as self-responsibility for thinking and learning; awareness of social responsibility; thinking and acting using scientific processes; and relating group process and product with professional practice. In earlier research, Collis (1997) identified key indicators for the role of the instructor in providing effective scaffolding: (1) provision of learning resources to help students solve their own problems and share them with others; (2) offering multiple channels of communication to enable conversations, exchange of ideas; and discussion; and (3) provision of support for collaborative tasks and development of higher order cognition.

Concluding Comments

Curriculum design generated in an environment based on dialogue and interactions among learners is a basis for online constructivist theoretical application. For example, online constructivist instructors seek students' points of views and facilitate student learning rather than presenting themselves as the sole authoritative source of knowledge. Additionally, the research literature encourages multiple perspectives on definitions of constructivism, in both cognitive and social aspects of course content and process with an emphasis on a coherent framework, allowing learners to solve problems collaboratively and to develop critical thinking skills.

Therefore, for the purpose of this chapter, the theoretical viewpoint of constructivism is defined as the learner's active participation in constructing meaning, rather than passively acquiring knowledge. Within the body of research literature reviewed (e.g., Bagi & Crooks, 2001; Graddy, 2003; Hung, 2001; Maor, 2003; Tan & Hung; 2002), current research-based online constructivist design using a Vygotskian approach is termed *online social constructivism*. This term will be used for the purposes of this chapter. The term *online social constructivism* will also be used to define this perspective. Social constructivism in online learning reflects concepts of:

1. **Online learning:** Designed to facilitate instruction that is developmentally slightly ahead of the learner's development (scaffolding)
2. **Online social processes:** Necessary for knowledge exploration are facilitated (social mediation)

3. **Use of technology:** Creates tools for learning and development (cultural construction).

Analysis of Current Research Concerning Online Applications of Constructivism from a Vygotskian Perspective

Two perspectives emerged in a critical analysis of research concerning perceptions of constructivism in an online environment: (1) the context of constructivist design in online teaching and learning, and (2) the application of Vygotskian constructivist theory in online learning communities within higher education.

Context of Constructivism in Online Learning

Palloff and Pratt (1999) provide evidence for their argument for a constructivist approach to the online classroom based on an analysis of interviews with teachers and students for support of their positions. However, other studies (Klemm, 2000; Sage, 2000) suggest that students who are experiencing a constructivist approach for the first time may be different, "where they were expected to be active learners and problem solvers, they clearly floundered at first ... and found wading through multiple resources online group work, defining and conceptualizing the problem, and using past experience to be overwhelming at times" (Sage, 2000, p. 6). Several studies, including those of Tan and Hung (2002) and O'Reilly and Newton (2001), also emphasize the constructivist change of the faculty role to a facilitator, rather than a lecturer and the subsequent change to content and process. These studies support the idea that simply presenting information to learners in an online environment is not an optimum approach, rather the preferred approach is one that includes situated cognition, critical discussion, establishment of social communities, and self-directed learning.

Application of Vygotskian Theory in Online Learning

The research indicates that support for student learning through Vygotskian social constructivist theory using ZPD has been extended immensely through technological applications (McLoughlin, 1999). A variety of evolving research focusing on the specific nature of supports, especially online scaffold functions in specific contexts of online learning, has been reported. Studies reviewed include the following findings:

1. The use of quickly evolving and sophisticated online technologies requires the construction of more complex practice (Davidson, Schofield, & Stocks, 2001).
2. When presented with quality real-life experiences, students can make bridges between concepts and applicability (Lansdell, 2001).
3. Distance educators are incorporating active, collaborative, and constructivist learning strategies rather than taking a traditional directive tutorial model found in 20th century online offerings (Schrum, 1999).
4. A collaborative asynchronous (time-independent) online learning milieu where structure and dialogue are optimized can produce results comparable to those in a face-to-face traditional milieu (Wiesenberg, 2001).
5. The instructor's primary responsibilities are becoming constructing and maintaining focus on the core issues of the course, articulating a supportive knowledge maps, and ensuring the integrity of knowledge resources (Foshay, 2002).

Role of Content

Several studies (Collis, 1997, 1998; McLoughlin, 1999) have examined the concept of scaffolding as described by McLoughlin as a form of temporary support offered to content learning to assist in the process of becoming a skilled practitioner. Traditionally, one of the most common forms of scaffolding learning has been apprenticeship, where a novice learns through active participation in a content task, initially only peripherally, and then assuming more control and ownership.

The research reviewed indicates that the concept of scaffolding is a focus of constructivist technology-based content. However, existing studies indicate a need for a redefinition of the use of scaffolding as it is used in online communities, since it is not readily translated into contexts where the teacher is not present. While research in this area is still sparse, studies led by the work of McLoughlin (1999) and Collis (1998) indicate the following range of contexts where technology may be used to mediate the teaching interaction for content:

1. Reducing the scope for failure in the task that the learner is attempting
2. Enabling learners to accomplish a task that they would not be able to achieve on their own
3. Bringing learners close to a state of independent competence

Role of Instructor

Squires (1999) discusses the constructivist uses of educational software in distance learning and the importance of the instructor's role in choices of usage. Jonassen's (1994) examination of how technology in the online classroom can be used within a constructivist framework, again emphasizing the role of the instructor. Further, Odin (2002) demonstrates a clear and direct relationship between well-designed teaching activities and the quality of student online collaborative learning. Specifically, Odin's study indicates that multimodal teaching activities define the social presence of the teacher who serves as a guide to promote self-motivation and self-direction. The study concludes that the instructor's expert guidance manifested through multimodal teaching activities is indispensable in creating a shared context of learning where students are engaged in both constructing knowledge and applying it to other contexts. The diverse teaching-learning activities promote a complex mode of multilevel interaction among the learners, the instructor, and the content of the course, which creates a social context for constructing, exchanging, and transforming knowledge.

Role of Student

In defining the role of the student from a Vygotskian perspective, the research repeatedly reflects the need for the student learner to assume active responsibility for the acquisition of knowledge, to accept the complexity of the process of learning in a social milieu, and to understand the online learning environment as one in which self-directed, authentic academic problem-based activities and reflective practices are opportunities for learning.

The research also notes that for students, opportunities for collaborative learning and scaffolding are needed. These opportunities are suggested as needing to be characterized by:

1. Self-responsibility for thinking and learning
2. Awareness of social responsibility
3. Thinking and acting on scientific processes
4. Relating group process and product with professional practice

Vat (2000) also lists the following "enabling" (p. 23) roles that are the responsibility of the student: "goal setting, management of own learning activities, and committed contribution to peer learning." In a Vygotskian approach to online learning, Vat concludes that not all learners can respond to the "high cognitive demands" (p. 29) that include the testing of previous concepts with new knowledge, resulting in "a sense of dissatisfaction (that emerges) from online learning experiences that threaten existing conceptual structures" (p. 29).

Vat (2000) proposes that the subsequent adjustments for the learner in the structuring concepts and the needed exertion for social negotiation and testing new structures can be challenging for some learners. The literature also describes difficulties for some students in assuming responsibilities in such an online setting. For example, Bull and Greer (2000) focused on the following in a problem-based online environment: (1) students may not understand their social role in a problem-based group setting; (2) students may lack the social skills to make group interactions work; (3) students have different social interaction preferences; and (4) students have different cognitive styles.

Synthesis of Research Literature

The literature so far illustrates how constructivist theory has expanded to include many new forms of support, including Vygotskian applications such as (1) increased responsibility for students for their learning; (2) faculty responsibility for providing multiple resources and providing opportunities for focused discussion; and (3) less directive aspects of the constructivist approach in online design that previously had connected constructivist coursework with behaviorist principles found in more directive instruction.

Future Considerations for Research

A consideration for continued research of online social constructivism is suggested by the research studies reviewed. While the use of a Vygotskian perspective provides the theoretical constructivist online anchoring needed for making explicit connections between social interaction and cognitive development online, relevant and specific forms of support and design components must continue to be emphasized.

As distance learning becomes both a realistic and rigorous alternative to traditional settings, design considerations have become more sophisticated. For example, as the research continues to discuss asynchronous communication as supporting the constructivist approach of reflective thinking and Vygotskian perspectives of teaching and learning, such practices must be informed by research that considers its complex implications in online environments. Ortiz (2004) suggests that 21st-century communication theory includes technologically based learning along with Wertsch's (2002) assertion that current educational thinking considers not only action but thought is "reshaped by tools that support interaction" (p. 67). This suggestion also reflects that 21st century instruction online has gone beyond McLuhan's (1964) advocacy of the importance of media in the delivery of messages to suggest that now "media shape(s) their participants" and that "infrastructures shape civilization." The literature reviewed reflects an international understanding that communication technology "has a deep impact on the structuring of the knowledge production process" and suggests the profound impact of constructivist principles in a global community of learning with the benefit of multiple perspectives.

This background discussion has also served as an introduction to the authors' investigation of perceptions of Vygotskian approaches from both faculty and student perspectives, an area of scant specific study in the body of research reviewed. The findings from the literature were used to inform both the researcher/instructor design of online coursework and their investigative inquiry concerning perspectives of the roles of both instructor and student.

Investigative Inquiry: How are Constructivist Approaches Perceived by Students in an Online Experience?

The concept of the research inquiry to be reported here began with the authors' personal query: "Can online courses in teacher education be taught in a constructivist framework that values student-centered learning, collaboration, and discussion?" This query emerged from ongoing dialogue and subsequent investigation of the research literature concerning the challenge of translating face-to-face courses grounded in a constructivist pedagogical approach using Vygotskian applications into online format.

The three courses chosen for the focus of this study were three educational courses concerning curriculum and assessment, classroom management, and learning theory within a teacher education program for postbaccalaureate students seeking teaching licensure. The authors, having taught these courses in a face-to-face format, were both the designers and the instructors of the same courses in the online format.

Elements of Online Design

Based on the research literature, key elements for the online constructivist coursework design using a Vygotskian approach included the use of (1) a discussion board for peer support as a process for ZPD, (2) the provision of learning resources reflecting the constructivist approach of providing multiple resources for the building of knowledge, and (3) consistent opportunities for synthesizing assignments for the purpose of reflection and assessment.

The Discussion Board

The discussion board was utilized as a primary tool to provide opportunities for student collaboration, social interaction, time for reflective thinking, and active participation in constructing meaning. For each unit, the authors' online coursework included the following design elements: an initial discussion question based upon students' prior knowledge and experiences, which prompted student exploration of the unit theme, often encouraging the development of questions for further examination within the unit. Each unit also included a final discussion question, which not only prompted a sharing and reflection of individual student learning, again encouraging student-initiated development of questions for further examination, but also continued the process of collaborative construction of meaning as it related to the unit theme.

Learning Resources

A set of resources was created for each unit that might include chapter readings, articles, and a variety of Web resources (i.e., interactive materials and primary resources). Often students were also encouraged to explore additional sources of knowledge, such as literature, the Internet, and classroom teachers they identified.

Reflective Assessment Opportunities

Assessments for each unit were created that required students to apply, reflect on, and/or synthesize the knowledge they had gained from their peers (shared through the initial discussion question) and the unit resources. Assessments were designed so that students could make the knowledge meaningful in the context of their professional lives and demonstrate their understanding of the content in multiple ways.

Role of the Instructor and Student in Constructivist Online Coursework

As both designers and instructors of online courses, the major objective of the authors was to reflect a constructivist approach to an asynchronous, virtual teaching-learning environment. Through ongoing dialogue, along with a review of the current literature, the roles of both the instructors and the students in these online courses were defined.

One of the initial roles agreed upon as instructors designing and implementing coursework was the goal of building connections with and between students. In the teacher preparation program involved in the inquiry, teacher education candidates are initially asked about what they perceive to be challenges they will face in an online learning environment. Many express concern that they will not experience the same quality interaction with their instructor and classmates that they have had in a face-to-face course. Understanding that positive instructor and peer relationships are integral to the learning process, the researchers began their courses with all participants, including the instructor, posting introductions. These postings were available through the entire course and were accessed occasionally to gain perspectives on experiences and/or opinions shared in discussions and assignments. While the ongoing academic dialogue continued to build connections between students, the researchers recognized that often in face-to-face classrooms, students also have opportunities, before and after class, to connect. To provide a similar opportunity in the online classroom, e-mail for private communications was encouraged and a separate discussion thread was offered for class chat.

The development of student understanding of the online tools and their use in the coursework was another defined role of the instructor. When seeking to reflect a constructivist approach in online course content, one of the roles of instructors is to facilitate student understanding of the learning process through multiple means. One example of this type of support is facilitation of the discussion boards. The role of students was defined in the discussion boards to include not only their posting of responses to the discussion prompts, but to also the role of competent peers; (i.e., responding to other student postings with further examples, clarifying statements, or additional questions).

At the beginning of the courses, the role of the instructor included the need to model this Vygotskian concept of *competent peer* support with active participation in the discussion board that also included follow-up e-mails that provided additional clarification and examples of expectations for the student role of *competent peer*. However, as courses progressed and students gained independent competence, this instructor role became primarily limited to one expert consultant, providing clarification, examples, or additional resources when requested by the students. One level of instructor support that was maintained consistently throughout the courses was found within the assessment process. While students receive frequent peer feedback indirectly on assessment outcomes through the final discussion questions and responses, each student receives specific feedback from instructors, including comments and questions for further reflection for every assessment submitted to the instructors. Often this results in additional dialogue between the student and the instructor concerning the assignment submission.

Through course design and subsequent definition of the authors' role as instructors and its relation to the role of the student, the authors' conclusive perception was that their face-to-face courses, grounded in a constructivist framework, had been successfully translated into an online format.

In addition, what the authors' sought, in an investigative inquiry, the perceptions of students in newly developed online courses, specifically regarding learning experiences related to a constructivist framework using a Vygotskian approach as defined by the literature.

Methodology

Development of Research Questions

As the instructors/researchers probed their own experiences and reviewed the research literature, they found a paucity of research on the constructivist approach to online teaching from the student perspective. Thus, the inquiry question became: "How are constructivist approaches perceived by students in an online experience?"

Procedure

Prompts

Based on the foundational research question, key principles of constructivism and Vygotskian theory emerged as subsequent questions for students. Three prompts were developed to explore students' perception of how online learning was (1) continuous, (2) shaped by a competent peer, and (3) enhanced by technological tools. The prompts included an example of how the researchers, as the instructors, perceived their own constructivist learning instruction in response to the prompts. The prompts were administered at the end of each course, over a period of three semesters, to a total of 106 students who served as the research participants.

Initial Responses

Student perceptions of how learning was continuous in their online course centered on the scaffolding of course content, assessments, and discussion prompts. Students recognized that within the units and throughout the course, they were required to examine prior knowledge and experiences, develop new knowledge, apply the knowledge, and reflect and reevaluate their knowledge application as they experienced ongoing interaction with the content and their peers.

Of the 106 students surveyed, 100 (or approximately 95%) cited the *competent peer* as essential to their online learning experience. The competent peer was identified as providing perspectives on the content alternative to their own perspective, collaborative support in constructing meaning from unit resources and subsequent applications, and additional resources for future exploration. One student shared that because the course design created a dependence on learning from peers and discussion prompts required thorough exploration of unit resources, she became much more engaged in being a competent peer who could contribute to the intellectual conversation.

Only a few of the students surveyed (n = 5) were critical of others in their role as competent peers indicating that some discussion responses were "superfluous and not well thought out." Reflective of constructivist approaches to teaching, several students also identified the instructor as a competent peer who shaped their learning.

Over half of the students expressed that the opportunity to learn from their peers was significantly heightened in the online course compared to face-to-face learning experiences. While students generally cited the design of the course as essential to this experience, 21 students (or approximately 20%) also explicitly shared that online discussion provided greater opportunity for them to act as competent peers because of a perceived sense of safety in expressing opinions in this format and the allowance of time for reflective thinking. One such student stated:

I think the online experience enhances the participation of peers. I was able to read what each student thought about a unit and respond without fear of being judged. I could take the time to analyze how I felt about what each student wrote and respond in agreement or offer a differing opinion. This made me more comfortable in exploring new ideas.

Additionally, the online discussion board tool was repeatedly cited as one that enhanced student learning, and students' perception of being independent learners was mentioned as being enhanced by the freedom of the online format of when and how to engage in the learning process.

Data Analysis

The authors used qualitative data analysis to codify student responses and investigate themes that emerged from these responses.

Emerging Themes

Emerging themes from the data analysis included the students' perceptions of (1) the instructor as a facilitator, (2) students as independent learners, and (3) students as competent peers. To further the inquiry into these themes, the researchers randomly selected 14 online students to participate in a focus group setting in order to solicit thicker descriptions (Denzin, 1989) for each of the themed questions.

Each instructor/researcher had four students who agreed to participate in an online focus group for a total of eight students. Students were requested to post responses within a discussion board format to the following questions over a period of one week:

1. How did your online instructor act as a guide for learning?
2. How were you an author of your own learning?
3. How would you define *competent peer* in your online virtual community?

After their initial responses to these questions, student dialogue continued to peer postings and also in response to the continued facilitation of both researchers for the purpose of exploring the questions in more depth. The resulting data were then analyzed to frame the inquiry's principle conclusions.

Focus Group Response Analysis

Based upon students' perceptions of how the instructors acted as a guide for learning, how students were authors of their own learning, and how students defined competent peer in the online learning experience, focus group responses affirmed the instructors' perception that constructivist approaches were successfully translated into the online course design.

Role of Instructor

While student definitions of the instructor role were congruent with constructivist approaches to teaching, the researchers were surprised at the critique offered by students regarding this role and their perceptions of student roles. Specifically, students in the focus groups primarily identified the instructor as a guide for learning by citing her role in the discussion board. Although briefly mentioned, students did not include much commentary on instructors setting up assignments, defining scope and sequence of coursework, researching the appropriateness of assignments or readings or project work, and representing expertise in the field. Students did consider that the learning process was facilitated when the instructor demonstrated a caring, responsive, and supportive presence by utilizing the various modes of communication effectively, appropriately, and with sensitivity.

Acknowledgment of the instructor as the creator of initial discussion prompts was mentioned, but predominantly the instructor was identified as someone who facilitated and "monitored" discussion, "refocused" and "deepened" the dialogue, and was available as a "subject matter expert." What became evident in this discussion thread was that students did not perceive their own role as being one that could facilitate, refocus, and deepen discussion. While half of the students in the focus groups expressed appreciation for what they termed a "student-centered approach," the other half were critical of this approach, perceiving it to be a lack of involvement of the instructor, and expressing a desire of greater instructor direction and intervention in the discussions.

Role of Student

Interestingly, response to this question contradicted these same student perspectives on how both course design and the instructor role supported their own desire to be "authors of their own learning." For example, one student stated as follows: "in these courses they were able to construct their own learning through collaboration rather than the teacher dictating the knowledge (or their own opinions)." Six of the eight students in the focus groups expressed appreciation for the opportunity to be an author of their own learning. For this to happen, students recognized the need for the instructor to "step back and let go of some authority." Additionally, students felt that authority of their own learning was gained through "participatory options [that were] more expansive in the online course," increased reflective thinking supported by asynchronous discussion, required articulation of their thinking through writing responses to discussion prompts and assessments and their independence in being flexible in things like what time they would participate, what discussion threads they would respond to, and what resources they might explore.

In short, students viewed their learning as directly dependent on the level of their own engagement with the content and their peers in the discussion and were critical of those students that did not engage at the same high level.

Competent Peer

Student definitions of a *competent peer* included the following: "one that engages fully in the content," "develops connections between theory and applications," "provides constructive feedback and support," "adjusts to the learning needs of their peers," and "contributes to meaningful discussion." Contributing to meaningful discussion was further defined as the ability to challenge the opinions of others without being confrontational, responding to discussion postings frequently and critically, and staying focused and on topic. Again, students failed to identify the role of competent peer as one that acted as a discussion facilitator, asking clarifying questions, drawing out differing perspectives of their peers, provoking higher levels of engagement, and so on, even though these expectations had been expressed by the instructors.

Preliminary Findings

While students' readily perceived constructivist approaches in the course design and instructor and student roles, comments expressing a desire for more instructor voice and intervention in discussion contradicted their affirmation of learning experiences that provided both significant autonomy in the learning process and social construction of meaning. Students also consistently perceived their own responsibility in engaging in the content and discussion, but failed to view their authority/responsibility in influencing the level and/or type of engagement they desired from the instructor and each other.

Conclusion

The vast frontier of online learning in higher education continues to be explored by both seasoned and novice pioneers. Designing and learning in an online environment in higher education can be both challenging and rewarding. For example, both new and online seasoned instructors must continue to pay close attention to setting explicit course guidelines and developing structured parameters for each course in order to design course content for optimum learning and for a high quality of organized interaction with and among students.

Using a social constructivist approach in course design allows the learner to assume an active and reflective role in the learning process. This student-centered belief system suggests that students will participate in problem-based activities, inquiry activity dialogues that encourage making sense of the course material, exposure to multiple information sources, and participation in activities that demonstrate their understanding. For successful progress through such course content and development of knowledge, students participating in online learning must be committed to taking greater responsibility and self-direction than in their face-to-face classes.

Discussion of Review Findings

The review of research consistently reveals that the use of constructivist pedagogical online application in higher education reflects a deeper approach to learning than found in approaches not using such a focus. For example, Windschitl (1999) states that constructivism is more than a variety of teaching techniques and is a coherent pattern of expectations for building relationships among students, teachers, and ideas. He posits that any interpretation of constructivism, including online design and application, is based on the belief that learners actively create, interpret, and reorganize knowledge in individual ways. In such a setting, Berge (2002) believes the ideal situation for lifelong application of constructivist experiences is for independent learners to apply what they have learned and make it meaningful in the context of their own lives as they seek personal satisfaction and professional advancement.

From both the review of literature concerning online constructivist theoretical applications using Vygotskian principles and the authors' own investigative inquiry, it can be concluded that any use of online social constructivism in higher education is open to multiple interpretations. At the very beginning of the 21st century, Vat (2000) stated for online learning:

We believe that constructivist ideas ... make up what we might call pragmatic constructivism. Namely, constructivism could be viewed as a toolbox for problems of learning ... . In keeping with this flexibility, active, social and creative learning can play out in different ways, depending on the circumstances. Although the term constructivism suggests a single philosophy and a unique potent method, there is no such thing as one-size-fits-all. Rather, our suggestion is to look at constructivism like a Swiss knife with various blades for various needs. That is also the learner-centered philosophy behind ... support for online education. (p. 29)

Particularly in the authors' inquiry, it can be noted that interpretations even differ between instructor and student. However, it can be concluded that any interpretation and application of such a pedagogical approach in the online higher education environment must include in a constructivist toolbox with a Vygotskian perspective the following concepts: (1) student-activated learning that is attuned to both social processes and cognitive development; (2) student responsibility for exploring faculty offerings of multiple opportunities for acquiring information; (3) support from both peers and faculty for the enhancement of learning within their ZPD; (4) a multiplicity of faculty proffered open-ended query opportunities to motivate consistently high degrees of reflection, and clear and well-articulated definitions of the roles of both instructor and learner throughout the process; and (5) ongoing student reflection on the learning process that examines both the role of the instructor and the learner.

Contribution to the Field

In both the literature review and an investigative inquiry, the chapter content provides theoretical and practical understanding of the essential elements of the social constructivist approach to online learning in the higher education milieu in the 21st century, particularly in defining the roles of both the instructor and student. To reflect tenets of adult learning theory and lifelong learning, the chapter discussion of this active, collaborative paradigm provides specific elements of the multiple interpretations and examples of the vibrancy of this field of study.

The research findings support the view that social constructivism provides a powerful strategy to support students' active engagement with content and facilitates the development of high levels of conceptual understanding for students. However, further research is required to explore this approach in more focus groups and classes and within a variety of academic disciplines.

Suggestions and Challenges for the Principled Use of an Online Social Constructivist Approach

As new technology continues to emerge, further research needs to continue the examination of the multiple perspectives of the (1) application of constructivism in online higher education environments and (2) use of social constructivism in online learning. Factors of desired subject matter competencies, theoretical beliefs of the instructor, and prior experiences of the students need to be considered in these future studies.

In this 21st century frontier, deep and continued understanding by the online instructor for the principled use of a social constructivist approach rather than solely applying the power of technology must be the most important consideration for higher education constructivist distance education to be successful.

Comparisons and evaluations of such programs need to be considered as an important challenge. As each institution of higher education in the 21st century continues to make decisions concerning implementation and management of online instruction, they will continue to have an exhaustive range of possibilities. However, it will be important for them to include the research- based understanding that learning can be enhanced through the student experience of a shared online social constructivist environment for the purpose of critical discussion, knowledge building, and the establishment of supportive social communities.

References

Bagi, J., & Crooks, S. M. (2001). Synchronous WWW-based course-support systems: Tools for facilitating online constructivist learning. *United States Distance Learning Association Journal, 15*(4). Retrieved August 6, 2006, from http://www.usdla.org/html/journal/APR01_Issue/articles.html

Berge, Z. L. (2002). Active, interactive, and reflective learning. *The Quarterly Review of Distance Education*, *3*(2), 181-190.

Bozhovich, L., & Slavina, L. (1972). Fifty years of soviet psychology of upbringing. In J. Brozek & D. Slobin (Eds.), *Psychology in the USSR: An historical perspective* (pp. 161-180). White Plains, NY: International Arts and Sciences Press.

Bruner, J. (1966). *Toward a theory of instruction*. Cambridge, MA: Belknap Press of Harvard University Press.

Bull, S., & Greer, J. (2000). Peer help for problem-based learning. In S. Young, J. Greer, H. Maurer, & Y. S. Chee (Eds.), *Proceedings of the International Conference on Computers in Education* (pp. 1007-1015). National Tsing Hua University of Taiwan.

Collins, A., Brown, J. S., & Newman, S. E. (1989). Cognitive apprenticeship: Teaching the crafts of reading, writing and mathematics. In L. B. Resnick (Ed.), *Knowing, learning and instruction: essays in honor of Robert Glaser* (pp. 453-494). Hillsdale, NJ: Lawrence Erlbaum.

Collis, B. (1997). Supporting project-based collaborative learning via a World Wide Web environment. In B. H. Khan (Ed.), *Web-based instruction* (pp. 213-219). Englewood Cliffs, NJ: Educational Technology Publications.

Collis, B. (1998). New didactics for university instruction: Why and how? *Computers & Education, 31*, 373-393.

Crumpacker, N. (2001). Faculty pedagogical approach, skill, and motivation in today's distance education milieu. *Online Journal of Distance Learning Administration*. Retrieved August 6, 2006, from http://www.westga.edu/~distance/ojdla/winter44/crumpacker44.html

Davidson, A. L., Schofield, J., & Stocks, J. (2001). Professional cultures and collaborative efforts: A case of technologists and educators working for change. *The Information Society, 17*(1), 21-32.

Denzin, N. K. (1989). *Interpretive interactionism*. Thousand Oaks, CA: Sage.

Dixon-Krauss, L. (1997). *Vygotsky in the classroom: Mediated literacy instruction and assessment*. White Plains, NY: Longman.

Ermer, P. A., & Newby, T. J. (1993). Behaviorism, cognitivism, constructivism: Comparing from an instructional design perspective. *Performance Improvement Quarterly, 6*(4), 50-72.

Foshay, R. (2002, March). *An overview of the research base of PLATO* (Tech. paper #12). Bloomington, MN: PLATO Learning Inc. (ERIC Database #ED464601)

Graddy, D. B. (2003). Mapping online discussion with lexical scores. *Journal of Interactive Research, 14*(2), 209-229.

Hung, D. (2001). Design principles for Web-based learning: Implications for Vygotskian thought. *Educational Technology, 41*(3), 33-41.

Jonassen, D. H. (1994). Thinking technology: Toward a constructivist design model. *Educational Technology, 34*(3), 34-37.

Klemm, W. R. (2000, November). What's wrong with online discussions and how to fix it. In *Proceedings of the WebNet 2000 World Conference on the World Wide Web and Internet*, San Antonio, TX (pp. 335-340). (ERIC Database #ED448755)

Lansdell, L. (2001). Distance learning environment. *LTL Newsletter.* Retrieved August 6, 2006, from http://www.ltlinc.cm/LTL/newsletters/jan01/oln_article.htm

Maor, D. (2003). The teacher's role in developing interaction and reflection in an online learning community. *Education Media International, 40*(1/2), 127-137.

McLoughlin, C. (1999). Culturally responsive technologies use: developing an on-line community of learners. *British Journal of Educational Technology, 30*, 231-243.

McLuhan, M. (1964). *Understanding media.* New York: McGraw-Hill.

Merriam, S. B., & Caffarela, R. S. (1991). *Learning in adulthood: A comprehensive guide.* San Francisco: Jossey-Bass.

Noddings, N. (1992). *The challenge to care in schools: An alternative approach to education.* New York: Teachers College Press.

Norlander-Case, K., Reagan, T. G., & Case, C. W. (1999). *The professional teacher: The preparation and nurturance of the reflective practitioner.* San Francisco: Jossey-Bass.

Nunes, J. M., McPherson, M., & Rico, M. (2001). *Constructivist instructional design and development of a networked learning skills (NICLS) module for continuing professional education distance learning.* Paper presented at the ED-MEDIA 2001 World Conference on Educational Multimedia, Hypermedia and Telecommunications, Tampere, Finland. (ERIC Database #ED466132)

Odin, J. K. (2002). *Teaching and learning activities in the online classroom: A constructivist perspective.* Paper presented at the ED-MEDIA 2002 World

Conference on Educational Multimedia, Hypermidia and Telecommunicatos, Denver, CO. (ERIC Database #ED470077)

O'Reilly, M., & Newton, D. (2001). *Interaction online: Above and beyond requirements of assessment*. Paper presented at the 18th annual conference of the Australasian Society for Computers in Learning in Tertiary Education (ASCILITE), Melbourne, Australia. Retrieved August 6, 2006, from http://www.ascilite.org.au/conferences/melbourne01/pdf/papers/oreillym.pdf

Ortiz, B. I. D. (2004, October 19-23). *Problem-based learning (PBL) in distance education: A literature review of how distance education (DE) environments transforms the design of PBL for teacher education.* Paper presented at the Association for Educational Communications and Technology, Chicago, IL. (ERIC Database #ED485067)

Palloff, R., & Pratt, K. (1999). *Building learning communities in cyberspace: Effective strategies for the online classroom*. San Francisco: Jossey-Bass.

Palmer, P. J. (1998). *The courage to teach: Exploring the inner landscape of a teacher's life.* San Francisco: Jossey-Bass.

Richardson, V. (1999). Teacher education and the construction of meaning. In G. A. Griffin (Ed.), *The education of teachers. Ninety-eighth yearbook of the nation l society for the study of education: Part I* (pp. 145-166). Chicago: National Society for the Study of Educators.

Sage, S. M. (2000). *The learning and teaching experiences in an online problem-based learning course.* New Orleans: American Educational Research Association. (ERIC Database #ED442467)

Schrum, S. A. (1999). Introduction. In S. A. Schrum (Ed.), *Teaching in cyberspace: Issues of teaching, acting, and directing* (pp. 1-6). New York: Peter Lang.

Squires, D. (1999). Educational software for constructivist learning environments: Subversive use and volatile design. *Educational Technology, 39*(3), 48-53.

Stepich, D., & Ertmer, P. (2003). Building community as a critical element of online course design. *Educational Technology, 43*(5), 33-43.

Tan, S. C., & Hung, D. (2002, September-October). Beyond information pumping: Creating a constructivist e-learning environment. *Educational Technology, 42*(5), 48-54.

Vat, K. H. (2000). *Online education: A learner-centered model for constructivism.* Paper presented at International Conference on Computers in Education/International Conference on Computer-Assisted Instruction (pp. 22-44). Taipei, Taiwan. (ERIC Database #ED454832)

Vella, J. (2002). *Learning to listen, learning to teach.* San Francisco: Jossey-Bass.

Vygotsky, L. S. (1978). *Mind in society: The development of higher psychological processes*. Cambridge, MA: Harvard University Press.

Wang, C. Y.J., Resta, P.E., & Miller, P. (2001, November 8-12). The medium is the message: The design of an online collaborative learning community. In *Annual Proceedings of Selected Research and Development and Practice Papers* (pp. 521-529). National Convention of the Association for Educational Communications and Technology, Atlanta, GA.

Wertsch, J. (2002). *Voices of collective remembering*. Cambridge, UK: Cambridge University Press.

Whittle, J., Morgan, M., & Maltby, J. (2002). *Higher learning online: Using constructivist principles to design effective asynchronous discussion*. Paper presented at the Annual NAWEB Conference. Retrieved August 6, 2006, from http://naweb.unb.ca/2k/papers/whittle.htm

Wiesenberg, F. (2001). *The roller coaster life of the online learner: How distance educators can help students cope*. Retrieved on August 6, 2006, from http://www.extension.usask.ca/cjuce/articles/v27pdf/2722.pdf

Williams, S. W. (2000). Instructional design factors and the effectiveness of Web-based training/instruction. In R. N. Cervero, B.C. Courtenay, & C. H. Monagahan (Eds.), *The Cyril O. Houle scholars in adult and continuing education program global research perspectives, 2* (pp. 132-145).

Wilson, B. G. (1993). Constructivism and instructional design: Some personal reflections. In M. R. Simonson & K. Abu-Omar (Eds.), *Proceedings of Selected Research and Development Presentations at the 1993 National Convention of the Association for Educational Communications and Technology* (pp. 1131-1149). New Orleans, LA.

Windschitl, M. (1999). A vision educators can put into practice: Portraying the constructivist classroom as a cultural system. *School Science and Mathematics, 99*(4), 189-196.

Chapter VI

A Theoretical Model for Designing Online Education in Support of Lifelong Learning

Lawrence A. Tomei, Robert Morris University, USA

Abstract

The escalating infusion of online education to promote lifelong learning has triggered a re-examination of teaching and learning not witnessed since perhaps the advent of the printed textbook. Textbooks changed the landscape of individualized learning as professors added reading to their inventory of instructional strategies. Today, distance education, in all its manifestations from programmed instruction to Web-based courses, requires instructors to employ new strategies in course design and delivery in order to engage students and promote learner-centered activities. The rapid growth of distance education (especially for the adult learner) serves to challenge traditional methodologies in which education is designed, delivered, and assessed. This chapter introduces a new model for designing instruction using this state-of-the-art venue, an archetype for effective instructional design for lifelong learning.

Introduction

The rapid growth of technology now enables delivery of lifelong learning in ways that increase access and overcome traditional barriers of geography and time normally associated with conventional classroom instruction. The emergence of video and Web-based courses has thrust educational institutions into newer and more complex distance learning environments in order to link their students and instructors in cyberspace. The potential for sharing information, engaging in collective learning, and participating in reflective thinking has provided, according to Van Dusen (1997), opportunities for supporting "collaborative learning, heterogeneous groupings, problem-solving and higher order thinking skills—educational processes that a lecture format cannot facilitate" (p. 45). Such focus on student-centered teaching requires more than simply learning to use technology; it also requires learning new and different ways of teaching that engage the student in a virtual learning environment (DeNigris & Witchel, 2000; Kearsley, 2000; Knowlton, 2000; Ko & Rossen, 2001; Palloff & Pratt, 2001; Simonson, 2000; Young, 2000). Some would say such reorientation requires an entirely new model for designing and assessing such new instruction.

The objective of the chapter is to propose a new model for designing online instruction that incorporates state-of-the-art technologies. The research-based methodology presented in this chapter describes a process for designing effective online education that involves a simple five-step process. The model is offered to assist educators in developing online instruction for lifelong learning.

Review of the Literature

History of Instructional Design: Problems and Their Solutions

The word "model" is often used to represent theoretical or abstract concepts that exist in the real world. A model may be a prototype of a real-world object (e.g., an architect's model of a building) or merely represent an object with no real-world counterpart (e.g., a UFO spaceship). In the context of education, models have often presented fresh perspectives for educators seeking to construct a vision of new concepts or representation of experiences too large, too small, too dangerous, too distant, or, in the case of educational applications, too fragile for human experimentation. For the innovative educator, models have often served to provide the conceptual framework to pose solutions to practical problems.

Instructional System Design (ISD)

Designing instruction experienced its first taste of immediacy during the ramp-up of World War II. Military instructors needed a systematic, methodical, organized schema to produce training courses—and they needed it in a hurry. For the thousands of military instructors and the tens of thousands of their recruit-students, ISD was the answer to the problem quickly of creating results-oriented lessons.

ISD models have enabled would-be developers to tackle new lessons or curriculum in a systematic, methodical, organized manner. ISD models help visualize the inter-related tasks associated with the sequencing of discrete, manageable instructional units. Educational psychologists would ascribe behavioral learning styles to the ISD approach; that is, designers who prefer sequential, logical, hierarchical, and chronological instruction tend to steer towards using the ISD paradigm.

A variety of ISD models have been developed since the initial military ISD model came into wide spread acceptance in the 1940s. The Inter-service Procedures for Instructional Systems Development (often called the military ISD model) was approved by the Joint Chiefs of Staff in 1975 and remains the governing prototype for all military education and technical training.

The ADDIE model (Figure 1) represents the five basic phases of most ISD models, although terminologies may differ. Most ISD models propose an analysis phase followed by design, development, implementation, and evaluation. They begin with the analysis of tasks to be performed, content area learning objectives, timelines, and priorities and constraints. Designing lessons via ISD demands an understanding of the target learner and a hierarchy of instruction from simple to complex, least to most important, past to present—basically, the behavioral approach to learning.

Figure 1. ADDIE instructional systems design model

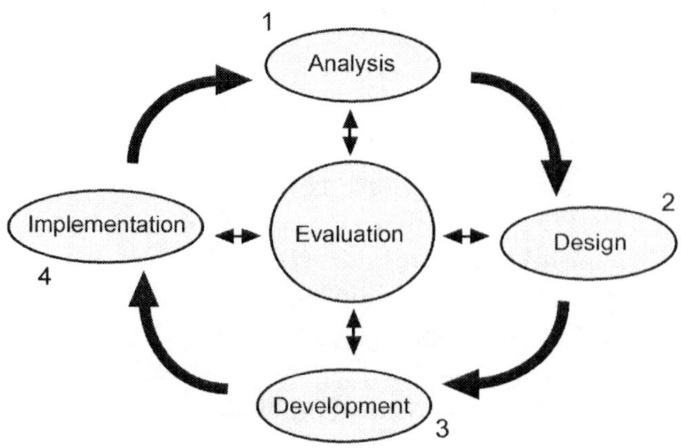

The development phase examines questions such as who will be responsible for the instruction, what resources will be needed to deliver the lesson, when the instruction will be delivered, where the lesson will be delivered, and how the instructor will know learning has occurred.

Implementation encompasses a critical distinction among the various target learners: traditional, adult, and distance learners. Traditional lessons are most often found in the classroom and employ more static learning materials such as textbooks, manipulatives, and workbooks. Lessons targeting the adult learner seem to favor group or collaborative activities with a healthy dose of experiential learning materials as instructional resources. Distance education integrates a wealth of multimedia materials to enhance learning with an inventory of technologies that is increasing geometrically every year.

Finally, the evaluation or assessment phase of the model ensures that instructional objectives have been met and a process of continuous improvement is in place to continually update and revise the lesson based on learner feedback that may take on a variety of forms such as traditional paper and pencil quizzes, authentic projects simulating real-world situations, or online tests that provide immediate reinforcement to the learner.

A half-century later, the ISD model remains intact and its standards for implementation still serve to address the time-honored problems of technical training and adult education.

Lesson Design Models

Lesson design models differ from their ISD relatives with respect to the educational psychology they espouse and the problems they seek to address. While the ISD approach is focused on behavioral principles, lesson design models find their strength in cognitive learning strategies.

In contrast to the behavioral perspective, cognitive psychologists focus on the learner (rather than the environment) as the active component of the teaching-learning process. They uncovered serious shortcomings when seeking to explain all learning as a simple response to environmental stimuli. Behaviorism, they conceded, offered an adequate explanation when designing a lesson for multiplication tables, for example. But, the psychology seemed to fall short when explaining how new knowledge was acquired apart from environmental stimuli without the requisite S-R-R experience. Understanding how prior knowledge is constructed and new information processed and structured in an individual's memory demanded a new model for lesson design.

The ASSURE model (Figure 2) is a popular prototype for designing lessons. The model assumes that instruction is delivered using a variety of media and has been

Figure 2. ASSURE lesson design model

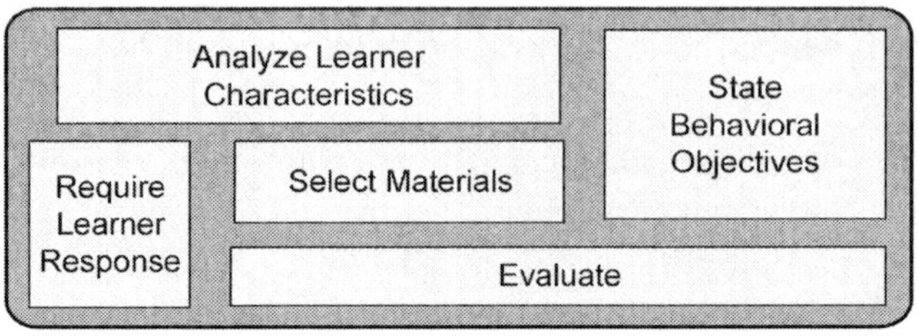

found to be especially helpful when designing technology-based lessons. It encourages incorporation of out-of-class resources and technology into its learning materials (Heinrich, Molenda, Russell, & Smaldino, 1996). Although critics (at least of the acronym) find the letters ASSURE somewhat contrived, the acronym conveys the importance and interrelationship of the six major steps in the design of cognitive-rich lessons: analyze learners, state objectives, select media and materials, utilize materials, require learner participation, and evaluate/review. Most discussions of the ASSURE model offer additional, specific criteria for selecting media that considers key features when infusing technology into successful lessons.

Universal Curriculum Design Models

The final school of educational psychology provides the foundation for the third generation of instructional design models. As educational learning theories evolved, the limitations of both behaviorism and cognitivism became more obvious. Neither psychology could satisfactorily portray how affective knowledge was mastered. The teaching of values, social interactions, or personal relationships required yet another paradigm. The new archetype attempted to take into account how a person feels about learning, how learning contributes to growth and individual satisfaction, and how all manner of instructional strategies combine to form a more effective universal curriculum.

The backward design model (Figure 3) is the foremost archetype of the universal curriculum design model. The backward design process begins with the end in mind. As the authors relate the concept: "One starts with the end—the desired results (goals or standards)—and then derives the curriculum from the evidence of learning (performances) called for by the standard and the teaching needed to equip students to perform" (Wiggins & McTighe, 2000, p. 8).

Figure 3. Backward design model (Source: Wiggins & McTighe 2000)

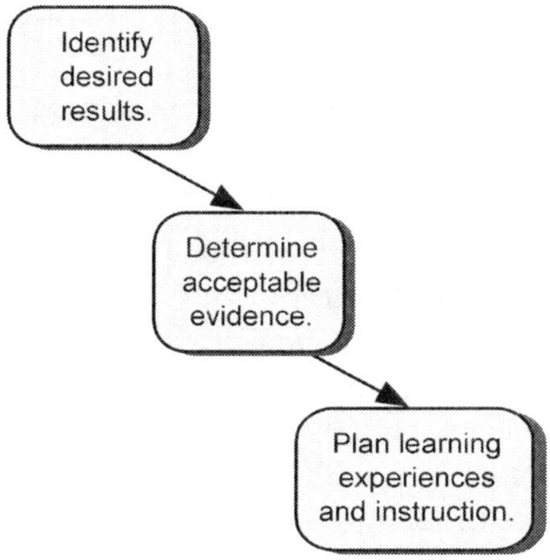

The design process involves three stages, each with a focusing concept. First, what is worthy and requiring of understanding? In this first stage, teachers focus on the learning goals and "enduring understandings" that students are to develop by the completion of the lesson. Guiding questionnaires are formulated and universal skills that focus on larger concepts, principles, or processes are devised.

Stage 2 examines the requisite evidence of understanding, deciding ultimately how students will demonstrate their understanding. The assessment tasks created in this step ensure that students develop an understanding of the content presented and demonstrate that understanding throughout the learning process (formative assessment) as well as at its conclusion (summative assessment).

The final stage of the backward design model develops the learning experiences, sequence of the instruction, and the actual subject area content to be taught.

Historically, ISD led the charge from advocates seeking an explanatory model for developing instruction. For its time (the 1940s and 1950s), education was well served. However, by the 1960s and into the 1970s, the shortcomings of ISD produced the next necessary schemata with its focus on lesson design. Finally, recognition of its shortfalls was hastened with the advent of the universal curriculum. Each model, in turn, served to address a recognized need m the design and delivery of instruction.

For the 21st century educator, evolution was replaced with revolution as technology sought to impact the classroom. And, as in the past, this change, too, was to precipitate yet another new model for instructional design.

The Engine for Designing Online Education in Support of Lifelong Learning

Each of the three previous approaches to lesson design offered a unique perspective for developing successful lessons. However, by fate or circumstance, each model would focus on the same set of five key elements: the learner, principles of learning, instructional resources, delivery methods, and learning outcomes.

In graphical depiction, Figure 4 illustrates the new model for designing online instruction in support of lifelong learning. Like its ancestors, the five foci remain unchallenged. The remainder of this chapter considers each component independently and presents arguments for moving from the more traditional perspective of the child-learner to one that considers the idiosyncrasies of the adult, and finally, to a perspective unique to the demands of distance education. The new engine for designing online education changes the way we design, develop, implement, and assess learning in this emerging virtual world of lifelong learning. We begin with learning theories and the many contributions of educational psychology to the design of traditional, adult, and distance-based lessons.

Figure 4. The engine for designing online education

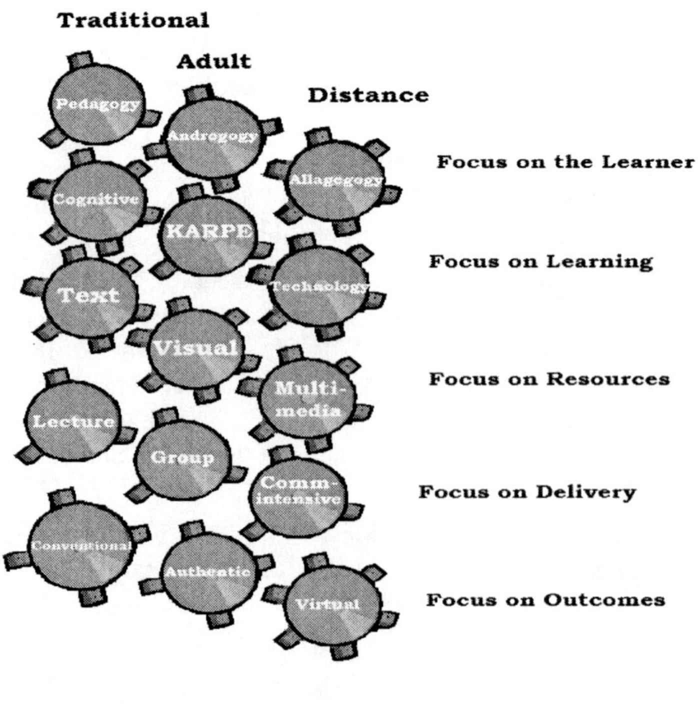

Focus on the Learner: Learning Theories

The primary responsibility of an educator is to promote student learning. Teachers select instructional strategies based in large measure on their own particular comfort and familiarity with learning theory. A popular model of teaching and learning depicts how the principles of learning contribute to the fabric of a successful lesson. One of the most important objectives of lesson design is to factor into course development the appropriate learning theories of the target learners be they traditional, adult, or distance learners (Dembo, 1991).

K-12 teachers, in particular, learn how to design lessons from the outset of their preservice undergraduate programs using boiler plate lesson planning tools. They mirror courses that they, themselves, take which celebrate the diversity of pedagogical learning styles associated with traditional preschool through high school students. Teachers of adult learners, on the other hand, are often not as well prepared to teach their particular strata of client. Andragogy, which attempts to describe how adults learn, is not often a prerequisite for undergraduate or postgraduate faculty education, or corporate trainers for that matter. Teaching at a distance adds yet another layer of learning, termed *allagegogy* ("teaching to transform") by Priest (2002), to describe a still newer approach to education that focuses on learner independence and the inherent changes that define lifelong learning.

Learning Theory for the Traditional Learner (Tomei, 2004)

Historically, learning theory for traditional learners has advanced through three evolutionary phases of what is typically referred to as pedagogy. The three schools of educational psychology (behaviorism, cognitivism, and humanism) were introduced briefly in the previous section and are now discussed in detail as they pertain to the traditional learner.

Years ago, teachers believed that the best way to learn was through repetition, a principle from behavioral learning theory that dominated educational thinking since the time of Ivan Pavlov and his experiment with animals. Contemporary behaviorists view the environment in terms of stimuli and its resultant behavior or response. Simply put, learning is a response to the environment. Teachers who accept the behavioral perspective assume that the behavior of their students is a response to their past and present experiences and that all behavior is learned.

Cognitive teachers, on the other hand, focus more on the learner as an active participant in the teaching-learning process. Those who adhere to this psychology of learning believe that teachers can be more effective if they know what prior knowledge the student already possesses and how information is processed and structured in an individual's memory. Cognitive-based teachers instruct students by using teaching strategies to help the learner acquire knowledge more effectively.

Humanists believe that how a person feels about learning is as important as how he or she thinks or even behaves. They describe behavior not from the viewpoint of the teacher as do behaviorists but rather from the vantage point of the student who is performing the activity. Teachers create an educational environment that fosters self-development, cooperation, positive communications, and personalization of information.

Learning Theory for the Adult Learner

Knowles' (1984) theory of andragogy redefined the previously child-only perception of learning. Adult learning is typically characterized as experiential, problem-based, immediate, and self-directed.

Unlike children, adults learn experientially using their considerable practice, knowledge base, and problem-solving skills. They must know why they need to learn something and they learn best when that topic is of immediate value. Adults approach learning, for the most part, as self-directed and expect to take at least some responsibility for their own learning. Adults expect that the learning environments fashioned for them accommodate these fundamental aspects of adult learning.

In practical terms, andragogy focuses more on process (how we learn) and less on content (what we learn). Strategies include case studies, role playing, simulations, and self-evaluation and are often enhanced with the infusion of the right blend of technologies. Instructors adopt the role of facilitator rather than lecturer.

Learning Theory for the Distance Learner

Although Lev Vygotsky died decades before the information revolution of the late 20th century, his work and that of other developmental psychologists was to become the foundation of distance learning theory. His theories stress the fundamental role of social interaction in the learning process and the importance that community serves in the process of "making meaning" (Vygotsky, 1978). Such concepts have come to form the basis of adult education, lifelong learning, and distance education. For example, teaching at a distance has come to be accepted as a natural outgrowth of Vygotsky's work on the more knowledgeable other (MKO) that refers to someone who has a better understanding or a higher ability level than the learner, with respect to a particular task, process, or concept. Electronic tutors as well as today's online learning management systems have been used in distance settings to facilitate and guide students through the learning process.

From these early beginnings came a growing research base that continues to identify qualities inherent to successful distance learners. Moore (1990) and Campbell Gibson (1990) examined the success rates of distance students and discovered that certain common characteristics seem to lend themselves to success at a distance. Others, typified by Holmberg (1995), discovered a nonhomogeneous population with respect to demographics of distance students. Regardless, research does contribute some broad demographic and situational parallels that help educators profile the "typically successful" distance learner. Characteristics vary but in general reflect a combination of demographic variables such as age, gender, and ethnic background as well as situational variables including disability, location, and life roles.

In addition, characteristics inherent to allagegogy include the ability to work independently or in a group, complete assignments and readings with minimal supervision, write in a clear and articulate manner, manage time, learn using different delivery formats, and work with technology tools (Lehigh Carbon Community College, 2006).

As the first component of the engine, learning theories encourage designers to consider developing lessons that combine principles from pedagogical, andragogical, and allagegogical learning theory to produce a lesson that truly targets the widest possible audience of distance learners. Lessons designed for the online environment should take into account that some of their target learners anticipate content that must be mastered (behavioral) as well as those who expect exposure to problem-based, real-world experiences. The first component of our engine produces lessons that consider these initial competencies while moving towards true online education designed with a set of prejudged skills, namely, the ability to learn either independently or in a cohort, writing and time management skills, and technology literate. Focus on the learner is the first stage of our engine for designing online education.

Focus on Learning: Taxonomies

A taxonomy is a classification system that presupposes an innate relationship or order among elements. A vocabulary is considered the simplest form of a taxonomy with only one level, that being its acknowledged register of terms, common expressions, and established lexis. More complex taxonomies form a hierarchical structure. At the highest level, terms and descriptive phrases are general in nature, followed by an increasingly more refined set of terminology at progressively more specific levels of articulation.

Taxonomies are typically categorized by domain. Historically, the more popular taxonomies have addressed a broad representation of educational objectives (cognitive, affective, and psychomotor): service-learning outcomes (academic, career, civic, ethical, personal, and social); developmental skills (cognitive, social/emotional, language/linguistic, and fine/gross motor abilities); lifelong learning skills (knowledge, application, and research/practice, and evaluation); or, more recently, instructional technology (literacy, communications, decision making, learning, teaching, and tech-ology) (Furco & Billig, 2002; Krathwohl, Bloom, & Masia, 1964; National

Center For Infants, Toddlers and Families, 2002; Tomei, 2005). A brief review of the more important taxonomies as they pertain to lifelong learning follows.

Taxonomy for the Traditional Learner

Benjamin Bloom created what is arguably the most famous classification for educators in his *Taxonomy of Educational Objectives* (Bloom & Krathwohl, 1956). In his landmark exposition, Bloom developed a theory of six progressively complex steps of cognitive development (Figure 5) to include knowledge, comprehension, application, analysis, synthesis, and evaluation. He offered educators a rubric for designing and implementing instructional objectives at increasingly advanced levels of higher order thinking. Following in his footsteps, Krathwohl and Kibler completed a trilogy of domains with similar classifications for the affective and psychomotor learner, respectively (Krathwohl et al., 1964). Supplementing Bloom's effort came a host of extraordinary contributions supporting the advancement of higher order cognitive thinking skills from the likes of Howard Garner, Jean Piaget, and Jerome Bruner, to name a few.

Taxonomy for the Adult Learner

Later, the *KAR-P-E taxonomy* (Figure 6) offered a schema for technology education encompassing adult education, corporate training, and professional development. Designing instructional learning objectives at the knowledge, application, research, practice, and evaluation (KAR-P-E) levels (1) applies to all learners in all disciplines; (2) develops the learner in progressive sequential steps; and (3) assumes mastery

Figure 5. Bloom's taxonomy of educational objectives

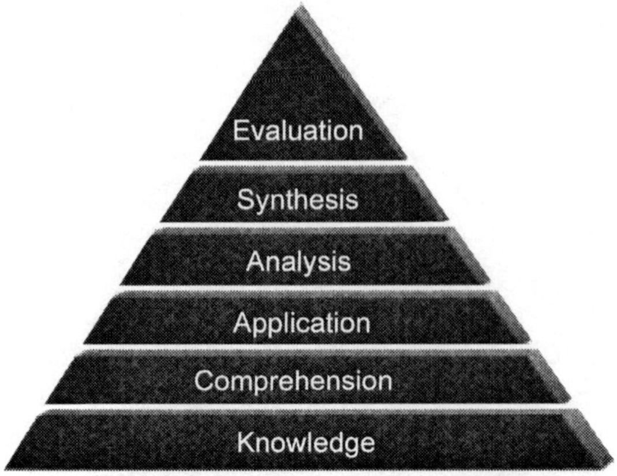

and competency at previous levels before advancing up the hierarchy (Tomei, 2005). Using the KAR-P-E model answers the perennial question from advanced learners who seek a distinction among undergraduate, graduate, and postgraduate courses that often sport the same course titles if not many of the same learning objectives, the model (and the research that supports it) proposes that typical undergraduate courses should construct learning focused predominantly on the knowledge plane. Graduate courses present learning on a more application level, while postgraduate programs (e.g., doctoral studies) should concentrate on research, practice, and evaluation. Of course, some overlap among all three program levels is not only expected but encouraged.

Taxonomy for the Distance Learner

The latest addendum to the classification of educational learning objectives came onto the scene with the introduction of *The Taxonomy for the Technology Domain*. Like its predecessors, technology classifications include a similarly progressive level of higher order thinking skills complete with action verbs that represented appropriate intellectual activity on each of the hierarchal levels (Figure 7). The six interconnected levels of literacy, communication, decision making, infusion, integration, and tech-ology matured into a paradigm for constructing technology-related lesson objectives and technology-based student learning outcomes (Tomei, 2005). It offers the most comprehensive classification system for designing distance online education. Online courses begin with the mastery of targeted technologies (literacy) and move quickly to communications (e-mail, word processing) and decision-making skills. True distance learning design begins with the infusion of existing

Figure 6. K-A-RPE taxonomy

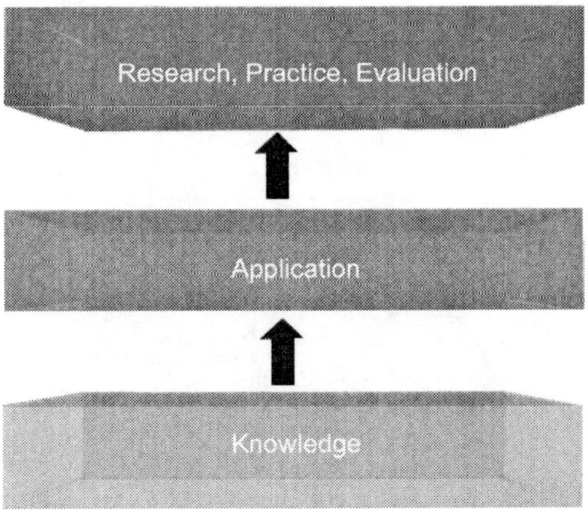

and available technology-based resources (e.g., files, audio and video, Web-based learning environments, etc.) and advances to the integration of new technologies and new technology-based learning materials created by a highly motivated and technologically-prepared instructor who tops the lesson by placing technology in its rightful place and priority in the learning equation (tech-ology).

Use of an educational taxonomy is considered appropriate either to establish a set of terms defined by a common rubric and accepted by a common body of knowledge or to confirm a progressively complex yet controlled set of possibilities. Especially useful for our purposes in conceiving the engine for designing online education is to emphasize the importance of selecting appropriate methods, media, and materials. In this step, the design of the lesson is a focus on learning that bridges the audience and the lesson objectives.

Focus on Resources: Selecting Learning Materials

Selecting Learning Materials for the Traditional Learner

Prototypically, traditional learners are provided with static-based materials that offer significant learning opportunities coupled with the advantages of extreme portability. The ability to use these materials in any instructional environment, plus their high recognition level, ensures most students have an acceptable comfort level using these materials. Add to these advantages, the cost-effectiveness and availability of materials readily created and duplicated with little expense, and it becomes immediately evident why text-based resources such as textbooks, handouts, worksheets and workbooks, manipulatives, encyclopedias, and lesson

Figure 7. The taxonomy for the technology domain (Source: Tomei, 2005)

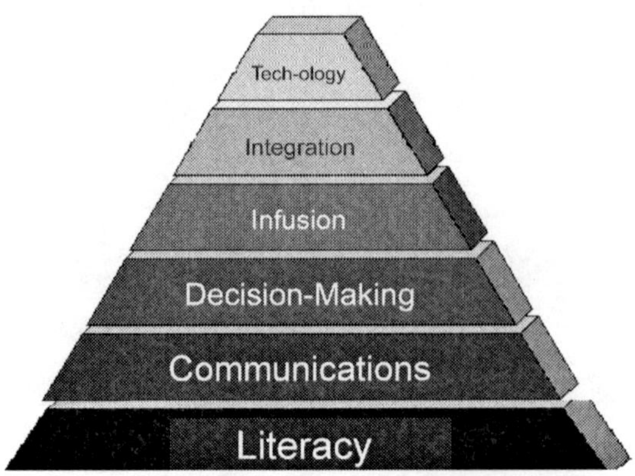

kits remain the instructional materials of choice for the traditional learner. Other learning materials, technology-rich but traditionally delivered, include CD-ROMs, VHS videotapes, and 35 mm slides.

Selecting Learning Materials for the Adult Learner

Adult learners are afforded a broad range of learning material alternatives categorized for purposes of this text as dynamic materials. They include, but are not limited to, visual-based graphic presentations, video and audio reproductions.

Experiential learning is adult learner-centered and operates on the premise that adults learn best when instruction combines experience with the theoretical; in other words, "learning by doing." Experiential materials engage the learner directly with the content being studied via case studies, clinical experiences, team-building, and decision-making exercises.

Self-directed materials encourage the learner to take responsibility for personal growth by diagnosing their own learning needs, setting individual goals, identifying appropriate resources, implementing successful strategies, and assessing the personal worth of learning outcomes. In 1999, more than 95% of adults participated in self-directed learning and spent an average of 15 hours per week on self-directed learning initiatives (Rager, 2003), enhanced by instructor facilitation. Adult learning occurs just as often in the isolation of a university library as it does in more interpersonal communication with experts and peers. Typical resources brought to bear to promote self-directed adult learning include printed and audiovisual materials; first- or second-hand experts; education-focused institutions such as museums; and involvement with professional associations.

Selecting Learning Materials for the Distance Learner

Distance learners command the widest assortment of learning materials in terms of quantity, format, and form. Multimedia-based materials are the particular forte of the distance learner, roughly divided across print, audio (voice) and video, and computer (data) objects. Several subdivisions and widely diverse applications of the same, many of the technologies extend this grouping into multiple categories.

Print technologies heralded the advent of the original form of distance learning—correspondence courses once integrated self-paced print materials mailed to students and returned upon completion for instructor assessment. Even though most, if not all, printed text for today's distance courses takes on an electronic façade, reading assignments remain a significant component of most courses. Lumped into print technologies comes electronic mail and many other forms of digital material (e.g., hyperbooks, e-journals, and e-books).

Audio or voice technologies offer less costly and yet very effective ways to enhance distance learning. The audio component of a distance learning course can be as conventional as voice mail or as complex as audio conferencing or live broadcasts integrated audio, chat rooms, presentation hardware, electronic polls and surveys, and computer sharing represent some current advancements in audio technologies.

The ability to see and hear an instructor offers opportunities for behavior modeling, demonstrations, and instruction of abstract concepts. Video technologies for distance learning are often characterized by the media on which they are hosted: videotape, satellite, cable vs. broadcast television, and desktop or Internet conferencing. Each of these media is further categorized depending on the path of the video signal (i.e., one-way audio/video, one-way video/two way audio, or two-way audio/video).

Computer (data) technologies comprise the broadest and fastest growing dimension of distance learning materials. The primary computer technologies used for distance education include both online environments and electronic tools that host a wealth of materials for the distance learner. Most state-of-the-art online environments host digital content, audiovisual presentations, and links to related Web content. If it is digital, it can be uploaded to distance courses hosted by Blackboard, WebCT, e-College, and other online forums.

In addition, a suite of ever-increasing technology tools can he dropped into online courses with a click of a mouse. Chat rooms with online logs, threaded discussion groups with multiple levels, online quiz editing and grading, whiteboards, gradebooks, calendars, drop boxes, and Webliographies are just a few of the tools available to the distance learner.

Future online instructors can anticipate even more advancements as two-way Web video, desktop video, and evolutions in assessment options are integrated into the list of multimedia-based learning (and teaching) materials.

The final cache of multimedia-based learning materials, often overlooked as a category in its own right, is multimedia software. Streamed audio and video software is as important as the hardware that drives it. CD-ROM and Web development software, along with advanced graphics and presentation applications, have incontrovertible influence on the discipline of media and fine arts. The abundance of distance learning applications validates the claim that multimedia software is one of the fastest growing branches of the computer industry (University Affairs, 1996).

The focus on resources accounts for the third rung in the engine for designing online education. With this step comes a shift from the predominantly theoretical considerations of the previous two steps to a more practical focus on the methodologies of teaching online. Our fourth level of the engine next examines presentation modes in general and, specifically, the most effective modes for teaching at a distance.

Focus on Delivery: Selecting Presentation Modes

Selecting Presentation Modes for the Traditional Learner

Historically, instructors of traditional learners have opted for classroom-centered presentations. In many respects, classroom lectures represent the "but we've always done it this way" approach to teaching. Such emphasis on the lecture-rich "sage on the stage" has rapidly diminished as research and technology combined to offer new and exciting venues for delivering instruction to contemporary students. Lectures are arguably the easiest mode for both the sender (teacher) and receiver (learner) requiring less student preparation and groundwork than more complicated modes of presentations. As educational psychology matured over the years since the 1940s, emphasis on behavior, research, and the literature have combined to uncover many of the major shortcomings of the lecture-based lesson. More importantly, the growing sophistication of learners (even at the K-12 level) and the infusion of technologies appropriate for traditional as well as mature learners have heralded the retooling of presentations away from the one-way, send-receive mode to a host of new and innovative modalities for learning.

Selecting Presentation Modes for the Adult Learner

Teaching adults demands the incorporation of a variety of instructional strategies, expanding an already complex inventory of diverse teaching tools. Andragogy places instructional emphasis on groupwork suggesting several new modes of participative, self-directed instruction, the most widely known being cooperative and discovery learning. Cooperative learning, as an adult mode of presentation, encourages a manner of interaction similar to how successful adults master many real-world experiences. A solid cooperative learning experience incorporates realistic tasks, shared leadership, predefined responsibilities, and often ill-defined outcomes to trigger the desired learning outcomes.

Discovery learning places the teacher in the role of facilitator, serving up a menu of resources from which the adult learner may pick and choose to enrich their personal learning experience.

Together, presentation modes for the adult learner are characterized by collaborative projects and shared endeavors, and other group-focused evaluation and assessment.

Selecting Presentation Modes for the Distance Learner

Distance learning adds still other strategies that provide a wealth of communications-intensive presentation modes including: asynchronous and synchronous communication, immersion/hybrid/repository online courses, and online learning management systems.

Asynchronous communication does not happen in collaboration; it is most beneficial when common meeting times are difficult to arrange (e.g., incompatible time zones or work schedules) or when the learner is required or would prefer to take time considering a response or forming opinions. E-mail, newsgroups, and bulletin boards are common examples of asynchronous learning tools.

Synchronous communications occurs in real time, back and forth between two locations, fostering socialization and discussion. Audio and video conferencing, chat rooms, and electronic whiteboards offer the best examples of this form of learning.

Most distance courses are constructed as immersion (totally online), hybrid (partially online), or repository (materials only online) presentations. Immersion courses are often referred to in their more generic term: e-learning. Defined by Wikipedia (2006), immersion or e-learning is computer-based training that incorporates technologies that support interactivity enhanced by technology. Hybrid, or partially online courses divide course content, collaboration, and assessment, offering combinations of these elements either online or traditional. Repository courses provide an online component for instruction but use technology narrowly to capture and store digital information. For example, an instructor might make available a list of favorite Web sites online or a digital journal article might be captured for download (assuming appropriate copyright permissions, of course). Finally, the newest category of comprehensive multimedia-rich distance courses is learning management systems (LMS) that manage essential learning activity such as registration, scheduling, reporting, and so forth. Instructionally, a typical LMS might provide course delivery and content authoring, student exercise and quiz item authoring, student grade book and progress tracking, and statistical analysis.

This focus on delivery comprises a review of appropriate presentation modes for the traditional, adult, and distance learner and covers an impressive range of instructional tools from the straightforward lecture to the virtual. Next, a discussion of assessment methodologies and their importance in measuring learning outcomes completes the introduction of a new model for designing online education.

Focus on Outcomes: Selecting Assessment Methodologies

Selecting Assessment Methodology for the Traditional Learner

Assessment takes many forms, typically extends over an extended period of time (class periods semesters, entire programs of study), and serves multiple purposes. Principally, assessment measures the quality of a student work and attainment of mastery. In its more robust roles, it is the stimulus for continuous course improvements, faculty development, and lifelong learning. For the traditional learner, conventional assessment often takes the form of a single-incident, unidimensional, timed exercise characteristically objective in its measurement, summative in its scope, and often limited to rote memorization, rehash of definitions, and reiteration of terms. Traditional assessments are commonly multiple-choice, true-false, or short-answer instruments and have garnered considerable criticism over the tears from teachers, students, and administrators alike.

However even its staunchest critics will concede that conventional assessments do have their advantages. They are less time consuming to construct, easier to grade, and much more straightforward to administer. They are also less problematic to validate for internal consistency and reliability. Past studies by Gaynor and Millham (1976) found that students who received weekly quizzes earned higher scores on final examinations when instruction was modified based on class results, a powerful testimony to more frequent student-centered feedback.

Selecting Assessment Methodology for the Adult Learner

Adult learners expect real-world challenges that require them to apply their personal skill and knowledge base. Proponents of andragogy have come to find that experience, communications, and interpersonal skills define the unique characteristics that blend to form the successful adult learner. For the adult learner, such expectations have come to mean authentic assessment.

Authentic assessment requires learners to build responses rather than choose from preselected options, thereby eliciting higher order thinking and a return to the educational learning objectives of Bloom. Authentic assessment focuses on students' analytical skills; abilities to integrate what they learn; creativity; capacities to work collaboratively; and written and oral expression skills. Assessing authentically values the learning process as well as the finished product and includes an inventory of tools such as portfolios, performance tasks, demonstration presentations, observations (formal and informal), discussions, and learner self-reflection and self-assessment.

Selecting Assessment Methodology for the Distance Learner

As a group, distance learners are probably more anxious about how they are doing than their traditional counterparts. Distance instructors use virtual assessment to provide the frequent feedback needed to track their learners' individual and collective efforts to complete assignments, master objectives, and gauge progress. Because distance learners are forced to read directions online, detailed information on how assessment will be conducted is highly recommended. Basic information such as the specific forms that assessment will take is paramount. For example, synchronous participation using chat rooms, videoconferencing, and Web conferencing is an excellent option when teaching at a distance. Distance learners should be prewarned that, even though a course may labeled as online or at a distance, participation during scheduled synchronous discussions may comprise a significant percentage of the final course grade. Likewise, timely submission of asynchronous contributions is important to keep most online courses within semester timelines. Strict adherence to issues of American Psychological Association (APA) style, copyright infringements, and academic integrity often contribute to final grades while e-mail, bulletin board posts, discussion forums, and listservs are integrated into formative and summative course assessment. Finally, the online versions of the more traditional evaluator instruments remain viable assessment tools and include digital documents (e.g., essays), other electronic files (e.g., spreadsheets), as well as online exams in the form of multiple choice, true/false, or short answer completion graded electronically online as soon as responses are submitted.

In addition (and somewhat beyond the scope of this chapter) are numerous other electronic tools that enhance the statistical dimensions of distance learning environments. Many online learning management systems provide instructors with standardized analytical data including rate of student progress, completion rates, access to course materials, quantity of instructor/student interaction, assignment completion tracking, examination item analysis, and more.

Our focus on outcomes is fraught with challenges as well as opportunities. For many learners, technology already places them in isolation from both their instructor and their peers. Even though technology has invaded every aspect of 21st century living, there remains uneven access to some resources necessary to learn at a distance. Finally, technical problems are common, variations in learner (and instructor) skills are endemic, and learner anxiety must all be factored into every consideration when selecting appropriate assessment methods for distance learning.

Recommendations

Applying the Engine for Designing Online Education

Using the new engine, designing online education embraces the structured approach of a sequential, step-by-step process that begins with the learner and flows through a considered examination of learning objectives, learning materials and presentation modes, and ends with appropriate assessment.

Focus on the Learner: Pedagogy, Andragogy, and Allagegogy

Define target learners by moving quickly through pedagogy and andragogy and focusing on the new concept of allagegogy. For best results, design a lifelong lesson based on adult learning strategies taken to its ultimate goal of "teaching to transform." Consider infusing traditional principles of pedagogy and themes of behaviorism, cognitivism, and humanism to appeal to the widest audience whenever possible while simultaneously developing online lessons that encourage independent learning and incorporate appropriate technologies.

Focus on Learning: Cognitive, K-A-RPE, and Technology

Bloom's taxonomy for the traditional learner as well as Tomei's KAR-P-E classification for adults have much to contribute to the formation of successful lesson objectives and should not be summarily dismissed. The engine's second gear emanates from the traditional and adult learner for a reason. However, designing lifelong learning at a distance demands conscious reflection on the technological elements of a lesson. Use the taxonomy for the technology domain to formulate successful learning objectives for online education.

Focus on Resources: Static, Dynamic, and Multimedia Materials

The third set of cogs petitions the designer to consider the various resources for learning. Again, designing for the distance learner moves us quickly past traditional materials and resources towards the infusion of digital content. Integrate as diverse a menu of multimedia resources as time, money, and best practice permit to produce a winning online lesson.

Focus on Delivery: Lectures, Groupware, and Communications-Intensive Media

The fourth set of gears for the new engine encompasses the medium of delivery. Lectures, whether they occur in the classroom or digitally via audio or video, remain a viable platform for any lesson. Groupwork, likewise, is now more accessible to a broader population and retains its attraction for the socially-receptive adult learner. But certainly, an ever-expanding inventory of innovative tools suggests that the designer of distance lessons should proceed with all due haste to the suite of communications-intensive delivery modes that will surely come to define the future of lifelong learning.

Focus on Outcomes: Conventional, Authentic, and Virtual

The final bank of gears to turn in crunching out a new lesson emphasizes learning outcomes. As before, consider the more conventional as well as electronic adaptations of authentic assessment tools. The digital portfolio, perhaps the mort authentic of the various evaluation instruments, bridges the adult and virtual learner. While more is not always better (especially regarding educational technology), when it comes to focus on outcomes, the more opportunities for assessing learner achievement in a virtual environment, the greater the chances of realizing successful learning outcomes.

Conclusion

The search for a research-based methodology for designing effective online education boils down to a simple five-step process. A new model has been offered to assist the educator in developing technology-based online instruction in support of the lifelong learner.

An anonymous educator expressed it best, "Learning is difficult. To better learn a subject, try teaching it. To truly master content, try teaching it using technology." The application of technology has moved lifelong learning past the traditional models of instructional design to a new paradigm for lesson development. The consequences of teaching with technology force teachers to simultaneously consider multiple instructional foci while demanding that learners recognize their own learning style and how technologies help or hinder their own ambitions.

To that end, we add one more level of definition to the aforementioned author's quip: "To truly understand subject content, try teaching it at a distance." The engine for designing online education in support of "lifelong learning" is learner-focused, theory-based, and resource-rich. It supports communications-intensive delivery and virtual assessment. And it incorporates a truly unique blend of traditional and contemporary tools for designing online instruction.

Turn all the gears. Follow the concepts and tools presented in this chapter. Infuse the wealth of information provided elsewhere in this text. And, develop successful online education lessons in support of lifelong learning.

References

Bloom, B. S., & Krathwohl, D. R. (1956). *Taxonomy of educational objectives: The classification of educational goals by a committee of college and university examiners* (Handbook I: Cognitive Domain). New York: Longmans Publishing.

Campbell Gibson, C. (1990). Learners and learning: A discussion of selected research. In M. Moore (Ed.), *Contemporary issues in American distance education* (pp. 121-135). Oxford: Pergamon Press.

Dembo, M. (1991). *Applying educational psychology in the classroom* (4th ed). White Plains, NY: Longman Publishing Group.

DeNigris, J., & Witchel, A. (2000). *How to teach and train online*. Needham Heights, MA: Pearson Custom Publishing.

Furco, A., & Billig, S. (2002). *Service-learning: The essence of the pedagogy*. Greenwich, CT: Information Age Publishing.

Gaynor, J., & Millham, J. (1976). Student performance and evaluation under variant teaching and testing methods in a large college course. *Journal of Educational Psychology, 68*, 312-317.

Heinrich, R., Molenda, M., Russell, J., & Smaldino, S. (1996). *Instructional media and technologies for learning* (6th ed.). Upper Saddle River, NJ: Merrill/Prentice Hall.

Holmberg, B. (1995). *Theory and practice in distance education*. New York: Routledge Publishers.

Kearsley, G. (2000). *Online education: Learning and teaching in cyberspace*. Belmont, CA: Wadsworth/Thomson Learning.

Knowles, M. (1984). *The adult learner: A neglected species* (3rd ed.). Houston, TX: Gulf Publishing.

Knowlton, D. S. (2000, Winter). A theoretical framework for the online classroom: A defense and delineation of a student-centered pedagogy. *Principles of Effective Teaching in the Online Classroom, 84*, 5-14.

Ko, S., & Rossen, S. (2001). *Teaching online: A practical guide*. Boston: Houghton Mifflin.

Krathwohl, D. R., Bloom, B. S., & Masia, B. B. (1964). *Taxonomy of educational objectives: The classification of educational goals* (Handbook II: Affective Domain). New York: David McKay Co. Inc.

Lehigh Carbon Community College. (2006). *Characteristics of successful online learners.* Retrieved August 6, 2006, from http://www.lccc.edu/default.aspx?pageid=470

Moore, M. (1990). Self-directed learning and distance education. *Journal of Distance Education, 1*(1), 7-24.

National Center for Infants. (2002). *Toddlers and families: Zero to three.* Retrieved August 6, 2006, from http://www.brighttots.com/domains.html

Palloff, R. M., & Pratt, K. (2001). *Lessons from the cyberspace classroom: The realities of online teaching.* San Francisco: Jossey-Bass.

Priest, S. (2002). *Technology think tanks in experiential learning*. Unpublished manuscript.

Rager, K. B. (2003). The self-directed learning of women with breast cancer. *Adult Education Quarterly, 53*(4), 277-293.

Simonson, M. (2000 Winter). Making decisions: The use of electronic technology in online classrooms. *Principles of Effective Teaching in the Online Classroom, 84*, 29-34.

Tomei, L. A. (2004). *Learning theories—a primer exercise: An examination of behaviorism, cognitivism, and humanism.* Retrieved August 6, 2006, from http://academics.rmu.edu/%7Etomei/ed711psy/1lngtheo.htm

Tomei, L. A. (2005). *Taxonomy for the technology domain: A classification of educational objectives for the technology domain* (pp. 90-108). Hershey, PA: Idea Group Publishers.

University Affairs. (1996). *Canada's magazine on higher education.* Multimedia makes its mark. Retrieved August 6, 2006, from http://donbergland.com/UAffairs/

Van Dusen, G. C. (1997). The virtual campus: Technology and reform in higher education. *ASHE-ERIC Higher Education Report, 25*(5). Washington, DC: The George Washington University, Graduate School of Education and Human Development.

Vygotsky, L.S. (1978). *Mind and society: The development of higher mental processes*. Cambridge, MA: Harvard University Press.

Wiggins, G., & McTighe, J. (2000). *Understanding by design.* New York: Prentice Hall.

Wikipedia, The Free Encyclopedia. (2006). *E-learning defined.* Retrieved August 6, 2006, from http://en.wikipedia.org/wiki/E-learning

Young, G. (2000). Dispatches from distance education where class is always in session. *The Chronicle of Higher Education, 46*(38), A41-A43, A45.

Chapter VII

Self-Regulation and Online Learning: Theoretical Issues and Practical Challenges to Support Lifelong Learning

Julia M. Matuga, Bowling Green State University, USA

Abstract

This chapter illustrates theoretical issues and practical challenges to support lifelong learning, namely the development and use of self-regulation within online learning environments. Self-regulation, or the ability of students to plan, monitor, and evaluate their own learning is a critical skill for lifelong learning (Longworth & Davies, 1996; Zimmerman, 2002) and online learning (Niemi, Launonen, & Raehalme, 2002). While self-regulation may be and has traditionally been viewed and investigated from a social cognitive theoretical perspective, this chapter proposes that a Vygotskian view of self-regulation may be more applicable to investigating self-regulation within the social and cultural context of online teaching and learning. Case studies, personal essays, and contemporary research focusing on self-regulation in face-to-face and online environments are utilized to examine, discuss, and illustrate key challenges and strategies to support lifelong learning within online environments.

Introduction

For a student to become a lifelong learner, it is critically important that they develop and utilize effective strategies for learning how to learn (Dohmen, 1996; Longworth & Davies, 1996). While other skills and knowledge, like creative thinking or being able to utilize evolving technological resources, may be important for students to engage in learning across the lifespan, the skills and knowledge that underlie one's own ability to effectively learn is perhaps most critical to lifelong learning. Scholars interested in lifelong learning may refer to skills and knowledge about "learning how to learn" in various ways. Self-directed learning (Conceição, 2002), self-knowledge (Longworth & Davis, 1996), and self-management (Longworth & Davies, 1996), for example, have been utilized to describe key processes and skills that are essential to becoming a lifelong learner. However, these terms related to "learning how to learn" fall under the conceptual umbrella within the psychological domain of self-regulation. Self-regulation, or the ability to plan, monitor, and evaluate one's own learning processes and strategies, therefore, is a key psychological feature of lifelong learning (Zimmerman, 2001).

The primary objective of this chapter is to discuss theoretical issues and practical challenges facing online educators to support the development and use of self-regulation by students within their courses. In particular, this chapter proposes a Vygotskian theoretical perspective to ground future investigations concerning self-regulation within online learning environments. A review of the research literature in the area of self-regulation and online learning illuminate gaps in our understanding of how online learning environments impact student self-regulation. Practical instructional strategies from the literature are presented and briefly discussed in an effort to support self-regulatory skills necessary for lifelong learning within online environments. This chapter also suggests a robust research agenda to investigate student development and use of self-regulation within online learning environments.

Self-Regulation and Online Learning

It is probably most accurate to state that self-regulation, as a psychological construct, encompasses categories of strategies that are utilized by students to plan, monitor, and evaluate their own learning (Zimmerman & Martinez-Pons, 1988). Self-regulatory behavior is actually the end result of effectively using a multitude of strategies (Brooks, 1997). For example, developing and utilizing good time management skills (i.e., adequately estimating the time needed for tasks) are very important for a student to effectively plan for their own learning. Therefore, self-regulation is really a collection of strategies that, together, greatly impact student learning.

Self-regulation has been found by researchers to be related to various affective and cognitive outcomes (Zimmerman, 2002; Zimmerman & Schunk, 2001). For instance, self-regulation has been found to influence student achievement within traditional brick-and-mortar educational environments (McCaslin & Hickey, 2001; Winne, 2001; Zimmerman, 1990, 1994, 2001; Zimmerman & Schunk, 2001). Zimmerman and Martinez-Pons (1998) investigated the self-reported use of self-regulation strategies by 80 high school students and found strong correlations with the performance on standardized achievement tests. Researchers (e.g., Clearly & Zimmerman, 2000; Schunk & Zimmerman, 1998) have also found critical differences in planning, monitoring, and evaluative strategies used by students with high and low degrees of self-regulatory expertise. While there appears do be a well-documented relationship between self-regulation and academic achievement within traditional brick-and-mortar classrooms, the relationships between self-regulation, lifelong learning, and online learning deserve further attention.

Brooks (1997) and McLoughlin and Marshall (2000) believe that becoming a self-regulated learner is the first necessary step to becoming a successful online learner. This is understandable given the fact that the "anyplace, anytime" affordance of online education requires that the student, rather than the brick-and-mortar school structure or classroom teacher, determine the place and the time for learning. Learning "how to do school," or mastering the implicit and explicit knowledge and skills needed to be a successful learner, within an online educational environments requires a fundamental shift in skills and knowledge from how students learn "how to do school" within a brick-and-mortar school. Westby (1997) stated that this shift may be like:

> *Coming from cultures that value interdependence, obedience to authority, and learning by watching rather than talking, [students] will be delayed in the development of self-control and self-regulation. Development of these skills will require not only environments that expect such skills but that also foster such skills by providing necessary scaffolding.* (p. 286)

This has several important implications for students and teachers regarding the development and use of self-regulation within online environments. First, just as learners enter an online learning environment with varying degrees of technological skills, learners enter an online learning environment with varying degrees of self-regulatory skills. I would argue, and my colleagues would probably agree, that postsecondary and graduate students in my face-to-face courses have and utilize varying degrees of self-regulatory skills. While some students illustrate a high-degree of self-regulation, others have very few skills or strategies to help themselves effectively regulate their own learning within a face-to-face learning situation, much less an online one.

Often potential online students are asked to take a "Are you a good candidate for online learning?" type of questionnaire before enrolling in a postgraduate online course. These types of questionnaires often try to assess whether or not a student is, indeed, self-regulated "enough" to be a successful online learner. While it is commendable to prescreen students to help them realize the expectations of an online course or to help them identify areas in which they may need help, there is almost an implicit expectation that a student must come to an online learning situation as a somewhat effective self-regulatory learner. To some degree this is very true since students must plan, on their own, when they want to learn. Traditional constraints within face-to-face learning environments that support regulatory strategies, like a standard or set class day and time, may also be viable in an online learning environment (i.e., a regularly scheduled chat). Online students, however, must be self-regulatory "enough" to engage in learning (i.e., get to the computer to log on).

Environmental affordances and constraints of online education have been found to influence the development and use of self-regulation of postsecondary students (Grabe & Grabe, 2001; McMahon, 2002; Nesbit & Winne, 2003; Niemi et al., 2002; Ng, 2002; Olgren, 1998; Song, Singleton, Hill, & Koh, 2004). For example, McManus (2000) found that students who had differing degrees of self-regulatory expertise were able to navigate online course structures of varying linearity. McManus (2000) investigated how the self-regulation abilities of 119 college students impacted their navigation through various online course structures over one semester. While not statistically significant, McManus' findings indicate that students with different levels of self-regulatory expertise seem to learn more effectively in different hypermedia structures. Students with apparently high self-regulatory expertise were not as successful in nonlinear hypermedia environments and students with a low degree of self-regulatory expertise were not as successful in "highly nonlinear environments where they are given too many choices" (McManus, 2000, p. 219). While important, the above mentioned studies are not without limitations and there does seem to be a general lack of empirical investigations examining the impact that online learning has on the development and use of cognitive skills over time. More disconcerting is the general lack of knowledge regarding the development and use of key cognitive and learning processes of K-12 online students.

The critical question of how the development of self-regulation by K-12 students is influenced by online learning is especially important as the number of K-12 students enrolling in online schools increases. This is related, in part, to the rate at which K-12 online schools are becoming available to students and parents as an alternative to traditional, brick-and-mortar schools (Cavanaugh, Gillan, Kromrey, Hess, & Blomeyer, 2004; Mehlinger & Powers, 2002; Zucker & Kozma, 2003). The number of K-12 online schools, or an exact number of students attending these alternative schools, is difficult to determine and remains somewhat elusive due to the rapidly expanding nature of distance education (Cavanaugh et al., 2004; Zucker & Kozma, 2003). A recent report by the National Education Association (2004) estimated that by 2006, a majority of high school students will have had an online course before graduating (Rose, 2001 cited in NEA, 2004). Therefore, it is not inconceivable for future face-to-face and online students to have had an experience as a K-12 online learner. For example, the Michigan State Board of Education will require new high school graduates take at least one online course before they can graduate, part of their rationale for this new high school requirement is to foster lifelong learning (Carnevale, 2006).

What are the long term benefits or detriments of online learning on K-12 students? How are K-12 online students learning (or not learning) self-regulatory skills? Will we find similar or different developmental patterns of self-regulation among K-12 face-to-face and online students? These are critically important questions that impact, not only current generations of online learners, but also online *and* face-to-face teachers. Online educators, which may have pedagogical experience rooted within brick-and-mortar classroom environments, must be knowledgeable about the role self-regulation plays in learning course content and becoming a lifelong learner. Furthermore, and perhaps more critically, online teachers must have the pedagogical skills to be able to scaffold student development and use of *effective* strategies for self-regulation. This is problematic in light of the belief that most teachers within brick-and-mortar educational environments rarely provide support and activities to help students to effectively learn on their own (Zimmerman, Bonner, & Kovach, 1996). Teachers who do exhibit self-regulatory expertise are often not able to make their knowledge and skills explicit for their students (Randi, 2004) and often students are left obtaining skills and strategies for self-regulation on their own. This often leads students to adopt self-regulation strategies that are ineffective. This chapter will investigate and illustrate a few practical strategies and challenges used to support the development and use of self-regulation for planning, monitoring, and evaluating student learning within online learning environments.

It is critically important to note that the appropriation of self-regulation strategies, however, is not sufficient for students to meet achievement goals and outcomes, students must also be motivated to utilize acquired self-regulation strategies. Student perception of themselves as being intrinsically or extrinsically motivated to engage in learning activities within educational environments is known as student goal orientation (Barron & Harackiewicz, 2001; Elliot & Thrash, 2001). Student self-regulation and goal orientation are tightly interwoven constructs that influence student learning and cognition (McWhaw & Abrami, 2001; Pintrich, 1989; Wolters, Yu, & Pintrich, 1996). Essentially, self-regulation addresses the strategies used by students to engage in learning activities (i.e., "skill"), while goal orientation provides a rationale as to why students engage in those activities (i.e., "will"). While it is important to note the connection between motivation and self-regulation, a thorough discussion regarding motivation and lifelong or online learning is beyond the scope of this particular chapter.

What is of particular interest, however, is the role that the social context plays in the development and use of self-regulation as it continues to challenge research findings seeking to clarify critical questions regarding self-regulation. As stated earlier, one limitation of studies investigating self-regulation, that Pintrich and DeGroot (1990) acknowledge, is that empirical findings may be greatly influenced by contextual and task-related variables within the classroom. The influence of the family, various social factors, and culture on children's self-regulated learning has been investigated by researchers (Boekaerts, 1998; Grolnick, Kurowski & Gurland, 1999). Additionally, the development and use of self-regulation of postsecondary students has also been shown to be influenced by technology (Grabe & Grabe, 2001; McMahon, 2002; McManus, 2000; Nesbit & Winne, 2003; Niemi et al., 2002; Ng, 2002; Song et al., 2004; Zimmerman & Tsikalas, 2005). The broader question of how self-regulation develops and is utilized within the context of online learning environments is an important question to explore.

Vygotskian Theory: Self-Regulation and Online Learning

Investigations highlighting the development and use of self-regulation are traditionally grounded in social cognitive learning theory in which researchers tend to focus on the "social influences on children's development of self-regulation" like teacher modeling, student goal-setting, or self-monitoring (Zimmerman, 2002, p. 66). The use of specific self-regulation strategies is also dependent upon what the student views to be salient characteristics of the social context in which strategies are employed. This view of self-regulated learning, that emphasizes "how students selectively activate, alter, or sustain their learning practices in home or school contexts," is known as an interactionist perspective (Zimmerman, 1998, p. 75). This perspective acknowledges that strategy use for self-regulation may vary according to contextual variables (Zimmerman, 1998; Zimmerman & Martinez-Pons, 1988). Instructing students to proactively utilize various strategies to help them actively plan, monitor, and evaluate their own learning, in the hopes that these are adopted by the student to maximize their own learning, is largely "contextual in its application" (Zimmerman, 1998, p. 75).

Investigating cognitive processes within social and cultural contexts is the hallmark of Vygotskian theory (McCaslin & Hickey, 2001; Vygotsky, 1986, 1978). In fact, Vygotsky and Vygotskian scholars have discussed and investigated the important role that private speech, or spontaneous self-directed speech for oneself, plays in the emerging development and use of self-regulation in young children (see Diaz & Berk, 1992). Private speech is utilized by children as a form and function of cognitive and behavioral self-guidance, a tool used to self-regulate (Berk, 1992). While the development and use of private speech as a tool for self-regulation was and is a principle focus of Vygotskian theory and research, few scholars have expanded upon the development and use of self-regulation from a Vygotskian perspective.

McCaslin and Good (1996) and McCaslin and Hickey (2001) have proposed a view of self-regulated learning from a Vygotskian perspective. This view holds that the sociocultural environment plays an important part in regulating student cognition and behavior. The ways in which environmental factors, like instructional support, pedagogical activities, and interpersonal dynamics contribute to self-regulation has been identified as "co-regulation" by McCaslin and Good (1996). They state that the concept of coregulation "integrates the social/instructional environment with the learner in mutual pursuit of a standard of excellence, within a setting of accountability" (p. 660). Their reconceptualization of self-regulation, as coregulation, is based upon the belief that neither learning nor motivation is an "individual struggle," that both are collaborative ones embedded in social educational contexts (McCaslin & Good, 1996). While the end goal may be self-regulation, coregulation connotes that there is a shared responsibility in the development and use of self-regulatory strategies (McCaslin & Good, 1996).

The idea of coregulation is aligned with the Vygotskian (1978, 1986) notion that learning is first and foremost a complex social activity. Perhaps the most important cognitive process from a Vygotskian perspective is internalization. Internalization refers to the transformation of external, or social, practices into "interpsychological functions," or thought by the individual. In other words, internalization refers to the process by which "interpsychological activity becomes intrapsychological activity" (Frawley, 1997, p. 94). It is important to remember that internalization is not a direct translation of social experiences, but refers to the "ingrowing of lived experience into personal meaning" (Frawley, 1997, p. 95).

The reconceptualization of self-regulation as coregulation from a Vygotskian perspective is theoretically different from the more traditional theoretical perspective of self-regulation described by social cognitive theorists. Social cognitive theorists support the use of teacher modeling, student goal setting, and self-monitoring as strategies used to support student development and acquisition of self-regulatory skills (Zimmerman, 2002). These social cognitive instructional methods are not impossible to utilize within an online learning environment. Zimmerman and Tsikalas (2005) utilized these approaches when designing a computer based learning environment to teach early adolescents how to conduct inquiry projects.

The difference between social cognitive and Vygotskian views of self-regulation, however, has practical implications for online instructional strategies. From a Vygotskian perspective, students internalize, from the social and cultural context of the learning environment, effective strategies for self-regulation that are embedded within that social and cultural context. A Vygotskian perspective, for example, supports the use of instructional support, pedagogical activities, and interpersonal dynamics to scaffold the shared development and use of self-regulatory strategies (McCaslin & Good, 1996; McCaslin & Hickey, 2001), these strategies can easily be incorporated within online learning environments. Furthermore, Vygotskian theory provides a robust and promising framework for discussing the role of technology in learning and teaching. Vygotsky's notion of psychological tools is particularly appropriate when discussing the how technology influences and is influenced by cognitive processes (Vygotsky, 1978, 1986). Vygotsky (1978) claimed that language, art, and technology, to name a few examples, are tools that individuals utilize for cognitive and/or behavioral activity. Vygotskian theory has often been utilized as a theoretical foundation to investigate the impact of technology on cognitive processes, and more specifically, how thinking, learning, and instruction influence and are influenced by technological tools (Duffy & Cunningham, 2001).

Supporting Student Self-Regulation within Online Learning Environments

A review of the literature regarding self-regulation illustrates few research-based strategies for supporting and promoting student self-regulation within online environments. Many self-regulation strategies are recommended or suggested for use within online environments based upon their effectiveness within face-to-face learning environments. In the following section of this chapter, the issues and challenges for supporting self-regulatory planning, monitoring, and evaluation within online learning environment are presented for discussion. While not all potential interventions for self-regulation are presented here, those that are have been aligned with a Vygotskian perspective of self-regulation (or coregulation) within online learning environments. The sampled instructional strategies, which may be used by expert or novice online instructors, are grouped and presented in three general categories: instructional support, pedagogical activities, and interpersonal dynamics.

Forethought: Planning Issues and Practical Challenges

The ability of students to identify salient characteristics of a task and environment to inform the selection of effective learning and cognitive strategies is known as self-regulatory planning (McWhaw & Abrami, 2001; Zimmerman, 1998). Promoting students to think about their strategies to plan for effective learning and implementing those strategies before they engage in learning is, perhaps, the most challenging collection of self-regulatory strategies (i.e., like time management) to implement

Table 1. Sample of strategies and research for self-regulatory planning

Online Components	Strategies (Research Support)
Instructional Support	• Provide clear "Rituals of Participation" for all members within the online course. • Promote individual, yet supported, responsibility (Perry & Drummond, 2002).
Pedagogical Activities	• Utilize activities or discussion to clarify student and teacher expectations for learning and teaching. • Break up larger project and assignments (i.e., research papers) into more manageable subassignments. • Ask students to set hierarchical and realistic goals (Schunk & Zimmerman, 1998; Zimmerman, 1998) and post these within online learning communities.
Interpersonal Dynamics	• Ask students or student groups to define rules for participation within the online course. • Provide students with an online "social" area for informal discussions.

within online learning environments. Why? Because, as stated earlier in this chapter, the first step toward planning effectively to learn is for a student to "come" to the learning situation, in other words, to turn on the computer.

However, there may be ways in which an online instructor may use instructional supports, pedagogical activities, and interpersonal dynamics to support and, in some cases promote, the self-regulatory planning of online learners. Table 1 highlights a sample of potential strategies (and in some cases related research) for instructional support, pedagogical activities, and interpersonal dynamics used to promote the development and use of effective planning, or forethought, of learning. While not all those listed in Table 1 will be illustrated in this chapter, a few examples will be used to discuss issues and practical challenges when implementing self-regulatory strategies into online courses: rituals of participation, asking students to design their own project due dates, and asking students or groups to define "rules of participation."

One of the ways in which an individual navigates or tries to make sense of new technological, social, and psychological contexts are what Courtney (2001) called "rituals of participation" (p. 236). These rituals for participation encompass the norms and behavior for participating in cultural activities, like engagement in online learning. Earlier when discussing learning "how to do school" the importance of mastering explicit and implicit knowledge needed to be a successful face-to-face students are learned within the context of the brick-and-mortar school. There may be, what you might call, a cross cultural interference between how students conceptualize "doing school" within face-to-face environments and how this concept is challenged and, by necessity, altered within online teaching and learning environments.

Educational environments that promote individual, yet supported responsibility for self-regulation, have been found to help students plan for their own learning (Perry & Drummond, 2002). In my own online classes, one of the ways that I try to hold individuals responsible for their own learning is establish clear and consistent "rituals of participation." I try to do this in several ways in the belief that it does help online students with self-regulatory planning. First, I try to make the overall course structure rhythmic, mimicking, in some sense, the rhythm of face-to-face schooling. My students rarely have to be online at the "same place/same time" as rarely use synchronous discussions (i.e., chats). I do, however, rely heavily on small group, asynchronous threaded discussions as an instructional strategy in my online graduate courses. For many of my online students, this is their first online class and they enter the class extremely anxious. I try to make discussions and assignments due at the same time over the course of the semester. Sunday at midnight, for example, seems to work the best for students in my online courses, as most of them are K-12 classroom teachers. Consistent due dates for discussions and assignments appear to help them establish, on their own, an effective pattern for participating in online learning that works for them. Preliminary results, from a small study currently in progress, indicate that out of 22 graduate students enrolled in one online class, 16 students had established a pattern of participation (posting and responding on the same day) by the fourth week of class. While the instructional support and design, like the consistent due dates for discussions and activities, for example, may have factored into this finding, interpersonal dynamics (as we will discuss in a moment) may have also contributed to this preliminary finding.

A pedagogical activity that has been found by researchers within face-to-face environments to aid in the development of self-regulatory planning is asking students to set hierarchical learning goals (Schunk & Zimmerman, 1998; Zimmerman, 1998). Within an online course structure, students may have a common area to share and/or monitor their personal goals throughout the semester. An instructor may also ask students to break up a larger project or assignment, like a research paper, into more manageable subassignments to help with self-regulatory planning within an online course. A colleague of mine asks students within her face-to-face class to develop a self-regulation plan at the beginning of the Educational Psychology course that she teaches, this plan focuses upon specific student behaviors and learning strategies. These self-regulation plans are used by students to self-assess their progress over the course of the semester. While these students are also learning about the concept of self-regulation by actually participating in self-regulation, it is important to note that self-regulatory skills could and should be incorporated into pedagogical activities within online courses.

As stated earlier, the primary instructional strategy that I utilize in my course is small group, asynchronous threaded discussions. The framework for discussions in my class is based upon the concept of collaborative inquiry (Bray, Lee, Smith, & Yorks, 2002). Collaborative inquiry "is a process consisting of repeated episodes of reflection and action through which a group of peers strives to answer a question of importance to them" (Bray et al., 2000, p. 6). Employing this method in my online class requires students to utilize storytelling, critical reflection, and questioning and feedback to explore how learning theory and research applies to their own classroom practice. For the weekly-required online discussions, students are required not only to post a response to questions related to course content but also to respond to peers within their small groups. These groups are kept intact the entire semester. To facilitate discussion and to help with rituals of participation, the due dates for these discussions are kept consistent. Students typically have one week to post their response to the original question and respond to peers.

One of the very first online activities that I ask students to complete, after posting introductions to each other, is very important to helping students plan for their participation in the course. First, groups are asked to negotiate and define rules for participating within their small groups. Discussion requires students to be interdependent within their group; they have to post and respond to others within a set time frame, I ask them to negotiate and create a "group" plan for participation. Students are also asked to establish criteria for peer responses, based upon what and how they themselves would like to receive feedback. In addition to these rules for participation, I also suggest that they generate a new "name" for the group. This final activity seems to establish a group dynamic that helps students plan for their own participation in the course and an identity that holds them accountable to each other within the group.

Performance: Monitoring Issues and Practical Challenges

Effort, on the part of the student, "to observe themselves as they evaluate information about specific personal processes or actions that affect their learning and achievement in school is called self-regulatory monitoring" (Zimmerman & Paulsen, 1995, p. 14). Students who have effective self-monitoring strategies are able to evaluate their own progress towards an established goal, making appropriate strategy changes as they proceed to regulate their learning effectively (Zimmerman & Paulson, 1995).

It has been argued by Courtney (2001) that students do not always develop effective monitoring strategies within traditional learning environments because "the teacher remains at the center of all pedagogic activity—figuratively if not literally—and how student activity in the pursuit of learning must always refer back to the teacher's actions" (p. 239). While this pattern of activity is interwoven into the fabric of

Table 2. Sample of strategies and research for self-regulatory monitoring

Online Components	Strategies (Research Support)
Instructional Support	• Provide students with a common area to "ask" questions. • Provide students with clear and specific feedback on their progress.
Pedagogical Activities	• Ask students to reflect in an online "Learning Diary" or Reflection log to self-record their own learning (Brooks, 1997; Shapiro, 1984). • Ask students to complete reflection papers concerning what they know and do not know about course content (Zimmerman, 2002).
Interpersonal Dynamics	• Generate discussion questions in online groups to clarify comprehension of course content (Zimmerman & Paulson, 1995). Participate in group reflection and critique regarding student learning in the course.

traditional classrooms, moving online alters the role of the teacher monitoring student learning and, perhaps more interestingly, the teacher monitoring his or her own teachning, and the role of each participant has in monitoring the activity of the other. One of the most prevalent ways in which a student views himself or herself as a learner, for example, is in comparison to others.

Online teaching environments often do not present students with the traditional social and environmental cues that they utilize within face-to-face environments to gage their own progress in a course in relation to others. While online pedagogy certainly has many advantages, one disadvantage, from a student's perspective, is being unable to assess how well they are doing in an online course in relation to other students (Matuga, 2001). A sample of strategies to support self-regulatory monitoring within online courses is presented in Table 2.

Instructional supports which could be utilized within online courses to help students monitor their own learning are creating a common area for students to ask course related questions and providing students with clear and specific feedback on their progress in class. Having a common area to "Ask the Teacher" and strongly encourage all students in the course to consistently use this course feature could help self-regulatory monitoring. For example, often online students will contact the teacher directly when they have a question about a course related activity or assignment. At least in my experience, this was the case when I first started teaching online. Even with face-to-face experience as a K-12 and postsecondary teacher I did not anticipate the sheer volume of questions from students sent directly to me via e-mail. I learned, rather quickly, to set up a common question area (somewhat different than the more proactive FAQ area which I also use) for students to ask course related questions and, perhaps more critically, rather strictly to enforce the use of it. This "Ask the Teacher" feature may replicate the interactions between the instructor and the entire class, when those housekeeping questions are asked. This may provide students with a method to evaluate where they are in relation to other students based upon the type of question posted. While there is no empirical evidence to support that this strategy supports self-regulatory monitoring, it may provide online students with instructional support that acts as a mirror through which they may observe their own understanding of activities and assignments in relation to others.

Zimmerman and Paulson (1995) described different pedagogical activities by which teachers may scaffold student development of effective monitoring strategies: baseline, structured, independent, and self-regulated monitoring. In the beginning phase, teachers may provide students with rudimentary monitoring activities, such as keeping a reflective journal or self-assessments. Online instructors may ask students to keep track of their own learning in a "Learning Diary," reflection log, or even a blog. Research has shown by asking students to simply keeping track of their own learning aids in the promotion of self-regulatory monitoring (Brooks, 1997; Finnish Virtual University, 2005; Shapiro, 1984).

In the second phase, an instructor may refine more general pedagogical strategies to encompass specific goals for activity, like providing students questions that will clarify comprehension. Zimmerman (2002) suggests that asking students to complete reflection papers about what they know, and perhaps more importantly, what they *do not* know is an effective way to clarify a student's comprehension of a topic and aids in self-monitoring. An instructor would slowly transfer monitoring responsibilities to the student in the next two phases outlined by Zimmerman and Paulson (1995): independent monitoring (have students generate their own strategies for specific activities) and self-regulated self-monitoring (have them try to develop monitoring strategies on their own for another activity). These phases may also be used within online learning environments to scaffold the development of effective monitoring strategies to be used in pedagogical activities by teachers to facilitate student learning.

There are a few strategies that utilize interpersonal dynamics to facilitate the development and use of monitoring strategies for self-regulation within face-to-face environments that can easily migrate to online environments. First, asking students to generate critical thinking or reflective questions for online discussions may help students clarify their own comprehension of course content (Zimmerman & Paulson, 1995). In the small group discussions that I utilize in my online classes mentioned earlier in this chapter, I begin the semester by providing students with the discussion questions then slowly transfer the responsibility of creating critical and reflective questions to students. I also include periodic formative group self-assessments, asking students to reflect and critique their own and their group progress towards learning in the course, revisiting their rules of participation.

Self-Reflection: Evaluation Issues and Practical Challenges

When a student reflects upon performance using effective evaluation strategies, a student may learn to improve performance and "proactively select, structure, and even create advantageous learning environments" (Zimmerman, 2001, p. 5). Students who are effective self-regulatory learners are able to evaluate their personal goals for learning in relation to the strategies that they used rather than their own ability (Zimmerman, 2002). In this way, they are able to utilize their own evaluation of their learning to plan for the use of more effective strategies in the future. Self-regulation is a critical vehicle for students taking responsibility of evaluating their own learning (Ames & Gahagan, 1995). At this point it is also important to note that the development and use of self-regulatory skills and strategies is actually a cyclical process of forethought, performance, and self-reflection (Zimmerman, 2000). The importance of self-reflection in the self-regulatory cycle cannot be understated. Furthermore, while supporting self-regulatory planning and monitoring within online environments may be challenging, incorporating self-reflection into instructional supports, pedagogical activities, and interpersonal dynamics is critical and, I would argue, as a hallmark of effective courses whether courses are face-to-face or online ones (see Table 3).

Self-reflection, as a critical component of both summative and formative evaluation, can be incorporated into the structure of a course via instructional supports in a variety of ways (Matuga, 2005). For example, instructors may embed self-assessments throughout the structure of the course providing students to periodically evaluate their own learning. Beatty, Wilson, and Branon (2001) found that embedding self-assessments within an online course structure allowed students to review and reflect upon how well they are learning the course material. One strategy, grounded in social cognitive learning theory, that may be particularly valuable to "borrow" here would be modeling. For example, in the structure of my course I provide students with my own reflections concerning course content. In my "Teacher Notes," I provide students with a personal and evaluative narrative of the ways in which I relate course material to my own teaching and various strengths and weaknesses of the theories and research we are investigating together. On average, 97 students (85%) in my classes in which I have used "Teacher Notes" strongly agreed that they helped their own understanding of the topics covered in class. And, 68 students (60%) stated in course evaluations that they read the "Teacher Notes" first to provide them with guidelines or questions to guide their own engagement with the assigned readings, course activities, or small group discussions.

Student-constructed assessments or reflective electronic portfolios (McMahon, 2002) are beneficial pedagogical activities to utilize to encourage online students to self-reflect on their own learning. Additionally, the use of reflection writing or

Table 3. Sample of strategies and research for self-regulatory evaluation

Online Components	Strategies (Research Support)
Instructional Support	• Provide students with personal and evaluative comments on course material or activities ("Teacher Notes"). • Embed self-assessments throughout the course structure (Beatty, Wilson & Branon, 2001).
Pedagogical Activities	• Ask students to evaluate their own learning or construct course assessments. • Ask students construct electronic portfolios (McMahon, 2002) and/or provide feedback to other students' portfolios. • Ask students to keep an online journal (Andrusyszyn & Davie, 1997; King & Rocco, 2006).
Interpersonal Dynamics	• Provide opportunities for students to provide peers with feedback on learning outcomes/goals or projects and assignments.

papers to explore student understandings is another popular pedagogical activity widely utilized in both face-to-face and online learning environments (Buehl, 1996; Reed & Koliba, 1995). Another fairly common strategy to encourage self-reflection within online courses is interactive journaling (Andrusyszyn & Davie, 1997; King & LaRocco, 2006). There are two primary benefits of online journaling as compared to traditional journaling, according to King and LaRocco (2006). First, online journals are far less cumbersome than paper journals. Second, it is much easier for a teacher to access and provide feedback and comments when journals are accessible electronically. These are just a few pedagogical activities that online instructors may consider when designing online learning environments to support the development and use of self-regulation for evaluation.

Utilizing interpersonal dynamics to provide support for students to develop and use self-reflection to evaluate their own learning can be done in various ways as well. One strategy is to provide students with opportunities to provide peers with feedback on learning outcomes (defined in planning activities) or on class projects and assignments. One activity that I ask my online students to participate in, for example, is a critique of final research papers within their groups. Not only are students asked to provide summative evaluative comments to each other, but they are also asked to provide strategies and helpful hints to other students for future research projects and further learning regarding course topics. In this manner, the interpersonal dynamics of each group members aid in providing alternative perspectives to help each student with future learning activities.

Conclusion and Future Empirical Directions

As a critical component of lifelong learning, self-regulation and how it influences and is influenced by learning within online learning environments deserves more attention by researchers. While there is a general lack of research regarding online teaching and learning, self-regulation should be a priority for robust research agendas due to its role in successful online teaching and lifelong learning. Specifically, the lack of research on K-12 online learning, the "no significant difference" phenomenon, and lack of longitudinal studies represent significant challenges to our knowledge about online teaching and learning and indicate future trends for empirical investigations concerning online learning.

There may be a variety of factors that have influenced the lack of research on student learning within K-12 online environments (see Zucker & Kozma, 2003). One possible explanation is that research concerning online education has largely been restricted to investigating the cognitive processes and learning of postsecondary students (McIsaac & Gunawardena, 2001; Ng, 2002; Song et al., 2004; Zucker & Kozma, 2003). Empirical investigations and programs of research within the realm of online education appear to be based on the supposition: "distance education serves mainly adults" (McIsaac & Gunawardena, 2001, p. 423). Therefore, it is possible that attention has been limited to postsecondary online learners and has not yet been expanded to encompass the population of learners within K-12 online education (Zucker & Kozma, 2003) or investigate the different needs and characteristics of K-12, postsecondary, and nontraditional students. Future research on self-regulation within online learning environments should encompass K-12 students, especially as online courses become available for high school students.

Second, the study design and methodology employed by many empirical investigations within online educational environments has also been criticized. The validity of these criticisms has contributed to a perception that there is a lack of empirically sound findings to contribute to our understanding of student learning and cognition within online educational environments (Zucker & Kozma, 2003). For example, a number of empirical investigations of online learning have sought to compare postsecondary student cognition and learning within traditional, face-to-face, and online educational environments (see Bernard, Abrami, Lou, et al., 2004). Likewise, the few studies that have looked at K-12 education have sought to compare and contrast learning outcomes of students within online environments with students within traditional brick-and-mortar environments (Cavanaugh et al., 2004). Many of these studies report "no significant differences" found between learning online and in traditional classroom environments (Cavanaugh et al., 2004). These studies have been viewed as problematic for a number of reasons, most notably, a lack of ecological validity (see Bernard, Abrami, Lou, et al., 2004). There is little ecological validity in comparing two environments (face-to-face and online) that have very different affordances and constraints, making it difficult to compare student learning and cognition with achievement outcomes.

Empirical studies regarding student learning and cognition within postsecondary online education have also been criticized for focusing on relatively short-term interventions involving a small number of students (Cohen & Ellis, 2003; McIsaac & Gunawardena, 2001). In other words, empirical investigations regarding online teaching and learning tend to focus on the learning and cognition of students while they were enrolled in one particular online class over the course of one quarter or semester, typically at postsecondary institutions. Longitudinal studies, investigating the development and use of self-regulation of online students over time and, perhaps, within multiple online learning environments, are critical to understanding the impact online course structure and instructional strategies have on lifelong learning.

The empirical methods employed in designing single cohort, short-term studies have also been criticized by McIsaac and Gunawardena (2001) for not utilizing randomized sampling of participants. In addition, it has been noted that these studies rarely contribute to systematic programs of empirical research (McIsaac & Gunawardena, 2001). There are many potential avenues of research suggested in this chapter that will contribute to our understanding of self-regulation, an important and critical aspect of online learning.

In conclusion, this chapter presents a theoretical foundation for self-regulation and online learning grounded in Vygotskian theory. This framework has potential for robust research agendas investigating the potential use of instructional supports, pedagogical activities, and interpersonal dynamics within online learning environments to support student development and use of self-regulation. Granted, the research concerning the development and use of self-regulation within online learning environments is limited and few insights can be made from currently available empirical investigations within online learning environments. It is still important to note that additional variables that impact self-regulation, like individual differences, communication competence, and motivation, for example, have been set aside in this chapter. For example, McSporran and Young (2001) found that women and older students were more successful online learners than males and younger students. These age and gender related differences in self-regulation within online environments warrant further investigation.

In addition to investigations regarding individual differences in self-regulation and suggested avenues for exploration mentioned above, additional research regarding what are the most effective instructional supports, pedagogical activities, and interpersonal dynamics to foster the development and use of self-regulated learning are necessary within K-12 *and* postsecondary online learning environments. Studies investigating how the affordances and constraints within online learning environments impacts self-regulation of students over time is also critically important given the potential popularity of K-12 online schooling. The opportunity to explore self-regulation within online learning environments can only provide insights into one of the most critical skills for lifelong learning, *learning how to learn*.

References

Ames, C. K., & Gahagan, H. S. (1995). Self-reflection: Supporting students in taking ownership of evaluation. In C. Dudley-Marling & D. Searle (Eds.), *Who owns learning? Questions of autonomy, choice, and control* (pp. 52-66). Portsmouth, NH: Heinemann.

Andrusyszyn, M. A., & Davie, L. (1997). Facilitating reflection through interactive journal writing in an online graduate course: A qualitative study. *Journal of Distance Education, 12*(2). Retrieved August 10, 2006, from http://cade.icaap.org/vol12.1/andrusyszyndavie.html

Barron, K. E., & Harackiewicz, J. M. (2001). Achievement goals and optimal motivation: Testing multiple goal models. *Journal of Personality and Social Psychology, 80*(5), 706-722.

Beatty, B. J., Wilson, J., & Branon, R. (2001). Embedded self-assessments in executive education courses: Improving participant learning and perceptions of course quality. In *Proceedings of WEBNET 2001*(pp. 60-61). Orlando, Florida.

Berk, L. E. (1992). Children's private speech: An overview of theory and the status of research. In R. M. Diaz & L. E. Berk (Eds.), *Private speech: From social interaction to self-regulation* (pp. 17-54). Hillsdale, NJ: Erlbaum.

Bernard, R. M., Abrami, P. C., Lou, Y., et al. (2004). How does distance education compare with classroom instruction? A meta-analysis of the empirical literature. *Review of Educational Research, 74*(3), 379-439.

Boekaerts, M. (1998). Do culturally rooted self-controls affect students' conceptualization of control over learning? *Educational Psychologist, 33*, 87-108.

Bray, J. N., Lee, J., Smith, L. L., & Yorks, L. (2000). *Collaborative inquiry: Action, reflection,and meaning making*. Thousand Oaks, CA: Sage.

Brooks, D. W. (1997). *Web teaching: A guide to designing interactive teaching for the World Wide Web.* New York: Plenum.

Buehl, D. (1996). Improving students' learning strategies through self-reflection. *Teaching and Change, 3*(3), 227-243.

Carnevale, D. (2006, January 6). Michigan considers requiring high-school students to take at least one online course. *The Chronicle of Higher Education, 52*(18), A45.

Cavanaugh, C., Gillan, K. J., Kromrey, J., Hess, M., & Blomeyer, R. (2004). *The effects of distance education on K-12 student outcomes: A meta-analysis.* (Tech. Rep. No. ED-01-CO-0011). Naperville, IL: Learning Point Associates, North Central Regional Educational Laboratory & Institute of Learning Sciences. Retrieved August 10, 2006, from http://www.learningpt.org

Clearly, T., & Zimmerman, B. J. (2000). Self-regulation and differences during athletic practice by experts, non-experts, and novices. *Journal of Applied Sports Psychology, 13*, 61-82.

Cohen, M. S., & Ellis, T. J. (2003, November 5-8). *Predictors of success: A longitudinal study of threaded discussion forums.* Paper presented at the 33rd ASEE/IEE Frontiers in Education Conference, Boulder, CO.

Conceição, S. (2002). The sociocultural implications of learning and teaching in cyberspace. In M. V. Alfred (Ed.), *Learning and sociocultural contexts: Implications for adults, community, and workplace education* (pp. 37-45). San Francisco: Jossey-Bass.

Courtney, S. (2001). Technology and culture of teaching and learning. *To Improve the Academy, 19*, 232-249.

Diaz, R. M., & Berk, L. E. (Eds). (1992). *Private speech: From social interaction to self-regulation.* Hillsdale, NJ: Erlbaum.

Dohmen, G. (1996). *Lifelong learning: Guidelines for a modern education policy.* Bonn: Federal Ministry of Education, Science, Research and Technology.

Duffy, T. M., & Cunningham, D. J. (2001). Constructivism: Implications for the design and delivery of instruction. In D. H. Jonassen (Ed.), *Handbook of research for educational communications and technology* (pp. 170-198). Mahwah, NJ: Lawrence Erlbaum.

Elliot, A. J., & Thrash, T. M. (2001). Achievement goals and the hierarchical model of achievement motivation. *Educational Psychology Review, 13*(2), 139-156.

Finnish Virtual University. (2005). *The IQ form: A pilot project from the Finnish Virtual University.* Retrieved August 10, 2006, from http://www.edu.helsinki.fi/iqform/default_eng.htm

Frawley, W. (1997). *Vygotsky and cognitive science: Language and the unification of the social and computational mind.* Cambridge, MA: Harvard University Press.

Grabe, M., & Grabe, C. (2001). *Integrating technology for meaningful learning.* Boston: Houghton Mifflin.

Grolnick, W. S., Kurowski, C. O., & Gurland, S. T. (1999). Family processes and the development of children's self-regulation. *Educational Psychologist, 34*, 3-14.

King, B. F., & LaRocco, J. D. (2006). E-journaling: A strategy to support student reflection and understanding. *Current Issues in Education*, *9*(4). Retrieved August 10, 2006, from http://cie.ed.asu.edu/volume9/number4/

Longworth, N., & Davies, W. K. (1996). *Lifelong learning: New vision, new implications, new roles for people, organizations, nations, and communities in the 21st century*. London: Kogan.

Matuga, J. M. (2001). Electronic pedagogical practice: The art and science of teaching and learning on-line [special issue]. *Educational Technology & Society, 4*(3), 77-84.

Matuga, J. M. (2005). The role of assessment and evaluation in context: Pedagogical alignment in online courses. In D. D. Williams (Vol. Ed.), S. L. Howell & M. Hricko (Series Eds.), *Online assessment, measurement and evaluation* (pp. 316-330). Hershey, PA: Information Science Publishing.

McCaslin, M., & Good, T. L. (1996). The informal curriculum. In D. C. Berliner & R. C. Calfee (Eds.), *Handbook of educational psychology* (pp. 622-672). New York: Simon & Schuster Macmillian.

McCaslin, M., & Hickey, D. T. (2001). Self-regulated learning and academic achievement: A Vygotskian view. In B. J. Zimmerman & D. H. Schunk (Eds.), *Self-regulated learning and academic achievement: Theoretical perspectives* (pp. 227-252). Mahwah, NJ: Erlbaum.

McIsaac, M. S., & Gunawardena, C. N. (2001). Distance education. In D. H. Jonassen (Ed.), *Handbook of research for educational communications and technology* (pp. 403-438). Mahwa, NJ: Erlbaum.

McLoughlin, C., & Marshall, L. (2000, February 2-4). Scaffolding: A model for learner support in an online teaching environment. In A. Herrmann & M. M. Kulski (Eds), *Flexible Futures in Tertiary Teaching, Proceedings of the 9th Annual Teaching Learning Forum*. Perth, Australia: Curtin University of Technology. Retrieved August 10, 2006, from http://lsn.curtin.edu.au/tlf/tlf2000/mcloughlin2.htm

McMahon, M. (2002, July). *Designing an on-line environment to scaffold self-regulation*. Paper presented at the Annual Meeting of the Higher Education Research and Development Society of Australasia, Perth, Australia. Retrieved August 10, 2006, from http://www.ecu.edu.au/conferences/herdsa/main/papers/ref/pdf/McMahon.pdf

McManus, T. F. (2000). Individualizing instruction in a web-based hypermedia learning environment: Nonlinearity, advanced organizers, and self-regulated learners. *Journal of Interactive Learning Research, 11*(3), 219-251.

McSporran, M., & Young, S. (2001). Does gender matter in online learning? *Association for Learning Technology Journal*. Retrieved August 10, 2006, from http://hyperdisc.unitec.ac.nz/research/ALTJpaper_9.pdf

McWhaw, K., & Abrami, P. C. (2001). Student goal orientation and interest: Effects on students' use of self-regulated learning strategies. *Contemporary Educational Psychology, 26*, 311-329.

Mehlinger, H. D., & Powers, S. M. (2002). *Technology and teacher education: A guide for educators and policymakers*. Boston: Houghton Mifflin.

National Education Association (NEA). (2004). Guide to online high school courses. Retrieved August 10, 2006, from http://home.nea.org/www/htmlmail.cfm?type=printer

Nesbit, J. C., & Winne, P. H. (2003). Self-regulated inquiry with networked resources. *Canadian Journal of Learning and Teaching, 29*(3). Retrieved August 10, 2006, from http://www.cjlt.ca/content/vol29.3/cjlt29-3_art5.html

Niemi, H., Launonen, A., & Raehalme, O. (2002, September). T*owards self-regulation and social navigation in virtual learning spaces*. Paper presented at the European Conference on Educational Research, Lisbon, Spain. Retrieved August 10, 2006, from http://www.leeds.ac.uk/educol/documents/00002589.htm

Ng., C. (2002, December). *Relations between motivational goals, beliefs, strategy use and learning outcomes among university students in a distance learning mode: A longitudinal study*. Paper presented at the Annual Conference of Australian Association for Research in Education, Brisbane, Australia. Retrieved August 10, 2006, from http://www.aare.edu.au/02oao.ng02462.htm

Olgren, C. H. (1998). Improving learning outcomes: The effects of learning strategies and motivation. In C. C. Gibson (Ed.), *Distance learners in higher education: Institutional responses for quality outcomes* (pp. 77-96). Madison, WI: Atwood Publishing.

Perry, N., & Drummond, L. (2002). Helping young students become self-regulated researchers and writers. *The Reading Teacher, 56*, 298-310.

Pintrich, P. R. (1989). The dynamic interplay of student motivation and cognition in the college classroom. In C. Ames & M. Maeher (Eds.), *Advances in motivation and achievement: Vol. 6. Motivation enhancing environments* (pp. 117-160). Greenwich, CT: JAI Press.

Pintrich, P. R., & DeGroot, E. V. (1990). Motivational and self-regulated learning components of classroom academic performance. *Journal of Educational Psychology, 82*(1), 33-40.

Randi, J. (2004). Teachers as self-regulated learners. *Teacher College Record, 106*(9), 1825-1853.

Reed, J., & Koliba, C. (1995). *Facilitating reflection: A manual for leaders and educators.* Retrieved August 10, 2006, from http://www.uvm.edu/~dewey/reflection_manual/

Schunk, D. H., & Zimmerman, B. J. (1998). *Self-regulated learning: From teaching to self-reflective practice*. New York: Guilford.

Shapiro, E. S. (1984). Self-monitoring procedures. In T. H. Ollendick & M. Hersen (Eds.), *Child behavior assessment: Principles and procedures* (pp. 148-165). New York: Pergamon Press.

Song, L., Singleton, E. S., Hill, J. R., & Koh, M. H. (2004). Improving online learning: Student perceptions of useful and challenging characteristics. *Internet and Higher Education, 7*, 59-70.

Vygotsky, L. V. (1978). *Mind in society: The development of higher psychological processes*. Cambridge, MA: Harvard University Press.

Vygotksy, L. V. (1986). *Thought and language*. Cambridge, MA: The MIT Press.

Westby, C. (1997). There's more to passing than knowing the answers. *Language, Speech, and Hearing Services in Schools, 28*(3), 274-286.

Winne, P. H. (2001). Self-regulated learning viewed from models of information processing. In B. J. Zimmerman & D. H. Schunk (Eds.), *Self-regulated learning and academic achievement: Theoretical perspectives* (pp. 153-190). Mahwah, NJ: Erlbaum.

Wolters, C. A., Yu, S. L., & Pintrich, P. R. (1996). The relation between goal orientation and students' motivational beliefs and self-regulated learning. *Learning and Individual Differences, 8*(3), 211-238.

Zimmerman, B. J. (1990). Self-regulated learning and academic achievement: An overview. *Educational Psychologist, 25*(1), 3-17.

Zimmerman, B. J. (1994). Dimensions of academic self-regulation: A conceptual framework for education. In D. H. Schunk & B. J. Zimmerman (Eds.), *Self-regulation of learning and performance: Issues and educational applications* (pp. 3-19). Hillsdale, NJ: LEA.

Zimmerman, B. J. (1998). Academic studying and the development of personal skill: A self-regulatory perspective. *Educational Psychologist, 33*(2/3), 73-86.

Zimmerman, B. J. (2001). Theories of self-regulated learning and academic achievement: An overview and analysis. In B. J. Zimmerman & D. H. Schunk (Eds.), *Self-regulated learning and academic achievement: Theoretical perspectives* (pp. 1-38). Mahwah, NJ: Erlbaum.

Zimmerman, B. J. (2002). Becoming a self-regulated learner: An overview. *Theory into Practice, 41*(2), 64-72.

Zimmerman, B. J., Bonner, S., & Kovach, R. (1996). *Developing self-regulated learners: Beyond achievement to self-efficacy.* Washington, DC: American Psychological Association.

Zucker, A., & Kozma, R. (2003). *The virtual high school: Teaching generation V.* New York: Teachers College Press.

Zimmerman, B. J., & Marinez-Pons, M. (1988). Construct validation of a strategy model of student self-regulated learning. *Journal of Educational Psychology, 80*(3), 284-290.

Zimmerman, B. J., & Paulsen, A. S. (1995). Self-monitoring during collegiate studying: An invaluable tool for academic self-regulation. *New Directions for Teaching and Learning, 63*, 13-27

Zimmerman, B. J., & Schunk, D. H. (Eds.). (2001). *Self-regulated learning and academic achievement: Theoretical perspectives.* Mahwah, NJ: Erlbaum.

Zimmerman, B. J., & Tsikalas, K. E. (2005). Can computer-based learning environments be used as self-regulatory tools to enhance learning? *Educational Psychologist, 40*(4), 267-271.

Section IV

Tech-Knowledge and Communication Technologies for Lifelong Learning

Chapter VIII

Building Powerful Online Synchronous Communications: A Framework for Lifelong Learning in Distance Education

Volkan T. Yuzer, Anadolu University, Turkey

Gulsun Kurubacak, Anadolu University, Turkey

Abstract

Digital citizens have been using online synchronous communications (OSCs)-based milieus since the last decade. OSCs can provide these online communities with new and challenging opportunities via instant interactions, which are OSCs' dominant nature, in lifelong learning. OSCs, therefore, help online learners, as lifelong learners, and communication workers (online communication designers, media coordinators, online managers, technology-support staff, multimedia designers, etc.) understand this milieu better to have more benefits. In this study, media richness theory and four cultural issues (biases, stereotypes, ethics and values) are discussed together to highlight the communicational characters of the OSCs. To utilize the communicational prospects of OSCs, this communication theory provides communication workers with useful guidelines related to cultural issues, which expand on future directions for OSCs. Finally, the researchers develop a framework according to the strategies of media richness theory, which declares that there must be a fit between technology and communication structures to reduce task-related ambiguity.

Introduction

Online synchronous communications (OSCs) in distance education have the potential to deliver global knowledge around the world. The location independent communication opportunities become a consequence of the philosophy of dynamic and democratic lifelong learning. OSCs are therefore powerful means to generate logical online possibilities and flexible contents. In order to build appropriate flexible lifelong content for OSCs, professionals and learning communities must focus on methods, techniques, and principles, as well as barriers to share and exchange knowledge in distance education. According to the philosophy of lifelong learning, a framework can design and maintain effective OSCs thus providing professionals and community with flexible collaboration contents in distance education. Besides, this framework can help them become engaged citizens, informed individuals, and dynamic members in their online society to improve their communication styles and abilities with each other. However, there are limited research studies and theoretical articles about online learners' communication styles and abilities to assist lifelong learning with real-life experiences through OSCs. Therefore, this topic will bring a new ground by addressing key questions about learners' *communication styles* and *abilities*, as well as about OSCs and real-life experiences. Based on the main purpose of this chapter and the concerns discussed above, the key inquiries in the study reported in the present chapter are as follows:

1. To what extent do online learners' skills continue to improve their communication styles and abilities with OSCs?
2. What kind of online learning experiences are associated with developing communication styles and abilities with OSCs?
3. What are online learners' patterns of participation in communication styles and abilities with OSCs in distance education?
4. What is the impact of communication styles and abilities with OSCs on their lifelong learning outcomes?

The authors will build a framework based on the constructivist OSCs approach to improve the learners' communication styles and abilities related with real-world problems. In this case, online communications must be an active process to obtain, evaluate, and produce knowledge. That is, individuals can become active participants in their knowledge constructions rather than passive receptacles. In this constructivist milieu, these learners can work on complex lifelong learning projects and build their own understandings with their communication styles.

Background

The main purpose of this chapter is to discuss the design principles of OSCs in distance learning and to introduce a framework about how to design OSCs for lifelong learning. There is an urgent need to investigate clearly how to produce collaborations among online professionals, communities, and global resources with OSCs. This framework will help online professionals and community understand how to manage their communication roles, and to play important roles to integrate new digital technologies in their lifelong learning activities with OSCs. Further, this theoretical framework will have multidimensions to design OSCs for lifelong learning in distance education to share and exchange knowledge among online professionals, learners, and community, and to develop a strategic technology plan to produce successful online synchronous environments. OSCs will help online communication designers find creative solutions to build quality online communication contents based on the needs and expectations of individuals from around the world. This framework will also show the new ways of online communication styles and abilities and organize multicultural global resources and the various strategies, principles, and suggestions of lifelong learning by respecting culturally diverse people via OSCs.

The OSC evaluation can help online communication designers understand how to manage their role tasks, give careful attentions to diverse online community, and understand their important roles to integrate new digital technologies in their activities via OSCs. However, involving people to become involved in the evaluation process is often difficult. Therefore, this chapter addresses the Media Richness Theory as the theoretical and philosophical foundation of the evaluation of OSCs. This theory can help online communication workers be aware of the strengths and limitations of OSCs.

Media Richness Theory

Media richness theory is based on contingency theory and information processing theory (Galbraith, 1977). The first proponents of the theory were Daft and Lengel

(1984). The theory of media richness, one of the most widely used media theories, asserts that task performance is improved when task information needs are matched to a medium's richness or its "capacity to facilitate shared meaning" (Daft, Lengel, & Trevino, 1987, p. 358). Media richness theory points out that media vary in certain uniqueness that affects personal ability to communicate rich information. According to Daft and Lengel (1986), information richness can be defined as the ability of information to change understanding within a time interval; and, media capable of sending *rich* information are better suited to tasks with equivocal information. Moreover, they mentioned that this theory theorizes which media should prove most effective in what situations. Based on this concern, this theory does not focus on conjecturing how managers *choose* media. Furthermore, according to Daft and Lengel (1986), the theory of *media richness* explains the impact of various types of media demonstrating that these are the basic foundations of interactive online communications. According to this theory, the various communications media differ in richness. Rich communications media allow the transmission of a multiplicity of cues, provide immediate feedback, allow communications with both natural language and numbers, and facilitate the personal focus of messages.

Kydd and Ferry (1991) highlight that existing communications media can be viewed on a continuum of rich to lean, with face-to-face communications being the richest, followed by electronic meeting systems, video-conferencing, and audio-conferencing, with electronic mail, voice mail, and computer conferencing being the leanest. In other words, it is vague that the use of richer media improves the performance of equivocal or uncertain tasks. Empirical researchers of media richness theory have not been terribly convincing, particularly for *new media* such as computer mediated communication (Burke & Chidambaram, 1999; Ngwenyama & Lee, 1997). However, it is quite clear that the new Internet-based technologies generate radical revolutions in the area of OSCs that build not only multicultural and but also democratically interactive online communications. OSCs-based communications provide people with dense communications milieus, both technically and socially, more so than do face-to-face environments. The media richness theory, posited in this chapter, helps online communication workers concentrate on significantly decreasing the boundaries of time and space in OSCs about which the media richness of a channel is concerned. This research examines the following four main aspects:

1. Capacity for immediate feedback determined by the amount and the promptness of the feedback the receiver can give to the sender (Timm & Detienne, 1995)
2. Ability to support natural language regarded to have the ability to support natural language if the sender can structure and send the message in the most intuitive manner or as if it were in a conversation (Chua & Ngee, 2001)

3. Number of cues it provides by the channel includes both verbal and nonverbal cues such as tone of voice, hesitation, facial expressions, vocal cues, dress, and posture that help the individuals to interact more effectively (Parks & Floyd, 1996)
4. Extent to which the channel creates social presence for the receiver provided by a channel influences individuals' motivation to engage in interpersonal communication (Williams & Rice, 1983)

The evaluation and assessment of OSCs must be viewed as a primary means for solving interactive online problems dealing with communication. The theory of media richness can play a vital role in developing and implementing successful OSCs to provide a foundation for decision making and policy formation and to accredit the program. Media richness theory can also help to define achievement strategies and boundaries. As noted by Worthen and Sanders (1987), there are three important reasons for planning and conducting evaluation of OSCs:

1. **Planning** new procedures, programs, and products to contribute to decisions about program adjustments
2. **Improving** existing procedures, programs, and products to contribute to decisions about program installation
3. **Justifying** existing or planned procedures, programs, and products to contribute to the understandings of basic social and communicative processes

Online Synchronous Communications (OSCs)

OSCs are one of the communication types in the Internet-based learning environments near asynchronous communications. According to Hofmann (2004), *synchronous* refers to training that is delivered to a geographically dispersed group of participants at the same time. Driscoll (2002) highlights the importance of the communication types as real time interactions, and these communication types reveal the tone and personality of learners and generate a greater sense of presence. These explanations indicate that two main groups (i.e., online learners and communication workers) come together in the internet-based learning environments. There should be, at least, one communication worker as an instructor in synchronous meetings, simply because of helping and guiding the online learners for better learning and preventing the discussions which are not on point and which may affect the other learners' learning process.

There are different styles of interactions among participants in OSCs. Internet relay chat (IRC) is one of these forms. Turkle (1997) has stated that IRC is a widely used conversational forum in which any user can open a channel and attract guests to it, all of whom speak to each other as if in the same room. In other words, this structure is well known by the online learners who interfaced with the Internet environments before and they can encourage the others to use it easily. Although IRC interactions have only written communications in general, they can be very useful in learning-based OSCs. For instance, an instructor may want to have the answers or comments of all the online learners at the same time. If all the learners write their answers or comments, the instructor and the learners have a chance to read all of them. Creating this real time event is very hard with another application in OSCs. Moreover, IRC communications scrolls on the screen. All participants have a chance to check the previous comments, questions, and answers if needed.

The second one is real time audio. Hofmann (2004) asserts that everyone dislikes listening to a monotonous voice. This assertion is valid even if there are important topics in the distance learning. Strategies such as using voice in an effective tone with the increasing and decreasing of the level to clarify the essential points in a conversation or narration, using humor to gain the attention of the online learners, continuing as if speaking, even if the person were reading, are very crucial for the communication worker. If the online learners used these criteria, others would be more inclined to listen to and pay attention to them.

There may be real time video with the audio as a third style in the OSCs. Although real time videos need broader bandwidths from the real time IRC and voice connections (Preece, Rogers, & Sharp, 2002), they create a unique condition for the OSCs. Since there are vast distances among participants in OSCs meetings, there is no eye contact between online learners and communication workers. Contrary to this, using video connections provides a *virtual eye contact* between OSCs participants. It is considered a virtual eye contact, because there is no need to have a video of all online learners (Driscoll, 2002). Bandwidths may not be broad enough to provide this opportunity, but one video signal can be used to show the instructor's real time video. In this situation, all online learners can see the image of this person on their screens and think that this person is looking directly at them from the screen. This communication worker looks at the Webcam in front of him or her. Also, the eye contact has only one-way communication, from the communication worker to the online learners. These factors make this eye contact virtual. Besides, online learners have a chance to see the reflections of this person when speaking, listening, and answering. These reflections may create sympathy between the communication workers and online learners. If online learners have Webcams and enough bandwidths, they can use their real time videos in OSCs. This situation provides that the other learners and communication workers should know this person not only from the name or voice but also from the look. This application also resembles traditional video-conferencing, and because all the participants can see each other, there may be eye contacts with the help of Webcams and screens in spite of distances.

The forth style of using OSCs is the application sharing. Whiteboard applications are an example of this style. There are pencils, erasers, text boxes, colors, and shapes in the whiteboards. The online learning participants use whiteboards with using these tools. They can write, draw, and paste items onto the whiteboard. One or more participants can use the whiteboard at the same time. Communication workers can prepare their special whiteboards before the OSCs start. They save time with using these prepared whiteboards during synchronous meetings. Presentation slides, spreadsheets, and Web pages are the other application sharing examples. Using only application sharing in OSCs is gross underutilization. All of these applications can be used with other synchronous styles like IRC or real time audio-video such as in virtual classroom programs.

The style of OSCs used depends on the dominant technology. If persons have Webcams, headsets, and broad bandwidths, they can easily use one of these styles without any technological problem. This situation is important to provide technically good communication and interaction environment (Hofmann, 2004; Preece et al., 2002). However, there are different dominant issues when users start to communicate with each other. Culture and its subtitles begin to rise as a dominant issue after the technology provides a communication environment for the participants.

Rising of Cultural Issues in OSCs

There are different communication technologies that bring people, societies, and cultures together in spite of the distances in the world. Mass media are examples of

Figure 1. The relationships of OSCs with biases, stereotypes, ethics, and values

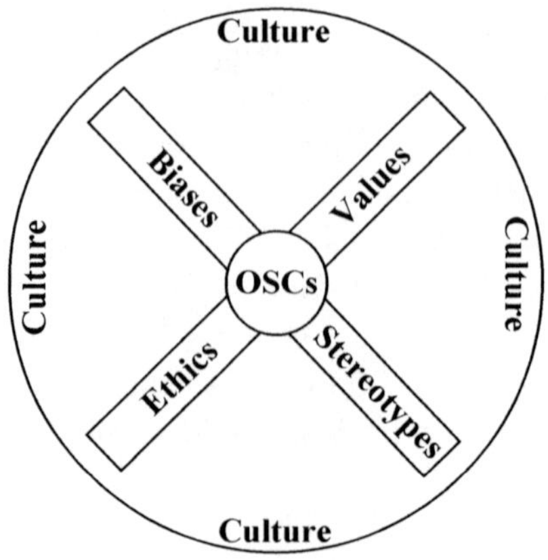

these. For instance, people can watch the news and have information from any place in the world at any time from the screens of their television. The other example is the Internet. According to Kendall (2003), there are different people from different countries, societies, cultures, and subcultures in the Internet. OSCs enable them to interact with the others in real time meetings. Culture and some of its conventions, behaviors, and practices like biases, stereotypes, ethics, and values are shared at the same time because of the two-way communication of persons in OSCs (see Figure 1).

Biases in the OSCs

"Bias" is defined as a partiality that prevents objective considerations of an issue or situation (WordNet Search, 2006). Furthermore, any factor that distorts the true nature of an event or observation generally has a bias in it (Medsearch, 2006). There are biases in OSCs. It is possible to divide and examine the *bias* concept into two main parts in the synchronous communications. First, there are biases in the media (Innis, 1991). Second, there can be biases in the minds of persons and they can show these biases when communicating in OSCs. Although it is possible to find these two bias concepts in all communication technologies and all communications, there are some special aspects of these in OSCs as illustrated in Figure 1.

Adeogba (2003) claims that communication helps to maintain relationships close and far-distanced, and helps to nurture a sense of community among the technology users. According to Shade (2006), Innis was one of the first researchers who explicated how communication is biased in terms of its control over time or space. Innis (1991) categorized media into two main biases: (1) time-binding media and (2) space-binding media. Time-binding media covers oral communications and manuscripts. These communications have limited distribution potential around the world. Close communities and traditional authorities use them (Shade, 2006). Space-binding media covers print and electronic media in which communications are enabled to expand to the larger areas and many communities found easily in the world. OSCs have a capacity to allow persons to interact with oral communications with the help of headsets. If people have Webcams, they can even see each other when they are speaking despite distances at the same time. Moreover, some people constitute special communities, and they do not allow anyone to join them when they are interacting in OSCs. These events indicate the time-binding media characteristics of OSCs. On the other hand, there is another capacity of OSCs, which covers the carriage of real time messages around the world written or spoken-based interactions. IRC interactions are the example of this capacity. Many people from different societies, cultures, and subcultures can come together and share instant communications with the help of OSCs. This situation highlights the space-binding characteristic of OSCs. The electronic infrastructure of OSCs is another of the characteristics towards space-binding media. OSCs have the either side of media approaches of Innis. Their usages among persons indicate on which side they are.

The biases can also appear in OSCs. Although this situation is valid in all communications, it is hard to find people to come together in any place of the world in real time communications randomly (like IRC meetings) or consciously (like computer-based video-conference meetings) in OSCs. This characteristic signifies that individuals have a capacity to interact in real time with other people of a society, culture, or subculture in the world. Biases can appear at any time of this instant communications. Persons including online learners and communication workers should stay away from destructive bias-based conversations and instead engage in constructive interactions. Communication workers should especially always be ready to obstruct destructive communications among online learners. According to Rosenberg (2001), the Internet has a greater capacity to create a *learning culture* where everyone can learn from the other than a *teaching culture*. If there are destructive interactions in the Internet including OSCs, people and online learners may have bad and unwanted biases about the Internet; and learning cultures can not be constituted by some of these users. Chandler (1996) talks about a medium which closes some doors as well as opens others, destroys as well as creates. Because of the instant interactions in the OSCs, there is more jeopardy for the bad parts of this explanation.

Stereotypes in the OSCs

"Stereotyping" is an oversimplified conception, opinion or image, often held in common by people (Equalcitizen, 2006). It is also defined as a conventional or formulaic conception or image. (WordNet Search, 2006). Although they are often used in a negative or prejudicial sense, there are also genuinely positive stereotypes about groups (Wikipedia, 2006). Positive or negative stereotypes depend on the point of view and relationship of the persons, societies, and cultures to the others. Stereotype-based points of view and interactions can take place among participants in OSCs as in all kinds of communications, like technology-supported or face-to-face communications. On the other hand, the power of OSCs enables persons, societies, and groups to come together at the same time as mentioned. This situation provides an opportunity for people to better understand the other (i.e., persons, societies, and cultures) better in an instant interaction and changing their ideas in a short time period. Although this situation may not be fulfilled every time by the participants of OSCs, OSCs have a potential to realize this idea, changing stereotypes and the other thoughts and opinions. People can easily search and find the other people for whom they have some stereotype-based thoughts to discuss and share their ideas in real time and reach some enlightenment or understanding with the help of OSCs.

Communication workers should be careful when they prepare the learning sessions and choose examples for the OSCs. If the topics or examples in the sessions reflect some dominant stereotypes and make some online learners feel bad or hurt, they can be destructive by reinforcing negative attitudes. This consideration is valuable for the asynchronous communications as well as the synchronous ones, but OSCs have their own character for this condition. Because of the instant interactions, if some online learners become reactive to these stereotypes, the others may include to the discussion and all learners can affect from this unwanted situation. It is hard to estimate the ending time and destructiveness of this real time communications. Besides, somc online learners want to show their stereotypes during the sessions, even the contents do not cover any stereotypes in the OSCs. The attitudes of the others can be different. They may tolerate these stereotypes, try to end the real-time communication, show their stereotype-based behaviors, or try to understand the reasons of the stereotypes. The communication workers must be ready for these kinds of interactions in the OSCs.

Values and Ethics in the OSCs

"Values" and "ethics" are fundamentals to OSCs that focus on the aspects most relevant for strategic planning and decision-making strategies. Values are important to or valued by the members of digital societies. One place where values are important is in relation to vision ("Strategic Leadership," 2005) that one of the imperatives for OSCs-based vision is that it must be based on and consistent with the community's core values. Furthermore, the values in OSCs are the embodiment of what this society stands for, and must be the basis for the behavior of its members. There is a disconnection between personal and OSCs-based values that can be dysfunctional. Therefore, it is very difficult to verify what is right and wrong. There is close connection between values and ethics that are tied to the online laws and the customs of OSCs. In this context, as pointed out by Solomon (1984), the main concern is that not all laws and customs approved by the entire society are equally acceptable. Ethics attempt to clarify digital citizens about general ideas, opinions, goals, and principles that are the study of the rules of right and wrong. These lifelong learners also admire the appreciation and justification of OSCs-based goals and ideals.

The strategic management actions and the way they deal with ethical issues must be determined based on OSCs-based values to make overt ethics policies. Working on how to deal with situations with ethical dimensions and how to predict circumstances that generate radical ethical choices can go a long way toward online ethical practices. Therefore, probing the salience of ethics can respect the diverse backgrounds to concentrate on areas where ethics may come into play ("Strategic Leadership," 2005). Understanding what essentially is going on in OSCs is indispensable to accepting the ethical principles and strategies that manage intentions. Online ethics must be that part of OSCs which is concerned with communicating well, being a respectful person, making right decisions, and generating new codes of online ethics and values for OSCs that would better reflect the issues and concerns of a complex and diverse digital society.

The appropriate procedure of democratic OSCs for lifelong learning requires that multicultural decision makers be independent, impartial, and accountable to the digital society in which they communicate. Consequently, online ethics, and values must promote and maintain the highest standards of digital citizens' conduct in collaborative communications. All registered members of OSCs who would like to participate in digital worlds must appreciate what their specific responsibilities and practices are in their communications. Looking for public confidence and trust in OSCs, the collaborations and interactions of digital citizens must congregate the most demanding ethical standards and demonstrate the highest levels of achievements that endeavor to:

- Make any OSCs communities better by building on mutual respects and trusts to promote and maintain the highest standards of personal and professional conduct among all involved in collaborative communications that describe the critical faithfulness to ethical codes that is expected of all members of a group or society to function for the collective goods
- Ensure that the public interest comes first and one does not advance her or his own personal interests at the expense of OSCs that ensure the digital members' actions serve the public, and that the power they wield in OSCs is used only for the purpose that concerns making moral judgments about the policies
- Look at different points of view to decide what is right or wrong in a particular set of communications to set the diverse values and ethics of OSCs that guide and support online communications in all their professional activities to maintain and enhance public confidence in the integrity of the digital society perfectly
- Set out the strategies that plan and clearly articulates their commitment towards collaborating with OSCs through diverse vision and mission to concentrate on developing and transmitting multicultural knowledge about ethical and value dimensions associated with the conduct and impacts of OSCs
- Foster toleration of disagreement and ambiguity without ending in moral relativism to gain diverse understandings and abilities to analyze ethical concepts within online communications

In brief, lifelong learners in OSCs must realize and appreciate the dynamic relationships between the values and ethics that help participants be aware of other participants' morals, and how they can judge each other more carefully.

Solutions and Recommendations

OSCs have different dimensions from their richness as a media and from their cultural issues like biases, stereotypes, ethics, and values. All of these dimensions have their own importance because they include very valuable clues for the communication workers and digital citizens. If communication workers understand and try to use all of these clues as mentioned on the previous pages, it will be easier to create powerful synchronous and interactive meetings in the Internet environment for the digital society. Moreover, this kind of approach should help them improve their self-confidence and willingness to use OSCs in distance learning applications.

Digital citizens have a chance to have better instantaneous and interactive experiences of Internet environments in which they are involved with the help of these clues. Noted below are steps of interactions in a synchronous meeting, which will be shared more consciously by users because of understanding better the actions or reactions of the other OSCs participants. These users can more easily determine what course of action they will follow in OSCs.

It is possible to bring together the main concepts of the media richness theory and the four cultural issues in a framework for generating powerful OSCs. Media richness theory, as part of the framework, covers the capacity for immediate feedback, supports natural languages, regards the number of clues provided by the channel, and also the extent to which the channel creates social presence for the receiver. Furthermore, stereotypes, ethic codes, and values as cultural issues in the OSCs are the other part of the framework (see Table 1).

Summary and Conclusion

The purpose of the present chapter is to help individuals to rethink OSCs by focusing on the more pressing educational and social problems of our time and to understand the achievement challenges and assessment concerns of online communication. This research addresses the questions and concerns of lifelong learning for educators, policymakers, stakeholders, and scholars. Not only does this chapter provide a constructivist-based approach to improve online learners' communication styles and abilities to look at practices and experiences from the real-life situations, but it also provides a discussion of pedagogical knowledge and design guidelines required for the education-oriented design of lifelong learning resources in constructivist OSCs. Additionally, this study provides important information about the changing needs of online learners toward lifelong learning in distance education.

There are different types of using OSCs applications in the Internet-based, real-life educational experiences. First, online learners and communication workers have

Table 1. The framework for generating powerful OSCs

	OSCs		
Cultural Issues Media Richness Theory	**Biases**	**Stereotypes**	**Values-Ethics**
Capacity for immediate feedback determined	There is instantaneous meetings around the world with OSCs and this situation enables understanding of the biases of the other persons, societies, cultures, and subcultures	Instant meetings can be creative (if they have the similar stereotypes) or destructive (if they have different stereotypes) with the stereotype-based communications of OSCs participants (the danger of destructiveness is always high in stereotype-based interactions)	Synchronous communications and interactions provide sharing of cultural or subcultural values and ethics around the world
Supports natural language	People meet with the biases of others, which they may have in the same language but different cultures or different languages and cultures	Communication workers should be careful about stereotypes of themselves and the other cultures when they prepare online synchronous meetings for participants within any languages	Visions or behaviors are shared instantly among the persons or cultures of the Internet society with the elimination of the distances (considering that all of these are sent with different languages and solving these codes depends on knowing of these languages for the others)
The number of cues provided by the channel	Biases can be shared and discussed with the persons, cultures, and subcultures with verbal or nonverbal communications based on the technology used in OSCs meetings	People, societies, or cultures can tolerate but show their stereotype-based behaviors; they try to understand or try to end a synchronous interaction when they face with the stereotypes of the others in verbal or nonverbal communications	It is difficult to verify what is right or wrong among OSCs participants on values and ethics issues in verbal and nonverbal communications (however there may be an attempt to clarify general ideas, goals, principles, and behaviors among digital citizens)
The extent to which the channel creates social presence for the receiver	People create communities or join different communities which are provided by the OSCs meetings and biases are able to be reshaped positively in this social groups	Conventional conceptions or images can be changed with instant communications or stereotype-based interactions may be a reason for limiting the presence of the receivers and the willingness for ending the communication	People come together based on interactions in OSCs; and fostering toleration about ethics and values is important for better instant presences and communications

enough time to think and generate content parts before the meetings. They can come together within some special platforms prepared for synchronous meetings such as audio, video, chat-based communications, and/or mix of them. These platforms allow communication workers to generate diverse content parts like slide shows, diagrams, animations, videos, or questions before online synchronous meetings. This situation helps them to focus ongoing communications and interactions during the meetings. Second, learners have a chance to interact their communication workers instantly via text-based interactions. Institutions can use these two types of applications because pre-prepared content parts can help the learners study the sessions. Third, online learners can come together with using ordinary applications of the Internet. For instance, IRCs provide them to share and discuss their ideas instantly. However, there are not prepared content parts and prepared education flows in these synchronous meetings. Even communication workers may not be in the meetings of the learners. The ratios of bias or stereotype-based communications may increase in these kinds of meetings. Prepared (formal or structured) and unprepared (informal or unstructured) OSCs meetings and mix usages can be varied in the future with the help of new communication technology and the imagination of human. However, the first two seem to remain.

It seems that time is the most important barrier to build and manage powerful OSCs. This can be true somehow, but the social backgrounds of the members of OSCs are more crucial issues than managing time to communicate on the Net. Finding answers to the time related problems cannot be the only solution to strategize for OSCs-based developments. Therefore, online communication workers must focus on the obstacles related to stereotypes, biases, values, and ethics. OSCs can be designed based on the respect for the diversity of communication and intellectual styles of digital citizens for lifelong learning. Besides, to build effective OSCs, these online workers also must improve their critical thinking skills to become the citizens of the world, and provide online learners with radical democratic opportunities to get ready to meet the real world without hiding their feelings, ideas, attitudes, opinions, and isolating themselves in their digital societies. This perspective can tend to put emphasis on strengthening and advancing the establishment of specialized OSCs which handle cultural issues.

The growing up process of the Internet has not ended for the first decade of the 2000s. It started to grow up worldwide in 1993 (Smith & Kollock, 1999). There were 25 million people in 1995 and 605 million people in 2002 (Benschop, 2005). These conditions signify that not only more and more persons but also more and more cultures, subcultures, biases, stereotypes, values, and ethics of people enter the Internet environment. While the potential of educational opportunities are increasing, the ratios of facing with the cultural issues are also increasing. The Internet has a potential to empower of understanding the others instantly with the help of the communication workers in the OSCs meetings.

The world is rapidly becoming more technologically complex. Distance education or online education must prepare learners to become active members of this changing society and to adapt these transformations as they occur. OSCs provide online learners with powerful digital learning resources and engage them complex communications activities. This chapter has discussed the main characteristics of OSCs to promote learners' communication styles and abilities to learn with online communication components which are diverse applications of new technologies. This process can allow online professionals and communities to make right decisions on the ethics and values of OSCs. The framework will help them examine their communication styles and abilities to share and exchange knowledge rather than to memorize and reproduce it. Additionally, the learning activities of the framework encourage learners to motivate other learners to learn effectively and efficiently.

Most professionals in online learning communities must reap global knowledge from diverse learning resources. They must also plan and manage their communication styles and abilities by having a high degree of personal control and autonomy and reflect on their learning experiences. OSCs, based on the ideas of the framework, can help online professionals actively engage in their communication progresses and critically reflect upon what they share with each other online. These, in essence, help them effectively transfer their communication styles and abilities to new contexts. As a result, online participants can produce and demonstrate their knowledge in OSCs. This framework can also provide rubrics for assessment criteria to promote collaborations and interactions among professionals and communities via OSCs. Moreover, the profession can involve innovation in assessment to meet their changing needs and to realize new opportunities for lifelong learning in distance education. As digital citizens maintain their developments into pluralistic and multicultural OSCs, there are increased prospects for effective communications among diverse online learning communities.

References

Adeogba, E. (2003). *Notions and practices of spirituality: An etiology of technology, education and teacher preparation.* Doctoral dissertation, New Mexico State University, Las Cruces. Retrieved August 11, 2006, from http://reta.nmsu.edu/tunbi

Benschop, A. (2005). *Internet users: Demography and geography of the Internet.* Retrieved August 11, 2006, from http://www2.fmg.uva.nl/sociosite/websoc/demography.html

Burke, K., & Chidambaram, L. (1999). How much bandwidth is enough? A longitudinal examination of media characteristics and group outcomes. *MIS Quarterly*, *23*(4), 557-580.

Chandler, D. (1996). Engagement with media: Shaping and being shaped. *Computer Mediated Communication Journal*, *3*(2). Retrieved August 11, 2006, from http://www.aber.ac.uk/media/Documents/short/determ.html

Chua, A., & Ngee, A. P. (2001). Relationship between the types of knowledge shared and types of communication channels used. *Journal of Knowledge Management Practice*. Retrieved August 11, 2006, from http://www.tlainc.com/articl26.htm

Daft, R. L., & Lengel, R. H. (1984). Information richness: A new approach to managerial behavior and organizational design. In B. Staw & L. L. Cummings (Eds.), *Research in organizational behavior* (pp. 191-233). Greenwich, CT: JAI Press.

Daft, R. L., & Lengel, R. H. (1986). Organizational information requirements, media richness, and structural design. *Management Science*, *32*(5), 554-571.

Daft, R. L., Lengel, R. H., & Trevino, L. K. (1987). Message equivocality, media selection, and manager performance: Implications for information systems. *MIS Quarterly, 11*(3), 355-366.

Driscoll, M. (2002). *Web-based training*. San Francisco: Jossey-Bass/Pfeiffer.

Equalcitizen. (2006). *Stereotype*. Retrieved August 11, 2006, from http://www.equalcitizen.org.uk/glossary.htm

Galbraith, J. (1977). *Organization design*. Reading, MA: Addison-Wesley.

Hofmann, J. (2004). *The synchronous trainer's survival guide*. San Francisco: Pfeiffer.

Innis, H. (1991). *The bias of communication*. University of Toronto.

Kendall, L. (2003). Cyberculture. In S. Jones (Ed.), *Encyclopedia of new media* (pp. 102-104). New York: Sage.

Kydd, C. T., & Ferry, D. L. (1991). Computer supported cooperative work tools and media richness: An integration of the literature. In *Proceedings of the 24th Annual Hawaii International Conference on Systems Sciences, 3* (pp. 324-332). Los Alamitos, CA: IEEE Society.

Medsearch. (2006). *Bias*. Retrieved August 11, 2006, from http://www.gulflink.osd.mil/medsearch/glossary/glossary_b.shtml

Ngwenyama, O. K., & Lee, A. S. (1997). Communication richness in electronic mail: Critical social theory and contextually of meaning. *MIS Quarterly*, *21*(2), 145-167.

Parks, M. R., & Floyd, K. (1996). Making friends in cyberspace. *Journal of Communication, 46*(1), 80-97.

Preece, J., Rogers, Y., & Sharp, H. (2002). *Interaction design*. New York: John Wiley & Sons.

Rosenberg, M. J. (2001). *E-Learning: Strategies for delivering knowledge in the digital age*. New York: McGraw-Hill.

Shade, L. R. (2006). *Is technology neutral? Space, time and the biases of communication.* Retrieved August 11, 2006, from http://www.cfp2000.org/papers/shade.pdf

Smith, M. A., & Kollock, P. (1999). Communities in cyberspace. In P. Kollock & M. A. Smith (Eds.), *Communities in cyberspace* (pp. 3-25). New York: Routledge.

Solomon, R. C. (1984). *Ethics: A brief introduction*. New York: McGraw- Hill.

Strategic leadership and decision making Web page of National Defense University. (2005). Retrieved August 11, 2006, from http://www.au.af.mil/au/awc/awcgate/ndu/strat-ldr-dm/cont.html

Timm, P. R., & Detienne, K. B. (1995). *Managerial communication*. New York: Prentice Hall.

Turkle, S. (1997). *Life on the screen*. New York: Touchstone.

Wikipedia, The Free Encyclopedia. (2006). Stereotype. Retrieved August 11, 2006, from http://en.wikipedia.org/wiki/Stereotype

Williams, F., & Rice, R. E. (1983). Communication research and the new media technologies. In R. Bostrom (Ed.), *Communication yearbook, 7* (pp. 200-224). Beverly Hills, CA: Sage.

Wordnet Search (2006). Stereotype. Retrieved August 11, 2006, from *http://wordnet.princeton.edu*

Worthen, B. R., & Sanders, J. R. (1987). *Educational evaluation: Alternative approaches and practical guidelines*. White Plains, NY: Longman.

Chapter IX

Tech-Knowledge: How Children and Early Childhood Education Teachers Develop Knowledge Through Technology

Satomi Izumi-Taylor, University of Memphis, USA

Ann F. Lovelace, University of Memphis, USA

Abstract

This chapter describes how early childhood teachers can support the development of young children's love for learning through technology, and how one early childhood education program promoted college students' learning through online video conferencing technology. Useful suggestions for educational software for children as well as Web sites for both children and teachers are included. Recommendations on how to use technology for higher education are also described.

Introduction

"Any sufficiently developed technology is virtually indistinguishable from magic": This famous quote from author Arthur C. Clarke vividly demonstrates just how much we have advanced technologically in recent years. It has advanced so much that technology has influenced all levels of society (Morrison, 2001), and many early childhood educators warn that children and their families without access to computers and other high technology will have a hard time succeeding in our society (Morrison, 2001; Taylor, 2000). Technology is defined as "the application of scientific, material, and human resources to the solution of human needs" (Morrison, 2001, p. 386). According to the position statement of the National Association for the Education of Young Children (NAEYC), today technology is a big part of American life (1996), and its potential benefits for young children's development are well documented (Fisher & Gillespie, 2003; Wright & Shade, 1994). All young children need an opportunity to experience and to explore technology at early ages in order to prepare for life in a modern society and to deepen their creative problem solving and thinking skills (Bowman, 1998). Since technology plays a great role in young children's learning and development (Ashikawa, 1991; Morrison, 2001), early childhood educators need to know how to implement technology in their programs and to develop technological literacy for their charges as well as for themselves.

This chapter is twofold: how teachers can support the development of young children's love for learning though technology, and how one early childhood higher education program promoted college students' learning through online video conferencing technology in 2003 and 2004 (Taylor & Hsueh, 2005). The two issues mentioned above will be discussed from the perspective of constructivism which is defined as "the learner constructs knowledge through self-initiated exploration" (Taylor, 2004, p. 20). We consider constructivism as an approach to teach young children, and constructivist teaching includes authentic tasks for learners by providing them with real materials, equipment, and supplies (Branscombe, Castle, Dorsey, Surbeck, & Taylor, 2003). Also, we consider technology such as computers to be included as children's everyday materials in the classroom; and if teachers understand and implement technologies in their classrooms aligned with constructivist teaching, children can actively engage in authentic learning experiences and can create their own knowledge. Moreover, if we are to understand how children construct their own knowledge by interacting on their environments, teachers must understand the process of how they themselves construct their own knowledge. Therefore, by interacting with top researchers/educators through the use of technology, college students can actively engage in their own learning experience and can thus understand how children construct their knowledge (Taylor & Hsueh, 2005). The recommendations regarding the use of technology for higher education are also included.

Children's Construction of Knowledge Using Technology

When children encounter new information, they use their own existing knowledge to relate to that new information in order to make sense of it (Branscombe et al., 2003). During the process, children construct their own knowledge, and to engage in such a process, children need ample opportunities to explore, to investigate, to gather information, to create new categories, and to rethink their thinking. Teachers need to consider and support this process by which children learn, and because children learn in different ways, teachers should consider each child's own unique way of learning. Constructivist teachers value individualized instruction according to each child's needs (Branscombe et al., 2003), and through the use of technology, teachers can provide each child with individualized instruction (Goldberg, 2006; Hertzog & Klein, 2005). Technology can broaden and enhance children's thinking as well as their products by providing them with tools such as graphing, charting, illustrating, data collecting, and analyzing (Means & Olsen, 1994). Likewise, by using technology children can expand their own ways of thinking (Goldberg, 2006) as well as develop their abstract thinking skills (Hertzog & Klein, 2005; Nir-Gal & Klein, 2004). Constructivist teachers promote in children these thinking skills that include multiple learning skills and nonlinear thinking, and technology opens up many windows of opportunities for children to develop such skills (Goldberg, 2006).

Another important issue of how technology can relate to children's construction of knowledge is the development of a community spirit in children. Constructivist teachers are firm believers in developing children's community spirit in the classroom (Branscombe et al., 2003; Brooks & Brooks, 1999; DeVries, Zan, Hildebrandt, Edmiaston, & Sales, 2002; Taylor, 2004) in which children and teachers feel physically and emotionally safe by sharing and expressing their own ideas with everyone. Using technology teachers and children are able to create such a community spirit and have ownership of their products (Thomas, 2005). Another example of technology and community spirit is a recent study involving kindergartners who used technology to lead their own parent-teacher conferences (Young & Behounek, 2006). With a little help from their teachers, a group of kindergartners created their own PowerPoint presentation to show their parents what they do at school. Young and Behounek explained that by conducting this project using technology, these children as a group were able to make sense of what they know about their school experiences, and they learned about their school as well as about themselves by discussing their own strengths and weaknesses. Others also found that children can use technology collaboratively to "produce reflections of their own learning and representations of their thinking" (Hertzog & Klein, 2005, p. 31).

How Teachers Can Support the Development of Children's Love for Learning through Technology

Since technology is constantly changing, the goals of education have changed, and in turn, technology has changed the notion of what it means to be educated (Morrison, 2001). Therefore, early childhood teachers need to be aware of the influence of technology on children and also need to develop their skills in using technology to benefit children (NAEYC, 1996). The influence of technology on early childhood education is reflected in research indicating that developmentally appropriate educational computer programs promote young children's social, emotional, and cognitive development (Blagojevic, 2003; Clements & Sarama, 2003; Fisher & Gillespie, 2003; NAEYC, 1996; Wortham, 2006). In this section, the issues of how the use of developmentally appropriate technology can promote children's learning and development will be discussed. How teachers can promote children's construction of knowledge using technology will be also addressed. We will describe some educational software programs that young children enjoy, including children's comments about the software. Then we will list helpful Web sites where teachers can find suggestions for implementing technology in the classroom.

The Use of Developmentally Appropriate Technology

According to the position statement of NAEYC, when teachers use technology appropriately, it can enhance children's cognitive and social development (1996). Likewise, when children use computers, have a variety of choices, and are pleased with the products (Blagojevic, 2003), even children who have had difficulties in succeeding in other areas of learning are able to increase their self-esteem through the use of computers (Moore, 2003). The use of technology can help teachers design a curriculum that meets the diverse needs of learners (Blagojevic, Twomey, & Labas, 2002). However, when integrating technology into the curriculum, teachers need to make sure that children's use of technology is developmentally appropriate (Haugland, 2000). To that extent, it must be asked, what is developmentally appropriate technology?

According to the NAEYC (1996), teachers can ask the following three questions in order to determine what developmentally appropriate technology is: Is it age appropriate? Is it individually appropriate? And is it culturally appropriate? The NAEYC recommends that teachers take time to evaluate and to select software based on children's development and learning, and that teachers closely observe children when using software in order to "identify both opportunities and problems and make appropriate adaptations" (1996, p. 12).

To determine age appropriateness of technology, teachers need to keep in mind that children are active learners who need the opportunity to explore, to make choices, and to discover the impact of their actions (Prairie, 2005; Shade, 1996). The best software needs to provide children with opportunities to "incorporate their ideas into the software experience" (Prairie, 2005, p. 164). Open-ended software provides children with such opportunities (Clements & Sarama, 2003; Fisher & Gillespie, 2003; Prairie, 2005; Shade, 1996), and through the use of such software, teachers can encourage children to become independent computer users (Shade, 1996). According to Shade (1996), the following characteristics of software should be considered when choosing appropriate computer programs: software that promotes a child's own pace, active learning, controlled interaction, possible experimentation, initiative in ceasing the program, ability to operate from a picture menu, and independent use of the computer.

To carry this issue of age appropriateness further, software should be suitable for children's developmental stages. For example, three-year-old children may be using a specific software because of its easy access, while seven year olds may enjoy the same program because of the more complex knowledge and skills provided to them (Shade, 1996). However, Prairie (2005) also notes that some drill-and-practice software can be helpful to certain children who have had no opportunities to work with computers because those children may become more confident with a structured program.

In addition to the age appropriate use of technology, individual appropriateness of technology must be considered, and it can be determined by ensuring that technology is being used most efficiently by children (Morrison, 2001). Teachers need to keep in mind children's individual differences when considering how to get them involved in learning activities using technology. Some children may need more encouragement, while others may find it easy to participate in activities using technology (Morrison, 2001). Teachers need to find out each child's needs, interests, and abilities as regards technology in order to facilitate his/her learning. Likewise, teachers need to select activities involving technology in relation to their students' learning goals. Every classroom has its own educational goals, values, themes, schedules, lesson plans, unit plans, and activities, and the use of computers should support these existing educational directions (NAEYC, 1996). By integrating computer-related activities into the daily routine in the classroom, teachers can observe children's reactions and interactions with computers and will be able to provide appropriate activities based on each child's needs.

In keeping with the importance of developmentally appropriate technology, when teachers promote equitable access to technology, cultural appropriateness can be addressed. Providing all children and their families with access to technology is a vital issue in the field of early childhood education (Becker, 2000; Morrison, 2001; NAEYC, 1996). Supporting culturally appropriate technology in the classroom can be accomplished when teachers evaluate and select "nonbiased technology-based materials" (Morrison, 2001, p. 395). When choosing technological materials, teachers need to think about depictions of other people of different abilities, ages, gender, and socioeconomic and cultural backgrounds. According to Haugland (1992), such materials should have multiple language availability, diverse environments, gender equity, and a wide representation of many cultures. Haugland's perspective on technology is congruent with the NAEYC's position stating that teachers need to pay attention to the important issues of "eliminating stereotyping of any group and eliminating exposure to violence" (p. 1996, p. 14).

Another imperative issue related to culturally appropriateness through the use of technology is meeting the needs of children with disabilities as well as with limited English proficiency. NAEYC (1996)'s position on technology states that "children with special needs should have increased access when this is helpful" (p. 13). To meet such needs, many early childhood professionals are implementing assistive technology to help children and their families (Morrison, 2001; Mulligan, 2003). According to Public Law 100-407, the Technology-Related Assistance for Individuals with Disabilities Act of 1988 (Tech Act), assistive technology refers to any materials or device that can be used to support, improve, and sustain functional abilities of persons with disabilities. Assistive technology includes a variety of products, "from simple devices such as adaptive spoons and switch-adapted battery-operated toys to complex devices such as computerized environmental control systems" (Morrison, 2001, p. 398).

To determine which assistive technology program is appropriate, the following criteria can be helpful to teachers (Holder-Brown & Parette, 1992): (1) technology should have the capability of responding to each child's educational goals; (2) technology should be practical in that resources and training should be taken into consideration; thus, allowing children, their families, and teachers to use it; and (3) technology needs to provide users with specific and desirable outcomes.

To reflect further on culturally appropriate technology, teachers need to provide software with multiple language capabilities (Haugland, 1992; Morrison, 2001). The importance of such software can be understood by looking at the fact that during the 21st century, "traditionally underrepresented groups—often called 'minorities'—will constitute a new majority within the United States" (Trawick-Smith, 2003, p. iv). Early childhood classrooms are constantly becoming diverse, and teachers must meet the unique needs of children from multiple language backgrounds (Clements & Sarama, 2003; Morrison, 2001). To meet such needs, teachers can use appropriate software to support the development of language for children with limited English proficiency.

In summary, because of technology, the concept of the classroom has expanding for early childhood educators (Blagojevic, 2004). It is time to discuss how technology can be used to enhance early childhood educators' professional development opportunities (Donohue & Neugebauer, 2004). However, according to Bewick and

Kostelnick (2004), "there is strong evidence that many teachers basically ignore the computers in their classrooms or use them in a limited fashion" (p. 26). Likewise, Plowman and Stephen (2005) found that many preschool teachers in Scotland voiced the need for training and technological support when implementing computers in the classroom. When teachers understand developmentally appropriate use of technology and the importance of equity, technology can enhance children's development and learning. Therefore, Haugland (1999) recommends that teachers need to explore, to experience, and to discover the positive power of developmentally appropriate computer programs, and after experimentations with such programs, teachers can comfortably integrate particular software in their classrooms.

Software for Children

Reading Success by Smithson-Berry Publications

(Available from Smithson-Berry Publications at 1-877-732-3935 or www.smithson-berry.org)

"Reading Success" is a software program that takes children on a journey through the "Itty Bitty City" while offering them multiple interactive visual and auditory learning experiences. The research-based program focuses on early literacy skills including phonemic awareness, language development, phonics, fluency, comprehension, and vocabulary. Prereading skills addressed in the program include sequencing, categorizing, rhyming, recognition of letters, development of language and vocabulary, and identification of colors and shapes. Reading readiness activities include categorizing, vocabulary and language development activities, patterning, letter sequencing, capital and lower case letter identification, consonant and vowel identification, blending letter sounds, and sight word identification. Early readers can practice previously learned skills while increasing their sight vocabulary, creating simple sentences, exploring homophones and diphthongs, practicing verb tense, and actually reading early readers.

The following are comments made by children and their teachers while playing this game:

- One four-year old commented, "Look! 'Nine' and 'Vine'—they rhyme! I can rhyme!"
- Another preschool child stated, "I wish I could go into the Itty Bitty City. It is fun there!"

- According to a teacher who implements the program in her classroom, "I have had to start using a timer in the classroom since I have started implementing the Itty Bitty City program. The children never want to quit!"
- One child's motivation to continue playing is the "fireworks" that occur when a level of play is successfully completed. He stated, "I can't quit until I get the fireworks. I want to get fireworks!"

Reader Rabbit Learns to Read with Phonics by the Learning Company

(Available at www.learningcompany.com)

The software program is suitable for children ages three to six. The software uses a dual approach, using both phonics and sight word identification, to encourage reading readiness skills. Activities included in the program support the development of letter sound recognition, blending skills, and patterning ability. The program also aids in the development of vocabulary skills. The *Road to Reading* mission, a component of the software program, features Mat the Mouse. Mat the Mouse is a young mouse who wishes there were no more words in the world during a moment of frustration at her inability to read. The children help Mat the Mouse restore the alphabet to the world, one letter at a time.

Alphabet Express by School Zone Publishing Company

(Available at www.schoolzone.com)

After logging on to this program, children can choose to listen to an alphabet song, play early literacy games, or select a letter of the alphabet to learn about via games and coloring pages. Printable handwriting pages are available for each letter of the alphabet. The bright colors and lively music captures the interest of the very youngest learners. The program is recommended for children from ages three to six.

Adobe Photoshop by Adobe

(Available from Adobe at 1-800-279-2795 or www.adobe.com)

Adobe Photoshop can be used to create slideshows and class books using digital photos taken in the classroom. Slideshows are a great way to document a school year, or special event, in pictures. Slideshows can be saved to disk and are keepsakes that parents are sure to enjoy. By making class books using Adobe Photoshop, teachers can help students retell their own classroom experiences through writing. Children love to take the books home to share with friends and family!

Kid Pix Studio Deluxe by Broderbund (the Learning Company)

(Available from the Learning Company at 1-800-825-4420 or www.broder.com)

Kid Pix allows children to create artwork using the computer. The creativity toolbox provides resources so that children can draw, paint, and animate artwork. Their work can also be accompanied by movement and sound. Artwork can be saved, combined to form a slideshow, or sent to friends and family via e-mail. Skills addressed in the program include colors, shapes, numbers, and letters. Early vocabulary usage is also encouraged.

Kidspiration by Inspiration Software, Inc.

(Available from Inspiration Software, Inc. at 1-800-877-4292 or http://www.kidspiration.com/productinfo/kidspiration/index.cfm)

Kidspiration allows children to create graphic organizers using pictures, texts, and spoken language. The program can help children to develop study skills by helping them to create visual representations of important concepts. Kidspiration can aid students in the development of the following skills: categorization, communication, and estimation. The program is intended for children in kindergarten through fifth grade.

Bailey's Book House by Edmark

(Available from Edmark at 1-800-362-2890 or www.edmark.com)

Bailey's Book House is recommended for children from the ages of two to five. When interacting with the software, children select from seven early literacy activities that focus on letter recognition, rhyming, and vocabulary development. Children also can create printable cards for various occasions and "write" stories. The program also encourages the development of basic computer skills.

Sammy's Science House by Edmark

(Available from Edmark at 1-800-362-2890 or www.edmark.com)

Sammy's Science House encourages children to think scientifically while learning about the weather, seasons of the year, animal habitats, and other basic concepts. Sequencing, sorting, and classifying skills are addressed. The children love that the program allows them to manipulate various characteristics of the environment to create different animated scenes. For example, children can select different precipitation and wind levels and observe their effects. Creativity is encouraged throughout the program.

Web Sites for Children (www.starfall.com)

At this site, parents and educators can find activities, handouts, and interactive games that support children's learning at the pre-reading, beginning reading, intermediate reading, and advanced reading levels. Very young children can discover the letters and the sounds that the letters make while exploring the site. Animated pictures that reinforce the sounds made by the particular letters are available for each letter, and short jingles help to teach the sounds. Beginning reading acquisition is encouraged by the interactive books available at this site. The students can manipulate the pages of the available books while working on the computer, and the computer will "read" the books to the children, highlighting each individual word as it is read. Printable books and skill-building worksheets are available to reinforce the skills learned via the computer. For more advanced readers, various genres of interactive books are available including plays, comics, myths, folk tales, and fables. Fictional and nonfictional works are also available.

http://www.sesameworkshop.org/sesamestreet/

At this site, children can learn about letters, numbers, shapes, sorting, the weather, and many other topics while playing interactive games and listening to stories. Digital coloring pages are available as well as printable games. A special section of the website is designed just for parents. While visiting, parents can get tips on parenting and educational issues and find suggestions for enjoyable activities to complete with their children.

http://www.bbc.co.uk/cbeebies/

An underlying belief of CBeebies is that children learn through play. Interactive stories and games are available at this site. Several games and stories have been modified to meet the needs of special needs children.

http://www.storyplace.org/

Available in both English and Spanish, this Web site provides children with an opportunity to explore interactive books. The digital library contains selections for preschool and elementary-aged children. Both online and printable activities are available at this site.

http://www.bookhive.org/

The site is designed to offer information on various children's books to children ages birth through 12, as well as parents and teachers. Book reviews, along with parental notes, can be found for a wide variety of books. Searches may be conducted based on author, illustrator, title, interest area, reading level, or number of pages.

http://www.literacycenter.net/

Started with a small business innovation research (SBIR) contract from the U.S. Department of Education, LiteracyCenter.net offers free resources for parents and educators to aid in the development of early literacy skills. Resources are available in English, Spanish, Dutch, and French. Interactive activities available at this site provide young children with the opportunity to learn about colors, letters, numbers, shapes, phonemes, rhyming, and writing. At the site, additional information on the importance of each skill addressed is available.

Web Sites for Teachers (www.internet4classrooms.com)

From this site, educators can access a wide variety of educational resources including:

- Assessment assistance to aid in test preparation
- Practice modules/tutorials to support the development of technological skills needed to use multiple software programs including PowerPoint, Word, Excel, Inspiration, Internet Explorer, Dreamweaver, HyperStudio, Macintosh, Windows/PC, WebQuest, Works, Netscape, and Claris
- Links to frequently updated sites containing notable quotes, trivia questions, and other interesting facts
- Guidelines for effective searching of the Internet
- Links to numerous sites that can be used to enhance learning in the classroom (the links are grouped according to subject area, grade level, and topic)

http://school.aol.com/

Resources for students, educators, and parents are available at this site. Students can access information including games, lessons, and tutorials to enhance learning in math, science, language arts, social studies, the arts, and other elective subjects. Reference tools such as atlases, almanacs, dictionaries, and encyclopedias are available as well as news sources, educational games, and weather forecasts. For educators, lesson plan builders, flashcards, worksheet, and puzzle makers, clip art resources, and rubric generators are available. Tips for integrating technology into the classroom, creating Web sites, online collaborative projects, and Internet safety can also be found at this Web site.

www.PlayhouseDisney.com/Educators

Educators can search for classroom activities, recipes, puzzles, games, and songs at this Web site. When at this site, the educator is able to search for information by selecting specific skills to be addressed, themes to be reflected, and age levels (from two to five) to be included in the activities. Each search generates age-appropriate activities that can be used in the classroom.

http://teacher.scholastic.com/

Subject-related online activities, lesson plans, and teaching tools are available at this site. Teachers can generate flashcards, make rubrics, create a class home page, and find age-appropriate lesson plans. With Scholastic's Global Classport, educators can connect with classrooms and collaborate with teachers in 182 countries!

http://netc.org/earlyconnections/

Developed by the Northwest Educational Technology Consortium, the site provides resources and information for educators on the use of technology in early childhood education. Information on how technology relates to children's development during different stages can be found at this site. Also, information on how to incorporate technology into the classroom and links to additional information can be found.

www.techandyoungchildren.org

The official site of the NAEYC Technology and Young Children Interest Forum, the Web site offers information on the best practices for using technology with children, a technology information exchange, research references on the use of technology with young children, resources for funding technology, and tips for using the internet.

http://school.discovery.com/

At this site, educators can find lesson plans, create puzzles, download free clip art, and create custom quizzes and worksheets. By signing up for an online account, teachers are able to store their online creations for future use. An entire section of this site focuses on Science Fairs, offering project ideas and multiple links where further information can be found. "Brain Booster" word puzzles that require higher order thinking skills are also available for educators to use in their classrooms.

http://educationworld.com/

Educators can find a plethora of information organized according to the following topics: lesson planning, professional development, technology integration, school issues, and Education World at home. Tips for the classroom, management tools, and printable ideas and activities can be found here. Links to other professional resources are also available at this site.

http://www.alphabet-soup.net/

At the site, educators can find thematic units, games, activities, recipes, and lots of free printables. Alphabet coloring pages, thematic writing paper, bulletin board borders, and printable books are among the resources available to educators. The site is well-organized and updated frequently.

http://www.teachersandfamilies.com/index.html

From the site, teachers and families can access preschool theme-based activities, projects, and printable practice pages. Links to valuable study resources relating to subject and grade level can be found for students in grades K-12. Articles on current issues and links to further information are available for parents.

Incorporating College Students' Learning Through Technology

We agree with the notion: "constructivist teachers study how young children think" (Branscombe et al., 2003, p. 313); and this sets the base for this section. In order to create an appropriate learning environment for children, constructivist teachers must understand how children understand and think. To understand children's way of thinking, Papert (1990) created his own theory entitled "constructionism" which includes the role of technology, and he considered children to be makers, designers, and producers of their own projects, especially through using technology (Forman & Landry, 2000). His theory is based on that of Piaget and is redefining learning environments and education using technology. Just as Papert believed that learners need to be actively involved in constructing their own knowledge, we also wanted our college students to be directly involved in their processes of understanding their own knowledge construction through online video conference sessions.

Online video conferencing sessions can provide early childhood education students with an authentic learning environment using technology. These students should actively construct their own professional knowledge by interacting with their educational materials and with their social and intellectual environments (Taylor & Hsueh, 2005). Video conferencing technology via the Internet affords an enriched environment in which students can interact with other educators at different sites. The use of online video conferencing in conjunction with teacher education courses can be an effective way to facilitate students' understanding of constructivism. This view is congruent with a basic understanding of constructivism because to understand how children construct their own knowledge by interacting with their environment, teachers should experience the processes of how they themselves construct their own knowledge. Online video conferencing sessions promote students' understanding of constructivism by providing opportunities for them to interact with renowned educators in the United States. The 2003 and 2004 sessions made available a world of ideas and intellectual resources that were not otherwise accessible from one university. This teaching method of opening up the world for teacher education students is based on Duckworth's (1996) notion: "people must construct their own knowledge and must assimilate new experiences in ways that make sense to them" (p. 150).

The purpose of this section is to describe how incorporating technology into teaching methods (including the stages of organizing the 2003 and 2004 video conference sessions) for college students promoted their construction of knowledge. The phases of organizing such sessions, the teaching strategies, the students' responses to these sessions, and the recommendations as to how to use technology in college classrooms will be discussed accordingly.

Stages of Organizing Online Video Conferencing Sessions

In order to provide Internet-protocol-based (IP-based) video conferencing sessions to graduate students majoring in early childhood education, the first required step was to obtain Technology Access Fee grants in 2003 and 2004 through the University of Memphis to support the efforts, followed by: (1) writing letters to nationally and internationally accomplished scholars in the field of early childhood education, including one educator in Japan and one educator in Sweden, asking them to participate in video sessions as well as asking about the availability of IP-based video conferencing via the Internet; (2) scheduling the scholars' appearance in class and testing the network connectivity; (3) redesigning an existing course on constructivism in early childhood education in order to include the video conferencing sessions as well as gathering new course materials from invited scholars; and (4) retesting the network connectivity just prior to the beginning of the semester. The stages of creating such sessions have been described in detail elsewhere (Taylor & Hsueh, 2005).

Although efforts were made to include two international scholars in the 2003 and 2004 sessions, they were unable to join because of time differences. Also, two scholars in the United States were unable to accept the invitation to participate in the conferencing sessions because of their personal circumstances. In the 2003 sessions, six scholars participated, and in the 2004 sessions, seven scholars participated. The participating scholars included Kathryn Castle of Oklahoma State University, Arleen Dodd of Long Island University, Rheta DeVries of the University of Northern Iowa, Eleanor Duckworth of Harvard University, Stephan Graves of the University of South Florida, Constance Kamii of the University of Alabama, Birmingham, Joseph Tobin of Arizona State University, and Dorothy Sluss of Clemson University. Some of these educators participated in sessions occurring in both semesters, and one participated in two video sessions occurring in one semester.

Teaching Strategies

During the two fall semesters between 2003 and 2004, 25 graduate students majoring in early childhood education participated in 14 different IP-based video conferencing sessions. 11 of the students in these classes were early childhood teachers, early childhood education college instructors, or administrators in early childhood settings. In order to make their learning more active and meaningful, the students were assigned articles or book chapters written by that week's guest lecturer, and were asked to prepare questions for the experts based on the readings. Each session lasted approximately two hours, and except for the first, each session was videotaped and made available for students to review later. During the 2003 and 2004 sessions, each guest lecturer was asked to discuss his or her current involvement in research, and then the students asked questions of them (Taylor & Hsueh, 2005).

The first phase of teaching is based on Duckworth's (1996) notion of engaging students in some problem with which they could connect their experience. In other words, students were engaged directly with current issues regarding constructivism in early childhood education through participating in online video conferencing sessions presented by experts in the field. Students then asked questions based on their reading materials, and the experts responded to them directly, thus allowing students to experience their own ways of interacting with the experts and to construct their own knowledge through the sessions (Taylor & Hsueh, 2005). In addition, through these sessions more questions were generated by students as they interacted with the presenters. Some questions were spontaneous and some were well thought out in advance.

Since the main focus of this course was on constructivism, students were encouraged to reflect on their learning by responding to a reflection form asking about their experiences with each guest lecturer after each session. Each student's reflective form was returned with written responses from the first author. At the end of each fall semester, the forms were collected from students, and then all forms were reviewed in their entirety. This perspective is congruent with the description of Duckworth's (1996) second phase of teaching and learning which states that by writing their reflections on the forms, students will be encouraged to make sense of what they have learned over the course of the semester.

The reflection form included the following items: (1) Discuss three issues that were important to your understanding of constructivism discussed during today's video conferencing session; (2) Discuss your reflection on your learning and development in today's class: Be sure to include what you have to do to improve your learning; (3) Is the TV screen large enough for the interactive purpose? (4) What are the advantages of using video conferencing in the seminar? (5) What are the disadvantages? (6) What did you enjoy most in regarding interacting with Dr.________? and (7) What suggestions do you have for future video conferencing sessions?

Students' Responses to the Sessions

"I couldn't sleep last night! I was so excited and motivated by the video conferencing sessions with Dr. Steven Graves! He reconfirmed my belief in constructivism!" (Taylor & Hsueh, 2005, p. 127). Such was the comment of one excited student after the first session in 2003. Just as this above mentioned student described the excitement of participating in the sessions, many students discussed their enjoyment of the opportunities to communicate directly with top educators. Other comments included: "It has been one of the most meaningful experiences for me as a professional teacher," "I have a chance to learn some great things from some very interesting people," and "A chance to interact with the movers and shakers of our field."

When asked to discuss the advantages and disadvantages of online video conferencing sessions, the students' comments were overwhelmingly positive. One student said, "The advantage is you are able to connect a face with the articles and materials that you read." Two students noted, "We have access to the world!" and "We can benefit from experienced professionals who are geographically inaccessible." Also, one student commented, "This is good exposure to technology that is hardly used" (Taylor & Hsueh, 2005, p. 131).

The advantages of online video conferencing sessions were evident not only in the comments made by students but also in those of the guests. Arleen Dodd of Long Island University said, "I have to explore this use of technology. It has been fun and educational." Likewise, Constance Kamii of University of Alabama, Birmingham commented, "Now, you have put a bug in my head about how great this video conferencing connection is. I will explore the possibility of using it myself and with my colleagues in Japan" (Taylor & Hsueh, 2005, p. 131). She also noted, "Today, I invited one Japanese student to this video session so he can observe and inform my friends in Japan of this session."

There were few comments on the disadvantages of online video conferencing sessions, but the disadvantages were noted: "The wait time was frustrating," "Slight time lag is a little distracting," and "The disadvantage is the noise interference that occurs occasionally." Still, the following comment of one student provided strong evidence of how important it is to continue offering these sessions to students, "The disadvantage would be that we would probably never be able to experience this again."

In summary, these online video conferencing sessions were based upon the notion that a college classroom is "a potential learning community of people with varied experiences, worldviews, cultural values, language backgrounds. When everyone has a voice, learning is richer" (Magee & Jones, 2004, p. 17). Just as Magee and Jones (2004) and Blagojevic (2004) found distance learning for college courses to be beneficial, Taylor and Hsueh (2005) found online video conferencing sessions with educators off campus to be meaningful and helpful to students' learning. The positive use of technology in distance learning can shape learning and development. Likewise, Prairie (2005) considers "communicating with people near and far" (p. 10) using technology can be beneficial to everyone involved.

Recommendations

Based on these online video conferencing sessions, the following are recommendations as to how to implement a constructivist approach in higher education using technology:

1. State clear course objectives in the class syllabus indicating the use of technology as a means of promotion of constructivism, and go over these objectives with students in order for them to understand what is expected of them during the videotaping of each session. By informing students of appropriate behavior during sessions, inappropriate behavior such as arriving late and chewing gum could be eliminated.
2. Prepare students to ask questions or to make comments on each guest's writing that they have read in advance of the session. Although students generated interesting new questions during sessions, preparing some of them could help guests and students to get started as well as to avoid awkward moments of silence.
3. Inform the guests of what is expected of them, since one guest's expectations were not aligned with those of the students. There was some confusion as to how to start the session with the guest. Good advance communication with guests will further promote opportunities for students to connect with the ideas with which they have become familiar through readings (Taylor & Hsueh, 2005).
4. Make sure to allocate a sufficient amount of time for interaction during the session. Some sessions could go over the allotted time; thus, informing guests of the expectations is crucial.
5. Consider "the possibility of providing students three-way video conferencing sessions in order for two or more guest lecturers to interact with each other" (Taylor & Hsueh, 2005, p. 131). This was suggested by one of the guests during the second fall semester in 2004; however, because of limited time to prepare for this possibility, three-way video conferencing sessions were not possible at that time.
6. "Make sure that each university has a broadband network infrastructure with access to the Internet" (Taylor & Hsueh, 2005, p. 132). The classrooms on both sites need to have an Internet-Protocol-based (IP-based) video conferencing camera with a large screen monitor. IP-based connectivity does not require any cost to access sites. According to Taylor and Hsueh, "the quality of this video conferencing interaction depends largely on the compatibility of the technical equipment and connectivity through the network on campus and between the two connected universities" (2005, p. 132).
7. Communicate with guests in advance about planning their sessions to accommodate their busy schedules. In one case, a willing guest could not participate because she had to be out of the country. In another case, due to the lack of clerical support, one session had to be rescheduled.
8. Explore possibilities of offering online video conferencing sessions in an auditorium in order to give lots of students the opportunity to participate.

References

Ashikawa, T. (1991). *Oya, kyoshi, jukuga kodomoodamenishita* [parents, teachers, and after school schools ruined children]. Tokyo: Gendaishorin.

Becker, H. (2000). Who's wired and who's not: Children's access to and use of computer technology. *The Future of Children, 10*(2), 44-75.

Bewick, C., & Kostelnick, M. (2004). Educating early childhood teachers about computers. *Young Children, 59*(3), 26-29.

Blagojevic, B., Twomey, D., & Labas, L. (2002). *Universal design for learning: From the start.* Retrieved August 11, 2006, from http://www.ume.maine.edu/~cci/facts/facts6/udl.htm

Blagojevic, B. (2003). Funding technology: Does it make cents? *Young Children, 56*(3), 28-33.

Blagojevic, B. (2004). World class learning. *Young Children, 59*(3), 42-44.

Bowman, B. (1998). Equity and young children as learners. In *Proceedings of the Families, Technology and Education Conference.* Retrieved August 11, 2006, from http://ericeece.org/pups/books/fte/general/bowman.html

Branscombe, N., Castle, K., Dorsey, A., Surbeck, E., & Taylor, J. (2003). *Early childhood curriculum: A constructivist perspective.* Boston: Houghton Mifflin.

Brooks, J., & Brooks, M. (1999). *In search of understanding the case for constructivist classrooms.* Alexandria, VA: Association for Supervision and Curriculum Development.

Clements, D., & Sarama, J. (2003). Young children and technology. *Young Children, 58*(6), 34-40.

DeVries, R., Zan, B., Hildebrandt, C., Edmiaston, R., & Sales, C. (2002). *Developing constructivist early childhood curriculum.* New York: Teachers College Press.

Donohue, C., & Neugebauer, R. (2004). Innovations in e-learning: New promise for professional development. *Young Children, 59*(3), 22-32.

Duckworth, E. (1996). *The having of wonderful ideas and other essays on teaching and learning*. New York: Teachers College Press.

Fisher, M., & Gillespie, C. (2003). Computers and young children's development. *Young Children, 58*(4), 85-91.

Forman, G., & Landry, C. (2000). The constructivist perspective on early education: Applications to children's museums. In J. L. Roopnarine & J. E. Johnson (Eds.), *Approaches to early childhood education* (pp. 149-174). Upper Saddle River, NJ: Merrill/Prentice Hall.

Goldberg, M. (2006). *Integrating the arts: An approach to teaching and learning in multicultural and multilingual settings.* Boston: Allyn & Bacon.

Haugland, S. (1992, Winter). Maintaining an anti-bias curriculum. *Day Care and Early Education*, pp. 44-45.

Haugland, S. (1999). What role should technology play in young children's learning? Part 1. *Young Children, 54*(6), 26-31.

Haugland, S. (2000). What role should technology play in young children's learning? Part 2. *Young Children, 55*(1), 12-18.

Hertzog, N., & Klein, M. (2005). Beyond gaming: A technology explosion in early childhood classrooms. *Gifted Child Today, 28*(3), 24-65.

Holder-Brown, L., & Parette, H. (1992, September). Children with disabilities who use assistive technology: Ethical considerations. *Young Children,* pp. 74-75.

Magee, J., & Jones, E. (2004). Leave no grownup behind: Coming to terms with technology. *Young Children, 59*(3), 13-20.

Means, B., & Olsen, K. (1994). The link between technology and authentic learning. *Educational Leadership, 51*(7), 15-19.

Moore, C. (2003). *With computers, children learn the 3Rs plus the S: Self-esteem.* Retrieved August 11, 2006, from http://www.Mainecite.org/funding.htm

Morrison, G. (2001). *Early childhood education today* (8th ed.). Upper Saddle River, NJ: Merrill/ Prentice Hall.

Mulligan, S. (2003). Assistive technology supporting the placation of children with disabilities. *Young Children, 58*(6), 50-51.

NAEYC position statement: Technology and young children-ages three through eight. (1996). *Young Children, 51*(6), 11-16.

Nir-Gal, O., & Klein, P. (2004). Computers for cognitive development in early childhood-the teacher's role in the computer learning environment. *Information Technology in Childhood Education Annual,* 97-119.

Papert, S. (1990). *A critique of technocentrism in thinking about the school of the future* (Epistemology and Learning Memo No. 2). Cambridge, MA: MIT.

Plowman, L., & Stephen, C. (2005). Children, play, and computers in pre-school education. *British Journal of Educational Technology, 36*(2), 145-157.

Prairie, A. (2005). *Inquiry to math, science and technology for teaching young children*. Clifton Park, NY: Thomson Delmar learning.

Shade, D. (1996). Software evaluation. *Young Children, 51*(6), 17-21

Taylor, S. I. (2004). Let it be! Japanese preschoolers rule the classroom. *Young Children, 59*(5), 20-25.

Taylor, S. I., & Hsueh, Y. (2005). Implementing a constructivist approach in higher education through technology. *Journal of Early Childhood Teacher Education, 26*(2), 127-132.

Technology-Related Assistance for Individuals with Disabilities Act of 1988 (PL100-104). (1988). Retrieved August 11, 2006, from http://pursuit.rehab.uiuc.edu

Thomas, A. (2005). Children online: Learning in a virtual community of practice. *E-Learning, 2*(1), 27-38.

Trawick-Smith, J. (2003). *Early childhood development: A multicultural perspective*. Upper Saddle River, NJ: Merrill/ Prentice Hall.

Wortham, S. (2006). *Early childhood curriculum* (4th ed.). Upper Saddle River, NJ: Merrill/ Prentice Hall.

Wright, J., & Shade, D. (1994). *Young children: Active learners in a technological age*. Washington, DC: NAEYC.

Young, D., & Behounek, L. (2006). Kindergartners use PowerPoint to lead their own parent-teacher conferences. *Young Children, 61*(2), 24-26.

Chapter X

Building Online Knowledge Societies for Lifelong Learning: The Democratic University-Community Partnerships in Turkey

Gulsun Kurubacak, Anadolu University, Turkey

Abstract

New communication technologies have the great potential to construct very powerful paradigm shifts that enhance university-community partnerships (UCPs) in Turkey. Therefore, the purpose of this chapter is to focus on how to build online knowledge networks between university and community for lifelong learning. Further, in this study, the strategies and principles of UCPs based on media richness theory through a critical pedagogy approach is discussed to generate a theoretical framework that provides everyday examples and experiences for probing social justice issues. Online learners can find the diverse resources, multicultural experiences, and egalitarian opportunities that broaden their perspectives via new communication technologies. This chapter therefore concentrates on discussing the characteristics of the UCPs for lifelong learning to build online communities with new communication technologies.

Introduction

New communication technologies can provide the vehicles to build a very powerful paradigm shift to enhance the university and community partnerships (UCPs) in Turkey. These technology-based collaborations allow the partners to interact with each other, sharing the global knowledge and resources. While this is unquestionably not a new concept, it is one that needs to be revisited, refreshed, and strengthened as distance education is developing critical concerns for lifelong learning. The UCPs are recognized as an integral part of social justice issues that theories, models, and strategies of online communications must lead these entities to carefully redesign and to revolutionize their new roles in the communication milieus. The standards and rubrics for lifelong learning must direct their partnerships in the milieus as well. As noted by Baum (2000), universities must be redirecting their social, economical, educational and intellectual resources, facilities, and other assets to benefit their community in many innovative ways for lifelong learning. Basically:

1. UCPs can be deeply engaged in diverse activities to build global knowledge networks effectively.
2. Participations can generate strong theoretical frameworks to bring democratic changes in online communities.
3. Social, cultural, and educational interactions and collaborations between them can provide guidance for the public good.
4. Possibilities, potentials, and implications of moving beyond transmission model of communication can generate social justice issues.
5. Attitudes, beliefs, and expectations of the UCPs can address important cultural and social problems.
6. UCPs can explore how to bring social justice into diverse real-life experiences and build comfort for them.
7. Effective practices can empower democratic intercultural decision making and dialogic leadership between the university and community.

A theoretical framework can provide everyday examples and experiences in Turkey for enhancing the UCPs. Therefore, to build strong online knowledge networks, the main concern of this chapter is to focus on producing explicit definitions for lifelong learners' roles and understanding their changing responsibilities. The UCPs must be a realistic road map of increasing resources by addressing community problems. This chapter discusses not only strategies and principles, but also pitfalls and barriers for the UCPs in Turkey. This highlights the importance of starting partnerships with certainty about outcomes and resources but maintaining flexibility in process. In short, this chapter proposes to illustrate how the Turkish university and community can work together to learn in such a way that develops a common vision for social justice issues, and is engaged as part of their online societies working toward that vision for lifelong learning.

Theoretical Framework

There is a need for investigating clearly how to build effective collaborations between the university and community for lifelong learning that constructs new diverse schemas in their minds. Online partnerships can interact with a wide range of viewpoints by reverencing individual cultural differences and giving more attentions to diversity issues. Therefore, as highlighted by Bates (2000) and Stephenson (2001), it is important that the UCPs must (1) understand how to manage their role tasks, (2) give careful attentions to diverse online community, and (3) understand their important roles to integrate new digital technologies in their activities. However, involving these people to become a part of the communication process is often difficult in Turkey. This chapter addresses the *media richness theory* as the theoretical and philosophical foundation of the UCPs. This theory can help the university and community become aware of the strengths and limitations of online collaborations.

Empirical researchers of *media richness theory* have not been terribly convincing, particularly for *new media* such as computer-mediated communications. However, it is quite clear that the Internet-based new technologies generate radical revolutions in the area of the UCPs. Online communications provide these people with more dense communications milieus than face-to-face ones both technically and socially (Powazek, 2002; Rovai, 2002). *Media richness theory* can help the university and community concentrate on significantly decreasing the boundaries of time and space in their partnerships. The UCPs, therefore, can achieve scholarly challenges and concerns for diverse learners that provide them with sharply opposed viewpoints on enduring social activist issues in Turkey.

Media richness theory can play a vital role in developing successful online communications to provide a foundation for decision-making process and policy formation. Not only do open and flexible online knowledge societies modify critical thoughts, feelings and actions to solve complex real-life problems for lifelong learning, but also they provide university and community with powerful and innovative solutions and perspectives (Bonk, Kim, & Zeng, 2006; Burge, 2000). Based on these concerns, in Turkey, using various channels to interactive online communications can:

1. Engage their partnerships in lifelong learning projects designed to be realistic, intriguing, and relevant to real-life experiences
2. Promote their partnerships to model how theory translates into practice
3. Integrate authentic partnerships by clearly stating the pedagogical guidelines to build online societies
4. Encourage their partnerships to take ownership and responsibility for lifelong learning processes
5. Become cognitive coaches to build online knowledge societies from a pedagogical perspective
6. Improve independent communication strategies and principles by utilizing lifelong learning

Encouraging the UCPs can plan, develop, and implement interactive communication milieus with real-life experiences, ideas, opinions, and discussions through *media richness theory* as a critical approach. It is quite clear that the UCPs can break down the walls of the traditional environments and gain worldwide communications and knowledge online. The failures of online collaborations can be alleviated by employing richer media. As emphasized by Powazek (2002) and Schrum and Benson (2002), the university and community appraise the quality of online communications whereas they decrease ambiguity about authentic practices. In the complex times ahead, the multiple and diverse areas of social concerns, juxtapose conceptions, practices, ideologies, and epistemologies, therefore, can investigate opposed definitions and visions for lifelong learning in Turkey. In this context, Figure 1 shows online collaborations through the proper selections of communication media for the UCPs.

This critical pedagogy approach can decrease ambiguity through media richness theory for empowering online communications. Online communications are rich media and can have significantly positive impact on partnerships quality by reducing isolated relationships (Benson & Harkavy, 2000). Capacity building in social justice issues, therefore, can focus on their leaderships, and develop collaborative communications between the university and community in Turkey. They can interact with each other especially regarding the educational progress of lifelong learners (Frabutt, Forsbrey, & MacKinnon-Lewis, 2003). It is an extremely essential concern for professional constituencies and the public to make decisions about how to build online societies with new communication technologies in distance education. These partnerships can provide the lifelong learners with powerful digital resources and engage them in complex communication and learning activities.

Figure 1. The basics of a critical approach through media richness theory for UCPs

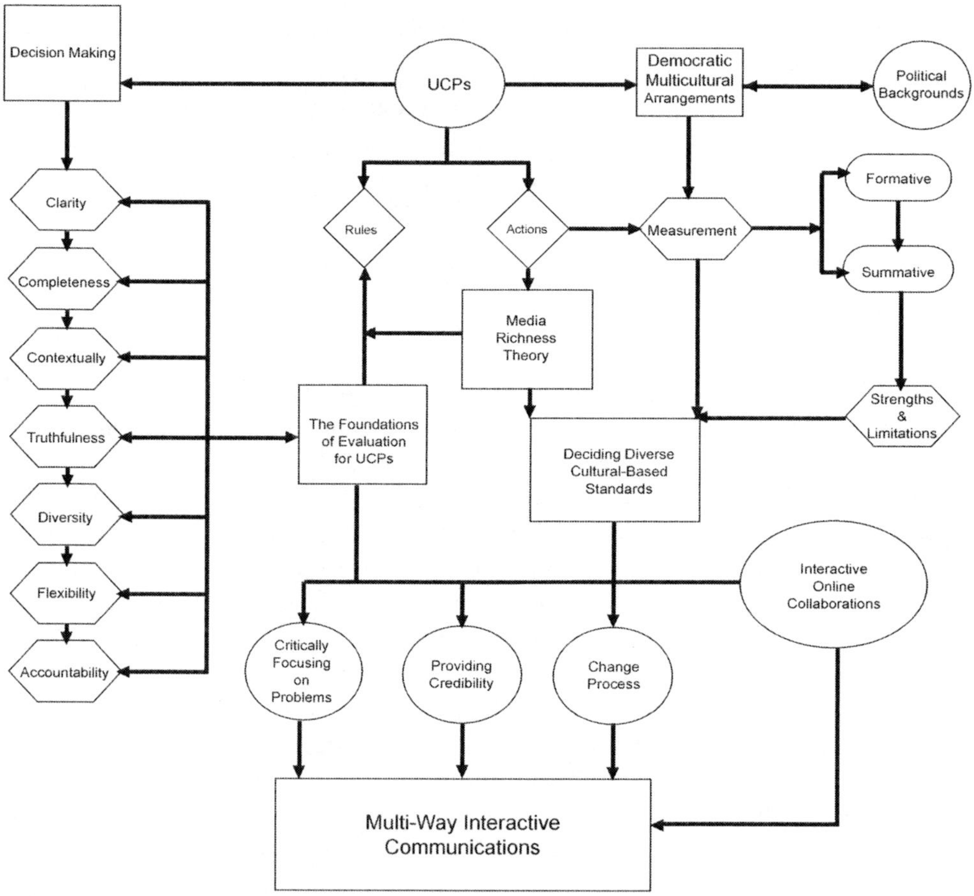

Continuity and Change of the University-Community Partnerships

The UCPs must investigate the nature and the future of online knowledge networks and consider ways to resolve the tensions generated by the need to change and to be responsive to novel needs and conditions. As highlighted by Farmer (2004) and Rovai (2002), improving the UCPs must be a continuing concern of online knowledge network that explores obstacles to good communications and offers a pragmatic analysis of how to develop successful changing. The emergence of new approaches in these partnerships, within and among virtual communities, can be marked by conflicts between autonomy and interdependence. The UCPs must discuss the changing milieus of lifelong learning and its institutional modifications, multicultural agreements that contain useful guidelines in the critical evaluations of these partnerships (Anderson & Elloumni, 2004). To increase in the public attentions and/or to be better accepted by the public, the Turkish UCPs must understand the potentials and powers of online societies, as well as the open, flexible and distributed approaches of the new communication technologies. Therefore, a clear conceptual framework can increase the public attentions and provide them with constructive methods, approaches, and models in lifelong learning. This framework can be able to:

1. Analyze the experiences of the UCPs toward sharing knowledge online
2. Generate open and flexible online communication milieus by encouraging constructivist thoughts, feelings, and actions for lifelong learners
3. Investigate their positive and negative online communication experiences and break down the diverse cultural barriers
4. Develop new organizational concepts and structures to ensure coherent and creative future-making procedures
5. Determine the feature needs and priorities of distance education, which are beyond unrealistic controls by online community
6. Envision and shape the common future with new approaches, and also multicultural policy-making and planning
7. Include critical thinking, decision making, and problem solving via real-life experiences, ideas, opinions, and discussions
8. Interpret and cope with the foreseeable impacts and effects of the emerging communication technologies
9. Define the most important expectations and dilemmas of lifelong learning in the near future clearly

This theoretical framework for building online communities, therefore, can allow the UCPs to generate interactive activities and enables them to understand problems and perspectives from the real world. As noted by Brook and Oliver (2003) as well as Garrison and Anderson (2003), with this framework the UCPs can address the problem of closing the gap between the university's enormous promise, prestige, and power and its actual performance in producing knowledge, personnel, and democratic practice required to solve the problems confronting Turkish society. In this case, the UCPs are active relationships to obtain, evaluate, and produce dynamic online communications for lifelong learning. On the other hand, as discussed by Ralston,

Lerner, Mullis, Simerly, and Murray (2000), the UCPs should provide ideas for training human development professionals in the integration of education, public policy, and community service. Otherwise, the changes and connections in lifelong learning can be qualified as hazardous duties. These situations move so fast that description can be difficult and analysis nearly impossible.

Changing Structures of the University-Community Partnerships

The functions and workings of the universities and communities in Turkey are constantly being revised in the light of changing social, economical, political, and cultural dilemmas. Thompson and Lerner (2000) note that online knowledge networks have accepted in putting concepts of democracy and multiculturalism into practice that the purposes of UCPs must be well defined to engage in the pursuit of knowledge, transmitting knowledge, giving public services, and expending great effort toward the goal of improving online knowledge networks. Internally, the UCPs should be able to encourage diverse participations in practices to protect individual rights. The universities and communities should voluntarily investigate the critical aspects of their partnerships by respecting diverse cultural identities and backgrounds.

Within the professional partnerships of the universities and communities, the objectives of reform must be approached by bringing together the various communities to gain the contributions of all to the evaluation of the adequacy and relevancy of lifelong learning in Turkey. In the recent years, the UCPs have been faced with designing and updating distance education programs to find new resources and to plan collective actions and justify new partnerships. As mentioned by Moore and Brooks (2000), the increasing complexities of these corporations in which they live and communicate require online knowledge networks to continue the search for ways, methods, and techniques to improve their ability to make better decisions for social justice activism. In this case, there must be fundamental multicultural approaches to discuss the identification and definition of actual and potential real-life problems transcend the separate capacities of online knowledge networks. These approaches are pursed with a dynamic variety of schemes that promise the UCPs how to build global knowledge networks, support social, cultural, and educational communications in order to emphasize the attitudes, beliefs and expectations, and document effective lifelong learning practices in Turkey.

Building global knowledge networks can help university and community who are deeply engaged in lifelong learning activities in distance education to develop strong theoretical frameworks for adult participations with each other in bringing about democratic changes in online communities. As mentioned by Harkavy (2000) and Smith (2000), in most the UCPs, however, there can be a hierarchy of social status that dominant power represents high controls and political authorities. These power elites can decide what valuable and fundamental for the UCPs are that online communications involve forceful structures and process of meaning making for lifelong learning. Therefore, UCPs expose completely the needs, expectations, beliefs, and desires of all diverse groups to collaborate within these social contents. This is extremely imperative for alien cultures, nondominance groups to communicate with the power elites in distance education due to the influences within the dominant cultures' social, political, economic, and religious arrangements.

The UCPs designed by the ideas of public interest about lifelong learning help individuals actively engage in their learning progresses and critically reflect upon what they share with each other. Furthermore, these collaborations encourage individuals to effectively transfer their knowledge to the new contexts of public goods. As a result, the members of these UCPs can improve their complex critical thinking skills to generate, produce, or demonstrate their knowledge, which provides rubrics for assessment criteria to promote collaborations and interactions among professionals, learners, and community (Burniske & Monke, 2001; Cawelti & Protheroe, 2003). They can involve innovative assessments to meet their changing needs and realize new opportunities by sharing knowledge toward online researches.

Finally, the UCPs can help their members to rethink about public interest, focus on the more pressing educational and social problems of our time, and understand the achievement challenges and assessment concerns of lifelong learning. As noted by Porter (2004), therefore, the UCPs must provide important information about the changing needs of online learners toward conducting both qualitative and quantitative researches toward publish interest for distance education that can address the questions and concerns of public good for educators, policymakers, stakeholders, and scholars. Moreover, the UCPs must look at practices and experiences from the real-life situations for probing public interests that are extremely crucial for lifelong learners to be engaged citizens, informed individuals, and dynamic members of their virtual society in Turkey.

Supporting Social, Cultural, and Educational Communications

Supporting social, cultural, and educational interactions between university and community can build spaces for them to see possibilities, potentials, and implications of moving beyond transmission model of communicating about educational and social justice issues for lifelong learning in Turkey. The people in online knowledge networks have different communication styles and strategies (Stephenson, 2001) so that they need diverse opportunities and encouragements to improve their critical thinking skills during their interactions. Each individual must assist *lifelong learning* experiences with real-life situations, which cover global knowledge and technology resources. The UCPs must address key questions about learner critical thinking skill developments through realizing some of the more pressing political, educational, ethical, economical, and social dilemmas of our time. Universities and communities must compete to realize online communication encounter they have to appreciate the idea that there is much more to communications than the mere analyses of messages. One of the most important aspects of human communication is the fact that the experimental backgrounds participants bring to a communication experience can affect their intentions during the encounter. There should be three main focuses of the UCPs in Turkey:

1. UCPs should provide easy and inexpensive as well as quick access to indispensable knowledge and information with high-tech communication media for their online members in the programs.
2. UCPs should encourage these online participants to develop their critical thinking skills by owning knowledge acquisition to become their knowledge constructors; articulating intentions, collecting and interpreting knowledge to build and represent new understandings; thinking critically about their learning processes and reflecting about what they were taught to scaffold their ideas and opinions, and discovering how to empower meaning-making with empowering their dreams with abstract mental images.
3. UCPs should support more collaborative shared powers in lifelong learning, which is implemented in control over the hidden curriculum. These multiway interactions in distance education can empower UCPs to share and exchange the ideas, beliefs, and facts of others from the real-life experiences. Needless to say, the development of UCPs does only occur in mutuality with others from the world.

Emphasizing Attitudes, Beliefs, and Expectations

Emphasizing the attitudes, beliefs, and expectations of university and community partnerships addresses important cultural and social problems for lifelong learning to build comfort for them to explore how to bring educational and social justice into real-life experiences in distance education. The models and approaches of the UCPs provide their members with wide variability in cultural differences during intercultural communications that range from interactions among them. The main purpose of the Turkish UCPs, therefore, is to focus on constructing interactions between the university and community to build critical and creative knowledge networks for lifelong learners. The strategies and principles of these online collaborations based on constructivist learning theory must be discussed and analyzed in UCPs. The pedagogical and communicational dimensions of lifelong learning can affect the design of collaborations between groups (Garrison & Anderson, 2000; Salmon,

2000). Accordingly, the degree of differences between these cultural groups depends on their relative social uniqueness. The members of UCPs are able to:

1. Encourage e-providers and e-communication designers to plan, develop, and implement interactive knowledge networks
2. Provide them with real-life experiences, ideas, opinions, and discussions
3. Make more efficient inventions and build up multicultural online infrastructures for achieving scholarly multi-way and multilevel e-texts and e-contents for diverse learners
4. Generate open and flexible online knowledge milieus that modify diverse thoughts, feelings, and actions
5. Recognize the existing contributions and predict future potentials, opportunities, and obstacles of UCPs

The Turkish universities, therefore, can be able to bring together a community of people committed to social justice and social equity, and eventually can be able to represent a range of experience in their community work and critical praxis.

Documenting Effective Lifelong Learning Practices

Documenting effective lifelong learning practices of the UCPs in a democratic decision-making process can promote dialogues and dialogic leaderships among practitioners. Critical analysis for lifelong learning is balanced with real-life practices (Burge, 2000; Powazek, 2002). The UCPs are able to encourage the contributions of their members so that they understand their own well-defined experiences of race and racism to practical and essential concerns with social justice coping with of racism and elite supremacy within the online milieus. Thus, the UCPs develop practical responses to the impact of race and diversity on their consciousness and practice, and on the associated online communicational experiences of lifelong learners that can inform new models and approaches to diversity communication. Moreover, increasing critical pedagogical and communicational responses interrupt existing mandates and the reproduction of power and privilege in and beyond UCPs in Turkey. The diverse perspectives and concerns of their partnerships recognize their own various race, ethnic, class, gender, sexual, and ability experiences that can become more important than ever for online knowledge networks.

As mentioned by Haefner (2000) and Rovai (2002), the UCPs can be able to bring together a community of people committed to social justice, and represents real-life experiences in their community works. These partnerships must reflect deeply and critically on their own assumptions, actions, and ways of critical thinking for lifelong learning. This is important to take leadership in communicating all members to become intercultural proficient, deeply informed about lifelong learning, and empowered to achieve and perform dependably in interdependent online milieus. The Turkish UCPs must be not only activist communication processes but also complex decision-making progressions in culturally diverse communities. The UCPs also discover online critical dialogues that show their awareness of cultural biases, stereotypes, and prejudices in online collective activities. Therefore, the members must be educational activists for lifelong learning to investigate the social constructions of dominant elites and social inequality groups (Brook & Oliver, 2003; Smith, 2000; Thompson & Lerner, 2000). The critical communication approaches for social justice activism can develop culturally responsive, social justice-oriented, and critical communication plans. These partnerships can go beyond elite power mandates that challenge the communicational constructions of social inequities in their online interactions. This help their members (1) develop culturally responsive, integrated, social justice communication plans for lifelong learning, and (2) empower their partnerships to engage in antiracist, social activism, and alternative communication practices through the critical dialogues.

The UCPs must demonstrate the relationships between diverse cultures and multicultural insights that they have memberships. Effective action plans, constant evaluations, and a sensitive awareness can help the UCPs understand needs and pressing problems that take all account of all major aspects of lifelong learning in distance education.

Solutions and Recommendations

Over the past few years, "lifelong learning" is explosively popular in Turkey, which is dealing with the enormous growth of the electronic communication environments. The distance education opens its doors to build online milieus where university and community can communicate with each other electronically. As emphasized previously, the UCPs must promote interactive collaboration environments for lifelong learning based on a theoretical framework. This collaboration must enable them to understand problems and perspectives from the real world. The communicational activities can help the UCPs focus on preparing lifelong learners related problems in their online societies. In this case, building online societies via these partnerships becomes a dynamic social and cultural activity and goal-oriented process in distance education (Cawelti & Protheroe, 2003; Moore & Brooks, 2000). In Turkey, therefore, all practitioners must work together to embrace this constructivist perspective to:

1. Describe and analyze lifelong learning projects for the effective UCPs in educational and social justice issues
2. Examine real-life experiences of their partnerships in pedagogical situations that seek to implement collective actions for lifelong learning
3. Move beyond transmission model for educational and social justice issues and implications for pedagogy to build online knowledge societies by involving their partnerships in distance education
4. Examine the multifaceted responsibilities of the university in supporting community actively engaging in building their communities for lifelong learning
5. Investigate how the university and community, theoretically and practically, work with lifelong learners to recreate more dialogical and democratic forms of pedagogy and community engagements
6. Focus on conscious and unconscious barriers and possibilities that the UCPs can promote the engagements of educational and social justice in distance education

The problem is to combine the support from diverse sources into a pattern of lifelong learning that must be adequate and consistent with the essential objectives of UCPs. In addition, these partnerships can influence the use of diversity resources, and the attached conditions and restrictions on building knowledge networks powerfully. The UCPs can be able to achieve their fundamental objectives, balanced programs, excellence performance, and openness of opportunity for lifelong learning. In this case, building knowledge networks help the UCPs encourage the development of distance education in multiple directions required by the public interests and public needs. The gains from building knowledge networks via UCPs are considerable to reduce discriminations against under at risk groups and deal with injustices and frustrations arising out of the racial problems in lifelong learning. UCPs must provide technologically and socio-economically disadvantaged groups with new opportunities to become the active members of their online knowledge networks. This can be faced simply with social, political, economical, and cultural gaps that yield power elites and also with a radical crisis in values that profit from diverse manners in which online knowledge networks resolve these conflicts democratically (Ralston et al., 2000).

As indicated Table 1, the Turkish UCPs have begun to change the roles and responsibilities of lifelong learners; the UCPs embrace online communications to incorporate the new ways of accessing to global knowledge and information democratically. The framework presented in Table 1 summarizes the main characteristics of the UCPs-based activities related to the foundations of *media richness theory* and *new communication technologies*.

Table 1. The UCPs framework for lifelong learning

University-Community Partnerships (UCPs)			
The Strategies and Principles of Media Richness Theory / New Communication Technologies		**Building Online Communities**	
		Lifelong Learners' New Roles	**Lifelong Learners' Changing Responsibilities**
Online Collaborative Communications	**New Communication Skills**	• Asking dynamic questions under diverse considerations • Exploring various opportunities to learn concepts, apply information, and represent their knowledge • Making active investigations to empower their cognitive tools in learning milieus that support them in the representation of their ideas, belief, opinions, attitudes, and intentions • Highlighting on their own artifact knowledge constructions to represent what they learned • Sharing knowledge and communicating with other learners, professors, and the course owner in the community to build an online knowledge network	• Exploring diverse points of views to learn from their mistakes and also successes in collective actions • Becoming flexible to seek and provide reasons for what they are communicating • Remaining relevant to the main point of a discussion to consider the new ideas and opposite information and knowledge • Following their own critical thinking skills to be sensitive to others' ideas, opinions, feelings, expectations, and needs • Seeking appropriate solutions to distinguish between concrete objects and abstract constructs
	New Communication Strategies	• Accepting constructivist strategies and principles for altering their communication processes and developing critical thinking skills • Producing the suitable real-life experiences and practices for answering critical questions related to learning with lifelong learning in distance education • Adapting the new technology-based communication environments powerfully to improve their higher-order thinking skills • Generating the number of new possibilities and strictly logical thinking perspectives to take the ownerships of their communication processes	• Using multi-way communications when interacting with each other • Preferring to be active contributors rather than be be passive receivers • Find diverse answers that were just as good as the ones they had suggested • Articulating their communication problems when they state the absence of other possibilities • Asking right questions to develop completely new ideas • Being careful about where they direct their attentions that strongly connect with their previous communication structures on how and what they think
Negotiate the Meanings of Flexible Online Communications	**Common Visions of Educational and Social Justice**	• Building global online knowledge networks to help UCPs that are deeply engaged in the service of the public good to support social, cultural, and educational communications between them to redefine their roles in collective actions • Emphasizing the attitudes, beliefs, and expectations of universities and communities to address some of the more pressing cultural and social problems of lifelong learning • Developing their critical thinking skills to become deeply engaged in the service of the public good to address complex problem solving activities enhanced democratic and multicultural e-contexts in lifelong learning • Delve into the communication patterns of UCPs to consider critically ethical dilemmas and their diverse solutions	• Promoting excellence through continous process improvement and the creative pursuit of new ideas and systems in lifelong learning • Communication experiences and skills associated with critical thinking developments to appreciate public interest for lifelong learning that builds knowledge networks via distance education • Gaining diverse and multicultural knowledge about their partnerships to plan, communicate, motivate, manage, and lead effectively in professional developments and lifelong learning endeavors in distance education • Generating and supporting democratic and multicultural communication milieus that focus on working collaboratively with their colleagues, learners, and global partners for lifelong learning

Online knowledge networks have the potential to support the real-world experiences of universities and communities (Salmon, 2000). With the use of these milieus as supplements to on-campus face-to-face collaborations as well as its use to support fully online interactions, there is no doubt that the UCPs are no longer bound by *time* and *space*. These partnerships provide increasing numbers of convenient and relatively inexpensive communication environments. The UCPs through building a virtual community by sharing knowledge online have become an important medium for addressing problems. Essentially, online knowledge networks have brought about new ways for the UCPs to allow accessing, delivering, sharing, and exchanging knowledge to each other. To deliver communicational knowledge via online, universities and communities together must carefully redesign and revolutionize their new roles around online communication methods, techniques, and strategies in an interactive and collaborative virtual community. Their experiences toward building online knowledge networks need to be more clearly defined, examined, and analyzed in order to integrate and implement the emerging technologies into their daily interactions efficiently.

There are drastic changes in the strategies and organization within building knowledge networks for lifelong learning. The new advancements and approaches of the cutting-edge communication technologies force the UCPs to develop and integrate diverse and multicultural resources in Turkey. As mentioned by Powazek (2002) and Stephenson (2001), these partnerships can provide richer interaction and more collaboration among lifelong learners. Needless to say, many traditional and contemporary distance education programs turn their attentions in growing numbers to the computer-based technologies to build knowledge networks for the Turkish UCPs.

Summary and Conclusion

Although increasingly academic institutions are beginning to offer distance education, the UCPs toward building online knowledge networks for lifelong learning are relatively new phenomena. This study defines, examines, and analyzes the partnerships to design and deliver real-life experiences for lifelong learners. This chapter has provided a theoretical framework to encourage the UCPs by highlighting the comprehensive challenges of the radical reform movement in distance education. Moreover, this chapter redefines new assessment techniques, increased standards, and more accountability issues for lifelong learning that conduct various researches to serve lifelong learners better in distance education.

In the future planning for lifelong learning, reasonable compromises must be sought between university and community autonomies as represented by multicultural and egalitarian resources from diverse groups, and response to social needs as represented by various kinds of distance education programs (Moore & Brooks, 2000; Schrum & Benson, 2002). The UCPs must devote more efforts to enhancing and demonstrating educational productivity. They must their knowledge networks as scholarly communities and demonstrate sincere concerns about how the educational communications are structured for lifelong learning. On the other hand, the UCPs can play the dominant roles that power elites and their values can play an important role in aristocratic knowledge networks in lifelong learning. Therefore, criticism of the UCPs to write their own manifesto in distance education must be extremely effective to reflect diverse perspectives and concerns on lifelong learning that reduce to hegemonic elite powers and exercises in discriminatory manners.

Learners in distance education must involve academic activities in meeting their changing needs and realizing new opportunities for lifelong learning. The UCPs must prepare these lifelong learners to become active members of online knowledge societies. Therefore, this study is to investigate the principles and strategies of the UCPs that lifelong learners actively engage in their education progresses and critically reflect upon what they share with each other. Building online societies encourages these learners to effectively transfer their knowledge to the new contexts of educational and social justice. As a result, all the lifelong learners can enhance their complex critical thinking skills to construct, produce, or demonstrate their knowledge in distance education. They can discover critical rubrics to assess lifelong criteria and promote partnerships between university and community. Building online knowledge societies must be the most important educational goals of university and community partnerships in distance education today.

In this chapter, the framework focused on the UCPs to build online knowledge societies to explore and discover the reflections and experiences of lifelong learners in Turkey. Exploring examples, principles and values, skills and competencies, action-oriented methods, and facilitative relationships between university and community (1) generate powerful enthusiasm for lifelong learning, (2) foster multigenerational partnerships, and (3) encourage democratic leaderships in distance education. The UCPs in this framework can help lifelong learners face with the educational and social issues effectively.

This study shows that the key points of building an online community are to offer online communication techniques and to provide reliable and regular technical support. In addition, encouraging universities and communities to take advantages of virtual communications is also a necessary measure to insure effective utilization. An essential step in building online knowledge networks productively in distance education is starting with an explicit definition of the educational role of lifelong learning and understanding the changing roles of universities and communities in online milieus.

Postscript

The UCP must build powerful knowledge networks within their community to construct greater communication, research, and funding opportunities through multidisciplinary collaborations. The mission of the UCPs must address a wide variety of important societal issues, with a focus on four main areas to achieve a variety of important outcomes:

1. **Faculty-learner interactions:**
   - Increasing youth civic engagement
   - Improving college student critical thinking
   - Preparing learners in a wide range of disciplines and professions for practice
   - Improving college learner mental health
   - Understanding the possibilities and potentials of democratic decision making and dialogic leadership
   - Decreasing college learner alcohol and drug use
   - Promoting critical communication activities for adult-youth engagements in democratic decisions
   - Promoting scholarship-based engagements
   - Making to promote authentic and high quality lifelong learning experiences
2. **Faculty-faculty collaborations:**
   - Engaging in community-based research and evaluation
   - Conducting effective community-based researches
   - Increasing the relevance of research
   - Engaging them in critical civic responsibilities, dynamic academic curriculums, and powerful social actions
   - Reconciling the pressures for diversity and difference with the models of dialogic leaderships
3. **Faculty-community communications:**
   - Solving important issues to individuals, families, groups, neighborhoods, and communities
   - Eliminating racial and ethnic diversity
   - Discussing the philosophical foundations and backgrounds of concepts, insights, and skills needed to accelerate democratic transformations

- Translating research into practice and policy
- Building healthier societies

4. **Faculty-community-learner partnerships:**
    - Integrating authentic partnerships by clearly stating the pedagogical guidelines
    - Taking ownership and responsibility for lifelong learning process
    - Building knowledge networks from a pedagogical perspective in distance education
    - Improving independent living strategies and principles
    - Providing unique and diverse perspectives with their own methodological strengths and weaknesses to obtain genuine equal opportunities and democratic participations
    - Building knowledge networks not characterized by power, dominance, hierarchy, and competition
    - Sharing power and cultures to help them deeply engage in lifelong learning activities
    - Examining the dynamics of democratic changes in online community by improving reflective practices for greater impact

The UCPs should explain the needs and expectations of their engagements in bringing about democratic decision making for dialogic leaderships. This is an important role in affecting deep community changes to examine the multifaceted responsibilities of the UCPs in supporting youth and community actively engaging in building their online knowledge networks. Therefore, they can become well-rounded knowledge-workers to shape a society based on authentic and participatory decision-making. In Turkey, the UCPs must discuss egalitarian decision making of how their engagements facilitate learning from each other, and develop a common vision of social justice by dismissing power and cultural oppressions.

The partnerships should ultimately build knowledge networks via new communication technologies. The technology-based collaborations encourage them to be altruistic to make democratic decisions for dialogic leaderships, which have a direct relevance to their own lives. These engagements increase awareness of their own identities and differences, and help to define the democratic values associated with equalizing of access to human rights. In addition, this new model provides their engagements with alternative holistic forms and scaffolding strategies of social justice to fight the hegemonic power of capitalism and its unfair structure. Within the context of these concerns, the UCPs should seek to empower their engagements to build progressive knowledge networks for lifelong learning.

To build global knowledge networks and authentic learning milieus can definitely bring democratic changes in universities and communities by implementing collective action to investigate real-life experiences in pedagogical situations. Furthermore, understanding critical communicational possibilities and potentials about educational and social justice issues for lifelong learning may be able to recreate dialogical and democratic forms of pedagogy and community engagement. Finally, exploring powerful democratic communicational practices by providing specific ideas can promote dialogues between the university and the community.

References

Anderson, T., & Elloumni, F. (Eds.). (2004). *Theory and practice of online learning.* Athabasca: Athabasca University Press.

Bates, A. W. (2000). *Managing technological change.* San Francisco: Jossey-Bass.

Baum, H. S. (2000). Fantasies and realities in university-community partnerships. *Journal of Planning Education and Research, 20*(2), 234-246.

Benson, L., & Harkavy, I. (2000). Higher education's third revolution: The emergence of the democratic cosmopolitan civic university. *Cityscape: A Journal of Policy Development and Research, 5*(1), 47–57.

Bonk, C. J., Kim, K. J., & Zeng, T. (2006). Future directions of blended learning in higher education and workplace learning settings. In C. J. Bonk & C. R. Graham (Eds.), *Handbook of blended learning: Global perspectives, local designs* (pp. 550-568). San Francisco: Pfeiffer Publishing.

Brook, C., & Oliver, R. (2003). Online learning communities: Investigating a design framework. *Australian Journal of Educational Technology, 19*(2), 139-160.

Burge, L. (2000). *The strategic use of learning technologies*. San Francisco: Jossey-Bass.

Burniske, R. W., & Monke, L. (2001). *Breaking down the digital walls: Learning to teach in a post-modem world.* Albany, NY: State University of New York Press.

Cawelti, G., & Protheroe, N. (2003). *Supporting school improvement: Lessons from districts successfully meeting the challenge*. Arlington, VA: Educational Research Services.

Farmer, J. (2004). Communication dynamics: Discussion boards, Weblogs and the development of communities of inquiry in online learning environments. In R. Atkinson, C. McBeath, D. Jonas-Dwyer, & R. Phillips (Eds.), *Beyond the comfort zone: Proceedings of the 21st ASCILITE Conference*, Perth, Australia (pp. 274-283). Retrieved August 11, 2006, from http://www.ascilite.org.au/conferences/perth04/procs/farmer.html

Frabutt, J. M., Forsbrey, A. D., & MacKinnon-Lewis, C. (2003). A university-community partnership's use of qualitative methods to foster community engagement in adolescent research. *Journal of Higher Education Outreach and Engagement, 8*(2), 105-118.

Garrison, R., & Anderson, T. (2003). *E-Learning in the 21st century: A framework for research and practice*. New York: Routledge.

Haefner, J. (2000). *Opinion: The importance of being synchronous.* Academic writing. Retrieved August 11, 2006, from http://aw.colostate.edu/teaching/haefner2000.htm

Harkavy, I. (2000). Historical evolution of university-community partnerships. *Community News & Views: A Publication of the MSU Center for Urban Affairs, Community and Economic Development Program, 12*(2), 1-3.

Moore, A. B., & Brooks, R. (2000). Learning communities and community development: Describing the process. *Learning Communities: International Journal of Adult and Vocational Learning, 1*(1), 1-15.

Porter, L. R. (2004). *Developing an online curriculum: Technologies and techniques*. Hershey, PA: Information System Publishing.

Powazek, D. (2002). Design for community: The art of connecting real people in virtual places. *Philosophical Perspectives on Constructivist Views of Learning, 29*(1), 37-48.

Ralston, P. A., Lerner, R. M., Mullis, A. K., Simerly, C. B., & Murray, J. P. (2000). *Outreach scholarship series, Vol. 3: Social change, public policy, and community collaborations: Training human development professionals for the twenty-first century*. Boston: Kluwer Academic Publishers.

Rovai, P. A. (2002). Building sense of community at a distance. *International Review of Research in Open and Distance Learning, 3*(1), 1-16.

Salmon, G. (2000). *E-moderation: The key teaching and learning online*. London: Kogan Page.

Schrum, L., & Benson, A. (2002). Establishing successful online distance learning environments: Distinguishing factors that contribute to online courses and programs. In R. Discenza, C. Howard, & K. Schenk (Eds.), *The design & management effective distance learning programs* (pp. 190-204). Hershey, PA: Idea Group Inc.

Smith, B. (2000). As we sow ... A pragmatic analysis of how to build successful partnerships between the university and the larger community. In R. M. Lerner (Series Ed.) & P. A. Ralston, R. M. Lerner, A. K. Mullis, C. B. Simerly, & J.

P. Murray (Eds.), *Outreach scholarship series, Vol. 3: Social change, public policy, and community collaborations: Training human development professionals for the twenty-first century* (pp. 59-70). Boston: Kluwer Academic Publishers.

Stephenson, J. (Ed.). (2001). *Teaching and learning online: Pedagogies for new technologies*. London: Kogan Page.

Thompson, L. S., & Lerner, R. M. (2000). Pursing policies promoting healthy youth development: The role of university-community collaborations. *Policy, Politics, & Nursing Practice, 1*(1), 68-75.

Section V

Case Studies in Online Education for Lifelong Learning

Chapter XI

Promoting Lifelong Learning Online: A Case Study of a Professional Development Experience

Danilo M. Baylen, Florida Gulf Coast University, USA

Joan Glacken, Florida Gulf Coast University, USA

Abstract

The introduction of computers and emerging technology applications has changed the learning landscape, especially in higher education. From traditional university classroom learning to community-based adult continuing education programs, it is common to see the delivery of instruction that is now supported by online or distance learning technologies. Online learning has become a common strategy to deliver instruction, enhance access to educational resources, and achieve success in higher education. This chapter focuses on practical applications of emerging technologies in the delivery of professional development programs.

Introduction

The introduction of computers and emerging technology applications has changed the learning landscape, especially in higher education. From traditional university classroom learning to community-based adult continuing education programs, it is common to see the delivery of instruction now supported by online or distance learning technologies (Huang, 2002). Online learning has become a common strategy to deliver instruction, enhance access to educational resources, and achieve success in higher education (Glacken & Baylen, 2001).

This chapter focuses on practical applications of emerging technologies (e.g., Internet, asynchronous communication tools, and course management systems) in the delivery of professional development programs. The goal of this chapter is to identify, discuss, and illustrate to individuals with professional interest in lifelong learning strategies how online technologies, such as a course management system called Authenticated Networked Guided Environment for Learning (ANGEL) can support the course design, implementation, and evaluation at a distance.

Overview

What is the essential link between "lifelong learning" and "online distance education"? First, after reviewing how other researchers like Aspin and Chapman (2000), Field (2001), and Griffin (1999) define lifelong learning, Koper and Tattersall (2004) state it "refers to the activities people perform throughout their life to improve their knowledge, skills and competence in a particular field, given some personal, societal or employment related motives" (p. 689). The successful implementation of lifelong learning activities could be hindered by mental, financial, access, learning design, and information (Longworth, 2003). It is important for those involved in designing and implementing these activities to have a thorough understanding first of their impact or influences.

Koper and Tattersall (2004) argue that barriers involving access, learning design, and information could be resolved with the use of existing and emerging technologies. Networked learning technologies could support lifelong learning activities "anytime, anyplace, and anywhere" (p. 698) as well as traditional learning contexts (Baylen & Zhu, 2005; Koper & Tattersall, 2004). Also, Edwards (1993) states that the use of electronic tools makes learning a private and personal experience that appears to motivate learners.

Examples from the literature of networked technologies supporting lifelong learning include the Semantic Web, interactive communication technologies, and e-portfolios (Friesen & Anderson, 2004; Zhu & Baylen, 2005). These technologies seem to fit well "with those characteristics of lifelong learning that constitute its 'eclectic' and 'holistic' nature" (Friesen & Anderson, p. 683). Furthermore, Gorard, Selwyn, and Madden (2003) argue that the use of these technologies could in some way alter patterns of participation in educational experiences for some, if not many, individuals, and should be embraced cautiously.

Also, new technologies like blogs, podcasts, wikis, social bookmarking, and instant messaging embraced by the younger generations are becoming visible and available to adult learners. These new tools are starting to redefine the way adult learners engage in teaching and learning activities, especially outside the classroom. Blogs and wikis provide virtual spaces where learners engage with each other to express thoughts and generate interest on specific issues (Downes, 2004; Engstrom & Jewett, 2005). Many university students are finding the value of podcasting by downloading class lectures in audio or video formats. Social bookmarkers (e.g., *del.icio.us* at http://del.icio.us/) are becoming useful tools for archiving and sharing Web resources. Also, instant messaging as a tool has found uses beyond personal communication and slowly gaining ground in enhancing professional activities (Farmer, 2005).

Online or distance education is a growing force in lifelong learning. Due to the rapid development of Web-based technologies, increasing bandwidth, decreasing costs and widening access, online versions of distance education programs are becoming increasingly popular teaching strategies for universities to adopt (Townsend & Wheeler, 2004). At the same time, confusion could be created with the advent of new terminology (such as virtual, open, distributed, and distance education), new technologies, new audiences, and new commercially competitive providers; these innovations present enormous challenges for educators to make sense of the distance educational options available (Garrison, 2000).

Given these changes in the learning landscape, the use of course management systems has become a prevalent tool in supporting online learning delivery. Morgan (2003) describes a course management system as a software system specifically designed and marketed for use in teaching and learning. Common course management systems include, but are not limited to, WebCT, Blackboard, and ANGEL. Course content, organization and presentation modalities, communication tools, student assessment tools, grade book tools, and functions that manage class materials and activities are common components of a course management system (Zhu & Baylen, 2005).

Theoretical Framework

Since learning through the use of these technologies has a different structure and format than the conventional classroom, educators need to use some special techniques and perceptions that would lead to a successful educational experience.

Designing instruction involves the application of instructional design principles (Dick & Carey, 2004) and online course design models (Sorensen & Baylen, 2004). Various theoretical frameworks involving authentic learning (Herrington & Oliver, 2000), case-based learning (Kreber, 2001), and vicarious learning (Rummel, Spada, Hermann, Caspar & Schornstein, 2002) appear to be some of the common frameworks utilized by instructional designers and course developers in online course development.

Huang (2002) proposes "instructional guidelines using the constructivist approach in online learning for adults" (p. 27). Herrington and Oliver (2000) suggest that using a situated learning framework appears to provide effective instructional design guidelines for the design of an environment for the acquisition of advanced knowledge. Kreber (2001) argues that experiential learning could foster students' learning on a higher-order level—critical thinking ability and openness to self-directed learning. Stenning, McKendree, Lee, et al. (1999) investigated the role of dialogue in learning and argue for the importance of learners benefiting from opportunities to "overhear" other learners. On peer-to-peer collaboration, Murphy (2004) states as follows: "the higher-level processes in an online asynchronous discussion (OAD) may need to be more explicitly and effectively promoted in order to counteract a tendency on the part of participants to remain at the level of individual rather than group or group collaborative effort" (p. 430). Murphy further elaborated that:

Promoting collaboration in the context of an OAD can be facilitated by conceptualizing collaboration in terms of processes and their indicators along a continuum. Participants in a discussion, the aim of which is to promote collaboration, can benefit from supports and scaffolds that guide them along the continuum through these processes. Promoting collaboration can also be facilitated by determining ways in which individuals can share goals and purposes and finally create or produce a tangible artifact or even an intangible one, such as a solution to a problem. Finally, promoting collaboration in an OAD will necessarily involve an appreciation for the context in which individuals interact in virtual environments. In these environments, individuals interact without sharing spatial or temporal presence. Producing a shared artifact and even sharing goals and purposes represent processes that may occur and manifest themselves differently in an online environment than in one in which individuals interact in real time and in each other's physical presence. (p. 430)

Finally, Huang (2002) summarizes that instructional principles of interactive learning, collaborative learning, facilitating learning, authentic learning, learner-centered learning, and high quality learning should be incorporated to design instruction, especially to promote learning at a distance.

Current Practice: Anatomy of an Online Course

The discussion of current practices on lifelong learning online could be better understood by observing and investigating an online course delivery. Understanding the background, motivation, and learning goals of learners, as well as strategies, issues, and feedback on the online delivery would be helpful. An online graduate course on designing instruction is reviewed for this chapter. Degree and non-degree seeking students registered for this course to satisfy requirements for their graduate program or for professional development.

In this context, nine adult learners registered for the online course designed to provide them with knowledge and skills for designing instruction for their selected learning environment. Five were currently teaching in K-12 classrooms (two elementary schools, one middle school, three high schools) and three were involved in teaching and/or administrative capacities not necessarily in a formal K-12 structure. However, all were involved in facilitating educational experiences for various student levels.

Five started their careers in industry or nonprofit organizations while the remaining members started as teachers. Seven were enrolled in a graduate degree program while two were taking the course for certification. Gender distribution identified three males and six females. Ethnicity identification was attributed to seven whites and two nonwhites.

Format and Structure of the Course Experience

The online delivery format of the course was designed to engage students in enhancing not only their knowledge about instructional design, online learning and teaching, and curriculum development, but also developing their skills in creating instructional units that can be delivered online as a component of a professional development program for adult learners. Table 1 illustrates the types of activity, instructional strategies used, and the delivery format that facilitated online teaching and learning.

The course structure involved students in multiple ways: from case analyses, reflective asynchronous discussions, and synchronous presentations (chat) among others. The course facilitator used several instructional strategies to promote self-directed learning and technology-supported interactions, implement activity-based sessions online, and achieve reflective learning outcomes. According to Knowles (1975), self-directed learning is a process that engaged "individuals take the initiative, with or without the help of others, in diagnosing their learning needs, formulating learning goals, identifying human and material resources for learning, choosing and implementing appropriate learning strategies, and evaluating learning outcomes" (p. 18).

Table 1. Types of activity

Strategy Used to Facilitate Teaching and Learning	Online Delivery Format	Types of Activity			
		Self-Directed Learning Activity	*Technology-Supported Interaction*	*Activity-Based Session*	*Reflective Learning Activity*
Content Knowledge Facilitation (One time experience per student)	Synchronous	X	X		X
Content Knowledge Discussion Participation (At least once per term)	Synchronous	X	X		
Case Analysis Facilitation (One time experience per student)	Asynchronous	X	X		X
Case Analysis Participation (Four experiences per student)	Asynchronous	X	X	X	X
Project Design Creation (Five sections per student)	Asynchronous	X		X	X
Project Design Proposal Review (Three reviews per student)	Asynchronous	X		X	

Figure 1. Course process between and among course facilitator and students

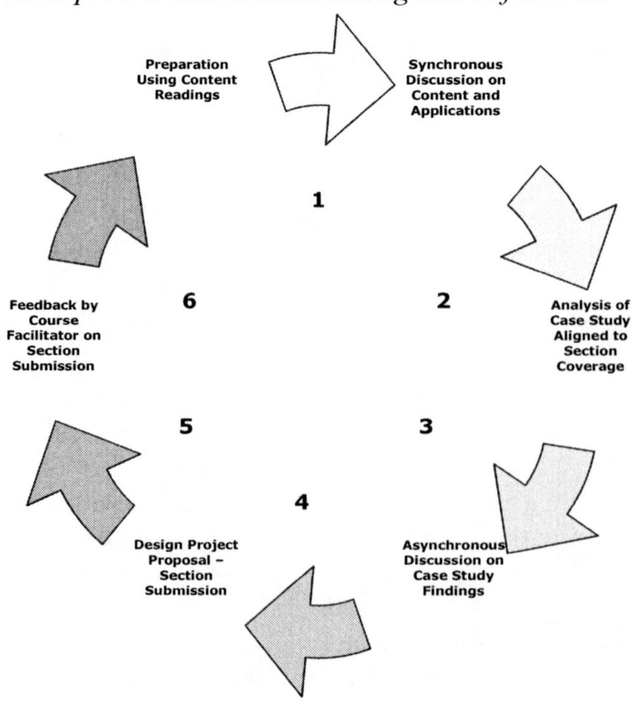

Given the online delivery format, the students' only means of interacting with each other was through the use of asynchronous and synchronous tools embedded in the course management system. Without online interactive activities, there was no difference between completing the exercises at the end of a book chapter and posting responses to questions for each online module. On activity-based sessions online, a case study seemed to lend itself well in promoting critical thinking, problem solving, and small group discussions. It became a natural flow of online interactions that generated reflective and thoughtful summations of what transpired. Figure 1 illustrates this process.

Online Strategies Used

Content Knowledge Facilitation and Discussion Participation

In supporting students to comprehend course materials relevant to the online activities and the design project, students were paired with each other to co-facilitate a one-hour synchronous session scheduled every two weeks during the semester in the early evening hours. Other members of the class participated in discussing the concepts and clarifying concerns and issues pertaining to the course expectations and implementation. This was also a good time to engage the course facilitator at the end of the session for a quick question and answer session. Students were expected to participate in at least one synchronous session during the course of the term. As shown in Table 2, at least two-thirds of the class participated in synchronous sessions (chat) held every other week during the term.

For this course experience, the synchronous sessions alternated between Tuesday and Wednesday to allow those with conflicts to participate at least once during the term. These one-hour sessions were usually conducted after 8:00 P.M. to allow those with families to tend to their activities but not too late for those who had to wake up early the following morning to go to work. Student feedback received involving these synchronous sessions was positive:

With awesome encouragement by my peers through our threaded discussion and online chats, I learned that I was not the only one with these struggles. I think that we became motivated as a group. I have brought that motivation into my classroom encouraging my students. I have been able to share with my students that I could relate with them on difficult classes or assignments that they might be faced with. Encouraging them, and myself, if we try and don't give up we can get through it. (Student H)

Table 2. Distribution of student participation during synchronous discussions

Synchronous Session	# of Student Facilitators	# of Student Participants N = 9	Course Facilitator	Total # of Students
1	0	6	1	6 (67%)
2	2	7	1	9 (100%)
3	2	6	1	8 (89%)
4	1	5	1	6 (67%)
5	2	4	1	6 (67%)
6	2	6	1	8 (89%)

Table 3. Learning goals of online case analysis and discussion

Case	Title	Learning Goals in Each Online Case Discussion
1	The Anxious Nurse Intern	Compare and contrast the details of the case study content to one's academic and/or professional experience.
2	Volunteering for the UEO Project	Develop a design project idea and identify changes made (added, edited, or revised) in each stage of the design project process.
3	Meeting of the Minds	Demonstrate understanding of the instructional design concepts and principles addressed by each case study.
4	To Be or Not to Be	Identify relevant aspects of the case and its accompanying discussion to one's design project.
5	Through the Looking Glass	Discuss content of the students' postings that help the thinking process about the development of one's design project. Apply lessons learned and insights gained from the case study relevant to the requirements of the design project.

Case Analysis with Discussion Facilitation and Participation

One of the driving forces in facilitating student learning of course content and skills development was the five case studies that were created by faculty members from both Colleges of Education and Health Professions (the authors). Each case addressed concepts and skills that students needed to learn and develop through online discussions and applications as students completed a design project proposal (see Table 3).

For some students, the use of this instructional strategy was familiar to some, while for others it was not. After the first case study, however, everyone seemed to know what was expected of them as appropriately stated by one of the students.

The use of case studies to further the learning process was new to me as a means to introduce concepts. In the first case of the Anxious Intern we looked at a scenario of an intern who had difficulty delivering an injection. I am a fixer, ready to work on a problem immediately without stopping until it is resolved. Often, I think I do not always stop to see what the true problem is. The value of discovering the problem is essential! (Student D)

Participation in the online case discussion required each student to post at least 10 messages that initiated new threads of conversation as well as replies to existing messages. 10 postings seemed to be the magic number to get students engaged in an online discussion. Based on online course delivery experiences by the authors, they found that after posting between 5 to 10 messages, the students had read most of what transpired in an online discussion and were involved in adding their own opinions and insights to what was discussed. The student facilitator assigned to a specific case usually began the online discussion with an initial post.

This class required a great deal of interaction with my peers' throughout its entirety. At first I found this interaction to be tedious and obtuse. However, as we advanced further into the design process, I found that each of my peers had established an area of expertise and aspired to share this knowledge with one another. Some of my peers were good at finding web pages with valuable information; some had a knack for APA references, while others had background knowledge with technology that was beneficial to all involved. From the beginning of the course, some of my peers' strengths became noticeable while others were not so obvious. However, by the end of the course, everyone's assets had been discovered and contributions had been made by all, me included. (Student G)

Examples of initial postings and replies (see Appendix A) demonstrated the depth of sharing among students in the course. References to prior experiences were evident. Also, there seemed to be a developing connectedness between students as personal feelings and perceptions were shared during the online exchange.

Project Design Creation and Proposal Review

In alignment to the case studies' discussions, students were expected to create a section of the design project proposal in response to an identified instructional need. A member of the class appropriately captured the connections between sections of the course and its relationship to the whole design project as a learning laboratory.

If you approach the course in a linear, sequential, conquest mode, you fail to make the connections and corrections that come from viewing the instructional problem as a whole, integrated and thoroughly unique event. I found that this course encouraged me to approach the material holistically and not simply as a means to an end. (Student F)

Table 4 illustrates the alignment of each case discussion to the section that needed to be completed by the students.

Students posted each completed section to the course Web site so other students could review the work. The course facilitator provided feedback on each section posted. This allowed nonduplication of feedback as well as learning vicariously among students in seeing the strengths and weaknesses of everyone's work.

After all the sections were completed, the course facilitator asked students to post a draft of the design project proposal. Then, each student was assigned to review three design project proposals created by their peers. The students reviewed each proposal using the following questions as a guide:

- **What do I believe to be the excellent features of this section and why?**
- **What do I want you to see changed or revised in this section and why?**
- **What do I believe does not belong in this section and why?**
- **What do I want to see added to enhance this section and why?**

In addition, the students were asked to comment on the overall design proposal document's clarity, creativity, appropriateness, alignment, out-of-box solutions, and formatting of resources, references, and appendices.

The peer review process allowed students to apply what they had learned from the readings, case discussion, and initial work on section completion. The ability to

Table 4. Concepts and principles addressed by case studies

Case	Section Coverage
1	Problem Statement, Need Analysis, Goal Analysis
2	Audience Analysis, Context Analysis, Initial Task Analysis
3	Clustering and Sequencing, Pre-Instructional Activities, Testing or Assessment of Student Learning, Follow Up Activities, Instructional Strategies for Objectives
4	Online Module Information, Online Module Content & Strategies, Online Module Assessment
5	Evaluation: Context, Input, Process, Product, Logistics, Cost

see three different design project proposals and elicit feedback allowed students to assume the role of instructional designers or consultants. From the course facilitator perspective, it became apparent how much students learned about instructional design concepts and principles and how well they succeeded in the role of an instructional designer or consultant. Finally, the students were asked to rank their own design project proposal submitted against the three other proposals they reviewed.

Issues and Challenges

Given that the course experience was open to degree seeking students and those seeking professional development, diversity in areas of knowledge, facilitation skill, and technology literacy was an issue at the beginning of the term. Students who were in the middle of their degree program found the initial expectations manageable while those who were registered for professional development saw the need to have immediate face-to-face or phone conversations with the course facilitator for some clarification.

Students who had taken core education courses in curriculum and educational research expressed confidence in tackling new concepts and principles addressed by this course. They stated that the language and terms used were familiar which allowed them to digest the readings with ease. Other members of the class who did not have similar experiences communicated that they struggled a bit in making connections between theory and practice as they applied concepts and principles from their readings to the case analysis and discussion and design project proposals. This sentiment had been expressed appropriately by one student.

As the class began, I struggled with the concepts feeling that I had no background or experiences in which to connect meaning with the material. I had hoped that I would be able to draw on my high tech background to compensate for my lack of background knowledge as a teacher. I continued to struggle through the first few sections along with most of my fellow classmates. (Student E)

Students who had taken online courses in the past found the use of the course management system (thus ANGEL) helpful in accessing materials and interacting with the course facilitator and class members. Students who were taking an online course for the first time expressed degrees of difficulty in mastering the technological features of the course management system, both synchronous and asynchronous. As the course progressed, however, the impact of this issue became minimal on student performance.

One important aspect of offering online learning is the target population otherwise known as a class of students. According to Mager (1997), target population information is a useful starting point to help shape a course. It helps determine vocabulary, examples that are most likely to fit, and the types of media and procedures to adopt. A more diverse student population requires more work for the course designer and instructor as presented in the case study. Learning activities and readings need to be developed at a level that all students can comprehend, as well as challenging so that the advanced student is not easily bored. Diverse student populations require a variety of teaching strategies to accommodate different student learning styles. Knowledge of the target population is essential in dealing with the technology learning curve. Not all students will be proficient in navigating an online course. Students with little or no experience with technology and online learning will consume a large part of the instructor's time. It usually takes about three weeks for these students to become comfortable with the technology and online format. Students with experience in online learning will fair well and usually serve as mentors to students with less experience in online courses. The importance of knowing your target audience cannot be stressed enough in the design and development of online courses.

Finally, available time was always an issue and a challenge when implementing a process-oriented activity such as this course experience. Given the location of the institution that delivered the course, forces of nature (e.g., hurricanes) disrupted access and availability of electronic resources. During the period of implementation of this particular experience, the course was disrupted for more than a week. Some students had problems accessing the course management system and participating in online activities for almost two weeks due to loss of power in their respective locations.

When offering any online course for lifelong learning, the limits of technology are always a factor. As mentioned previously, forces of nature caused power outages at the home site of the course and course facilitator. Extended power outages occurred at the home site of the students even after power was restored to the course home site. Technology issues such as these are not common but may occur during the course. Instructors must be prepared to address as many of these issues as possible before they occur. Including policies and procedures in the course syllabus related to technology issues will alleviate many problems in the future. If students are truly at a geographic distance, then course instructors need to have a plan of action to deal with these problems.

Another technology issue to consider is the system parameters of the students' computers. Instructors should inform students of the minimum hardware and software requirements needed for computers to properly function in online courses. If students are required to open PDF files, their computers should be equipped with the proper software program to do this. Students will become frustrated if the computer does not have enough memory or the proper Internet service provider to access or download lessons and assignments.

Implications to Online Teaching and Lifelong Learning

Various factors that impact successful learning experience have been identified through the review of the course experience, such as (1) prior experience, (2) authentic learning experiences, (3) connections between text, content, teacher, and technology, and (4) online role playing, facilitation, and collaborations.

Prior Experience

As adult learners, students in this course used their prior experience to help them get started during case analysis and discussion as well as meet expectations in producing a design project proposal. Some of them shared how they designed instruction prior to taking this course. Others shared how they were able to see how the pieces fit together based on things they learned not only from life/work experiences but also from previous courses taken at the university.

If asked to characterize my design process of the past, I would have to say I used the McDesign process. After studying and employing a variety of design models in this course, I now believe I can employ a more robust systematic process to instructional design. Time may not afford me the luxury of employing a "full blown" process, but at least I now have a better concept of what I need to do, and how in the past I may have cheated the process and the learner. With a clearly stated theory of education and instructional design, I can better design instruction that will produce quality learner outcomes. (Student B)

I found myself using bits and pieces from other classes that I had taken. I used some of what I learned in my assessment class to help design my formative and summative assessments. I used what I learned in my hardware class to make sure the design could work with a standard computer and server configuration. I used what I had learned in web and human interface design to help make my interface easy to use and user friendly. I used what I learned in my research class to review literature and finally I also used what I have learned about educational theory to differentiate instruction and appeal to different learning styles. As I was doing my rewrites it finally occurred to me that the seemingly disparate pieces of my education had all masterfully been pulled together into this one class. (Student E)

Authentic Learning Experiences

Throughout the course experience, the students read and analyzed details of a case study, discussed ideas related to the case study and the design project proposal, and shared personal or professional experiences and online resources (see Figure 2). Each of these activities or events not only enriched the online conversation but more so deepened each student's understanding of what they are learning and what is expected of them.

During the course, we encountered certain principles at work in the case studies. These same principles were named and described in our text readings. We discussed these components and their implications online and used them to lend substance to our own instructional design projects. So when I speak of the iterative process in the course, part of it has to do with the constant revisiting and recasting of our thoughts and how we expressed these, that participation in this course required. (Student F)

Through the text reading, the case studies, the threaded discussions, and the design project process, I now have a clearer understanding of the instructional design process. The case studies helped me to realize the weaknesses that existed in my past and present designs. Recognizing the gaps and weaknesses in designing instruction, I was also better able to see the potential design weaknesses in the ... design project. (Student B)

I had always believed that designing instruction, when done with care, will usually result in desired learning outcomes. However, I came to an even greater appreciation of this when reading the Anxious Intern Scenario. The same scenario taught me the consequences of improper assessment of student learning which can later have an adverse impact on both the learner and institutions impacted by the learner. (Student C)

Connections Between Text and Technology

The course was designed to make sure that technology supported student learning. The five case studies served as core teaching and learning material for the students. The text and related readings were divided to complement each case study, establishing a common ground and language for students and course facilitators to work with during the course. The synchronous (chat) and asynchronous (threaded discussion) communication provided venues where students were able to share ideas,

Figure 2. Case analysis and discussion process between and among course facilitator and students

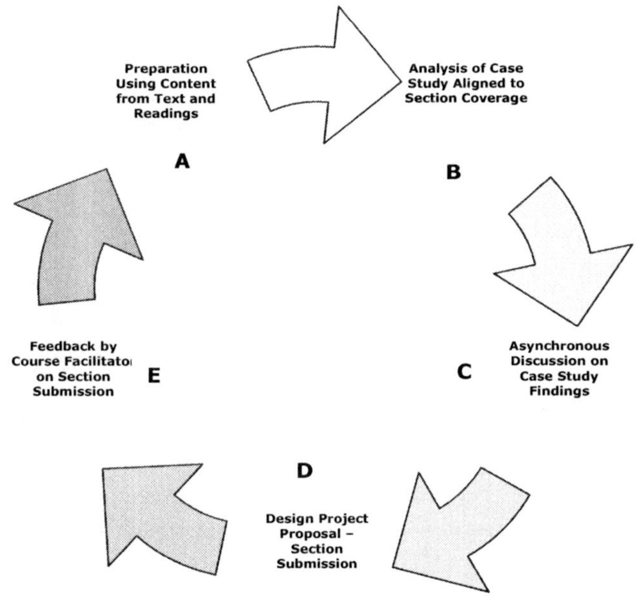

test assumptions, and converse on issues related to the topic at hand. Finally, after these exchanges, students were able to gather their thoughts and reflect upon what knowledge and skills they gained to what they learned about themselves in trying out new roles—as instructional designers or course developers.

Case Four helped me refine aspects of instructional strategies and materials for my own project. I considered the struggles that the trainers in the case scenario might endure as they developed engaging instructional components, and I realized that I must ask myself one especially important question regarding my project – "Would I want to take my own course?" When forced with considering my project in this dispassionate manner, I realized that it was not only important to incorporate properly sequenced instruction, but instruction that grabs the learner's attention and is creative in as many ways as possible. (Student C)

This has been a learning process from beginning to end with each case study that we have done. I thought at first, why are we doing things like this, but now I see the rhyme to the reason. The case studies have shown me things to do and not do in the future when designing an instructional design. They have been wonderful tools that have shown light on many areas that I was in the dark on. I truly do not believe I would have walked away with the knowledge I have without the cases and discus-

sions with the class on them. I think that these were great tools that I utilized in the course. The combination of discussions and cases really helped. (Student A)

The threaded discussions were most helpful to my professional career as a teacher. Exchanging ideas with other teachers on how to apply the course to my everyday situations was very beneficial. Another area was the use of technology. I have evolved beyond the use of the overhead and e-mail! I now know how to participate in a threaded discussion, and an on-line chat and how to upload files. (Student D)

By participating in this course, I learned that I truly learn best when I must communicate with others. It has always been a daunting proposition for me when required to communicate with others within a learning community. There is the fear of failure and not doing as well as the others in the class, but in this class, I finally realized, this is the best way to learn. When I am required to communicate and contribute to the learning community, the concepts and the learning take center stage and all other considerations are secondary. Although I resist it, I am always happier conversing with my peers and working towards a better understanding cooperatively. (Student F)

Online Role Playing, Facilitation, and Collaborations

As the course progressed, the students realized that the class had become their community—a source of support when times were rough, the body was tired from juggling demands at personal and professional levels, and forces of nature (e.g., hurricanes) interfered with course progress. Role playing as instructional designers or consultants became "real" as section after section of the design project proposal evolved into a coherent piece of intervention responding to an identified instructional need. Facilitation of learning events came from all fronts—from course facilitator to fellow students. Finally, collaborations became the norm between and among students, instead of individual work, as they each completed their own design project proposals.

For me, the most useful aspects of this course were the instructor's availability for questions and feedback, the emphases on vicarious learning and the peer review process. It was extremely helpful to be able to consult with the instructor via email or face-to-face to ensure that I was on the right track. It was also helpful for me to read others' observations, postings and papers. I came to a very clear understanding of various aspects of instructional design through this vicarious learning process. (Student C)

I'd have to say though that the most powerful learning tool we had were the chats. I learned so much from my peers that I wouldn't have made it through knowing what I know now without them. The chats utilized what we learned in our text and combined it to parallel our own projects so that we can see the direct correlation. Many times after a chat, I would think to myself "Now I understand!" (Student A)

Some aspects of this class were well within my comfort zone. I worked for years with Japanese companies where most of the communication was done via email as a member of an online community. I learned the importance of wording messages very carefully to avoid misunderstanding from the absence of body language and intonation in verbal speech. I also learned how important it was to give frequent feedback and support to other members of the online community. These skills and experiences served me well in this class as well as my other online classes. (Student E)

... when we were given our peer reviews, one of my classmates was able to clear up a confusion I had regarding assessment and evaluation. My classmate and reviewer pointed out my error with kindness and guided me to the section in the textbook which cleared up my difficulty and allowed me to see something I had been missing up until this point. It was a true "AHA" moment for me as I realized I had been using assessment and evaluation interchangeably. (Student F)

Conclusion

Offering lifelong learning courses online is challenging. Most courses attract a diverse student population with each student having different needs related to the reasons for taking the course, technology, socialization, and feedback.

When I first started out in this project and course I saw myself as a subject matter expert, not an instructional designer. Over time, I began to see myself transform and slowly become the designer. There are times I would see myself as one or the other or sometimes both. Now, I can truly say I am an instructional designer. I am what could be called an amateur designer. (Student A)

Working through the case studies, I learned the importance of considering the perspectives, needs, and issues of all stakeholders in searching out the root of the problem. I found it challenging to hone in on the actual problem for the case study as well as for my design project and work-related projects. (Student B)

The successful online instructor will realize that each student is different and will plan for these differences in the development of the online course. Instructors must take into consideration the previous experience of the students in the class and the importance of knowing the target population.

I came ... with an unstructured "method" for designing instruction. I leave an aspiring instructional designer with a toolbox filled with processes, tactics, strategies, assessments, research, and the confidence to use these tools in a systematic way to design effective instruction for students and adults. (Student B)

This course taught me also not to compromise your values or your self worth. A lot of time and energy goes into designing a project and I will not be selling myself short. It has shown me that I am worth every penny that I may charge. In regards to values, it showed me that hard work pays off. You get a sense of satisfaction when you know that you have put forth your best. (Student A)

Authentic learning is an important concept that allows the students to bridge the gap between theory and practice. Every part of the online course needs to be connected so that students understand the relevancy of all the assignments. Students need to become an active participant in online courses through role playing, facilitation, or collaboration.

One of the greatest benefits from this course was the impact on my attitudes, disposition, and orientation. While extremely valuable, the peer review process was an extremely tough pill to swallow. As a direct result of this process, I reaffirmed my belief that no one has all the answers. Robert Frost said it well when he said: "Education is the ability to listen to almost anything without losing your temper or your self-confidence." (Student C)

Communities can be developed online. Relationships can be formed and an actual bonding can take place. I was impressed by the learning that occurred and the degree of quality and degree of assistance provided by each member. I am deeply appreciative of the insight I gained from my peers. (Student D)

Technology will always be an issue in online classes and the more an instructor can plan for technology issues with policies and procedures, the easier life will be. Instructors that keep these concepts in mind during the development and implementation of online courses will be successful.

For the first time, I witnessed first-hand, how distance education can achieve a level of communication that is sufficient to support the topics being discussed. I always had a bias against distance education because I felt that it lacked the essential human presence. My experience in this course has provided me with living proof that distance education, by means of threaded discussions and chats, is able to achieve a high level of sophistication and communication. (Student F)

In retrospect, the experience as described reaffirms the belief that lifelong learning could happen in an online delivery format. It highly suggests that existing technologies could support interactive and engaging exchanges among those who want to develop themselves—to develop a knowledge base, appropriate skills, and competencies in a particular field—amidst a rapidly changing environment.

In conclusion, online education is a growing force in the delivery of lifelong learning experiences. The use of an emerging technology such as a course management system has become a prevalent tool in delivering professional development opportunities at a distance. The literature reports that successful instructional experiences supporting and encouraging lifelong learning online use interactive and engaging activities. Given these, online educators need to develop, design, and utilize a variety of instructional strategies that promote self-directed learning, technology-supported interactions, and activity-based sessions, as well as achieve reflective learning outcomes. Integrating these elements as demonstrated in this case study improve the quality of online instruction, attract a diverse audience, and assist students in bridging the gap between theory and practice as they become active participants in their professional development and as practitioners.

References

Aspin, D. N. & Chapman, J. D. (2000). Lifelong learning: Concepts and conceptions. *International Journal of Lifelong Education, 19*(1), 2-19.

Baylen, D. M., & Zhu, E. (2005). "Going online": Challenges and issues. In P. L. Rogers (Ed.), *Encyclopedia of distance learning: Distance learning technologies and applications* (Volume II, pp. 969-974). Hershey, PA: Idea Group Reference.

Dick, W., & Carey, L. (2004). *The systematic design of instruction* (6th ed.). Boston: Allyn & Bacon.

Downes, S. (2004). Educational blogging. *EDUCAUSE Review, 39*(5), 14-26.

Edwards, C. (1993). Lifelong learning. *Communications of the ACM, 36*(5), 76-78.

Engstrom, M. E., & Jewett, D. (2005). Collaborative learning the Wiki way. *TechTrends, 49*(6), 12-15.

Farmer, R. (2005). Instant messaging: IM online! RU? *EDUCAUSE Review, 40*(6), 49-62.

Field, J. (2001). Lifelong education. *International Journal of Lifelong Education, 20*(1/2), 3-15.

Friesen, N., & Anderson, T. (2004). Interaction for lifelong learning. *British Journal of Educational Technology, 35*(6), 679-687.

Garrison, D. R. (2000). Theoretical challenges for distance education in the 21st century: A shift from structural to transactional issues. *International Review of Research in Open and Distance Learning, 1*(1), 1-17.

Glacken, J., & Baylen, D. M. (2001). Health professions education online: A case study. *Journal of Allied Health, 30*(3), 183-187.

Gorard, S., Selwyn, N., & Madden, L. (2003). Logged on to learning? Assessing the impact of technology on participation in lifelong learning. *International Journal of Lifelong Education, 22*(3), 281-296.

Griffin, C. (1999). Lifelong learning and social democracy. *International Journal of Lifelong Education, 18*(5), 329-342.

Herrington, J., & Oliver, R. (2000). An instructional design framework for authentic learning environments. *Educational Technology Research and Development, 48*(3), 23-48.

Huang, H. M. (2002). Toward constructivism for adult learners in online learning environments. *British Journal of Educational Technology, 33*(1), 27-37.

Knowles, M. S. (1975). *Self-directed learning. A guide for learners and teachers.* Englewood Cliffs, NJ: Prentice Hall/Cambridge.

Koper, R., & Tattersall, C. (2004). New directions for lifelong learning using network technologies. *British Journal of Educational Technology, 35*(6), 689-700.

Kreber, C. (2001). Learning experientially through case studies? A conceptual analysis. *Teaching in Higher Education, 6*(2), 217-228.

Longworth, N. (2003). *Lifelong learning in action: Transforming education in the 21st century*. London: Kogan Page.

Mager, R. F. (1997). *Making instruction work*. Atlanta: Center for Effective Performance, Inc.

Morgan, G. (2003). *Faculty use of course management systems.* Retrieved August 12, 2006, from http://www.educause.edu/ir/library/pdf/ecar_so/ers/ERS0302/ekf0302.pdf

Murphy, E. (2004). Recognising and promoting collaboration in an online asynchronous discussion. *British Journal of Educational Technology, 35*(4), 421-431.

Rummel, N., Spada, H., Hermann, F., Caspar, F., & Schornstein, K. (2002). *Promoting the coordination of computer-mediated interdisciplinary collaboration: Vicarious learning from worked-out examples and the effects of different technical settings*. Paper presented at the Computer Support for Collaborative Learning (CSCL) 2002 Conference. Retrieved August 12, 2006, from http://newmedia.colorado.edu/cscl/26.pdf

Sorensen, C. K., & Baylen, D. M. (2004). Learning online: Adapting the seven principles of good practice to a Web-based environment. *Distance Learning, 1*(1), 7-17.

Stenning, K., McKendree, J., Lee, J., Cox, R., Dineen, F., & Mayes, T. (1999). Vicarious learning from educational dialogue. In C.M. Hoadley & J. Roschelle (Eds.) *Proceedings from Computer Support for Collaborative Learning (CSCL) 1999 Conference* (pp. 341-347). Mahwah, NJ: Lawrence Erlbaum Associates.

Townsend, M., & Wheeler, S. (2004). Is anybody out there? Teaching assistants' experiences of online learning. *Quarterly Review of Distance Education, 5*(2), 127-138.

Zhu, E., & Baylen, D. M. (2005). From learning community to community learning: Pedagogy, technology, and interactivity. *Educational Media International, 42*(3), 251-268.

Appendix A: Examples of Initial Postings and Replies to a Post

Case	Examples of an Initial Post	Examples of a Reply to a Post
1	I had two first thoughts. The first is that it was a training problem. If she had more training on the procedure she would have performed it better. The second, however, is that knee jerk reactions are very common in most industries. 10 complaints might not be a large number when viewed in context. Do they have interns at non geriatric facilities? If so, how does the complaint rate (and problem rate) compare to those facilities? (Student E)	You made interesting comments. In was mentioned that she did not feel comfortable with the procedure and that Dr. Shoemaker made her practice this procedure a dozen times because she knew that she feared the procedure. She commented that she needed to not rush, that she was getting better. To me that didn't sound like she had mastered the procedure. Why was the intern left alone to do a procedure she had not mastered and felt uncomfortable doing? Do you feel that she should have been aloud to do this on her own, without the supervision of the doctor? Do you feel that the instructional design should incorporate anticipated or future needs into the analysis? (Student A)
2	According to our text, page 56, we should decide early in our design stages which characteristics of our learners/trainees are most useful to identify. We have dabbled in this as we have discussed the case study volunteers. We have looked at general characteristics, entry competencies, learning styles, academic information, and personal and social characteristics. We have also been reminded to consider learners with disabilities even though we do not seem to have this consideration for the case study. Our peers have cautioned us not to overlook the non-conventional learners. As you proceed through the discussions, the readings, and the preparation of Section 2, consider this question: "How are the learners Holly and Ray are designing instruction for alike or different from your potential learners/trainees?" (Student B)	Yes, there are two sets of learners, but the trainers only have one set of learners to teach, the volunteers. The children would then be considered the volunteers learners. Right? Also, you brought up a great point that the children come from a diverse background and from a variety of situations that the volunteers might not have knowledge about. You said they may not be able to relate to their experiences or to them. Yes, maybe, but the children may find stability within the volunteers. This will then give them someone to hopefully depend on and maybe open up to. (Student A)

3	Remember those times that while you were eating something cold you experienced a brain freeze? Well, I have been having a brain freeze for about five days now! I sent in my two sections, started working on case 3, and began thinking about instructional objectives. That's when my brain FROZE. I reread my two sections. I reread the components for section three over and over. I read articles and visited web sites offered by my classmates, but yet my brain remained frozen. Tonight, the thaw began. Using the source that AR posted and my project proposal, I began to really evaluate what the heck I wanted this training to accomplish. On paper I thought it looked doable and "spectacular". Who wouldn't want to attend this training? It would be full of things to do and learn, and I was going to dazzle my participants with group interactivity, hands on experiences, and new tools they just could not live without. They would be transformed, in the span of about 6 weeks tops, into technology integrators who couldn't wait to finish the training so they continue in their culture of communication, change their curriculum, and teach in ways they never dreamed of. (Student B)	... thank you for sharing your heart, thoughts, and for being so vulnerable to us. I must admit that looking at your project (and your writings) has made me quite intimidated. I now can see that you are a real person that has struggles like me, but that you have the wonderful gift of formulating your thoughts (and our thoughts) and can put them in writing. Thank you, thank you, thank you! (Student H)
4	I am about to call it quits for today, but I wanted to share an experience I just had while working on the assessment piece of my project. When I wrote out the lessons for Module One, I indicated that I would be using a rubric to evaluate the assignments. Well, designing the rubric lead to refining the assignment. What I thought had been clear assignment directions and content was not very clear when I sat down to create the evaluation rubric. I found the rubric experience rewarding in that I refined the assignments and I feel much bette[r] about what my participants will be doing in each of the lessons. (the outcomes/ products) (Student B)	I agree about how helpful a rubric can be. I often start a project or assignment with the rubric. That allows me to make it clear in my mind what constitutes an A, B, C etc before I write the specs for the students. It ends up saving me a lot of time. The other thing I have noticed is that my good rubrics change with time. Every time I use them I have to evaluate them. It's amazing how many loop holes the students will find that I had not dreamed of. I once described a good rubric as similar to a fine wine—it gets better with age. I have been using them more and more as I have seen how powerful they are for both me and the students. (Student E)

5	As an experienced program designer you are preparing for the evaluation process. In creating your evaluation plan, what are some questions you may need to consider within the final steps of your design project? (Student H)	Please indulge me for a moment to play devil's advocate. :) It was mentioned in earlier posts that it was not acceptable to use people as a training ground for nurses. Should our training be any different? In the past I have used summative evaluations in the development phase or with a small test group. Why? For many the same reasons posted here. If the first implementation of the product has too many problems, then it may be doomed to fail even if it turns out to be wonderful. Take Microsoft for instance. Most people I know will not get anywhere near an early release of their software. Why? Because they know it's full of bugs. We wait until it's been reviewed before us wary customers will jump in. Thoughts? (Student E)

Chapter XII

"Life in the Round" and the History of Libraries in Micronesia

Nicholas J. Goetzfridt, University of Guam, Guam

Abstract

This chapter uses the importation of an American institution of information—"the library"—into the Pacific region of Micronesia as an example of a contextual-less, cross-cultural information transference that suggests the autonomous impact of distance education technology and protocols on indigenous and other interpretative communities. Such an impact negates the innate values of these communities as they pertain to concepts of "knowledge" and "information" derived from tenacious cultural and social values. Conflicts between indigenous values and the transferences of "the library" and subsequent information technologies are considered along with individualizing values exhibited by early Christian missionaries in Micronesia. Based upon these issues and cross-cultural tensions, the chapter appeals for the inclusion of indigenous contexts into discussions of online educational development and access to better understand and serve these communities and to provide an exemplary situation from which to recognize the importance of cultural contexts in the provision of distance educational opportunities.

Introduction

This chapter will focus on a case perspective of the transference of American libraries and librarianship into oral based societies of Micronesia. Libraries provide just one example of American cultural agencies whose introductions into Micronesia were historically guided by political and economic perceptions of what was right for Micronesia. The relevance of this cross-cultural transference for open and lifelong learning through expanding electronic horizons should not be seen simply through the stereotypical idea of the library as a depository of information. To do so is to accept the history and the presence of the institution of the American library in Micronesia without a context and specifically an indigenous context that is itself an historical and contemporaneous realm of information and protocols for sharing it. Its relevance is made clearer by acknowledging its historical and indigenous contexts as part of a contemporary discussion of the use of technology for learning in the Pacific today. Without this historical context, the idea of "online education for lifelong learning" in Guam and Micronesia and within other indigenous communities exists without critical thought given to the transference of foreign institutions of information—a transference pursued without critical thought as its resources develop and are used in future educational needs.

Stretching across a Pacific Ocean area broader than the continental United States, the islands and atolls of Micronesia were settled by Austronesian speaking peoples moving out from Southeast Asia over 3,000 years ago. Voyaging thousands of miles with only cognitive navigational aids in wooden outrigger canoes, the Austronesians likely reached the Mariana archipelago first, followed by the three other large archipelagoes that make up Micronesia: Carolines, Kiribati, Nauru, and Marshall Islands. British colonial possession and influence in Kiribati has, however, essentially divorced Kiribati and Nauru from events and discussions of Micronesia from an American context of influence.

Centuries after the discovery of most of the islands in Micronesia by canoe, French geographer Gregoire Louis Domeny de Rienzi received permission in 1831 from La Société de Géographie in Paris to label the islands as Micronesia, meaning "tiny islands" from the Greek. Domeny de Rienzi thereby completed the European labeling of Oceania, with all of Melanesia and Polynesia having already been labeled in European cartography. By this time, the American Board of Commissioners for Foreign Missions (ABCFM) had already been printing missionary material in Hawaii for nine years, establishing an important precedent for eventual movements to the Micronesian islands of Pohnpei and Kosrae 30 years later.

Although it claimed the Mariana Islands for itself in 1565, Spain actually began its efforts in 1668 to establish its authority in the Mariana Islands in the northwest region of Micronesia among the indigenous Chamorro people, essentially ignoring the Caroline Islands that form much of Micronesia to the south of the Marianas until an increased German presence prompted Spain to stake its claims in the Carolines in the 1880s. The Chamorro Wars of the late 1600s in the Mariana Islands demonstrated Chamorro resistance to outside efforts to interfere not only in territorial terms but in a people's system of communal life, values, and spiritual convictions. Father Diego Luis de San Vitores (1627-1672) is the most frequently acknowledged Catholic martyr on the island of Guam, providing a tenuous connection between a period of cultural loss and the contemporary religious devotion of much of the island and the rest of the Mariana Islands to Jesus Christ. San Vitores is credited with establishing Catholic missionary efforts in the Mariana Islands, which began a major force of acculturation and cultural change among the Chamorro people. A *chamorri* or high caste Chamorro speared de San Vitores in 1672 after de San Vitores' baptism of his newly born daughter angered him. De San Vitores was thrown over the reef in the Tumon area of Guam upon which hundreds of five star hotel rooms designed primarily for Japanese tourists now face (Rogers, 1995, p. 55).

The "history" of Micronesia is contested because of contemporary movements in Pacific historiography to challenge European interpretations that use time chronologies and measure events by what are essentially economic development milestones. The few events mentioned above are but distant stars in a diverse collection of histories. They become much more diverse when these movements are supplemented by the acknowledgment and use of indigenous histories that are not only based upon oral stories but which also reflect the cultural dynamics of a particular society. These stories sometimes reflect developments in spiritual and moralistic senses rather than the standard movement of time across calendar years. And they are sometimes impacted by local political and social tensions or preferences that either change or strategically emphasize some part of a traditional story.

Each district in the Federated States of Micronesia and the atolls closely associated with the main islands are culturally and socially distinct with a pan-Micronesian identity expressing itself only on occasions when outside pressures mandate such unity. Each Micronesian society typically reverts back to its own familiar terms in normal living circumstances. Although most Micronesian inheritances related to land and power are matrilineal in nature, historical and social factors have made each culture area tenaciously distinct. The failure of the U.S. effort to unify Micronesia into a single entity, which was reflected in the successful efforts of Palau, the Northern Mariana Islands, and the Marshall Islands to break away from the Trust Territory of the Pacific Islands and form their own, distinctive political statuses, is indicative of these cultural differences.

Controlling Systems

Pacific historian David Hanlon (1998) examined the "remaking" of post-World War II Micronesia by federal government agencies and their programs that promoted "development" under capitalistic terms and values. Much of this "remaking" involved the creation of an economy of consumerism under the umbrella of American democracy, reflecting much of the same desires the first Congregationalist missionaries in Micronesia had in the 1850s when the eradication of native "socialism" was a part of evangelistic strategies. Central to this "remaking" of postwar Micronesia was the envisioning of a culturally, socially, and linguistically diverse Micronesia restructured as a singular entity that was sometimes cartographically blanketed by a map of the United States (Richard, 1957). By showing that Micronesia stretched from the western islands of Palau in California to the Marshall Islands in North and South Carolina, conveyers not only relied upon a familiar physical form of reference to express space and distance but also implied a desire to make Micronesia a product of American development, reality, and values primarily for the sake of its military strategic position in the Pacific.

Hanlon (1998) notes that the assumption that what worked well for a developed America could work just as well anywhere else was unquestioned with Micronesia providing America a foreign postwar territory upon which to employ this assumption. What developed, however, was a mode of economic dependency "as a strategy of domination" to satisfy postwar military and political agendas. American efforts to remake and administer Micronesia as the U.S. Trust Territory of the Pacific Islands from 1947 to 1986 appears to reflect much of the same desire to individualize Micronesians that the earliest American missionaries to Micronesia had experienced almost a century earlier. In missionary minds, the reception of Christianity depended upon the eradication of native "socialism" just as American efforts at postwar economic development "would reveal what it meant to be productive, prosperous and free, what it meant to be American" (p. 6).

To early protestant missionaries in Micronesia during the 1850s, 1860s, and beyond, "socialism" was often seen as a central cause of communal depravity. Communal foundations of complex systems ruled by chiefs were antithetical to missionaries' notions of a "Christian civilization" that supported individualism and individual ownership of property (Hanlon, 1998). The communal system of land and material ownership controlled by native chiefs therefore had to be replaced by one in which individual ownership would encourage individual thought and actions. Without this individualism and concepts of democracy, a native rejection of indigenous gods deeply ingrained in Micronesian history and identity and the subsequent acceptance of a Christian god would be very difficult to achieve. American agencies of culture therefore seem to have had a perennial source of hope upon which to draw since at least the 1850s.

David D. Hall's (1996) precept for understanding a culture's social history through an understanding of the "production and consumption of books" is hardly a viable option in "Micronesia," or in the same "Micronesia" when it was the U.S. Trust Territory of the Pacific Islands, or in Africa for that matter. A small pocket of literature on African librarianship has appeared over the past 20 years to question Africa's reliance on British values and mechanisms of librarianship and is reflective of Michael Harris' (1976) call to American librarianship to reevaluate its own principles and standards. Most of this literature equates the foundation of African libraries to the social and political practices of colonialism by Great Britain in which African cultural contexts have been unacknowledged. Adolphe Amadi (1981) maintained that the book itself, libraries, and formal education were introduced into Africa by Britain as a tool for Christianizing the heathens and teaching them the way to salvation, as a means for educating the target people in order to achieve the social and political and economic objectives of the colony, and to acculturate or brainwash the natives into European ways.

Libraries as such attempted to force a transition:

From an oral pedagogy with its emphasis upon practicality and the nurturing of indigenous cultural elements, and experiential values, to a literary education that resulted in reflective values, the inculcation of alien cultural elements and an emphasis on paper qualifications and jobs. (Amadi, 1981, p. 70)

Amadi's book on the library as an ideological instrument, *African Libraries, Western Tradition, and Colonial Brainwashing*, remains a lonely monograph in this critical literature. For the most part, the literature of African librarianship continues to pursue foreign technological mechanism of access without considering sociocultural contexts, which is also often the case with American librarianship and information science.

The "strategy of domination" through economic dependency identified by Hanlon allowed numerous entanglements of colonialism, cultural change, and acculturated responses that may make libraries and texts viable instruments to those who can and wish to either submit to this domination or to manipulate it. And the positioning of Micronesia as a participant in a global economy by American officials (despite the poverty of most of its residents and the dire condition of basic health services) may suggest modernity and acculturation.

But this reality deposits Micronesians into the controlling systems, which Hanlon (1999) maintains adds "silent testimony to the distinction between the primitive and the modern" and dismisses "traditional" concepts of knowledge in favor of the readable written ones (Hanlon, 1999, p. 15). Librarianship passively participated in this dominance and yet at the same time, catered to those Micronesians who sought the benefits of Western education. Many did so to benefit from the acculturated state of affairs that, considering the impact of American programs and economic values, structures, and expectations, are likely to persist. They have done so, however, under the tenacious standards of indigenous communal values and as people with communally surrounded, individual plans.

The existence still of autonomous *wehi* chiefdoms in Pohnpei, for example, and their people's resistance to the historical brunt of capitalistic and political attachments of foreign involvements through a significant portion of its "post-contact" history, says something definite about the inner and outer products of these involvements and about the resiliency with which cognitive and perceptual values and workings continue to conflict in an unknown epistemology of librarianship in Micronesia. "Literacy," "information," and "knowledge" are terms that continue to tug at fabrics of indigenous contexts because of the American cultural foundations through which they have been introduced. No doubt literacy is important for Micronesians in a "modern" world and libraries in schools and public reading promotions (such as the promotion of children's literature in Pohnpei's public library) may provide important routes to that end. But such foreign inheritances can also make indigenous roots become untenable and a Micronesian epistemology a distant and esoteric idea.

Micronesian Epistemologies and Lives in the Round

Michel de Certeau's (1988) ideas about the centrality of controlled space in forming "strategies" of control in everyday arenas of life" and the "tactics" the less powerful use to subvert these spaces and strategies in moments of manipulative opportunities are useful in extending the Micronesian construct beyond localized issues in Micronesian studies. The distinctive political spaces in the five *wehi* or paramount chiefdoms of Pohnpei where there is no common history serve as examples in which the context of each space and the indigenous tactics that surround them explain "knowledge" and life as they will never be changed (or for that matter, challenged) by federal programs. De Certeau explains that although the user of spaces and goods cannot escape from the environment of the powerful, the trickery and subversive choices the user makes often reverses and drains the formal logic of the creators and proprietors of space, thus lessening the power of a space's locus of control. An established strategy, de Certeau stresses (1988), "postulates a *place* that can be delimited as its *own* and serves as the base from which relations with an *exteriority* composed of targets or threats (customers or competitors, enemies, the country surrounding the city, objectives and objects of research, etc.) can be managed." As such, a strategy relies upon a strong sense of predictability and the ability to survey the field so as to notice tactical ways of time in relation to this place and to subsequently force "the uncertainties of history into readable spaces" (Certeau, 1988, p. 36).

Perhaps it would be fair to say that Micronesia's current social epistemology is derived from a tension that exists between traditional knowledge and values and the contemporary demands of a very influential Western world and its knowledge. Perhaps the result is acculturated knowledge. Or perhaps knowledge in Micronesia is adjusted to fit the situation. Or perhaps the forces of change are so strong in Micronesia that it is very difficult to keep traditional and contemporary knowledge and values distinct from each other. Because Micronesia's libraries were created in the context of non-indigenous sources, it subsequently becomes imperative to search for a new history and a keener appreciation of how the social and cultural contexts of Micronesia distinguish Micronesian libraries from the American past in many ways. To fail to think seriously about the historical and social and cultural contexts of librarianship in Micronesia is to obscure the impact of a technological age that has increasingly placed greater professional value on processes than upon people.

An important perspective to consider in dealing with this problematic cross-cultural transference of information systems is the one taken by Elfreda A. Chatman (1999). In her studies of what she described as the "information poor" and the "information outsiders" (as opposed to the gate keeping forces of the "information insiders"), she found among janitors of a southern U.S. university, women at a crisis center, women at a retirement community, and in a maximum-security prison for women. Perhaps her most interesting findings were from the retirement community and the prison's information environment, both of which are dictated by what she described as "life in the round" (Chatman, 1999). Although Chatman (1992) had expected to find networking among retired women for sharing information and interacting between same age peers, Chatman instead found a strong tendency among these retired women to engage in secrecy and deception in order to appear normal when their lives and health were under strain. The extent to which these elderly women shared their knowledge about certain events or situations was determined by situational relevancy and the extent to which they were willing to engage in risk taking.

In creating her conceptual framework for comprehending the world of information insiders and outsiders, Chatman stressed that it is the mores and norms of the information insiders that determine what information is important and what is not. "Information insiders" exist in many situations and environments but the most important characteristic of information insiders is their capacity to "reinforce information poverty by neglecting to accept sources and information not created by themselves" (Chatman, 1996, p. 193). Consequently, one must accept, understand, and participate in common assumptions and values in order to know and benefit from a pool of knowledge, which insiders accept as the most valuable and, really, the only acceptable source of information. Is not accepting the importation of an American institution—the library—with its standards for determining and defining information and information storage and access systems without acknowledging the cultural contexts of indigenous knowledge and information, similar to undertaking the role of the "information insider" as Chatman describes it?

In her study of female maximum-security prison inmates, Chatman (1999) expanded upon the importance of a centrally accepted system of what is considered "normal" behavior and values. In the prison environment, Chatman found that information is used to change behaviors to fit the environment and that in this process, private viewpoints become assimilated to a communal view of life. She notes that a particularly noteworthy characteristic of this information is as follows: "it is produced within a specific context for use within that context. Consequently, it easily fits into the everyday reality of life" (p. 208). And it is from this shared experience of reality that meaning occurs. Life is in a sense played out in a small world and its horizons that are determined by these norms. Chatman calls this informational bound reality "life in the round," borrowing the phrase "total round" that P. G. Cressey employed in his classic 1932 study *The Taxi-Dance Hall*. Cressey used the taxi dance hall to describe how one encounters a distinctive world upon entering the hall and leaves this world only when one steps physically outside of it. Cressey writes as follows:

For those who attend the taxi-dance hall, even irregularly, it is a distinct social world, with its own way of acting, talking, and thinking. It has its own vocabulary, its own activities and interests, its own conception of what is significant in life, and—to a certain extent—its own scheme of life. (p. 29)

There is a difference, of course, between communal lives and perspectives in Micronesia and those of female prisoners or taxi-dance hall dancers. But one also needs to acknowledge that they are similar in the basic ways in which acceptable values and behaviors are established and maintained. Micronesia's communal environments are marked by the simple historical fact that colonial powers have wrought changes that female prisoners, elderly women in a retirement community, or janitors in a southern university have never had to react to. The norms, standards, and values created by these latter populations were institutionalized in response to a particular situation in which they found themselves. Micronesians, on the other hand, have communal roots that developed from forces originating from themselves—roots that generated social structures and expectations that were indigenous in nature. The American governance of Micronesia and the subsequent introduction of its grounded institutions—including the library and its foundational concepts of "information" and "knowledge"—carried on a colonial tradition of influencing and transforming these indigenous norms of communal information and information protocols—albeit at a more intensive pace in the American administrative take-over following World War II. This is a basic influential principle in relation to the implementation of educational technologies that now receives little if any attention and leaves a Micronesian "life in the round" (and those lives in the round of other indigenous peoples) typically unacknowledged and unaccounted for.

Falgout (1984) emphasizes the centrality of the concept of "person" in Pohnpeian epistemology—particularly in relation to types of persons and their relationship to knowledge, its possession, and the social negotiations involved in its disbursement. The Pohnpeian "person" is a direct contradiction to the Western concept of person that conceives of a person's appearance and behavior in the duality of that person's outside and inside environments. In the Pohnpei person, form or appearance can be more important than the inner content of a person, but they are not a direct reflection of inner content.

The social negotiations necessary to understand someone's true intentions and knowledge of something is affected by the associations Pohnpeians make between ancestral spirits who must not be offended unless the power of those spirits is to be given license to create misfortune. The *manaman*—the power and authority of a person—must not be violated in communal relationships. Glenn Petersen (1993) has also examined the function of *kanegama* in Pohnpei's politics of concealment, which enable members of the society to express respect toward authority without necessarily being controlled by that authority. He argues that hierarchical and egalitarian structures of society subsequently become interdependent rather than diametrically opposed ways of organizing a community:

One of Falgout's informants stressed that knowledge is the inner content of a person and:

A person who is filled with knowledge serves a purpose and is useful. An emptied person, like an emptied basket, serves no purpose. He is no longer important and Ponapeans believe that the person will weaken and die. Knowledge, then, is the life force of the human body. Furthermore, it gives reason and purpose to an individual's existence... Fear of reduced vitality or even death due to depletion of inner content is very real for Ponapeans. Another informant likened the giving away of knowledge to the giving away of one's life. Losing knowledge for a Ponapean man, he said, has a similar effect as that of losing a much loved wife; a man's thinking declines, he is weakened, becomes sick and will eventually die. Actual cases of declining health, mental ability or even death allegedly resulting from giving away knowledge are fairly common occurrences. (Falgout, 1984, p. 135)

We find nothing like this in Melvil Dewey's ideas of "objective" knowledge and information in the "library spirit" mission that has centrally affected librarianship for generations nor do we find this in any chapter of the history of American librarianship. The formal promotion of the "library spirit" in Dewey's School of Library Economy at Columbia beginning in 1887 and which has extended into librarianship's contemporary values and practices, relied and relies upon the extensive availability and access to "information." While librarianship has had changing visions and expectations on what constitutes "good" literature and how that literature might impact the society the library serves, its practices have been based upon the sharing and promotion of information and knowledge. Although the extent and form of this information and knowledge in non-democratic regions is debatable, conceptualizations of indigenous societal consequences for sharing information as exemplified by this Pohnpeian example have not been part of the discussion—either from the foundations established by Dewey's school or from within contemporary professional literature of American librarianship.

Shera's Model of Social Epistemology

Even in the relatively recent scholarship that focuses on what is broadly labeled as "user studies"—and specifically in relation to studies of users' cognitive approaches to information—we find a focus primarily on individual methods of searching for information and not communal standards for accessing and using information, which is clearly the case in Pohnpei, the Marshall Islands, and throughout the rest of Micronesia. Jesse Shera's (1976) *Introduction to Library Science: Basic Elements of Library Service* touches upon this very dilemma. However, he does not relate it to the cultural contexts of ethnic communities, which can have a defining impact upon the way in which people form their needs and values of information and appropriate protocols for sharing it.

Much of Shera's thought is concerned with what he calls a society's "social epistemology" which he defines as the study of "how knowledge has been coordinated, integrated and put to work" (p. 49) in a society. In attempting to outline how "the nature of culture" is associated with this social epistemology, Shera constructed a triangular representation of culture with one side of the triangle represented by "physical equipment," another side by "scholarship," and the third side represented by "social organization" (p. 44). In Shera's model, this social organization is composed of "institutions and their agencies that 'drive' or give reality to the culture." In order for a culture to survive, Shera argues that all three aspects—physical equipment (which in our day would certainly include computers and technology), scholarship (including knowledge, experience, "belief, myth, and legend"), and social organizations—must exist in relative harmony. For this to happen, Shera places a fourth element—communication—inside the triangle wherein the library serves an important role in integrating these three main elements of culture. But more than this, the library Shera says, "is, as it has always been, conditioned and shaped by the social milieu within which it functions" (p. 42).

Shera stresses that attempting to understand a society's social epistemology is fundamental to the librarian because it should provide an effective philosophical frame of reference within which can be viewed and understood the complexities of the intellectual processes of society—an understanding of how society as a whole seeks to achieve a perception of its *total* intellectual and social environment: "The focus of this discipline [i.e., social epistemology] should be upon the production, flow, integration, and consumption of all forms of communication operating throughout the entire social pattern" (p. 50). Shera asks:

How does society know what it knows, and how does that knowledge influence the total social environment? That question lies at the very heart of the role that the librarian plays in society and the role of the library as a social instrumentality. Only when armed with such knowledge can we make valid decisions about what the library should become. (p. 50)

Librarianship can become the great unifying agent that gives order to the intellectual life of our times and relates man to his total environment. It is this creation of synthesis of man's knowledge to the end of promoting wisdom that is one of the most important contributions the librarian can make to man's intellectual life; his is the gift of order and relationship. (p. 54)

What is the relevance of Shera's model of the library in Micronesia where secrecy and respect form the traditional cornerstones of the creation, storage, expression, and negotiation of "knowledge" and "information" on a communal level in Micronesia? Generally speaking, the influx of Western models and standards of education throughout Micronesia's colonial histories have ushered in a recurring and persistent tension between these cornerstones and the fundamental objective of Western education which seeks individual achievement, enhancement of the self, and, if possible, public recognition of that self. This tension represents a dilemma that an uncritical acceptance of American librarianship and other American institutions in Micronesia can make almost invisible, although it is critical to the lives of Micronesians in a rapidly changing world. Libraries in Micronesia function in the same general social context in which they were introduced by the Library Services and Construction Act (LSCA), which was itself created under that same social context—the advancement of democracy. Under the LSCA, rural libraries in America were ideally meant to close the gap between the "information poor" farm and rural village dwellers and the "information rich" inhabitants of the cities, which were the sites of unprecedented support for libraries following World War II and for the great explosion of research and knowledge that the war prompted. The idea was to make information access equal so that Americans could be equal on the pluralistic stage of democracy. This epistemology of social knowledge was transferred to "rural" Micronesia along with the American models and values of librarianship for which the LSCA was created in the first place. These are the roots of Micronesia's libraries.

But these are not the roots of indigenous societies in Micronesia. When one talks to Micronesians with the idea of forming some groundwork for understanding the epistemological elements of Micronesian societies in relation to the presence of both libraries and "information," one repeatedly hears the same valued, social components of Micronesian life expressed: the prominence of the ocean; the secrecy of knowledge related to navigation, canoes, and to herbal medicines; the importance of expressing respect in the exchange of "information"; and the extensive (usually negative) ramifications of money and material goods on the desire to preserve cultural knowledge and values. These shared, communally based values do not diminish when discussion turns to the impact of the migration of young people from atolls and islands to obtain a Western college or university education. Rather the subject of acculturation and its—usually negative—consequences comes up almost without fail (Goetzfridt, 1997).

Chatman emphasized that it is ultimately the common "grounding of a shared reality" between "information insiders" that supports the communal view of life. This is true whether this reality is shared between members of a Marshallese, Pohnpeian, or Satawalese community; a community of elderly women who know the risks of revealing their situations; janitors attempting to maintain or increase their work status in a work environment or known rules and regulations; or prison inmates interested in getting by until they have served their time.

However, successive Western and Japanese colonial powers essentially imposed a set of norms onto these existing indigenous structures. One is left with the basic question of whether or not librarians have and are participating in these forces of acculturation and ignoring Micronesian "lives in the round" for the sake of maintaining and promoting Western models of librarianship and Western sources of information. But no one has really ever effectively asked this question.

Hanlon's phrase "the chill of history" describes the implications of using Western standards for organizing, storing, and controlling access to records of knowledge that traditionally define Pacific societies (Hanlon, 1999). The same Western societies that supported colonialism and imperialism have also defined systems for classifying knowledge, overshadowing communal knowledge classification systems and protocols for access. By using these mechanisms, libraries lose their assumptions of credibility and neutrality. Hanlon maintains: "the existence of libraries and collections in the Pacific has been made possible by the intrusion, contact, displacement and colonization of then extant local epistemologies. Knowledge written down needed a place to be kept, while other modes of knowledge were left to be forgotten" (Hanlon, 1999, p. 15). Although the creation, preservation, and transmission of knowledge in indigenous communal societies are culturally determined, the imposition of organizational systems created under the values of Western librarianship fails to recognize this basic tenet of indigenous knowledge. Materials preserved by these systems—whether they are records or items of material culture in an American museum—become separated from their historical and cultural contexts. And not only do they convey a strong sense of exoticism within these controlling systems, they also "add silent testimony to the distinction between the primitive and the modern, and by their very placement in museums in metropolitan sites, to reaffirm the global historical transcendence of science, progress and capitalism" (p.15).

Historical References to Cross-Cultural Transferences

The implications and consequences of these cross-cultural transferences—particularly their one-sided movement from a dominant foundation—are not, or at least should not be restricted to the indigenous, historical contexts of the islands of Micronesia. In a broader sense, communal contexts involve a wide range of communities of interpretation that through elements of ethnicity, religion, economic status in a controlled environment, or through indigenous colonial histories, tug at the mechanical basis of the growing virtual phenomenon in "online distant education" and all the instruments and their transformations that are a part of growth in this educational approach. As virtual phenomena evolve and are embraced by educational institutions and professionals to address pressures of educational expansion and access, the practical levels of technology development and execution naturally take precedence over "interpretative communities" or "communal contexts" since it is this execution that eventually make these issues possible. On the other hand, these communal standards of interpretation and values of knowledge, and the social viability of information have always existed. The question becomes—as becomes evident in the colonial history of Micronesia and other areas of the world—whether or not technological development and execution become grounded in the origins of themselves or are capable of being transformed from these origins into the distinctive contexts that employ or attempt to employ them.

These Western based technological developments in Pacific contexts began a long road of one-sided, colonial transferences and transformations when nine native canoes helped struggle with and land a London Missionary Society printing press on Moorea in the Society Islands on March 18 of 1817. Print for the sake of saving native souls was implemented in Micronesia in January 1856 when the missionary ship, the Morning Star, brought a printing press ashore on Pohnpei in Micronesia where it sat unused until October. While the printing press was meant to be a tool for propagating Christianity, it also prompted an indigenous, oral-based response to print that went unrecognized by Pacific missionaries. Rather than experience change and conversion by reading scripture and prayer, islanders predominantly conceived of printed materials as material idols of the new religion and later as a practice in "reading" worth mimicking for indigenous political advantages. In response to missionary efforts to use print to transform souls, this mimicry by Pacific peoples followed opportunities for engagement with "the West" in ways that benefited social standings within their societies and played a part in cross-cultural negotiations. On occasion these responses (such as holding a missal upside down and reciting its apparent contents) also provided missionaries with material that was both humorous and self-justifying for serial publications back home (Smith, 1998, p. 73).

After 28 years of missionary work on Pohnpei, an aging Albert Sturges began to at least partially recognize that to become a Christian did not mean ceasing to be Pohnpeian. Sturges preached the gospel in Micronesia until 1884 and died the following year as Spanish authorities took control. In 1878, Sturges reflected upon what he had learned about the Pohnpeians during his 26 years. Although he continued to espouse a strong work ethic along with a free enterprise system that provides numerous business and farming metaphors for finding and training indigenous "embryo preachers" and planting them as seeds for spreading the Christian church throughout Micronesia, Sturges' thoughts about the redeemable, human-based values of Pohnpeians are a striking contrast to the disparaging characterizations that missionaries had written during the 1850s and 1860s. The overall theme of his reflections is the importance of allowing these "embryo preachers" to strike out on their own with the support of "white" missionaries and to enable the churches they establish to thrive through indigenous standards of communication and influence. "We are alone," Sturges writes:

> *... and want neighbors, if neighborly ourself we could hardly want kinder neighbors than some of our heathen become. Every where & in most things we find too much good, too much common sense, too much of the brother, the man the God in our people to allow of whole sale destruction ... . In the first place, the heathen are not the fools one takes them to be. I am not unfrequently reminded of the story told of Chief Justice Marshall, who broke down in his carriage—the fill was broke & he was about starting off to the nearest house, two miles away for help, when a plantation negro happened along who took his knife, cut a little sapling and withe and soon had the Judge all right. "Bravo! Sambo! Why couldn't I have thought of that?" "Only cause some folks naturally got more sense than others" was the quick reply!* (ABCFM, 1878, pp. 1-2)

Perhaps most striking however in terms of his evolving recognition of indigenous social structures and perhaps even an epistemology, was Sturges' assertion that the successful missionary must use "*thorough, systematic organization*" because "the condition of heathenism, which is not a chaos, or jungle, or broken heap, as some imagine it to be; but it is *a structure, a body, a system, an organization*, it is an out growth of human nature,and every where adapting itself to its surroundings." Although *kanegamah* is not mentioned in Sturges' paper and is never mentioned in missionary records, one might conjecture that under his newfound convictions of the structure and system of "heathenism" and its society, *kanegamah* might have been included had Sturges received instruction in it. Sturges' perspectives nevertheless suggest an evolution of responding to context and for an allowance of the subversive strategies Pohnpeians employed throughout his many years as a missionary in Micronesia.

The question of whether or not tremendous progress in virtual, online education can step back from its claims of omnipresent relevance for the future delivery of "information" and "knowledge" and consider these interpretative communities and these communal contexts of value seems simple enough. But the economic forces of educational delivery in a new world environment may very well make such inquiry seem irrelevant—somewhat in the same way that one might ask what studying Shakespeare or Walt Whitman has to do with making a living. It is a narrow view with dangerous parameters for excluding both the marginalized in our societies and for linking "growth" entirely with quantitative and individualistic means of measurement.

Acknowledging indigenous and other grouped contexts and values within the individualizing frameworks of education in a virtual environment will not lead to a measurable result shining somewhere in the concourse of a culture's core values and grouped means of sustenance. Given the paucity of inquiry in this area—particularly in terms of the role of librarianship—the results for acknowledging such and taking actions and developing responsive policies are actually unknown. The inquiry, somewhat on the other side of efforts to bring those early missionary printing presses ashore, could begin simply in the form of professional conversations. What comes after that depends on the will of those watching and using the mechanisms in which contexts of any kind easily become baseless and nonexistent. Professional educators and librarians would need to bring life to such inquiry and follow its progression of thought to whatever inspirational places and actions they might bring us.

Indigenous Contexts and Knowledge

One place to begin could be in the field of indigenous knowledge that has found a niche in the field of agricultural and international development in which the sole identification of science with Western culture belies its intended inclusion across cultures. Michael D. Warren (1996), for example, argues that rather than associating a focus on indigenous knowledge with the devaluation of science, a global distribution system of indigenously derived knowledge and information is actually a system that is striving toward a "mechanism that will value the contributions of every community to global knowledge" (p. 13). Such a mechanism could ultimately "change attitudes in such a way that nation states will begin to recognize the most important resource they have—the knowledge generated, but usually ignored, by their own citizens" (Warren, 1996, p. 13). Other writers cite the marginal regard given to indigenous knowledge as the cause for ongoing conflicts in communication between farmers and the officials and experts sent to help them. Dominance by these officials have also often led to a lack of comprehension of the physical environments that these farmers know best but are unable to convey because they cannot enter the authoritative structures that thwart the kind of encompassing mechanism that Warren describes.

In another example, Aletta Biersack (1982) has described and argued for the recognition of a "science among sciences" or a "science of the concrete" encapsulated in Paiela (Papua New Guinea highlands) counting systems in which the systems' communicational approach and a hierarchical pattern of multiplicity marks an alternative non-Western form of logic. However, like many other communal standards of thought and "knowledge," the Paiela approach to quantification becomes irrelevant in electronic forms of education that in themselves automatically inherit controlling "life in the round" standards of information and information access emanating from Western sources.

The inclusion of indigenous contexts into the discussion of online education in which access to and use of "information" and "knowledge" are indelible and central parts, does not in itself provide a solution to the issues of cross-cultural transferences that occur (and should be acknowledged) in such education for lifelong learning. The marginalization of indigenous knowledge has a long history in anthropology, education, and other fields, including library science. But making indigenous contexts a viable, cultural phenomenon does offer the means for its intellectual inclusion in the development of online education and for subsequent thought and policies related to these transferences and the epistemological values they affect. Without its inclusion, Chatman's concepts of information insiders and their design of an exclusionary and controlling realm of "life in the round" do not ultimately advance the basic objection of an all inclusive approach to intellectual enrichment that continuously developed, online learning environments potentially promise.

American librarianship in Micronesia was, in a sense, like Cressey's taxi-dance hall with its standards of what constitutes "information" and its standards for format and access. The "chill of history," as Hanlon describes it, comes from the exclusionary nature of these standards that continue from historical frames of reference in the American experience. And somewhat like the missionary imposition of the values of individualism in the 1850s and 1860s for the sake of converting Micronesians' spiritual concepts to encompass a long established Western figure of salvation, the American library held these standards of information, its format, and its access open only to those who would accept them as they have been developed at least since the first American Library Association gathering in 1876. Libraries and other sources of information become by default "information insiders" when these standards and the professionals who use them are unable or unwilling to pursue the need to know what Shera indeed referred to as the "total social environment" and its epistemology of knowledge. Although the objectives may be beneficial in nature, the offering nevertheless can easily become exclusionary. Because online education and technology offer an all encompassing stage of information access controlled by these "information insiders" functioning in a long propagated "life in the round," it is imperative that the potentially marginalized—in this case, indigenous peoples functioning in communal contexts and values—receive a place in the conversation on future developments.

Author Note

This chapter has benefited from helpful comments provided by Norman R. Yetman (University of Kansas) for which I am most grateful.

References

Amadi, A. O. (1981). *African libraries, Western tradition and colonial brainwashing*. Metuchen, NJ: Scarecrow Press.

American Board of Commissioners for Foreign Missions (ABCFM). (1878). *Letters and papers of the American board of commissioners for foreign missions: Mission to Micronesia, 1852-1909.* Honolulu, HI: The Hawaii Mission Children's Society Library.

Biersack, A. (1982). The logic of misplaced concreteness: Paiela body counting and the nature of the primitive mind. *American Anthropologist, 84*(4), 811-829.

Chatman, E. A. (1992). *Information world of retired women*. Westport, CT: Greenwood Press.

Chatman, E. A. (1996). The impoverished life-world of outsiders. *Journal of the American Society for Information Science, 47*(3), 193-206.

Chatman, E. A. (1999). A theory of life in the round. *Journal of the American Society for Information Science, 50*(3), 207-217.

Cressey, P. G. (1932). *The taxi-dance hall.* Chicago: University of Chicago Press.

de Certeau, M. (1988). *The practice of everyday life*. Berkeley, CA: University of California Press.

Falgout, S. (1984). *Persons and knowledge in Ponape*. Unpublished doctoral dissertation, University of Oregon.

Goetzfridt, N. (1997). *Tacking into context: The roots of LSCA public library services in Micronesia among the heritages and changes of an ocean world.* Unpublished doctoral dissertation, University of Wisconsin, Madison.

Hall, D. D. (1996). *Cultures of print: Essays in the history of the book.* Amherst, MA: University of Massachusetts Press.

Hanlon, D. L. (1998). *Remaking Micronesia: Discourses over development in a Pacific territory, 1944-1982*. Honolulu, HI: University of Hawaii Press.

Hanlon, D. L. (1999). The chill of history: The experience, emotion and changing politics of archival research in the Pacific. *Archives and Manuscripts: The Journal of the Australian Society of Archivists, 27*(1), 8-21.

Harris, M. H. (1976). Portrait in paradox: Commitment and ambivalence in American librarianship, 1876-1976. *Libri, 26*(4), 281-301.

Petersen, G. (1993). Kanengamah and Pohnpei's politics of concealment. *American Anthropologist, 95*(2), 334-352.

Richard, D. E. (1957). *United states naval administration of the trust territory of the Pacific Islands, 3*, 414. Washington, DC: U.S. Government Printing Office.

Rogers, R. F. (1995). *Destiny's landfall: A history of Guam*. Honolulu, HI: University of Hawaii Press.

Shera, J. H. (1976). *Introduction to library science: Basic elements of library service*. Littleton, CO: Libraries Unlimited, Inc.

Smith, V. (1998). *Literary culture and the pacific: Nineteenth-century textual encounters*. Cambridge, MA: Cambridge University Press.

Warren, D. M. (1996). Comments on article by Arun Agrawal. *Indigenous Knowledge and Development Monitor, 4*(1), 13.

Chapter XIII

A Case Study of the Adult Learner's Perception of Instructional Quality in Web-Based Online Courses

Terry T. Kidd, University of Houston-Downtown, USA

Holim Song, Texas Southern University, USA

Abstract

This study assessed the perceptions of adult learners in online distance learning programs regarding the instructional quality of Web-based courses via WebCT. The results showed an overall positive perception regarding the instructional quality of online courses delivered via WebCT ($M = 3.51$, $SD = 1.1362$). The mean obtained for students' perceptions regarding the instructional quality items ranged from 3.7 to 3.37. The visual appeal of Web site and appropriateness of the course materials received the highest rating ($M = 3.625$). Clarity and purpose in introduction to content components earned the lowest ratings ($M = 3.37$). These results were closely correlated to students' responses regarding the important aspects of instructional quality of online courses. The most important aspect indicated by students was the idea of having online course content and materials relevant to the course. The results of the study also indicated other perceived aspects that affect students' views of the instructional quality of an online course, including interaction, design, convenience, feedback, and usability.

Introduction

The terms *distance learning, distance education, online learning*, and *Web-based instruction* (WBI) have become buzzwords or catch phrases for the new phenomenon of learning for the adult learning population as well as the nontraditional student. These terms used to describe an ever-changing environment of learning represents approaches that focus on opening the access to education and training provision for adult learners, freeing the adult learners from the traditional constraints of time and place, and most of all this environment offers flexible learning opportunities to individuals and groups of nontraditional methods of learning. Distance education or distance learning is one of the most rapidly growing fields of education around the world, and its potential impact on all education delivery systems has been greatly emphasized through the development of WBI technologies, in particular, advancements in multimedia and communication technologies and more importantly in the World Wide Web (Web) through distance education and learning platforms such as WebCT, Blackboard, and Moodle.

Online and Web-based (WB) courses within the distance education environment have become popular with both students and educational institutions as the new media to deliver educational programs. For universities and other educational programs, they are an excellent way to reach students in diverse and distant locations. Some may also be used to supplement school enrollments since students can conceivably be anywhere and take the courses. Given their popularity and increased use, it is imperative that administrators and professors monitor students' perceptions of courses using these media for delivery. It is hoped that this type of feedback can help in modifying and improving the learning environment and education programs so that course can function as desired by all parties.

With these concepts in mind, the purpose of this case study was to identify the factors that affected the adult learner or nontraditional student's perception in regards to their ideas of the instructional quality of online and WB courses. This information presented in this chapter will lead to the development and implementation of innovative strategies to promote quality teaching and student learning online and with media. In order to effectively develop a conducive environment for the adult learner in a WB course, instructional designers, educators, trainers, and facilitators must pay particular attention to the design of instruction, the mode of delivery, and the technologies employed to disseminate the information to the adult student; only then can we begin to harness the power of online and distance learning.

Background

Distance learning has the potential to generate new patterns of teaching and learning for the adult learning and nontraditional students. This idea is strongly linked with developments in information and communication technologies (ICTs); furthermore, it is close to the development of new learning needs and new patterns of information access and application and learning. There is evidence that distance education and advances in technology can lead to innovation in mainstream education, and may even have effects beyond the realm of education itself. Distance learning, therefore, may play a decisive role in the creation of the global knowledge-based society (Michael & Tait, 2002).

In order to understand the environment online and distance education/learning and the factors that affect the adult learner or the nontraditional student and their perception of the instructional quality of the course, there must be an understanding of terms and concepts associated with these environments. A large component of this environment relates to the principles and theories of learning including the adult learning methodology, andragogy, active learning principles, and information processing theory that includes concepts on perception. Other words associated with distance and online learning environments include instructional design, distance education/learning, instructional quality, learning communities, learning management systems, and WBI.

It is evident that open and distance learning will be an important element of future education and training systems for adult learning in nontraditional environments. The emergence of new forms of distance learning based on new ICTs, in particular those supported by the Internet and using Web, have significant pedagogical, economic, and organizational implications, particularly for those in the nontraditional arena (Michael & Tait, 2002). Furthermore, there is a significant trend toward training, organization development, and community college programs where the adult learner is most prevalent. While major research has been conducted on distance learning environments, little research has been compiled on the adult learner or the nontraditional student in the context of distance learning and what factors affect their perception of the instructional quality presented from the course facilitator or instructor.

A thorough analysis of major research related to the adult learner's perception of online courses uncovered important factors that are involved in determining students' satisfaction of online courses (e.g., Anderson & Joerg, 1996; Cedefop, 2002; Hara & Kling, 2000; Polloff & Pratt, 2001). In order to paint a clear picture of instructional quality, current literature indicates instructional quality as being defined through nine dimensions: (1) learning, (2) enthusiasm, (3) organization, (4) group interaction, (5) individual rapport, (6) breadth, (7) examinations, (8) assignments, and (9) workload/difficulty (Marsh, 1982, 1987, 1997; Marsh & Roche 1997). With this view of instructional quality, we can begin to see the dimensions of online courses in their full totality and areas in which perception can be affected. The literature indicates that students' perceptions of online learning vary, but overall are positive (Daugherty & Funke, 1998; Morss, 1999; Polloff & Pratt, 2001). The top reasons for taking online courses were flexibility, convenience, and learning enhancement. Students could "attend" their online courses at any time and from anywhere. Convenient features of online courses include economy of travel, comfort, and family environment. Under learning enhancement, participants ranked technology factors and comprehension as the top reasons (Polloff & Pratt, 2001). The disadvantages of online courses were related to technology and isolation. Technology issues related to poor video quality and complaints about transmission delay over the Internet were included. As for isolation, students voiced they lacked opportunities for informal socialization with instructors and other students.

With regard to the interaction, participants rated interpersonal contact and self-monitoring of individual progress as the most highly rated indicators, followed by the timely responses by instructors. Although indicators existed in each of the interaction areas, self-regulating learning and having timely feedback from the instructor were reported as most valued by participants. Polloff and Pratt (2001) found that students are most satisfied with courses in which the instructors facilitate frequent contact between themselves and students, use active learning techniques, convey high expectations, emphasize time spent on specific tasks, and provide prompt feedback.

According to Anderson and Joerg (1996), students perceived online courses as a valuable delivery tool, and they reported that online courses changed the dynamics of access to class materials at any time from different locations. Students perceived online courses as a valuable educational improvement, according to one study (Anderson & Joerg, 1996). However, students hesitated to enroll in online courses due to problems associated with Internet access and ongoing questions related to the advantage of the technology. Students were also concerned about spending time on external Web sites. According to Cedefop (2002), online instructors tended to rely on external sources for materials or content that did not necessarily reflect the instructional standards of the course.

Web design issues are of concern to students as Polloff and Pratt's study (2001) indicated that students were moderately satisfied with the Web design of online courses. If students are not satisfied with the design of the course Web site, they may have negative perceptions of the effectiveness their online courses (Brush, 2001). As reviewed in the literature, Khan (1997) defined and explained WBI environments by providing two distinct classifications—namely, *components* and *features*. According to Khan (1997), components are integral parts of the Web, such as instructional design, multimedia, graphics, text, video, audio streaming, and asynchronous/synchronous communication modes. The findings indicated that these components of WBI contribute to the students' perceptions for online courses.

Multimedia elements, if designed properly, could have a positive impact on student achievement and the learning process (Ryan & Kasturi, 2002).

Chickering and Ehrmann (1996) proposed several principles of good learning and practices for online courses. The first principle of good practice encourages interaction between students and faculty. The students perceived the interactive course environment and frequent discussion as conducive to learning in online courses (Jiang, 1998). In fact, students identified more opportunities to interact with their instructors and peers as one of the main benefits of the online courses (Holmes, 2000). However, if interaction was not available, students became frustrated and unsatisfied with the course. According to Hara and Kling (2000), students' frustrations with online courses originated from two sources: technological problems and pedagogical issues. Technological problems included students' difficulty in obtaining technical support. Access to technical support was crucial to students' perceptions of their online course. The second principle of good practice encourages cooperation among students. Working together with other students increases involvement in learning and deepens understanding (Chickering & Ehrmann, 1996).

Schrum (1998) states that students find the notion of greater reflection required when typing than when speaking as a component of online communication and interactions. Asynchronous communication provides time for reflection and composition. Reading e-mail or bulletin board postings encourages reflection. The utilization of these strategies is important for the varied instruction of the online course. Electronic communication appears to foster collaboration and group interactions (Schrum, 1998). Learning management systems such as WebCT and Blackboard support this form of instruction. Through scaffolding learning, the teacher can create the conditions for collaboration. Organization and implementation of collaborative activities is important to be initiated and sustained by the instructor (McIssac, Blosher, Mahes & Charalombos, 1999). A key element of student collaboration is the support and monitoring by the online teacher. With the majority of communication in text format, the online environment operates differently than the face-to-face environment. Any form of communication has deficiencies; however, understanding them and capitalizing on the potential strengths can shadow the weaknesses. Understanding communication in the medium of the virtual learning environment allows for a more natural development of collaboration. Critics of online courses emphasize the isolation of learners through the lack of communication. Communication is very important in the virtual learning community; it is the actual brick and mortar of the community (Schwier, 2001). The online instructor must be conscious of this reality and stay in communication with the learner. It is also important that various forms of communication are fostered between learners, not just between the instructor and the learners.

Participation of the instructor in online discussions moderated by students provides more credibility to the discussion (McIssac et al., 1999). If the theoretical foundations of online learning are based on cognitive apprenticeship, it is important that the mentor be available to model proper discussion etiquette and to guide the discussion in a meaningful way. Involving participants from the periphery of the discussion can be achieved through public or private questioning by the instructor. Participants share tacit knowledge when they feel comfortable in the environment. The instructor moves towards the periphery of the discussion and monitors its progress with little input as the discussions quickly becomes student centered. Examination of the tacit knowledge when made explicit by the students helps the instructor evaluate what information and skills have been internalized. Since face-to-face meetings before meeting online cannot always be established, it is important for the promotion of interaction and social presence. Learners need to feel socially present interacting online (McIssac et al., 1999). As learners move from the periphery of a virtual learning community and engage the community, they can claim membership to the community and feel socially present when interacting.

The literature in WB courses and course interaction and communication (Chickering & Ehrmann, 1996; McIssac et al., 1999; Schrum, 1998; Schwier, 2001) indicates that communication and reflection is very important in retaining students. The initial meetings of the online course should include an activity for learning style assessment, an icebreaker, and open communication. Students need to recognize their personal learning styles. The instructor must also be aware of this latter information. Students and teachers need to compromise and accommodate each other in the teaching-learning process. When students understand how they learn, they can work on expanding ways of learning. The student who requires external motivation in an online course may look at ways of becoming internally motivated and learn independently. The teacher must be aware of this and help the student by being in constant contact with the learner as well as the teacher-supervisor. Frontloading engages the student immediately with the course. Allowing the student to talk about themselves is very important in the initial stages. Scaffolding the initial stages of the course brings the student into the learning environment, and makes the student feel a part of the group. Interaction throughout the course is important and usually results in engagement of ideas, people, and processes (Schwier, 2001). A third principle or good practice is prompt feedback. Although many aspects contribute to effective online instruction, prompt feedback consistently emerges as a powerful tool to promote student learning (Holmes, 2000; Polloff & Pratt, 2001).

Although studies have investigated student's perceptions of online courses, none have assessed the instructional quality of online courses specifically related to adult learning or the nontraditional student population. All online courses are not necessarily equal in terms of efficacy in delivery the course content. While most faculty assume that their online courses are good, this may not be the same assumption from the students' view. Little research has identified the factors that students use to form quality perceptions. Yet this is important due to the fact that perception could have long term implications to school programs given that online and WB delivery programs will continue to grow in the future.

Methodology

Data used to investigate the research questions in this mixed design exploratory case study came from a response to an online questionnaire that was designed to collect quantitative data on:

- Student's perception of online course instructional quality based on course content interactions, visual appeal, ease of use, and course materials
- Affects of Web design and visual aesthetics on students ability to interact with the course content
- Factors affecting course communication, feedback, and reflection
- Instructional design strategies for clear instruction

A set of ten questions were developed to assess student's perception of online and WB courses. Nine of the questions were closed-ended questions developed on a Likert scale model with the following choices:

- **No Basis for Judgment/Not Applicable**
- **Strongly Disagree**
- **Disagree**
- **Agree**
- **Strongly Agree**

The tenth question was an open-ended question that asked for the participants' opinions on what they thought the most important aspects were to the instructional quality of an online/WB course. At the end of each course offered in the summer I and summer II semester, which lasted six weeks, the survey was given to the students to assess their perceptions towards this learning environment along with the factors that affect the instructional quality of the online courses. The courses selected for this study were online courses offered during the summer I and summer II academic semester and were from the following academic units:

- **College of Business**
- **College of Education**
- **Hilton College of Hotel and Restaurant Management**
- **College of Liberal Arts and Social Sciences**

- **College of Natural Sciences and Mathematics**
- **College of Technology**

Of the 222 distance education courses offered during the summer I and summer II semesters, either through broadcast television, Web, or video, 169 of the courses were delivered online by a total of 32 faculty members. The participants of this study were adult learners in traditional university degree programs, taking part of the distance education online course offerings. An e-mail with a link to the Web site where the survey instrument was located was sent to the 32 instructors of the courses to share with the students at the end of the semester. Students were encouraged to be truthful in completing the survey and were assured that their grades would not be affected based on their responses. Of the 169 courses, which had a total number of 2,500 for both summer I and summer II semesters, a total of 291 (11.64%) valid responses were obtained. Female participants accounted for 54% of the participants, while males accounted for 46% of the responses.

Results and Discussion

Student Perceptions of Online Learning

Participants responded to nine questionnaire items to describe their perceptions regarding the instructional quality of online education using WebCT. Table 1 shows the descriptive summary.

Overall Perceptions

The results from this study indicated an overall positive response regarding the instructional quality of online courses delivered via WebCT. The visual appeal of online courses and the appropriateness of course materials received the highest perception ratings of instructional quality, followed by the tasteful use of colors for online courses. The results indicated that students had high rankings of visual design of the Web site for the instructional quality of online courses, and perceived that the visual display of content was an important factor that affected their view of online courses. Visual appeal of online courses may not seem to be critical to students' learning of the content of the course (Brush, 2001), but this study shows that this factor affects the students' level of interest and desire to use the site to obtain information. For the important aspects of instructional quality of online courses, several students identified the use of color in their online courses. They indicated:

Table 1. Factors that affect the instructional quality of online courses (N = 291)

Factors	No Basis		Strongly Disagree		Disagree		Agree		Strongly Agree		M	SD	Mean Rank
	n	%	n	%	n	%	n	%	n	%			
The course materials presented in the online course were relevant to the class.	7	2	8	3	120	42	107	37	46	16	3.70	1.06	1
The colors used in the course design were well coordinated and of good taste.	9	3	8	3	138	47	66	23	70	24	3.66	1.07	2
The use of appropriate graphics, sounds, pictures, animations made the Web site material visually appealing.	26	8.8	27	9.2	99	34	51	18	88	30	3.55	1.33	3
The combined use of text, graphics and/or sound to represent the information in different ways enabled you to better understand the material.	23	8	31	11	102	35	49	17	85	29	3.53	1.31	4
The Web site flow was easy to read and understand.	10	3	20	7	134	47	92	32	32	11	3.49	1.10	5
For each new section online course, there was a clear connection to the course objectives.	14	5	23	8	128	44	84	29	41	14	3.46	1.11	6
The specific tasks for every assignment were specifically stated.	17	6	29	10	102	35	108	37	34	12	3.45	1.14	7
New course content and material were well organized on the online WB course.	14	5	26	9	123	42	96	33	32	11	3.41	1.06	8
The introduction to content segments were well-stated with clarity and purpose.	11	4	30	10	133	45	86	30	31	11	3.37	1.04	9

Note: 1= No Basis for Judgment; 2= Strongly Disagree; 3= Disagree; 4= Agree; 5= Strongly Agree

"the colors on the website were not chosen in a professional and easily readable manner." Instructors are thus faced with the challenge of creating a functional and aesthetically pleasing Web site and they are responsible for the presentation of their online courses.

Perception of Web Design

Although respondents were satisfied with the Web design of this course, many were not satisfied with the Web design of most WB courses in general: 52% of the respondents said that they were satisfied with the Web design of online courses. However, nearly half of the respondents (46%) were not satisfied with the Web design of online courses in general. It is possible that instructors who use WebCT for their courses may not incorporate good design aspects for their online courses.

Factors Related to Instructional Quality

Approximately 15% of the respondents indicated that good Web design of their online courses was important. This was the third-highest ranking aspect of instructional quality. The results of this study confirmed that instructors need to take into consideration the architecture and user interface of an online site of the course (Brush, 2001). The site architecture determines the ease with which students can locate desired information. Brush (2001) emphasized that the site architecture establishes the sequence of the course, the organization of the information, the order of procedures that should be followed, and supplementary resources for students. From the study conducted by the research team, one student commented as follows: "The organization of materials is most important to me so that I can easily find what I need and see what is important." Others said that the "layout and presentation of material" helped them "coordinate class material." When a class Web site has poor site architecture, students become frustrated with their inability to locate the necessary information and navigate the site (Brush, 2001). Students who were confused and frustrated by their attempts to move from page to page would likely give up on the use of the Web site to locate desired information. This may lead to negative perceptions toward online courses. As reported by one of the respondents from one of the online courses indicated, "The organization of the class Web site is not streamlined, very busy and cluttered, this adds to the confusion and frustration of finding course materials and the appropriate content."

This study showed that the interface navigation scheme of the Web site should also be considered in online courses. Interface design influences students' focus on learning and their ability to obtain the necessary course information. When students can utilize the interface to navigate from one section of the site to another without too many distractions, the user interface design is effective. Approximately 73% of the respondents listed easy site navigation as an important aspect of online courses; specifically, "Ease of navigation through the site is an important aspect of online courses," and "It was easy to navigate through the site."

Nearly half of the respondents (47%) reported that they understand course material better when their online courses use multimedia components to represent the information. Regarding the important aspects of online courses, a student from the study the research team conducted commented: "animation helped me a lot to understand the concepts of this course." The idea is that if multimedia is not designed properly, it can have a negative impact. The results from the research study revealed that the time spent on downloading course materials and multimedia were factors that should be considered in the online course as well.

This study found that the links to new sections of the course should be clearly related to course objectives. Basically, 51% of the respondents were not satisfied with clarity of objectives in new sections. Study findings indicated that many instructors were not considering certain factors such as the objectives of the course and the objectives of each individual lesson when designing online courses. Clearly stated objectives (or the lack of them) affect students' perceptions regarding online courses, the results showed. The results were closely correlated with student responses regarding the important aspects of instructional quality of online courses, such as clear instruction, interaction, design, convenience, feedback, and usability. According to the survey conducted in this study, nearly 86% of the respondents indicated that the most important aspect of instructional quality of online course was the idea of having online course content and materials be relevant to the course.

Instructional Design Model

The clarity and ordering of online documents in relation to course content, according to the instructional design model (IDM), increased the students' sense of connection with the course (Dick, Carey & Carey, 2001). Dick et al. (2001) further identified a systematic process of designing instruction that ensures the quality of knowledge transferred from an instructor to a learner in their model. The findings from this study provided empirical evidence for IDM. The results of this study indicated that instructors should incorporate an IDM in their online courses because the model enables learners to learn effectively and to engage in activities that promote communities of practice. In the study, 22% of the respondents perceived clear instruction as the most important aspect in their online learning experiences. The result indicated that clear instruction is an instructional design issue, as commented by one student who valued "clear, concise, and detailed directions." Students called for "order and clarity of instructions," and "letting students know the due dates, where to read, which chapter is on the exam." If the instructions were not clear, students "didn't know what each assignment was worth," "didn't know how the final grade was computed"or even "felt lost the entire semester." Students' responses in this study indicated that clear instruction directly affects their learning, their understanding of content materials, and their participation in online learning activities.

Principles of Good Learning and Practice

The findings support Chickering and Ehrmann's (1996) principles of good learning and practices for online courses. The first principle of good practice encourages interaction between students and faculty. Online communication components such as e-mail, discussion boards, chat, and whiteboards available within the course management system (CMS) provide more opportunities for students and faculty members to interact and communicate online compared to traditional face-to-face instruction in the classroom. Interaction was the second most important aspect of instructional quality of online courses in this study (21%). Student comments from this study include: "communication from the professor is key" and "the message board and e-mail on WebCT help students and professors to communicate with each other." One respondent cited "frequent interaction with instructor" as a positive aspect. When students interacted with instructors frequently, they felt that "the online course was very successful," "the instructor was helpful to all students," and "[they] learned a lot from the teacher."

The second principle of good practice encourages cooperation among students. Another good practice is prompt feedback. Respondents (29%) in this survey stated that timely responses from peers and from their instructors were important factors in determining the instructional quality of online courses. The results support study that students have positive perceptions of online courses when the instructors facilitate frequent contact between themselves and students, use active learning techniques, convey high expectations, emphasize time on task, and provide prompt feedback.

Major Reasons for Taking Online Courses

Previous research mentioned flexibility, convenience, and accessibility and learning enhancement were the top reasons for taking online courses. Results of this study indicated that 12% of the respondents perceived "convenience" as an important aspect, especially for "students who are very busy and may not have the time to get to campus to attend class." Students felt that the convenience that online courses provide made them able to "access to material 24 hours a day," view "their assignment outside the classroom," and "attend class without leaving work or home," as well as "visit their course more often than they are able to sit in a class." The course offered "flexibility of work." This study concluded that convenience is a vital aspect of the online course. In this study, 62% of the respondents said that ease of use of WebCT was an important aspect in their learning; and 6% of them reported that "the old version of WebCT is easy to use," and "the older version of WebCT was clear and straightforward." Students' negative perceptions of online courses were often based on computer access (McMahon, Gardner, Gray & Mulhern, 1999). Students who did not have computers at home were often vexed by the additional time required to visit a computer lab and by the lack of convenience. Though computer access was an important issue at that time, in this study, only 15% of the respondents reported accessibility to class material as an important aspect of instructional quality. Other aspects reported from the results included the availability of instructors, the quality of content, and the personality of the instructor.

Future Trends

The Internet and Web offers a worldwide forum in which to teach courses. One can assume, for example, that each student at any time has an excellent encyclopedia at his or her disposal. Course material can be dynamically updated and linked across several related sources. Course text, examples, and exercises can be interactive in the sense of immediately illustrating equations with graphs, changing parameters and seeing the results, and linking to other Web sites according to the interests of the student. The WB learning environment or model is essentially free from limitations of space and time, while reaching adult learners and nontraditional students around the world with great ease. In addition, the WB learning model offers students a wealth of information that was never possible in the classical model. The possibility of linking to information worldwide in a multitude of formats creates a remarkably rich medium for learning. WB courseware is not merely an electronic duplicate of the original course material. It represents a new type of educational material which takes full advantage of the emerging Web and multimedia technologies in order to achieve an effective yet enjoyable learning process (Michael & Tait, 2002). That is, complex concepts are introduced in innovative ways—ways that involve the adult learner and integrate them into the learning process. Full linking to vast resources available worldwide introduces new levels of value to online courses in distance education. A WB course is envisioned as a dynamically evolving resource that will prove beneficial to both the adult learner and nontraditional students and instructors alike.

In the light of this research, it is evident that the design of a WB course is a multifaceted process that resembles movie making in cinema productions. That is to say, a WB course is developed through the efforts of *a team of professionals* with a complementary range of skills, as opposed to classical course design that is typically developed by *faculty alone*. Designer and instructors alike will have to take heed to principles in design, usability, and interaction in order to make online distance learning courses the top quality product for the next generation.

The richness of modern Web and multimedia technologies allow for unlimited creativity when it comes to electronic courseware development. Such richness offers educators new opportunities to develop very interesting course material while it also poses a substantial challenge in that it requires faculty to rethink their own course offerings in the light of the new technologies. In order to best serve the adult learner and nontraditional student population instructional designers, instructors, and course administration will have to take an active look at effective course design and communication strategies within online and WB courses. It is not enough for universities, colleges, and other educational institutions to just give financial resources, hardware, and software, but should fundamentally equip instructors to effectively teach, engage, extend, and enhance the adult learner's or nontraditional student's learning experience while in an online course offered via a distance.

The future entails faculty training and development in designing effective and efficient online courses for the adult learning population and nontraditional students. This trend can be seen at many major research institutions that offer online courses and e-learning training courses specifically for the adult learner or nontraditional student. By equipping the instructor to effectively design online courses in terms of online course interaction with both students and with the online content and materials, visual aesthetic in design and Web architecture, convenience and open access to materials, positive and useful user feedback, communication, and usability of both the course content materials and course Web site, students will develop a consensus toward a positive view on the instructional quality of the online course. It is important to understand that in order to foster an environment conducive to effective learning in the online atmosphere, we must pay close attention to the factors that affect instructional quality as discussed by Marsh and Roche (1997). For such research the future seems very bright and encouraging. There is a great of discussion on the effective and systematic design of instruction, effective design of visual aesthetics, design of communication structure, and the available of open access to course content and materials in online courses, specifically for adult learners and those individuals in nontraditional settings. This theme will be repeated as other aspects of online learning come under scrutiny. We know enough at this point to optimize quality in design and delivery, but the instructional quality of course content is more difficult to define and measure; that is why the more we discuss this issue, the more strategies, processes, and procedures will be developed to effectively engage designers and instructor in the development of online courses specifically for the adult learner and the nontraditional student.

Summary and Conclusion

The findings of the survey research in this chapter clearly show that Web design aesthetics and accessibility of the course information were all important factors that affected the instructional quality of online and WB courses. The survey results also revealed that the WB learning environment would allow students to be more active participants in their learning process, increasing their critical and creative thinking skills as well as improving their problem-solving skills. Furthermore, the results revealed that by adhering to the instructional design process and the effective design of the course Web site, students could learn to develop learning skills such as communication, teamwork, collaboration, and time management, which would assist them in achieving ownership of the course learning outcomes, but also master the online WB course environment. The use of online and WB tools for their online courses allowed them to be innovative in their coursework, making their learning experience valuable and rewarding. On the practical side, this research provides instructional designers, educators, and trainers with the necessary information on the aspects that affect the instructional quality of online and WB courses as well as innovative approaches to teaching with educational technology.

Online and WB learning environments in distance education are growing to meet the needs of the adult learning population or the nontraditional population. With advances in Internet and WB technologies reaching diverse locations, a diverse program can be offered to students throughout the world. The quality of instruction and the effective design of the online course will increase as the number of participants and the knowledge exchange among faculty and students. However, it must be understood that the instructional quality of WB and online courses in distance education programs is critical to the success of adult learners or nontraditional learners. Through utilizing the a variety of instructional design principles, Web design concepts, and virtual learning scaffolding model, instructors can incorporate multiple instructional routes to include all learners fostering active and dynamic learning environments.

As a whole, the results obtained in this project were positive and encouraging. Students in general enjoy the online and WB learning environment. Nevertheless, they were eager to indicate the critical factors that affect the instructional quality of online courses. The research examined in this study provides educators with the relevant factors to the instructional quality and overall success of the student learning outcomes via online and WB courses. This method of course design and learning engages students actively in participating in their own learning process, that is, leading to the promotion of quality teaching and student learning for a more consistent and dynamic WB educational learning environment. This case study has attempted to address the factors that affect the instructional quality of adult learners in online distance learning programs, as well as key strategies for designing online instruction and issues surrounding this form of education. Understanding this new educational milieu will help instructional designers and educators in the struggle to create and deliver successful inclusive online courses.

References

Anderson, T., & Joerg, W. (1996). WWW to support classroom teaching. *Canadian Journal of Education Communication, 25*(1), 19-36.

Brush, R. O. (2001). Effective Web design and core communication issues: The mission components in Web-based distance education. *Journal of Educational Multimedia and Hypermedia, 10*(4), 357-367.

Cedefop. (2002). *Joint Cedefop-European Comission study on e-learning in SMEs.* Brussel: CiRN.

Chickering, A., & Ehrmann, S. (1996). *Implementing the seven principles: Technology as lever.* Retrieved August 13, 2006, from http://www.tltgroup.org/programs/seven.html

Daugherty, M., & Funke, B. L. (1998). University faculty and student perceptions of Web-based instruction. *Journal of Distance Education, 13*(1), 21-39.

Dick, W., Carey, L., & Carey, J. O. (2001). *The systematic design of instruction.* Boston: Addison-Wesley Educational Publishers, Inc.

Hara, N., & Kling, R. (2000). Students' frustrations with a Web-based distance education course. *First Monday, 4*(12). Retrieved August 13, 2006, from http://firstmonday.org/issues/issue4_12/hara/index.html

Holmes, P. (2000). *Online and just in time: The change implications of implementing a strategy to use technology in the delivery of learning solutions in a large organization* (5th ed.). New York: Addison-Wesley Longman. Retrieved August 13, 2006, from http://www.t2b.com/au/resources/Final-Project-Paper.pdf instruction.

Jiang, M. (1998). *Distance learning in a Web-based environment: An analysis of factors influencing students' perceptions of online learning.* Unpublished doctoral dissertation, State University of New York, Albany, NY.

Khan, B. (1997). *Web-based instruction.* Englewood Cliffs, NJ: Educational Technology Press.

Knowles, M., Holton, E., & Swanson, R., (2005). *The adult learner: The definitive classic on adult education and resources development.* Burlington, MA: Butterworth-Heinermann.

Marsh, H. W. (1982). SEEQ: A reliable, valid and useful instrument for collecting students' evaluations of university teaching. *British Journal of Educational Psychology, 52*, 77-95.

Marsh, H. W. (1987). Student's evaluations of university teaching: Research findings, methodological issues, and directions for future research. *International Journal of Educational Research, 11*, 253-388.

Marsh, H. W. (1997). *Students' evaluations of educational quality (SEEQ): An overview*. Cambelltown, New South Wales: University of Western Sydney.

Marsh, H. W., & Roche, L. A. (1997). Making students' evaluations of teaching effectiveness effective: The critical issues of validity, bias, and utility. *American Psychologist, 52*(11), 1187-1197.

McIssac, M. S., Blosher, J. M., Mahes, V., & Charalombos, V. (1999, June). Student and teacher perceptions of interaction in online computer-mediated communication. *Education Media International, 39*(2), 121-131.

McMahon, J., Gardner, J., Gray, C., & Mulhern, G. (1999). Barriers to computer usage: Staff and student perceptions. *Journal of Computer Assisted Learning, 15*, 302.

Michael, M. M., & Tait, A., (2002). *Open and distance learning: Trends, policies, and strategy consideration*. Paris: United Nations Educational, Scientific, and Cultural Organization.

Morss, D. A. (1999). A study of student perspectives on Web-based learning: WebCT in the classroom. *Internet Research: Electronic Networking Applications and Policy, 9*(5), 393-408.

Polloff, R. M., & Pratt, K. (2001). *Lessons from the cyberspace classroom*. San Francisco: Jossey-Bass.

Ryan, R. C., & Kasturi, S. (2002). Instructional design and use of interactive online construction exercises. In *ASC Proceedings of the 38th Annual Conference* (pp. 61-70). Blacksburg, VA: Virginia Polytechnic Institute and State University.

Schrum, L. (1998). On-line education: A study of emerging pedagogy. *New Directions for Adult and Continuing Education, 78*, 53-61.

Schwier, R. A. (2001). Catalysts, emphases, and elements of virtual learning communities. Implications for research and practice. *The Quarterly Review of Distance Education, 2*(1), 5-18.

Appendix: Definition of Terms and Concepts

Active Learning

A set of processes and principles whereby learners are actively engaged in the learning process, rather than "passively" absorbing information through lectures. Active learning involves reading, writing, discussion, and engagement in solving problems, analysis, synthesis, and evaluation. Active learning is also known as cooperative learning. Refer to the adult learning theory and principles for more information.

Adult Learning Theory and Principles

A set of core principles developed by Knowles, Holton, and Swanson (2005) guide the teaching and learning of adults in educational or learning environments. Adult learning principles take into consideration the following assumptions:

- Adults have the need to know why they are learning something. There must be specified goals and objectives that can be measured and evaluated. The instructor must also show the participants how the course and its materials will help them attain their goals.
- Adults have a need to be self-directed and autonomous over their learning and learning environment(s).
- Adults bring more work-related experiences into the learning situation. The content must be valuable, relevant, and useful to what the adult is learning. This knowledge must be then connected to the adult's life experiences and knowledge base.
- Adults enter into a learning experience with a problem-centered approach to learning. The instructor must actively involve adult participants in the learning process and serve as facilitators for them.
- Adults are motivated to learn by both extrinsic and intrinsic motivators.

Adult learning theory is especially important to consider in developing online and distance learning programs because the audience for many such programs tends to be adults, most of whom have not spent a majority of their time in a formal education setting.

Andragogy

An educational approach characterized by learner-centeredness (i.e., the student's needs and wants are central to the process of teaching), self-directed learning (i.e., students are responsible for and involved in their learning to a much greater degree than traditional education), and a humanist philosophy (i.e., personal development is the key focus of education). Related concepts include the following: active learning, facilitated learning, self-directed learning, humanism, critical thinking, experiential learning, and transformational learning.

Distance Education

An educational process and system in which all or a significant proportion of the teaching is carried out by someone or something removed in space and time from the learner. Distance education requires structured planning, well-designed courses, special instructional techniques, and methods of communication by electronic and other technology, as well as specific organizational and administrative arrangements. Distance education can also be defined as related to the technology that drives instructional methods that allows the learner to study at sites physically removed from the instructor. Typically distance education environments employ video, data, print, and voice technologies.

Distance Learning

A system and a process that connects learners with distributed learning resources. While distance learning takes a wide variety of forms, all distance learning is characterized by the following: (1) separation of place and/or time between instructor and learner, among learners, and/or between learners and learning resources, and (2) interaction between the learner and the instructor, among learners, and/or between learners and learning resources conducted through one or more media; use of electronic media is not necessarily required.

Instructional Design

Also known as instructional systems design is the analysis of learning needs and systematic development of instruction. Instructional designers often use instructional technology as a method for developing instruction. Instructional design models typically specify a method, that if followed will facilitate the transfer of knowledge, skills, and attitude to the recipient or acquirer of the instruction.

Instructional Quality

The quality of the interaction between faculty and students, primarily taking place in a classroom and intended to either transfer information from faculty to student or facilitate self-motivated student learning processes. Marsh (1982, 1987, 1997) and Marsh and Roche (1997) described instructional quality as "teaching effectiveness." Marsh's instructional instrument includes nine constructs: learning, enthusiasm, organization, group interaction, rapport, breadth, exams, assignments, and workload.

Learning Communities

An approach to classroom instruction and organization based on democratic ideals, which is characterized by active teaching and learning, collaboration, belonging, shared decision making, and a strong sense of democratic participation. Learning communities are courses in which students and their professors experience a purposeful, coherent, and integrated learning environment together in a linked or interdisciplinary course.

Learning Management Systems (LMS)

LMS is a software application or Web-based technology used to plan, implement, and assess a specific learning process. Typically, a learning management system provides an instructor with a way to create and deliver content, monitor student participation, and assess student performance. A learning management system may also provide students with the ability to use interactive features such as threaded discussions, video conferencing, and discussion forums. The Advanced Distance Learning group, sponsored by the U.S. Department of Defense, has created a set of specifications called shareable content object reference model (SCORM) to encourage the standardization of learning management systems.

Online Learning

Defined as one where instruction and interaction are primarily based on the technologies available from the Internet and the World Wide Web. Students enrolled in a Web course interact with the class instructor and other classmates through Internet-based communications. See Web-based instruction for more information on this environment.

Perception

The acquisition and processing of sensory information in order to see, hear, taste, smell, or feel objects in the world; also guides an organism's actions with respect to those objects. Perception may involve conscious awareness of objects and events.

Web-Based Instruction (WBI)

A form of computer-based instruction which uses the Web as the primary delivery method of information. A textbook is usually required and all other materials, as well as communication with the instructor, are provided through the course Web site. The terms online courses and Web-based instruction are used interchangeably with WBT.

Chapter XIV

Lifelong Learning and Online Education: A New Framework for the Competence of Tomorrow's Educators

Marianthi Karatza, Bank of Cypress, Greece

Argiris Tzikopoulos, University of Athens, Greece

Niki Phillips, Bank of Cyprus, Greece

Abstract

In this chapter, the effects of lifelong learning and online education in the role of an educator are examined. Lifelong learning and lifelong education, as well as online learning and online education are terms that are located in a new context where flexibility has become a central demand. In such a framework, we identify the new capabilities and challenges that organizations, learners, and educators face. Moreover, we attempt to describe the role that an educator should adopt in order to be effective and able to support learning in this new environment. This review concludes with a framework of competencies necessary for the educators who practice their profession within new learning environments that already exist or that are going to appear in organizations, as needs for learning and knowledge management are continuously increasing. For this purpose, a specific case study is presented regarding the way an online training system can be implemented in order to support learning within a banking organization.

Introduction

Lifelong learning has become a central debate in academia and the policy context. This is not coincidental. The term "lifelong learning" reflects the need for continuous knowledge acquisition and update which characterizes our society—our knowledge-driven society. The term also reflects the rising stream of flexible ways of learning which gradually replace the old and traditional forms of education (Jarvis, 2001). Because of *globalisation* and *competitiveness*, we cannot neglect the need of every nation for continuous enhancement of its human resources' competencies (DFEE, 1998; Griffin, 2004). In this context, the role of practitioners is changing, regardless of the educational environment in which individuals work and move away from the traditional roles of teachers that provide knowledge to a group of people. This role of practitioners does change in terms of the competencies each person must initiate for lifelong learning (Cornford, 2002) as well as the kind of relationships each person should create within the learning group (Rogers, 2002).

Another factor that affects this change in different ways is the rapid growth of information and communication technology (ICT). ICT has become an important aspect of every day life, and educators/trainers must help their students in the use of ICT (Huysman & Gerrits, 1998). ICT can also provide new capabilities and means of supporting individualized educational needs in numerous ways (Karatza, Phillips, & Apostolakis, 2005a; Kirkpatrick & McLaughlan, 2000; Stites, Hopery, & Ginsburg, 1998). Concerning the growth of ICT and the relation with education and learning, there are those who believe that ICT should be applied to *every* discipline expecting that its penetration will improve the performance of *every* educational process (Tucker & Cordani, 1998). On the other hand, there are those who believe that the induction of ICT in education will not change things radically, so it should be dealt with cautiously, leaving no room for excitement (Tsolakidis, 2004). According to Mayes (2002), the argument appears to be that the power and potential of new technologies will mean that *new* methods become available, yet the evidence from past experience is that new technologies may *not* inevitably lead to change in education.

The growing hope for making changes in education using ICT has created a complicated environment with several contributors and vendors participating. Given the powerful role that technology applications can play in analysis and evaluation, there is a danger of underestimating the importance of pedagogic and adult education principles (Thorpe, 2005). In Mayes' (2002) words: "the failure of the technology to produce a real impact on education was due to a widespread misunderstanding about learning. This is the pervasive idea that the way in which information is presented to learners is somehow all important" (p. 164).

After the production of several e-learning systems in which large amount of money was invested with poor results (Paulsen, 2003), passionate discussions started to develop concerning *effectiveness*, *pedagogy*, *adaptability*, and *quality* of online learning in combination with new perspectives such as online communities and semantic Web, for example. It seems, although there is significant research and work from several institutions throughout the world, that there is still much questioning about the key factors that determine a successful online program.

Keeping the above situation mind, the purpose of the present chapter is to provide an analysis of the new online environment in which educators/trainers play a key role. It is important to identify the new environments in which learning is constantly supported. The role of educators is to help learners get accustomed with the new environment in which *learning*, *knowledge*, and *practice* are a constant need. That is to say, in this chapter, we introduce the context in which we define the terms and the environment individuals shape for *learning*, *education*, and *training*. We also examine the new capabilities and challenges that the aforementioned situation or framework shapes. Following, a case study of a banking organization is presented, with a focus on the way an online system enhances its vision for continuous development of human resources. Also, it is used as evidence of the flexibility that the system provides in the coverage of training needs. Finally, we propose a framework of competencies that educators must develop and attain. Our ultimate goal is to examine the competencies that educators need to work on, especially in order to support learners in the new learning environment that our knowledge society forms.

Defining a New Context for Learning: Lifelong Learning and Online Education

The discussion regarding the term "lifelong learning," its meaning, and the reason for its wide adoption has been particularly significant in the last few years. There are several factors that contribute to the shaping of a new framework concerning *learning*, *education*, and *training*. In this section, we try to identify the main directions that define the context of the contemporary knowledge society. We examine different sectors that are related to lifelong learning such as the research field, the related policies, and the final product of practice. Additionally, we induce the ways that "online learning" and "lifelong learning" can be combined effectively.

Most policy documents on lifelong learning are quite ambitious and motivating on engaging measures that will enhance more opportunities for individuals to learn. In the European Commission's (2001) document, *Making a European Area of Lifelong Learning a Reality,* we pinpoint the acknowledgment that people and their knowledge and competencies are Europe's future. Specifically, "lifelong learning is a life wide activity covering a wide range of areas such as personal, civic, social, and profession" (European Commission, 2001, p. 9). The aim of the Commission is to improve *knowledge*, *skills*, and *competencies* in particular. The framework consists of four categories: globalization, demographic change, digital technology, and environmental damage. These are the main factors that prescribe the need for lifelong learning and its methods of delivery. The necessity for a new approach to education is also recognized in the document. The key issues of the new approach are the focus on "the learner and the equality of the opportunities provided" (European Commission, 2001, p. 9). Field (1997) maintains, however, that no sign of any concrete proposals in the key issues was developed; the significance of lifelong learning has been defined, basically, in terms of *employment* and *economy*.

When it comes to government, the national policies seem to have a much more narrow perspective on lifelong learning. For instance, in the document of the Department for Education and Skills, *21st Century's Skills: Realizing Our Potential*, we see that the focus is on the demand for flexible workforce to meet the demands of the global economy (DFES, 2003, p. 22). The document further states as follows: "When people are better educated and better trained, they have chances to earn more and use talents to the full, both in and out of work" (DFES, 2003, p. 18). This statement, of course, is an indication that lifelong learning in such a context can help people gain a better quality of life. In this policy document, nevertheless, the central role is given to employers, putting their needs forward (DFES, 2003, p. 21). The question here, therefore, is whether it raises a danger of turning lifelong learning into a social control tool, refuting the perspectives of social inclusion, citizenship, and the right to choose (Coffield, 2002; Open University, 2002). Lifelong learning *is* in danger of becoming subsumed within pre-existing structures and interests rather than being the basis for the reform of the latter (Eraut, 1997). Although the policy discourse works hard to sustain a consistent and coherent vision capable of attracting support from a diversity of stakeholders—based on twin requirements for *economic competitiveness* and *social inclusion* (Edwards, Raggat, Harrison, McCollum, & Calder, 1998)—the most powerful voices frame lifelong learning as a strategy for *competitiveness* (Ashton & Green, 1996).

According to numerous researchers, the fact that we use the term "lifelong learning" instead of "education" or "training" has to do with a new perspective that assigns a central role to the learner and that individuals have to take appropriate initiatives in order to create their own learning path (e.g., Field, 2002; Kokkos, 2005a). Edwards et al. (1998), for instance, describe the ideal learner in the context of lifelong learning in the contemporary society as an autonomous customer, constructing a personalized pathway through a modular curricula leading to a tailored qualification. Although this description can have advantages towards the personalization of education and can help individuals design their own lives, it has no power to affect and deal with inequities that exist not only in the provision of opportunities but also in the society in general (Keep, 1997). Meanwhile, the funding for educational institutions that provide educational programs has been reduced and learners must undertake the cost for their development. This is the interpretation that many researchers and practitioners give when they identify the direction towards *individualization* (Kokkos, 2005a). In this unstable framework, regarding the meaning of lifelong learning for advantaged and disadvantaged, policy makers, practitioners, and researchers must add the concern about what "online learning" or "online education" means to us.

Terms used interchangeably here are e-learning, computer-based training, computer-assisted learning, Web-based education, and virtual education. What differentiates online learning with e-learning is the network. Online learning refers to the use of any kind of electronic forms of information, which deliver knowledge and courses, as well as to the use of a network's advantages. This means that there is a connection (which can be synchronous or asynchronous) allowing learners to communicate upon their course of study and discuss what they have gained already, and what practice they have been making based on the rules that the specific community has developed (Wenger, 1998, 2001). These rules can be set by the tutor or in collaboration with the members of the community. In the present chapter, when we use the term "online learning" or "online education," we refer to the exploitation of networks in the field of learning, education, and training. When we refer to the term "e-learning," we adopt the definition that the European Committee (2003) has provided as follows: "e-learning is the use of new multimedia technologies and the Internet to improve the quality of learning by facilitating access to resources and services as well as remote exchanges and collaboration" (para. 7).

There are several methodologies that have been used during the past years for the creation of e-learning systems. Multimedia, simulations, and adaptive environments, as well as expert systems, are the examples that have been considerably researched and experimented in various educational and learning environments. Some of them have been used in the classroom as educational tools for enhancing the learning process, other as stand-alone programs that have provided new knowledge to those who wanted to learn a given subject. According to Phillips (1998), for instance, there is a tendency for newcomers to this field to take the traditional objectivist approach used in the classroom and put it on the computer. Researchers have been trying to identify the characteristics that could make their systems more effective and help people learn better. Because of this, such a field as "human-to-computer interaction" has been brought at the center of interest and discussion.

Historically speaking, four different periods concerning the history of e-learning can be described. *First*, the instructor-led training era (pre-1983), during which an instructor was responsible for the learning process and the way in which any learning resource was used, had little to do with real e-learning situations. *Second,* the multimedia era (1984-1993) followed, which focused on the production of stand-alone applications. In that era, sophisticated environments and the way that knowledge was presented became important. *Third*, the Web infancy era (1994-1999) started with the development of the Internet particularly. The first online educational applications created hopes for increased communication and overcoming difficulties of space and time. *Lastly*, nowadays (1999-2005), a next-generation Web is fully developed to offer online courses provided by several educational institutions and with various aims and expectations (Leinonen, 2005).

According to numerous case studies, online education that has been offered so far has been transient, unsuccessful, and far from sustainable. Kruse (2003) argues that the e-learning industry followed the technology hype cycle. More specifically, Kruse describes that a blossom period (1995-2000) resulted in the funding of important and ambitious e-learning projects, while the same projects seem to close and conclude in poor results (2000-2002), and new ideas such as *blended learning* or *standards in e-learning* become extremely important.

Nowadays, significant working teams and organizations have developed e-learning standards to provide designers with guidance concerning specific attributes that e-learning systems should have in order to be effective and productive. There are numerous organizations which collaborate in several ways to produce specifications; and organisations such as ISO (International Standards Organisation) turn to standards (Apostolakis & Karatza, 2005). Additionally, serious efforts are made to measure the effectiveness of systems already implemented in several sectors. Workshops and various research teams and organizations are trying to deal with the difficult task of identifying the specific factors that prescribe the quality of e-learning systems. Presently, key issues that have been widely recognized include the following: motivation, making learning attractive, quality, content, and usability. Naturally, problems concerning the usability, sociability, and effectiveness of e-learning systems have risen to prominence. Researchers and practitioners question the ability of e-learning systems to solve problems related to learning. In other words, whether they are creating additional problems in connection with access to new technologies as well as building new boundaries between people who are computer literate and those who are not. Furthermore, there is the question of whether a learning system promotes isolation.

According to Nascimbeni (2005), there are several different dimensions of access that should concern us and may provide ways in which ICT can give some solutions:

1. Access to information on learning, meaning access to information on the available opportunities within formal and informal settings
2. Access to teaching, meaning access to what is considered traditional classroom-based learning
3. Access to infrastructure, meaning access to ICTs, learning materials, to the Internet
4. Access to studying facilities, meaning physical or virtual access to formal, nonformal, and informal learning settings
5. Access to learning catalysts, in terms of access to services as guidance, counseling, and orientation
6. Access to learning support, in terms of human or machine-driven support services, such as tutoring or mentoring
7. Access to learning motivation, meaning access to what motivate your learning experience
8. Access to funding, in terms of access to the economic support needed to take part in e-learning experiences

The above dimensions strongly connect the need for lifelong learning with the potential contribution of ICT and online education, training, or services.

New ideas of exploiting the opportunities of networks emerged. The new idea is that e-learning systems can create a connection between people within a learning community. Such a community can be originated from the resolution of new matters concerning everyday working practices. These communities can have different forms of organization and operation according to the sector in which they are active or the goals they aim (Preece, 2000). There is significant work on the function of these teams and the roles and rules that are developed within them (Tzikopoulos, Karatza, & Apostolakis, 2005a). It is widely accepted that there is important dynamics in e-learning communities' perspectives. Notions of (1) learning through practice and (2) the creation of knowledge in a social and producing-collaborative way are two of the most popular ideas that are expected to give new capabilities to the effectiveness of online learning (Wenger, 1998, 2001).

In reality, what seems to appear is a new notion about *space*, *time, communication*, and *learning*. The notion of lifelong learning and online learning can support people and solve problems giving more opportunities and challenges. Yet, we cannot guarantee a general solution for problems such as the need for inclusive education. Online education can support lifelong learning and enhance strategies to help people become computer literate and more effective in knowledge societies, but it must be used in combination with communities of learning, communities of practice, and determination from policy makers to promote lifelong learning.

As noted by Selwyn (2003), ICT has managed to "go deeper" more effectively than "go wider." That is to say, "people already endowed with an attitude to learning and already committed to learning through life have increased their participation thanks to ICT, but the most disadvantaged categories have not" (Selwyn, 2003, pp. 16-17). Some of the limitations that have been recognized are the access to ICT technologies (Tzikopoulos, Manouselis, Costopoulou, Yalouris, & Sideridis, 2005b), the ICT skills that people have (DFES, 2002; Selwyn & Gorard, 2003), and the nation that we cannot consider online education as the ultimate solution to every kind of learning need (Collis & Remmers, 1997; Damarin, 1998; Henderson, 1996), and that there are several limitations of specific tools. Thus, we have to keep our eyes open to new tools and be critical upon their use and usefulness.

New Challenges for Learners, Organisations, and Educators

Learners

It seems that individuals have to survive in a competitive environment facing many difficulties. In the level of individuals, they have to deal, not only with their career and employability, but also with their public and social life (Goleman, 2000). The new circumstances and the continuous changes demand from individuals for continuous searching and development to be competitive and employable. Moreover, changes in public life result in the need of citizenship, a subject not really developed in practice (Jarvis, 1999). This reality is connected with the inequalities that competitiveness produces. There is the necessity to have a complete life that will content individuals. At the same time, opportunities appear concerning policies of lifelong learning and online education. The trend in providing opportunities and policy making is individualization of learning, according to which someone can have the chance to design his or her own learning path according to special needs and interests, and eventually design his or her own life path. This idea presupposes that metaskills are already developed. The fact that not all citizens have the same opportunities to participate in learning programs, whether they are online or not, is a difficulty that prohibits the above capability. While online education has the ability to overcome difficulties of place and time, it has to deal with the digital divide. People must take initiatives on searching for learning opportunities concerning ICT literacy to facilitate their lives in multiple ways. Policy makers must take initiatives to provide such opportunities.

Organizations

In the level of organizations, public or private, there are some characteristics of practices and goals that are related to their needs for learning and development. There is a strong shift towards human capital. The competitive environment creates new dimensions for differentiation such as providing quality products and services, trying to produce innovative ideas. These circumstances demand employees with skills like creativity, communication, teamwork, flexibility, and leadership (Galvin, 2003). As a general requirement, employees have to have the ability to solve problems in demanding environments. Because of this, frameworks of social or "soft skills" are being shaped and employers realize that they have to invest on human capital if they want to remain competitive. There are researchers arguing that such circumstances may lead employees to exhaustion. In this context, lifelong learning and online education can provide some solutions, helping employees to develop their competencies and deal with complicated environments.

Learning organizations and learning management systems are two of the key systems concerning the reality of organizations (Deb, 2001). Discussions over learning organizations have produced a considerable literacy where advantages and disadvantages are identified (Fielding, 2001; Hawkins, 1994; Nyham, 2000). Of course, we must not ignore the fact that in the center of every organization is the people who work for it. Education and lifelong learning, whether provided in an online basis or not, cannot solve all the problems that an organization may have. When implemented in an appropriate way, however, according to the principles of fields such as adult education, humanistic education, and contemporary environments which can operate in the advantage of employees, lifelong learning can provide opportunities and applications for further development (Kokkos, 2005b).

Educators

The role of educators in an organization usually comes between the employees and the employers. In the eyes of an employee, the educator is someone who tries to achieve the goals of the employer, even though the educators' concern is to help their learners to operate effectively in the competitive environment. Differences appear when educators come from outside of the organization, even though they have come to serve specific goals. This contradiction is a challenge that an educator must overcome. Considering the fact that they need to settle an appropriate environment for learning and open communication, this may be a hard process, especially when employees are disappointed or concerned with additional problems.

Additionally, the new online environments provide educators with new challenges concerning their ICT literacy as well as their knowledge concerning the exploitation of new ways of providing support, knowledge, communication, and resources. Further, if an organization decides to implement online technologies to serve educational and learning goals, educators once more gain the role of helping employees appreciate the new opportunities in a positive way.

The Case of a Banking Organisation

Studying the above difficulties as well as opportunities concerning lifelong learning and online education in practice, we explore the case of a large banking organization, which operates in a very competitive European market and faces major needs of employee developments and productions of *new* methods and *new* products. After providing a historical sketch of this bank, the bank's training system is examined, and then the training needs within the organization are described. A proposal of an online training system can provide solutions in specific problems. Moreover, there are new aspects that the role of trainers should induce in their existing practices. It must be noted that the presentation of a thorough analysis of this case study is not possible. Such an analysis could be a separate chapter of its own. Nevertheless, we try to identify basic characteristics and to provide a framework for the design of an e-learning system based on the needs of a demanding and competitive environment and the people working in it.

Historical Sketch

The Bank of Cyprus was founded in 1899 and currently is the holding company of the Bank of Cyprus Group. The bank is the leading financial services organization in Cyprus with a dynamic presence in Greece and operations in the United Kingdom and Australia. The group offers a wide range of financial products and services which include banking services in Cyprus and Greece, United Kingdom, Australia, and Channel Islands; finance, leasing, factoring, brokerage, fund management, and general and life insurance services in Cyprus and Greece; and investment banking services in Cyprus. The bank has been operating in Greece since 1991. The dynamic expansion of the bank's Greek operations started in 1999. The bank operates 110 branches in Greece. The bank is well established in the United Kingdom, where it operates six branches to serve the sizeable Cypriot and Greek communities. The group's international activities were further enhanced in 2000 with the operation of a wholly owned subsidiary bank in Australia, which operates 10 branches. The bank has representative offices in the United States, Canada, South Africa, Russia, and Romania. The Bank of Cyprus Group employs 6,065 staff worldwide. The shares of the bank are listed on the Cyprus Stock Exchange (CSE) and the Athens

Exchange. The Bank is the largest listed company on the CSE in terms of market capitalization and has a well-diversified shareholder base.

Present Situation

Part of the organization's vision is connected to the continuous development of its human capital. The organization has a well-established training system operating for many years. There are two main different categories of training. The first one is "on-the-job training," which is provided to new employees by more experienced employees or expert trainers. On the other hand, there is training in the form of "short term seminars," with duration from one to three days. These seminars can be conducted in or out of the organization, and implemented by full-time trainers (organization's employees) or trainers from other corporations or educational institutions. These short term seminars are related to technical courses, connected with specific duties and responsibilities or may concern "soft skills" such as communication, team building, stress management, and time management. Employees may attend up to three seminars a year.

Challenges

During the last decade, the organization grew considerably. Because of this, many new employees have to be trained in limited time and training needs become very critical. New procedures needed to be established in order to operate effectively as the customers increased. Such a situation can be challenging due to the constant and continuous increasing of learning needs. The well-established training system seems to have exhausted its potential, as the seminars do not seem to provide enough opportunities for learning. Employees require more support and guidance in this changing environment. Boundaries concerning working hours, and travel and costs are difficult to overcome if more extended courses are proposed as a solution. Therefore, *distance education* and *blended learning* may provide a suitable solution.

Ideas

Online educational courses can be organized to help employees deal with various problems. The proposed system will be a portal in which every employee will have access. This portal will be a new opportunity for different teams to communicate and share knowledge considering everyday working practice. The short term seminars will be changed to distance learning courses, in which the learners will have the chance to continue to learn and receive feedback during an extended period of time.

Basic Principles

- The new system will be designed according to principles that have been established from organizations for the standardization of e-learning. This fact will enhance the reusability of our content and learning objects, helping tutors make better use of a well-organized database of available resources (Apostolakis & Karatza, 2005).
- Individualization opportunities according to different learning styles and preferences will be an important aspect of this work in order to enhance its effectiveness in an individual basis. Different learning styles and preferences are proved to be important for an educational program, especially when it concerns an online program where direct communication is not available (Karatza et al., 2005a).
- Construction of new knowledge through communication and experiential learning is one way that adults can learn and comprehend new knowledge. Through the sharing of everyday experiences and analysis of case studies with the support of online tutors, learners will find meaning and solutions to their everyday problems.
- An easy environment will be essential for our system. Learners already have difficulty in learning and becoming accustomed to new ideas concerning the field they have to learn. We should not add new difficulties by making them use complicated and not usable virtual environments.
- All substantial courses need to have interactions not only between trainees but also between the trainer and trainees. In online education, trainees and trainers can utilize blackboards, e-mail, chat rooms, and other methods to interact with each other (Mariani, 2001). Asynchronous communication is probably one of the biggest advantages to online education. The ability to post messages, read and respond to messages, reflect on responses, revise interpretations, and modify original assumptions and perceptions at a time convenient to the student is perhaps one of the biggest attributes of online learning (Chamberlin, 2001). Technology gives many opportunities to educators but the shift from traditional education environments to online education environments is not an easy one.

In this framework, we cannot expect that a new online platform can solve the problems the organization is facing today because of its growth as a whole. However, it can provide a new opportunity for employees to extend their learning outcomes and receive more support and guidance. It is apparent that while "e-education" is a valuable tool for both business world and academic world, and that it is not a panacea, it requires time, effort, and expertise to provide quality delivery.

Trainers

Instead of meeting every group once a year, by using an online system, educators increase opportunities for flexible ongoing learning support. Moreover, they can send more cases to be studied and discussed. Of course, for such a system to operate effectively, the trainer must develop specific competencies. Trainers must be capable of using network technologies without difficulties and have to help learners to use them. Trainers must understand the principles of distance education and the way it can provide effective learning to the group.

Principle One

Facilitating takes place in both a professional and a social context. A Net community does not just happen—it takes design and leadership practices to build (Collison, Elbaum, Haavind, & Tinker, 2000). It is the instructor's responsibility to teach learners how to create an effective Net course community. An online instructor also needs to be able to give up some control in the learning process so that learners are empowered and are able to build a learning community.

Principle Two

The style of "guide on the side" vs. "sage on the stage" is an important stance for online course instructors. A successful instructor is a facilitator who can *guide,* instead of giving expert answers, pushing learners to learn by doing instead of rote memory.

Principle Three

Online facilitating is a craft that can be learned. Facilitators must develop new strategies for interacting with learners (Collison et al., 2000). Another suggested addition to these competencies is the ability to design discussions that involve students. Students expect and enjoy having an instructor available for feedback, often even on the weekends (White, 2000).

A New Framework for the Competencies of Educators

We will now present a framework that we believe is essential for *tomorrow's instructors*. We examine the main directions that must concern them in order to be competitive and effective for their learners in similar circumstances. In unstable environments, trainers that are called to support the learning process take on new roles (Tuijnman, 2002). Six dimensions are identified among the views of several researchers concerning the new role of adult trainers. These six dimensions are selected to comprise an integrated model of a trainer that is in accordance with the basic principles of adult education and the need to enhance and support lifelong learning and competencies that are connected with it. In this framework (Karatza, 2005; Karatza, Tzikopoulos & Apostolakis, 2005b), we add a dimension connected with online education, and the need to support e-learning communities. We should note that the task of identifying the factors and practices contributing to the promotion of lifelong learning in a training process is not an easy one. Every good practice identified by educational researchers promotes *effective learning* and at the same time promotes *lifelong learning*. Good practices make the process of learning *rewarding* and *satisfactory*. It is thus possible that a trainee will be affected in a positive way towards lifelong learning. A conscious effort must be done on the behalf of trainers to enhance this occasional confrontation. For this purpose, we selected these dimensions and practices that are clearly connected with the promotion of lifelong learning as a conscious process and effort from the trainer.

It should be recognized that the trainer is an "example" of lifelong learning practices. The trainer must be in accordance with what lifelong learning mediates and be a "model" of lifelong learning (Courau, 2000; Knowles, 1980). The production of new knowledge and information is so rapid that trainers must continue to learn irrespective of the practices they must use to enhance the trainees' effort to become lifelong learners in order to gain up to date knowledge. Therefore, they must participate in the learning process (either formal or informal) having responsibility for their own learning path (Kokkos et al., 2005a). According to Todoulou (2005), trainers must study their own personality. Also, trainers must show their perspectives and experiences to the participants as a continuous and steady effort for effective and productive participation in social life. In a virtual learning team, trainers must demonstrate their effective practices for using ICT within the team regarding the learning object. This may be ways of searching effectively on the Net, ways of evaluating resources of information for validity and values, and ways of sharing practices, knowledge, and expertise within the team.

Moreover, trainers should engage practices that can create a suitable environment for their trainees to develop generic skills and basic competencies (Christofilopoulou, 2003; Karalis, 2003). According to European Training Foundation (1998), generic

Table 1. Key competencies (Source: European Commission, 2005, pp. 13-19)

Communication in maternal language	This competence refers to the ability to express and interpret thoughts, emotions, and facts in written and verbal form, and to communicate in a suitable way in a range of social and cultural contexts.
Communication in a foreign language	This competence is closely connected to the previous one and has the same dimensions.
Arithmetic literacy and basic science and technology skills	This competence refers to the use of basic arithmetic and technology skills and the emphasis is given to the process rather than the result.
Digital competencies	This area involves the use of electronic mediums for work, entertainment and communication. It is related with reflective thought, administration competencies, and well developed communication skills.
Learning to learn	Learning to learn means the willingness and competence to organize learning, individually as well as in teams. It includes the competence to manage time effectively, solve problems, as well as evaluate and assimilate knowledge in different contexts.
Interpersonal competencies	Interpersonal competencies involve all kinds of behavior that must be attained to be effective and participate creatively in social life.
Business dexterity	This competence involves the tension to change oneself and be flexible and adaptive in innovations that are imposed from the external environment.
Cultural countenance	Individuals must understand the importance of creatively expressing ideas, experience and emotions with the use of music, literature, and other kinds of arts.

skills are those which enhance lifelong learning, and specifically apart from basic skills (i.e., literacy and numeric). Generic skills include (1) communication skills, (2) problem solving, (3) collaboration, (4) decision making, (5) creative thinking, and (6) ICT and continuous learning (cognitive strategies and learning strategies). Key competencies are those which complete basic and generic skills and allow individuals to attain easily new qualifications, adapt to changing technological environments, and have mobility in the labor market with a developing career.

Irrelevant of the context in which trainers provide training, they should be able to support with specific practices the achievement of such educational aims. For example, to support ICT skills, irrespective if educators have available personal computers in a classroom, they can propose specific resources from the Internet, relevant to the subject and suitable for learners' needs. In the context of online education, such a goal is even more demanding. The trainer must be organized and prepared for participants' defensive behaviors or even difficulties that derive from technology and access to it.

For the purposes of the study in the present chapter, the key competencies defined by the European Commission (2005) are adopted. According to *Key Competencies for Lifelong Learning, a European Framework*, such key competencies are those which represent a set of transferee, multifunctional pack of knowledge, skills and attitudes that all individuals need for personal development, involvement, and employment. More specifically, these competencies are (1) communication in maternal language; (2) communication in a foreign language; (3) arithmetic literacy and basic science and technology skills; (4) digital competencies; (5) learning to learn; (6) interpersonal competencies; (7) business dexterity; and (8) cultural countenance (for the detailed description, see Table 1).

Furthermore, to support the development of such skills and competencies, it is important that trainers initiate the active involvement of the participants in the learning process. This active involvement can be gained with the use of several training techniques in which participants will have the chance to try and solve problems, collaborate with other participants, and exercise their creative thinking (Jaques, 2004; Noye & Pivetaeu, 1999; Silberman, 1998). According to Jaques (2004), the interchange of different views and the response to other participants' reactions develops the mind and deepens understanding. Moreover, trainers must help individuals to undertake personal responsibility of their own learning path, broadening their learning strategies (Kokkos, 1999; Rogers, 1999). According to Rahman (1993), every person has the ability of discovering and thinking creatively, but the transmission of information inhibits the development of such competencies. In any form of adult education, we should pursue the promotion of self-dependence, self-containment, and critical learning (Knowles, Holton & Swanson, 1998).

Since one of the key factors in adult education is the role of the "experience" that a participant already has, the role of the trainer becomes more of a *facilitator* (Knowles et al., 1998; Rogers, 2002) as previously stated. Practices of the trainer should have such a direction to support individualized learning. Another dimension of this new role concerns an effort to be honest and authentic during the educational process (Rogers, 2002). Trainers must be ready to accept the different views and ways of expressing, and understand those things deeply. Good practice enhances the relationship between learners and trainers. The relationship inside and outside of the training process is the most important factor to encourage participants to think of their own future goals (Jaques, 2004). Such a perspective includes dangers and may appear very difficult in comparison with the traditional view in which the trainer is the person who provides answers and does not pose questions. However, there is strong evidence that the relationship existing between the trainer and the trainee, nowadays more than ever, is similar to the one that exists between the psychotherapist and the client (Jaques, 2004; Mezirow, 1990; Rogers, 2002).

In a broader framework, a dimension of the new role we describe in this section is the awareness of the fact that individuals work in a *learning and knowledge society*. Trainers must adopt a conscious effort towards the implementations of the practice that enhance and support *lifelong learning* and *online education*. Furthermore, they must help the participants understand how important is the fact that throughout their lives they will participate in different learning environments and communities. It appears that *online tutoring* is a demanding task. The distance, which exists between the tutor and the learners in combinations with ICT and tools such as e-mails and forums, raises the expectations of trainees for more frequent and thorough interaction, mostly from their tutor. That is why it is important to help learners gain diverse understandings for the exploitation of new technology (Cooley & Johnston, 2000; Huysman & Gerrits, 1998; Lunch, 1998). Studies have shown that there is a difference between what learners and tutors perceive as frequent interaction and feedback (Tucker & Cordani, 1998). This is the reason why online programs must be well organized and online tutors must develop specific methods for effective "e-feedback" and "e-communication" to online learners.

From the above analysis and evaluation, it is obvious that new dimensions must be added in the role of the adult trainer to support *lifelong learning* in online contexts. We identify six separate factors that can comprise a model of competencies-aims of a trainer to attain. Figure 1 illustrates how these dimensions are interconnected. There are three dimensions that have direct effects in everyday training practices in which trainers design their own program: (1) active involvement of the participants in the learning process; (2) enhancement of the development of generic and basic skills in everyday practices; and (3) trainer as a facilitator. Supportively, there are two additional dimensions that must penetrate the trainers' attitude towards lifelong learning and the Learning Society in order to take an active stance towards these realities.

Figure 1. A framework for the development of tomorrow's educators' competencies

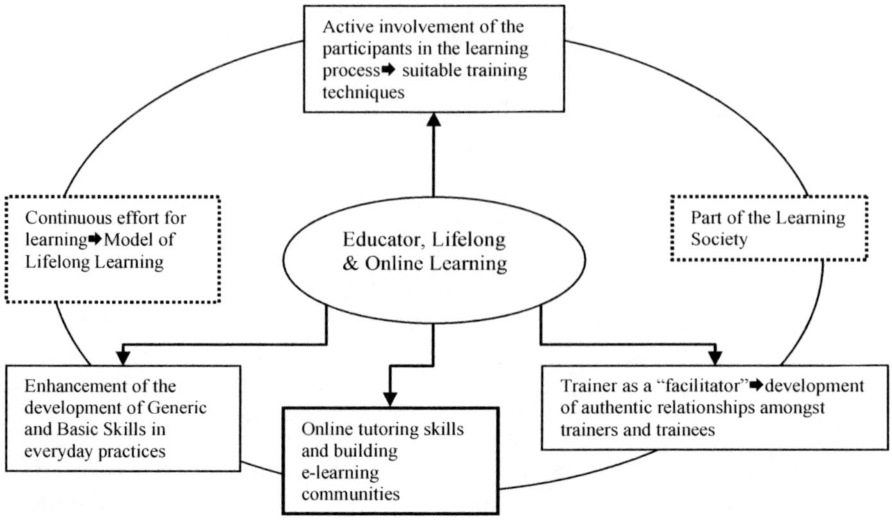

We can distinguish the above framework in aims of knowledge, skills, and attitudes. Trainers' knowledge in the field is important so that they can apply their knowledge to the different contexts. Trainers must know and study the subjects relevant to the dynamics developed within a team, as well as consultive psychology. Concerning skills, trainers must develop their own generic and basic skills and additionally develop skills that are related to the suitable use of training techniques. In addition, trainers must develop online tutoring skills and the ability to build online communities that can learn and work productively and effectively. Finally, trainers must be able to cope with the relations that will be shaped in the training process. In the field of attitude, the trainer must have a clear orientation towards *lifelong learning*.

Conclusion

It is apparent that the changing environment concerning *work*, *knowledge*, and *learning* does affect the role of educators. Online technologies confront difficulties such as distance and time and give new opportunities of communication and lifelong learning. However, an educational method alone cannot provide a solution to all problems. Online tutoring is a difficult and demanding task indeed, especially when one considers the difficulties connected with the complicated environments that are created in knowledge societies. We must mention that there are dimensions we did not include in our effort at least for the purpose of this chapter. The new circumstances that the knowledge society brings raise the need for global awareness and diversity concerns. Yet, these ideas and studies can be extended in a whole new chapter. The scope of our effort remained closely connected with the case study in order to find what is needed in a real environment with specific factors that seem to affect the role of a trainer.

In our work, we have attempted to identify the directions in which educators and trainers should try to develop their knowledge, skills, and attitude in order to be effective and productive. We have designed a framework based on the needs of a real, competitive, and demanding environment of a large banking organization, where training and development needs and expectations are extremely high. This broad framework is only a first indication of what an organization should do for its trainers to have contemporary and effective training. The next step that we have to develop is the "online" system itself with more details and the training program that trainers should take to gain the competencies needed to support it. This program will be organized with the same methods and tools that trainers will use for their learners to help them gain the experience of learning within online communities before they have to support one. After this implementation, it is expected that areas for the refinement of our model will be identified.

References

Apostolakis, I., & Karatza, M. (2005). The contribution of learning standards for the exploitation of ICT in education. In *Proceedings of the 3rd National Conference on Teaching Informatics*. Greece: University of Peloponnesus.

Ashton, D. N., & Green, F. (1996). *Education, training and the global economy.* Chelternham: E. Elgar.

Chamberlin, W. S. (2001). Face-to-face vs. cyberspace. *Syllabus, 15*(5), 10-11.

Christofilopoulou, E. (2003, November). *The contribution of training in the development of competencies.* Paper presented at the Meeting of EKEPIS for the National Program (Train the Trainers), Athens, Greece.

Coffield, F. (2002). Breaking the consensus: Lifelong learning as social control. In R. Edwards, N. Miller, N. Small, & A. Tait (Eds.), *Making policy work.* London: Routledge.

Collison, G., Elbaum, B., Haavind, S., & Tinker, R. (2000). *Principles that support effective moderation: Facilitating online learning*. Madison, WI: Atwood Publishing.

Collis, B., & Remmers, E. (1997). The World Wide Web in education: Issues related to cross-cultural communication and interaction. In B. Khan (Ed.), *Web-based instruction* (pp. 85-92). Englewood Cliffs, NJ: Educational Technology Publications.

Cooley, N., & Johnson, M. (2000, July-August). Beyond teacher bashing: Practical, philosophical, and pedagogical influences on educators' use of educational technologies. *The Technology Source: Commentary.* Retrieved August 13, 2006, from http://horizon.unc.edu/TS/default.asp?show=article&id=786

Cornford, I. (2002). Learning to learn strategies as a basis for effective lifelong learning. *Journal of Lifelong Education, 21*(4), 357-368.

Courau, S. (2000). *The basic tools of the adult trainer.* Athens: Metaihmio.

Damarin, S. K. (1998). Technology and multicultural education: The question of convergence. *Theory into Practice, 37*(1), 11-19.

Deb, S. (2004). *Reinterpreting the learning organisation.* Retrieved August 13, 2006, from http://www.business.vu.edu.au/mgt/pdf/working_papers/2001/wp3_2001_stewart.pdf

Department for Education and Skills (DFES). (2002). *Get on with IT: The post-16 e-learning Strategy Task Force report*. London: Author.

Department for Education and Skills (DFES). (2003). *21st century skills: Realising our potential.* Notingham: DFES Publications.

Edwards, R., Raggat, P., Harrison, R., McCollum, A., & Calder, J. (1998). *Recent thinking in lifelong learning.* London: DFEE, HMSO.

Eraut, M. (1997). Perspectives on defining "the learning society." *Journal of Education Policy, 12*(6), 551-558.

European Commission. (2001). *Communication from the commission: Making a European area of lifelong learning a reality.* Brussels: European Commission.

European Commission. (2005). *Proposal for a recommendation of the European parliament and of the council on key competencies for lifelong learning.* Retrieved August 13, 2006, from http://europa.eu.int/comm/education/policies/2010/doc/keyrec_en.pdf

European Committee. (2003). *Glossary, term: E-learning.* Retrieved August 13, 2006, from http://elearningeuropa.info/index.php?page=glossary&menuzone=1&int=1

Field, J. (1997). The European Union and the learning society: Contested sovereignty in an age of globalisation. In F. Coffield (Ed.), *A national strategy for lifelong learning* (pp. 95-111). Newcastle: University of Newcastle.

Fielding, M. (2004). *Learning organisation or learning community?* Retrieved August 13, 2006, from http://www.sussex.ac.uk/education/documents/learningorganisation.pdf

Galvin, T. (2003). Training top 100. *Training, 40*(3), 18-38.

Goleman, D. (2000). *Emotional intelligence in the workplace* (7th ed.). Athens: Ellinika Grammata.

Griffin, C. (2004). *Beyond the learning society.* Retrieved August 13, 2006, from http://www.adulteduc.gr

Hawkins, P. (1994). Organisational learning: Taking stock and facing the challenge. *Management Learning, 25*(3), 433-461.

Huysman, M., & Gerrits, H. (1998). *ICT and project-based education: Some finding from an explanatory research study* (Series Research Memoranda). Faculteit der Economische Wetenchappen en Econometrie, Amsterdam: vrije Universiteit.

Jaques, D. (2004). *Learning in groups*. Athens: Metaihmio.

Jarvis, P. (1999). *Adult and continuing education* (2nd ed.). London: Routledge.

Jarvis, P. (2001). *The age of learning.* London: Kogan Page.

Karalis, T. (2003). *The role of the adult trainer in the connection of training with employability.* National Program of Training the Trainers. Athens: EKEPIS.

Karatza, M. (2005). The role of adult trainer supporting lifelong learning. *Adult Education, 5*, 4-8.

Karatza, M., Phillips, N., & Apostolakis, I. (2005a). The use of ICT for the support of learning models in open and distance education. In *Proceedings of the 3rd International Conference on Open & Distance Learning: Applications of Pedagogy & Technology* (pp. 297-310), Hellenic Open University, Patra, Greece.

Karatza, M., Tzikopoulos, A., & Apostolakis, I. (2005b). *The role of adult trainer supporting lifelong learning*. Paper presented at the 1st National Conference on New Technologies and Lifelong Learning, Lamia. Retrieved August 13, 2006, from http://cosy.ted.unipi.gr/NT diaviou2005

Keep, E. (1997). There is no such thing as society ... : Some problems with an individual approach to creating a learning society. *Journal of Education Policy, 12*(6), 457-471.

Kirkpatrick, D., & McLaughlan, R. (2000). Flexible lifelong learning in professional education. *Educational Technology & Society, 3*(1), 24-31.

Knowles, M. (1980). *The modern practice of adult education.* New York: Adult Education.

Knowles, M., Holton, E., & Swanson, R. (1998). *The adult learner: The definitive classic in adult education and human resource development* (5th ed.). Houston: Gulf Publishing.

Kokkos, A. (1999). *Adult education: The field, the learning principles, the contributors.* Patra: Hellenic Open University.

Kokkos, A. (2005a). *Adult education: Detecting the filed.* Athens: Metaihmio.

Kokkos, A. (2005b). To develop social competencies: For what reason and in which way. In *Proceedings of the 2nd International Conference of Hellenic Adult Education Association: Adult Education and Social Skills* (pp. 5-23). Athens: HAEA.

Kruse, K. (2003). *The state of e-learning looking at history with the technology hype cycle.* Retrieved August 13, 2006, from http://www.e-learningguru.com/articles/ hype1_1.htm

Leinonen, T. (2005). *Critical history of ICT in education and where we are heading?* Retrieved August 13, 2006, from http://flosse.dicole.org/?item=critical-history-of-ict-in-education-and-where-we-are-heading

Lunch, M. M. (1998, December). Facilitating knowledge construction and communication on the Internet. *The Technology Source.*

Mariani, M. (2001). Distance learning in postsecondary education. *Occupational Outlook Quarterly, 45*(2), 1-10.

Mayes, T. (2002). The technology of learning in a social world. In R. Harrison, F. Reeve, A. Hanson, & J. Clarke (Eds.), *Supporting lifelong learning* (pp. 163-175). London: Routledge.

Mezirow, J. (1990). *Fostering critical reflection in adulthood.* San Francisco: Jossey-Bass.

Nascimbeni, F. (2005). *E-column: E-learning and access to E&T.* Retrieved August 13, 2006, from http://elearningeuropa.info/index.php?page=doc&doc_id=6677&doclng=5&menuzone=1

Nyham, B. (2000). Building learning organisations: Putting theory to test. *European Journal, Vocational Training, 16*, 14-23.

Open University, The. (2002). E845 *Supporting lifelong learning: Audio notes.* Patra, Greece: The Open University/Milton Keynes.

Paulsen, M. F. (2003). *Online education and learning management systems.* Retrieved August 13, 2006, from http://www.studymentor.com/studymentor/

Phillips, R. (1998). Models of learning appropriate to educational applications of information technology. In B. Black & N. Stanley (Eds), *Teaching and learning in changing times*. Proceedings of the 7th Annual Teaching Learning Forum, the University of Western Australia, Perth.

Preece, J. (2000), *Online communities: Designing usability, supporting sociability.* New York: John Wiley & Son.

Rahman, A. (1993). *People's self-development: perspectives on participatory action research.* London: Zed Books.

Rogers, A. (1999). *Adult education.* Athens: Metaihmio.

Rogers, C. (2002). The interpersonal relationship in the facilitation of learning. In S*upporting lifelong learning* (Vol. 1, pp. 25-39). London: Routledge.

Selwyn, N. (2003). *ICT in adult education: Defining the territory, international roundtable on ICT in non-formal and adult education.* Retrieved August 13, 2006, from http://www.literacy.org/ictconf/OECD_Selwyn_final.pdf

Selwyn, N., & Gorard, S. (2003, March). Reality bytes: examining the rhetoric of widening educational participation via ICT. *British Journal of Educational Technology, 34*, 169-181.

Silberman, M. (1998). *Active training: A handbook of techniques, designs, case examples, and tips*. San Francisco: Jossey-Bass.

Stites, R., Hopery, C., & Ginsburg, L. (1998). *Assessing lifelong learning technology (ALL-Tech): A guide for choosing and using technology for adult learning.* Walnut, PA: National Centre on Adult Literacy, University of Pennsylvania.

Thorpe, M. (2005). *New technology and lifelong learning, institute of educational technology.* Retrieved August 13, 2006, from http://www.open.ac.uk/lifelong-learning/papers/

Todoulou, M. (2005), *Methodology of adult education: The exploitation of the team in adult Education*. Athens: Hellenic Open University.

Tsolakidis, K. (2004, July 4-6). ICT in education: The dawn of new era or the development of an accessory? In *Proceedings of International Symposium on Advanced Technologies in Education,* Kefalonia, Greece.

Tucker, J. T., & Cordani J. (1998). Teaching teachers to teach online. In *Proceedings of the Annual ACM SIGUCCS Conference on User* (pp. 293-297). New York: ACM Press.

Tuijnman, A. (2002). Themes and questions for a research agenda on lifelong learning. In R. Edwards, N. Miller, N. Small, & A. Tait (Eds.), *Making policy work* (pp. 6-29). London: Routledge.

Tzikopoulos, A., Karatza, M., & Apostolakis, I. (2005a). The contribution of e-learning communities in Health. *Journal for the Quality of Life Research, 3*(2), 34-38.

Tzikopoulos, A., Manouselis, N., Costopoulou, C., Yalouris, C., & Sideridis, A. (2005b, October 12-14). Investigating digital learning repositories' coverage of agriculture-related topics. In *Proceedings of the International Congress on Information Technologies in Agriculture, Food and Environment (ITAFE05),* Adana, Turkey.

Wenger, E. (1998). *Communities of practice: Learning, meaning and identity.* Cambridge, UK: Cambridge University Press.

Wenger, E. (2001). *Supporting communities of practice: A survey of community-oriented technologies.* Unpublished manuscript.

About the Authors

Yukiko Inoue, PhD, is a professor of educational research and currently teaches both online and face-to-face courses in graduate studies at the University of Guam, where she is chair of the department of foundations, educational research, and technology. She was the recipient of the Faculty Award for Excellence in Research in 2000 and 2006. Inoue received a doctorate in educational psychology and research from the University of Memphis in the United States and a master's degree in business administration from Tokyo Keizai University, Japan. Her research interests include interdisciplinary studies on student learning and development, educational technology, online education for diverse learners, and the social contexts and learning with a higher education focus. Inoue is the co-author of *Teaching with Educational Technology: The Case of the Asia-Pacific Region* (2006), and the editor of *Technology and Diversity in Higher Education: New Challenges* (2006). She is also a poet and the author of *The Window That Reveals Tomorrow* (2000), and *Roses, You Must Be* (2002/2003). And Inoue is editor-in-chief of the journal of *Micronesian Educator*, a publication of the University of Guam.

* * * * *

Danilo M. Baylen, EdD, is an assistant professor in the College of Education at Florida Gulf Coast University. Baylen received his doctorate in instructional technology and master's degree in counseling from Northern Illinois University. His research interests include technology integration across the curriculum, media literacy, online learning and teaching, and instructional design. He is currently exploring the convergence of emerging technologies and children's literature and investigating the use of blogs in enhancing the educational experience of K-12 students and preservice teachers. Previous work experiences include posts in faculty development, instructional technology services, instructional design, and English as second language teaching.

Glenn Finger, PhD, is deputy director of the Centre for Learning Research and senior lecturer in the School of Education and Professional Studies in the Faculty of Education at Gold Coast Campus Griffith University, Queensland, Australia. Finger has specific research interests in examining the question: What new kinds of learning are needed to prepare people for successful engagement with a changing world? Prior to his appointment at Griffith University in 1999, Finger had 24 years experience as a primary school teacher, deputy principal, and acting principal in primary schools. He is a member of the Australian Council for Computers in Education, Australian Association for Research in Education, Australian Teacher Education Association, Australian College of Educators, Australian Council of Educational Leaders, and the Queensland Society for Information Technology in Education.

Joan Glacken, EdD, is a founding faculty member of Florida Gulf Coast University (FGCU) and serves as associate dean, curriculum and assessment and chair, Division of Health Sciences in the College of Health Professions. She earned her graduate degrees in health professions education from Rutgers University. She received her undergraduate degree in medical technology from Douglass College in New Jersey. Past work experiences include serving as supervisor at AccuMed Diagnostic Laboratory, and adjunct faculty at Rutgers University and the University of Medicine and Dentistry of New Jersey. At FGCU, she was recognized as Professor of the Year (2000-2001) and awarded the Team Faculty Service Excellence award (2002-2003).

Nicholas J. Goetzfridt, PhD, is a professor of library science and micronesian studies at the University of Guam. He has served as a library and college administrator, chair of the University of Guam's Micronesian Studies graduate program, and as chair and current member of the board of directors for the Guam Humanities Council. He was also recently a visiting fellow at the East West Center in Hawaii.

He has experience as a practicing librarian in the areas of collection development and reference and has published books on historical interpretations of Micronesia (with Dr. Karen Peacock), indigenous Pacific literature, and indigenous navigation and voyaging as well as various chapters and articles on information issues in Pacific communal contexts, pacific ethnomathematics, and Pacific library history. He is also editor-in-chief of the Guampedia online encyclopedia project at www.guampedia.com.

Satomi Izumi-Taylor, PhD, is a professor of early childhood education at the University of Memphis, Tennessee. She received her doctorate in family and child development from Virginia Polytechnic Institute and State University. She has been a teacher of young children for more than 12 years and has a special interest in early childhood constructivist classrooms. She has published articles on cognitive, social, and moral development in children, adults, as well as articles on Japanese early childhood constructivist approaches. Her current research interests included cross-cultural studies of Japanese and American teachers' mentoring skills.

P. Toyoko Kang, PhD, is an associate professor of Japanese and has been teaching Japanese language as a foreign language at the University of Guam since 1993. Kang was born in Japan, and educated in Japan and in the United States. She obtained her undergraduate degree in Russian and a master's degree in Russian linguistics in Kobe City University of Foreign Studies, Japan, and her doctorate in applied linguistics from the University of Texas at Austin.

Marianthi Karatza is a candidate (master's degree in lifelong learning) at the Open University. Her first degree is in technology education and digital systems of the University of Piraeus (2003). Karatza is a full time trainer in a large banking organization in Greece, teaching mainly soft skills such as effective communication, stress management, and organizational skills. As a member of the HAEA (Hellenic Adult Education Association), she is responsible for the contents of the association's portal and a member of the editorial committee of the journal *Adult Education* (Metaihmio: Athens). Her main research interests are focused on the area of lifelong learning and the ways in which online education can support related initiatives.

Candace Kaye, PhD, received tenure and the rank of full professor at California State University, Long Beach. Her current faculty service is in the College of Education at New Mexico State University, specializing in online educational design and teaching in graduate studies in the Department of Curriculum and Instruction. Her research and publications continue to focus on student-centered learning, constructivist philosophy and its application, and support for diversity in both traditional and distance learning classrooms. For her work, she has been recognized as a Country Alternate Fulbright Scholar and a Contemplative Practice Fellow by the American Council of Learned Societies.

Terry Kidd is lecturer in computer information systems and Web technology support coordinator at the University of Houston-Downtown. Kidd has presented at several international conferences on e-learning, information technology, and on cultural and urban studies. His research interests include designing technology-based learning environments, instructional design strategies for Web based instruction, the sociocultural aspect of information technology, performance improvement, and topics in organizational development and change.

Gulsun Kurubacak, EdD, is an assistant professor in distance education at the College of Open Education at Anadolu University, Turkey. She undertook graduate studies at Anadolu University, Turkey (master's degree in educational technology) and the University of Cincinnati (doctorate in curriculum and instruction) and has worked as a postdoctoral fellow at the College of Education at New Mexico State University (2001-2002). Kurubacak spent 20 years focusing on the democratic and multicultural aspects of distance education, finding answers and explanations for complex communicational problems through project-based online learning via online communications.

Ann F. Lovelace is a doctoral candidate in the Department of Instruction and Curriculum Leadership at the University of Memphis. Early childhood education is her area of concentration. She has five years of teaching experience in both public and private school settings. She is currently a prekindergarten teacher at a private, Catholic school located in Southaven, Memphis. She is also the graduate assistant for the Early Childhood Department at the University of Memphis. Her research interests include early literacy, phonemic awareness, and teacher reflection.

Julia M. Matuga, PhD, is an associate professor of educational psychology in the College of Education and Human Development at Bowling Green State University (BGSU) in Bowling Green, Ohio. As a graduate student at Indiana University in Bloomington, Matuga taught undergraduate online courses. At BGSU, Matuga teaches online and face-to-face courses in learning theory and online pedagogy. She has published several articles on private speech and articles and book chapters on online pedagogy, both from a Vygotskian perspective. She is currently engaged in research projects investigating the development and use of self-regulation of K-12 and postsecondary online learners.

Joyce K. McCauley, PhD, emeritus professor at the University of Guam, is currently teaching at Sam Houston State University in Huntsville, Texas. She earned her doctorate in reading from Texas Woman's University. Her research interests include multicultural and cross-cultural teaching strategies, drama and the language arts, and second-language acquisition.

Niki Phillips, PhD, teaches methodology of adult education in the Post Graduate Adult Education Program, Hellenic Open University. She received her doctorate in adult education with a specialization in the area of experiential learning and the development of social skills. Phillips is also head of the Department of Human Resource Development for the Bank of Cyprus in Greece. She has been training and facilitating adult teams of banking executives for 11 years to enhance their social skills particular. Phillips has designed and delivered numerous training programs in the train the trainer field.

Holim Song, EdD, is an assistant professor of instructional technology at Texas Southern University in Houston, Texas. Song received his doctorate in instructional technology from the University of Houston. His research interests include designing and sequencing of online interactions, instructional strategy for Web-based instruction, the impact of multimedia in online education, and designing and integrating multimedia learning objects to enhance instructional quality.

Lawrence A. Tomei, EdD, is the associate vice president for academic affairs and associate professor of education, Robert Morris University. Born in Akron, Ohio, Tomei completed his MPA and MEd at the University of Oklahoma (1975, 1978) and EdD from USC (1983). In his capacity as associate vice president, he directs the activities of academic services including the registrar's office, academic technology and Web site coordination, accreditation and curricular processes, and liaison responsibilities with financial aid, and information technology and services. His publications include *Taxonomy for the Technology Domain* (2005), *Challenges of Teaching with Technology Across the Curriculum* (2003); and *Technology Literacy Applications in Learning Environments* (Chapter 1: Defining Instructional Technology Literacy) (2004).

Argiris Tzikopoulos has been an associate of the Informatics Laboratory of the Agricultural University of Athens since 2004. His first degree is in technology education and digital systems of the University of Piraeus (2003) and he holds a master's degree in e-learning from the University of Piraeus (2006). Tzikopoulos is a PhD candidate in KM systems at the Informatics Laboratory of the Agricultural

University of Athens. His main research interests are adaptive and intelligent educational multimedia, learning objects and metadata, and online technologies that support learning communities, in the agricultural sector.

Erica Volkers is the chair of teacher education at Santa Fe Community College and teaches in the Teacher Certification Program, working with postbaccalaureate students seeking to become licensed teachers. She has conducted numerous workshops on three-tiered licensure, effective instruction, assessment and classroom management for educators in New Mexico and is working on her doctorate in education. The authors have co-taught and supported college faculty coursework in online design and instruction that supports constructivist approaches.

Susan J. Wegmann, PhD, is an assistant professor at the University of Central Florida in Orlando, Florida. She earned her doctorate from the University of Florida. Wegmann has extensive experience teaching online and face-to-face in elementary, middle school, and university settings. Her main research interests are online interactions and the teacher's stance as it relates to students' participation.

Volkan T. Yuzer, PhD, is an assistant professor in communication sciences at the Department of Distance Education, College of Open Education of Anadolu University, Turkey. Yuzer earned his doctorate in 2001. His research interests are new communication technologies, synchronous online communications, and new and interactive communication milieus in distance education. He particularly focuses on communication theories to explain them with new communication environments and technologies such as the Internet, interactive television, and interactive radio. He has participated in projects related to distance learning, online synchronous learning, and virtual classroom. He has been teaching courses in distance learning.

Index